Black Sociologists

THE HERITAGE OF SOCIOLOGY

A Series Edited by Morris Janowitz

Black Sociologists

HISTORICAL AND CONTEMPORARY PERSPECTIVES

Edited by

JAMES E. BLACKWELL *and*
MORRIS JANOWITZ

THE UNIVERSITY OF CHICAGO PRESS
CHICAGO AND LONDON

James E. Blackwell is professor and chairman of the Department of Sociology at the University of Massachusetts at Boston. Morris Janowitz is professor of sociology at the University of Chicago.
[1974]

The University of Chicago Press, Chicago 60637
The University of Chicago Press, Ltd., London

International Standard Book Number: 0-226-05565-5 (clothbound)
Library of Congress Catalog Card Number: 73-84187

Contents

v

Preface

On a day in mid-January 1971, Morris Janowitz and I lunched together in Washington, D.C. We were members of separate committees that had convened in Washington at the request of the Caucus of Black Sociologists and the American Sociological Association to determine means of cooperation between the two organizations. Following our morning session, Morris and I decided to talk to each other—to reach beyond the efforts toward rapprochement offered by official representatives—to search for some way of creating better understanding in the world of sociologists. The polarization that threatened the quality of internal relations among sociologists, evidenced at the annual meeting of the ASA in Washington (1970) and San Francisco (1969), could in our view be checked if we were able to generate more effective channels of communication.

The more we talked the more we realized that a knowledge gap existed between black and white sociologists about each other as well as within each of these groups about its members. One of our more salient points of consensus was that few sociologists, black or white, fully understood the scope of contributions by black sociologists to our discipline. The difficulties encountered and personal sacrifices involved in the process of making their contributions were immense. The conditions under which so many black sociologists worked have never been adequately explored and begged illumination. The near-confrontations and intense feelings of alienation observed at recent meetings of the American Sociological Association were only suggestive of the depths of misunderstanding and the failures of communication or meaningful interaction. The immediate question raised was how to effect an understanding of these contributions and conditions to a wide audience or, to phrase it differently, how to provide a systematic body of knowledge about black sociologists in a purely intellectual and objective way.

We agreed to request the University of Chicago to cosponsor a national conference designed to facilitate discussion and critical assessment of contributions by black sociologists to the field of sociology. The University of Chicago was chosen because of its reputation as an intellectual center, its long-established tradition of training sociologists and the leadership taken by its Department of Sociology in the training of black graduate students, its central location, its concern for social issues, and the presumed probability of a favorable response. The response from the University of Chicago was immediate and positive. The university agreed to host such a National Conference on Black Sociologists on May 5-6, 1972.

The University of Chicago provided financial support, and, as further manifestation of its generosity, the facilities of The Kellog Center For Continuing Education were made available as the conference site. The full sweep of media coverage was obtained through the courtesy of the television and radio staffs of the university.

Our purpose was not to quell disagreement but to stimulate candid discussion of the conditions out of which diversity is made. Nowhere is this more apparent than in the scholars selected as participants, either as formal presentors or as observers. Though perspectives differed, all who participated were held together by the common search for truth, intellectual honesty, and a willingness to share our understandings. The papers presented provoked lengthy discussion, and we soon discovered that time was against us as participants carried their polemics into the early hours of the morning.

This book is an extension of the national conference on black sociologists. It is our effort to systematize some of what we learned; not all of it. The understandings that came from one hundred interested people invited to join in learning more about a group and, consequently, about themselves, would, indeed, be beyond the reach of systematization.

On behalf of the Caucus of Black Sociologists and myself, I wish to express profound gratitude to the University of Chicago for its magnanimity, to the Center for Policy Study for hosting the conference, and to the Department of Sociology of the University of Chicago for its able assistance. My appreciation goes to former vice president of the University of Chicago, Mr. Eddie Williams, for his unqualified support, and to Mrs. Nancy Goldman for playing such an important role in helping to coordinate activities at Chicago. The authors of each selection are to be congratulated for their fine work and their patience at my cajoling to meet deadlines.

I owe an immense debt of gratitude to my secretary, Miss Maureen Hayes, who sacrificed so much of her time and who provided excellent secretarial skills to make this project come into fruition, and to Miss Judi Bean for her assistance in the earlier stages of the conference planning. I offer appreciation to Morris Janowitz for his intellectual insights, his humanity and capacity to understand the world of sociologists. Finally, I thank my wife, Myrtle D. Blackwell, for continued encouragement which has always meant so much to me.

James E. Blackwell

Introduction

The immediate circumstances which caused this volume to come into being were the efforts of black sociologists to gain full opportunity and acknowledgment in professional and university life in the United States. This includes full recognition of past accomplishments of black sociologists in the study of race relations. Therefore, the publication of this volume in the Heritage of Sociology series is intended as a particular response to these aspirations. The series had already included a volume on the contributions of E. Franklin Frazier prepared by G. Franklin Edwards.[1] An obvious need existed for a more comprehensive volume on the full historical scope of the work of black sociologists.

This volume is an effort at assessment and interpretation. The purpose of the Heritage of Sociology series is to assist sociologists to maintain a sense of continuity in their work and to appreciate what has been achieved by their predecessors. Awareness of past traditions is required so that sociologists can engage in the effective self-scrutiny and innovation required by any branch of social research.

This volume is also a collective effort. It was the ferment among sociologists—both black and white—about race relations which pointed to the desirability of preparing this volume. Without this ferment, the editors could not have mobilized the necessary collective effort, for sociologists are persons prone to follow their own inclinations. This assessment has the advantages of a collective work and thereby the attendant disadvantages as well. In due time, a single scholar will certainly take the next step to produce a more integrated effort.

In the spring of 1972, a national conference was held on the campus of the University of Chicago. The focus of that conference was on black sociologists; that is, on the work and achievement of black men and women in sociology. In the past, to become a sociologist, or to engage in sociological research, required a tremendous amount of initiative on the part of a black. Those who became engaged knew what they were about.

The history of black sociologists obviously is part of a larger history of the discipline. The initial period, the period of the founding, was dominated by three key figures. Gradually, in the second phase, starting in the late 1920s and early 1930s, an institutional base developed despite meagre resources and complete segregation as far as employment opportunities were concerned. With the emergence of an institutional setting, even within a highly segregated structure, the number increased. The third phase, since 1965, has come to involve the efforts of black sociologists, in conjunction with blacks in other occupational and professional spheres, to alter the institutional setting in which they work and teach.

The first section of this volume deals with the three founding figures: W. E. B. Du Bois, Charles S. Johnson, and E. Franklin Frazier. They were primarily concerned with the sociology of the black world in which they found themselves. They were men who had strong empirical interests and prodigious amounts of energy. While they were all skeptical of detached theorizing, they all sought to impose a general frame of reference on their empirical efforts.

W. E. B. Du Bois was the first major figure. The scope of his research accomplishments was heroic, given the resistance he had to face, and sociology took up only one segment of a most eventful career. Francis L. Broderick, in "W. E. B. Du Bois: History of an Intellectual," presents a biography of this man whose career combined academic teaching and research, journalism, fierce defense of the rights of blacks, and extensive international experiences. Elliott Rudwick deals specifically with the theme of "W. E. B. Du Bois as Sociologist." For a full understanding of the intellectual setting in which Du Bois worked and struggled to carry on his research, it is necessary to make reference to E. Franklin Frazier's article on "Sociological Theory and Race Relations." [2] In this essay, Frazier traced the efforts that were underway within sociology to throw over racial and biological theories of social organization, efforts which were pioneered by W. I. Thomas and which came to full consequence by 1920.

Du Bois's major accomplishment was his pioneering field research, *The Philadelphia Negro*.[3] Despite his achievements in sociological research, he did not receive an appropriate position within sociology or a significant degree of recognition. Within the system of black colleges and universities, there was no institution which could offer a proper base for a man of his talents and interests, and he was never appointed to a major university. His fate was not only the result of discrimination. The sociological discipline was not effectively organized on a national basis so that it could respond to a man in his position. Moreover, as Du Bois developed his civic and journalistic interests, he may well have recognized that a university, black or white, could not give him what he sought—a platform from which he could speak on behalf of black people throughout the world.

Charles S. Johnson, as portrayed in Richard Robbins's study, had early and extensive experience outside the university system. In time, he became fully committed to an academic career in order to conduct the research he believed essential for the development of sociology and for the pragmatic consequences of that development. *The Negro in Chicago*,[4] the penetrating and meticulous analysis of the Chicago race riot of 1919, was a study in which Charles S. Johnson played a central role, although it was publicly unacknowledged at that time. It established his reputation as an outstanding scholar. During his chairmanship of the Department of Sociology at Fisk University and, later, during his presidency of that institution, he energetically continued his own research and writing while at the same time helping to organize a vital center of social research.

By contrast, E. Franklin Frazier, although he carried the heavy responsibility of the chairmanship of the Department of Sociology at Howard University and was deeply involved in community affairs and on international bodies, saw himself primarily as a teacher and an intellectual. Frazier was the youngest of the three figures we are considering here. He acknowledged his debt to W. E. B. Du Bois and his life continually intersected with that of Charles S. Johnson. However, he moved in his own direction, as he was the most explicitly concerned to contribute to sociology within the prevailing theoretical tradition, and to train a new generation of black sociologists. He struggled to achieve that degree of objectivity which he felt essential and which culminated in the publication of his *Black Bourgeoisie*, with the resulting outcries which he fully anticipated.[5]

The second section, "Black Sociologists in a Segregated Society," deals with the institutionalization of the work of black sociologists. Such work during this period took place essentially in segregated institutions. There were some important cracks in the walls. Black sociologists were trained mainly at the University of Chicago and later at Ohio State University and Washington State University, with a scattering elsewhere. Limited but important foundation funds for black sociologists were available from the Julius Rosenwald Fund and the General Education Board of the Rockefeller Foundation, while some support came from the federal government, starting with the New Deal period. At the national meetings of the American Sociological Society, as it was then called, a few black sociologists had contact with each other and with some of their white colleagues.

The essays presented in this second section focus on the development and adaptation of intellectual life in such a setting. Butler Jones presents an account of "The Unheralded Professionals," those black sociologists who labored diligently to teach sociology to large numbers of students in black colleges. This essay is more than an analysis of the difficult conditions under which they worked. He has examined the intellectual attraction of sociology to blacks. While Elliott Rudwick searches for specific cases of racist content in the emergence of sociology in the United States, Jones explores the essential assumptions and logic of sociological investigation that attracted Du Bois and succeeding generations. They saw in sociology the intellectual tools for the redefinition of race relations and, in turn, a postive element for social change.

Along with their teaching responsibilities, these black sociologists sought to engage in empirical research, and Butler Jones describes the severe limitations under which they operated. The main centers of sociological research work were at Fisk, Howard, and Atlanta universities. It was at these places that Johnson, Frazier, and Du Bois were active.

Fisk University, under the leadership of Charles S. Johnson for a period in the 1930s and thereafter, became the center of notable ferment and achievement. Stanley Smith's study is a case study of the organization and content of teaching and research at Fisk University as a center of excellence. He probes the organizational and leadership factors which accounted for its emergence and persistence. The study by James E. Blackwell in the final section of this volume, on the participation of blacks in the American Sociological Association, is also relevant as it deals with the limited response, and thereby failure, of the national professional society to face its organizational responsibilities toward black sociologists.

From the earliest years of the discipline in the United States, black sociologists were not only scholars. They engaged in social and political protest against the treatment of blacks. The pattern of scholarly endeavors on the one hand and civic presence in the larger society was set by W. E. B. Du Bois and carried forward by Charles S. Johnson and E. Franklin Frazier. To be a black sociologist also entailed civic activity. Charles U. Smith and Lewis Killian have traced the linkages between "Black Sociologists and Social Protest" up to and through the contemporary period of militant black consciousness. Their underlying assumption is that the analysis of the patterns and consequences of black protest needs to be seen in terms of the political circumstances of each historical period. Each form of protest must be interpreted in terms of its deviation from existing political practice. In short, it makes no sense to apply current notions and concepts to previous historical periods. Their analysis brings a wide range of material in focus as they analyze protest as a form of collective behavior.

In the third section, "The Contemporary Setting," the subject matter is the dimensions and limits of professionalization for black sociologists in a period of expanded opportunities and resources. James E. Conyers and Edgar G. Epps review and analyze the findings on social background and educational careers of black sociologists who have achieved higher degrees in sociology. This analysis treats the problems involved in increasing the numbers of black sociologists. Jacquelyne Jackson investigates the characteristics of female black sociologists and their interests and professional orientations. The processes of discrimination and segregation worked with double impact on females who were black. Her account is a contribution to the sociology of knowledge and demonstrates that the type of research these black female sociologists undertook was influenced by the organization of graduate training and the particular disabilities under which they operated.

In the contemporary setting, many members of the newest generation of black sociologists have rejected the existing format of sociological endeavor. Nathan Hare deals with this generation in "The Contribution of Black Sociologists to Black Studies." In the view of these sociologists, the political and social injustices under which black people live render inapplicable the categories of sociological thought derived from white society. A revolution in intellectual content is required. Hare's contribution sets forth the sociological orientations which propelled him and others to participate in the creation of black studies.

Black sociologists in the period since 1965 have raised more than organizational and professional issues. To speak of "Black Sociologists" requires an examination of an intellectual dilemma: is there one sociology or is there a special category of black sociology? Moreover, some issues are not subject to closure but require ongoing debate for clarification. This issue cannot be limited to that of content. It is one of theoretical formulation and of the nature and consequences of the knowledge that sociologists generate.

For the founding fathers, Du Bois, Johnson, and Frazier, the issue seems never to be raised or addressed. Their answers are hardly definitive, not because their views were incomplete but because sociology implies continuous self-criticism. The debate at the conference and the papers on theoretical issues presented in this volume at least state the issues. Before the conference, I myself did not believe that there was a white sociology and a black sociology, although I am fully aware of the psychological and social distortions that can systematically enter any organized effort at social research. After the conference and after editing this volume, I remain convinced that the distinction is not a viable one but that some ongoing tasks remain to be dealt with.

The papers explicitly on theory construction, by Walter Wallace and William Wilson, are by members of the new generation of black sociologists with widely different academic training, professional interests and responsibilities. They both share, however, a commitment to the proposition that the role of sociologists as intellectuals is distinct from the role of sociologists as private citizens. Yet neither makes any such distinction between white sociology and black sociology. They regard the sociological study of black society as a part of the larger enterprise of understanding society.

Granting this position, it still remains that the universality of the scientific method in social research has been applied with less than perfection. In particular, the segregation—purposively or by organizational inertia—of blacks from the professional and corporate life of sociology has meant that valuable human and intellectual resources have been denied the sociological endeavor. The experiences, the insights, and the intellectual creativity of black sociologists have not been fully brought to bear on sociology. The full contribution of blacks to sociology will have its intellectual consequences, specialized in their origin but to be judged by the broad and still evolving standards of scholarship. Blacks have had and will have a role in the explication of these standards as they bring the scientific method to bear. The issue becomes one of demonstration of the consequences.

Each of these theoretical analyses departs from a different set of concerns. Walter Wallace's essay starts with a redefinition of the distinction between social organization and culture, a redefinition which differs from conventional usage in sociology and social anthropology. His goal is to present sharply delineated conceptual areas and propositions about race relations which can be the basis for empirical research. William Wilson is less interested in the potentials of black sociologists and more interested in their accomplishments, since, regardless of the segregation of the larger society, they have their accomplishments which can be thought of as being their own yet still part of the broader historical currents. His theoretical analysis is based on the importance of codification of knowledge. His analysis points out the analytical incisiveness and rigor of the founding black sociologists and others during the initial period of institutionalization of sociology. According to Wilson, the new generation of sociologists, who have been deeply involved in new currents of social protest, have yet to make substantive contributions to sociology. Because these contributions of two sociologists of the new generation reflect diversity and convergence based on rational debate, they contribute to the growth of sociology as an intellectual discipline.

The final section of the volume returns to the institutional setting of contemporary sociology. The contributions of both Wilson Record and James E. Blackwell present materials which black and white sociologists might prefer to avoid. Wilson Record presents his analysis of the impact of the black studies movement on the corporate life of universities in the United States. Obviously, his materials are a report on developments still in progress, but he offers his data for scrutiny and evaluation. His thesis is that the black studies movement forced some white sociologists to abandon teaching and research on race relations and restricted their professional scope. It has thereby weakened university life and also impoverished the study of race relations. His data deal with self-reported movement of white sociologists out of race relations teaching and research. No doubt, in any period, there would have been some changes in areas of specialization, as sociologists mature and change their focus of interest. However, even without a control group for comparison, Wilson Record argues the relevance of his findings.

"Role Behavior in a Corporate Structure: Black Sociologists in the ASA," by James E. Blackwell, is a careful, detailed, and objective account of the "second-class" citizenship under which blacks operated in the American Sociological Association through its long history. It can be argued that American colleges and universities had primary responsibility for altering the second-class citizenship of black sociologists. But such an assertion does not reveal the particular failure of the national association to make use of its resources and influences. Blackwell's essay describes the claims made by black sociologists on the American Sociological Association and the response by the society. It is a noteworthy piece of writing because of its objective reporting and assessment of a series of events of considerable tension in which the author was the principal actor.

The Heritage of Sociology series was launched with the assumption that sociologists could make use of continuous assistance to overcome their tendency toward parochialism, both intellectual and social, and their tendency to forget their points of departure. The experiences involved in preparing this volume have, I hope, served that purpose for me. I have always considered the task of editing the Heritage of Sociology series a form of personal education. I thought that I had had a good perspective on the writings of black sociologists, if only because an important aspect of this history is linked to the University of Chicago. Clearly, there was and still is a great deal about the scholarship of black sociologists about which I am ignorant. But the sociological issue is deeper and more complex. University life is partly a network of personal relations, a condition which complicates the university's internal race relations and which requires open and candid exploration. Long before contemporary tensions, Everett C. Hughes posed the dilemma. "While the standards of judgment among professional peers are in some respects objective and universal, yet the specialized colleagueship of the academic, scientific and professional world are small and relations are quite personal. People are loath to hire a stranger. This is the front on which Negro scholars and professional men have to move forward."[6] The papers on the institutionalization of black sociologists were pointed towards developing this complex theme.

As a graduate student at the University of Chicago, during the years 1946 to 1948, I naturally read the writings of E. Franklin Frazier and Charles S. Johnson. (I had known more of Johnson's work because, as an undergraduate, I had been interested in personality and culture and had read his work on Negro youth.) Through the writings of these men, I was in turn led back to those of W. E. B. Du Bois and the other lesser-known contemporary figures. In subsequent years, because of my friendship with G. Franklin Edwards, I was able to make the personal acquaintance of E. Franklin Frazier. Professional contacts put me in touch with Charles S. Johnson. I had completed my apprenticeship with Bruno Bettelheim, psychoanalyst and educator, and was therefore interested in Frazier's and Johnson's appraisal of our "Dynamics of Prejudice."[7]

Both men were studied in their "tolerance" of this effort. They accepted the idea that studies of prejudice were part of the academic effort, but they were hardly attracted to them. They were both driving in their concern to see that the main line of scholarship on the sociology of the black community would continue and be expanded. This was the period of the early 1950s in the aftermath of the publication of Myrdal's study. In retrospect, I believe that they were fully aware of emerging trends in scholarship about the black community. As Edward Shils has pointed out, the new centers of sociology in the 1950s, at Harvard, Columbia, the University of Michigan and the University of California at Berkeley, were not continuing the tradition of research into the negro community.[8] Even at the University of Chicago, with the departure of the older generation, this tradition was also coming to a temporary end.[9]

After I left the University of Chicago for the University of Michigan, my personal contacts with the community of black sociologists were mainly maintained through my students, particularly Albert McQueen and Mary Queeley. But throughout the 1950s no major university in the North or the West organized a broad and integrated research program on the sociology of the black community, although the need was obvious and pressing. Departments of sociology had transformed themselves so that they were mirroring each other rather than developing individual interests.

In the 1960s the explosive events of the civil rights movement and, subsequently, of the militant nationalist pressures, both of which involved black sociologists, pressed in on organized sociology. The initial response had to be political and organizational. But it was abundantly clear that for sociologists there had to be an intellectual dialogue as well. There were key intellectual issues which had to be clarified and debated. There was never any doubt in my mind that the format of sociological analysis of race relations and the contributions of black sociologists would supply a positive element in restructuring race relations in the United States. Naturally, I did not look forward to an episode of discovery or rediscovery, but a protracted refocussing of issues. I believed this had to come, but not from any precise solutions the research disciplines such as sociology offer, for they offer none. Rather, this would be the case because of the commitment to inquiry, communication, and rational discussion among sociologists.

When, in 1971, I had the opportunity to become acquainted with James E. Blackwell, it become immediately clear that an assessment of the contributions of black sociologists to sociology, both past and contemporary, would supply an appropriate vehicle for probing the intellectual dimension of race relations. I believe that the conference on which this volume was based can be taken as one specific example of the role of ideas in facing up to the issues of race relations in an advanced industrial society. The conference took place only because of the effective leadership of James E. Blackwell.

One can acknowledge limitations in the discussion generated by the papers, and gaps in the final papers. However, we do have an overview and acknowledgement of range of achievement of black sociologists prepared by a group selected on the basis of academic qualifications. As long as sociology has been in existence in the United States, despite the segregation of American intellectual life, there has been a powerful tradition of the study of the black community by blacks, and the record can be fully examined. The slogan has been offered that, in the United States, the black community has a future without a past. It is not for me alone to judge the importance of sociology for the black community in the United States, but so far as a self-generating stream of scholarly sociological research is concerned, I do not need to do so; there clearly exists a rich past.

I obviously believe that an academic discipline can not persist and develop by means of formal publications alone. There must be face-to-face discourse, even on the most difficult and controversial topics, as was the case at this conference and in the final preparation of these papers. As a result, many sociologists were brought together, sociologists whose converging interests should have meant that they would have known each other by direct contact, but who had been kept apart either by the remaining consequences of segregation or by the sheer size and weakness of sociological organizations. The freshness and candor of a whole set of new and intense contacts which have real intellectual significance were for me a powerfully stimulating experience. But my reactions were deeply conditioned by the enormous strength of character, intellectual toughmindedness, and sense of civility of James E. Blackwell, whom I came to know during this experience.

Morris Janowitz

Notes

1   G. Franklin Edwards, *E. Franklin Frazier on Race Relations* (Chicago: University of Chicago Press, 1968).

2   In *American Sociological Review* 12, No. 3 (June 1947): 265-71.

3   *The Philadelphia Negro: A Social Study* (Philadelphia: University of Pennsylvania, 1899).

4   *The Negro in Chicago: A Study of Race Relations and a Race Riot.* Chicago Commission on Race Relations (Chicago: University of Chicago Press, 1922).

5   E. Franklin Frazier, *Bourgeoisie Noire* (Paris: Plon, 1955). American edition, *Black Bourgeoisie* (Glencoe: The Free Press, 1957).

6   Everett C. Hughes, "Race Relations and the Sociological Imagination," *American Sociological Review* 28 (1963): 887.

7   Bruno Bettelheim and Morris Janowitz, "Dynamics of Prejudice," in *Social Change and Prejudice* (N.Y.: The Free Press, 1964), pp. 101-328.

8   Edward Shils, "Tradition, Ecology, and Institution in the History of Sociology," *Daedalus* (Fall 1970).

9   While I was a graduate student at the University of Chicago, the issues which were to be raised by black sociologists in the 1960s about the organization of sociology were dimly perceived within the department, but they were perceived. Sociologists of Jewish backgrounds were gradually being appointed to the social science faculties of ranking universities. In the Division of Social Science at the University of Chicago, Allison Davis had been appointed as professor in the Department of Education and Abraham Harris was one of the most esteemed members of the Department of Economics. One could not assert positive discrimination but rather slowness in awakening to the problem. In addition, the Department of Sociology had its special problem; it could not regenerate itself and it was unable to make any effective appointments. Clearly, in retrospect, E. Franklin Frazier was eligible, although he was very senior in age at that time and the department had a number of specialists in race relations. The general decline in effectiveness and clarity of purpose of the Department of Sociology accounts, in part, for the failure to make this and other appointments. But the failure served to continue a "segregated" pattern which might have been broken.

I. The Life and Work of the Founding Figures

1

Francis L. Broderick

W. E. B. DU BOIS: HISTORY OF AN INTELLECTUAL

W. E. B. Du Bois for two full decades, from 1915 to 1935, stood without peer in Negro America. From his desk at the National Association for the Advancement of Colored People, he made his periodical, *The Crisis*, the preeminent spokesman for black equality in the United States and for the rights of colored peoples all over the world, and he used the distinction of his position to deliver in Europe, in all parts of America, and, on one isolated occasion, in Africa as well, an unfaltering argument for the establishment of racial justice.

For the previous decade, from 1905 to 1915, he had been the mind and soul of the protest against the politics and the social policies proffered by Booker T. Washington as the path upward. First from Atlanta and then from New York, Du Bois had condemned the compromises that he believed contributed to the dead ends of disfranchisement and economic obsolescence, increasingly taking on himself responsibilities and opprobrium for which he had little taste.

In the ten years from 1895 to 1905, he had established himself as a pioneer in sociology; *The Philadelphia Negro*, the subsequent Atlanta University Publications, and his study of rural Negroes in Farmville, Virginia, provided the first reliable information about Negroes in America based on empirical sociological research.

Even in the decade prior to 1895, Du Bois had been a notable man, for his years at Fisk, Harvard, and Berlin had brought him under the tutelage of an array of scholars whose combined distinction touched few, if any, other young Americans.

After 1935, when Du Bois went into eclipse, he lost none of the fiery brilliance of his earlier years. For another twenty-eight years, he continued to study, to quarrel with injustice, to project himself into new areas, to stay abreast of the world that he saw changing to conform to the vision of equality that he had seen, however uncertainly, from his youth, even as he changed his own social vision to conform to what he regarded as the new reality. His retirement came only when he was buried outside Christiansborg Castle in Accra, Ghana, in 1963, the state funeral of his adopted land echoing the memorial tribute of the March on Washington that fate, with a kindly sense of poetic justice, had scheduled for the moment of his death.

Now, more than a hundred years since his birth and less than ten years after his death, Dr. Du Bois, as he was always called by all except the smallest handful of people, holds a unique place in American history. His long career took him to many places. His incessant writing on a wide range of topics left behind an extraordinary record, the scope of which began to be appreciated again in the 1960s and 1970s when revived black consciousness led to republication of book after book by Du Bois, books long out of print and in danger of being permanently forgotten. Du Bois has a word for nearly everyone: his sensitive response to changing reality through the years led him to occupy a wide variety of ideological and tactical positions; virtually any policy for racial justice in America can find a precedent in his writing. His fame having raced ahead of peoples' capacity to fathom him, his elusiveness makes more intriguing the process of trying to understand him.

Black and White America

A useful place to start is the recollection of Du Bois's insight into both black and white America. Du Bois spent his first fifteen years not in the rural south but in Great Barrington, Massachusetts, a rural white community where a black presence was long accepted as a matter of course. Du Bois's *Autobiography* describes his early years with detail and specificity not available in earlier works like *Darkwater*.[1] In such earlier work Du Bois made clear that if long-established residents in his community drew social lines, they were more likely to draw them against recent immigrants who worshipped in the Catholic church than against black neighbors. The *Autobiography* fills out its author's childhood with a wealth of detail that few people would remember into their twenties, much less into their eighties or early nineties. Du Bois knew his black community and those in the surrounding towns well, as his dispatches to the *New York Age* attest. At the same time, his life was fully lived in a preadolescent and adolescent culture where, as he said, he had "almost no experience of segregation or color discrimination." [2]

When he went off to Fisk, he "suddenly came to a region where the world was split into white and black halves, and where the darker half was held back by race prejudice and legal bonds, as well as by deep ignorance and dark poverty," [3] and where the norm of his daily experience was close contact with two hundred students from all parts of the South. During two summers he taught at rural schools in Wilson County, Tennessee. Yet even at Fisk, the all-white faculty and the young Du Bois's growing awareness of politics in a period when the move toward disfranchisement and legal segregation had not taken full hold kept him constantly aware of worlds both black and white. During his years at Harvard he lived two lives—the academic hours when his contacts with William James and Albert Bushnell Hart gave him a "vision of a commonwealth of culture open to all creeds and races and colors" [4] and the social hours when he moved easily in and out of the society of long-established black families. Gone now was the easy mutual acceptance he had known in adolescence—he resented his fellow students, their fixation on his race a constant reminder of the anomaly of his presence among them. Yet in class, where he did well (in history unusually well), and at public ceremonies, like graduations, where his addresses were vigorously applauded, and in the company of his professors, who measured his talent and not his hue, he belonged. For two years in Europe after Harvard, he was startled into escape from the "physical provincialism of America" and what he called the "psychical provincialism of any rather narrow race problem," [5] and he never again was fully recaptured by either. During his years in Atlanta, he taught at a Negro university, did research on Negro occupational groups, lectured across the country primarily to black audiences. But he worked with a mixed faculty under white presidents, and his articles appeared in magazines of general circulation. His research established him without American peer at the International Races Congress in London in 1911. His analysis of presidential elections, usually occurring in the context of advice on how to vote, showed how keenly he stayed in touch with dominant national trends. His conversion to socialism in the first decade of the century was a response to white American socialists— John Spargo, Jane Addams, Jacob Riis, Richard T. Ely, and, on a personal level, Mary White Ovington. Even his years at the NAACP kept him close to the white tradition of reform: throughout his twenty-five years there, the board of directors of the NAACP was controlled by white men and women, and only after the arrival of James Weldon Johnson as executive secretary in 1920 did the year-round operation of the group pass from white control.

Du Bois's insights into white and black worlds had their limits, to be sure. His was the scholar's and the publicist's role. He lacked Booker Washington's flair, in his genial migrations from county fair to conventions of black groups, for projecting an image of easy camaraderie, or Walter White's ebullient readiness to call everyone, up to and including residents of the White House, by his or her first name. He knew the rural poverty of Lowndes County, Alabama, just as he knew the discriminatory practices of craft unions; that is, he knew them as a scholar who studied them, not as a county agent or an organizer who lived with them. He knew John Spargo through his books. He knew Oswald Garrison Villard through correspondence and in formal board meetings; his friendship with Joel Spingarn of Columbia was unique in over nine decades of dealing with white men. Even when Du Bois went on his nationwide lecture tours, he was seen more than he saw: he tarried a day or two with an old acquaintance or a former student or a professional friend, gave his precisely arrayed speech at a local church or fraternal hall, then moved on. He had little interest in small talk, and scarcely enough time for minimal pleasantries. His reputation for abruptness, aloofness, and short patience was deserved; the judgment that he despised the masses or the intellectually inferior was not. He had his own style, and he gave of himself in his own manner: his deep knowledge came from study, and his wide influence came from formal speeches and from the carefully prepared printed word.

Du Bois knew the implications of his insight into both black and white worlds. In a famous passage in *The Souls of Black Folk*, he noted the conflict within: "One feels ever his two-ness,—an American, a Negro, two souls, two thoughts, two unreconciled strivings; two warring ideals in one dark body, whose dogged strength alone keeps it from being torn asunder."[6] The conflict was a source of anguish. It was also a source of strength that dealt with the anguish. Du Bois never ceased developing the insights that came from either part of his "two-ness."

Travel and Study

Du Bois brought those insights to a range of experience that touched four continents, that expanded continuously from constant study, and that took shape in a multitude of forms from statistical sociology to literary fantasy. A long life—ninety-five years for Du Bois—leaves much time for leisure, but he never learned about leisure; even as a young man at Harvard, he told the Boston black community that the five thousand dollars a year it spent on amusements would be better spent on a center for cultural uplift and on scholarships for young Harvard students. He set the same standard for himself: no justification for a trip to New York except to see the sights like the Statue of Liberty. The view persisted when pupil became tutor, and the stringer for the *New York Age* became editor and publisher in his own right. He stored information with relish and reached gluttonously for more.

His travels were only the beginning of his experience, but a solid beginning. When he went from Harvard to Berlin in 1892, he spent time to the limit of his money traveling in and beyond Germany; to England, France, Italy, and the Netherlands; to Vienna and Budapest, Cracow and Prague. In Eisenach he had an innocent affair with "Dora," and in Paris a tasteless one better forgotten but in fact remembered. He came to know Tannhäuser even before he broke in his taste on the Italians. He saw Sarah Bernhardt, and he "haunted" the Louvre. In territory that would later be called Poland he learned of an oppressed people, alien and subordinate in their own land. In Hungary, remote from the fair skins of Northern Europe, he was easily mistaken for a Jew, and he was treated accordingly, that is, he was put in his place. An English friend gave him an elegant last few days in England, "prattled finely" about selecting one transatlantic cabin rather than another, then sent his young American friend on his way—by steerage, of course, for if Du Bois had had enough money to go by cabin, he would probably have found time to see Scotland or circumnavigate the Azores.[7]

Du Bois went overseas as often as he could. Only six years passed before he went back to Paris, this time as creator of an exhibit on the American Negro for the World's Fair in 1900. In 1911 he returned to London for the Races Congress; he read a poem and gave two speeches. Just as World War I ended, he took passage to Europe to investigate the treatment of American Negro soldiers; he collected a significant mass of information, as yet unpublished. He went to Europe three more times in the 1920s, including one subsidized trip to Russia in 1926. He was awed by the Soviet Union: "I stand in astonishment and wonder at the revelation of Russia that has come to me. I may be partially deceived and half-informed. But if what I have seen with my own eyes and heard with my ears in Russia is Bolshevism, I am a Bolshevik."[8] In 1923, returning from Europe, he had first touched Africa, the homeland, and its breath of instant kinship changed an unexpected diplomatic assignment into a rush of emotion that covered three centuries and that eventually carried Du Bois into his final exile. All told, he visited Europe fifteen times.

Asia lagged well behind: he went through China on the way from Russia to Japan in 1936. Again in 1959, after years in which depression and war and Du Bois's own troubles with the American government curtailed his foreign travel, he entered China: "I have never seen a nation which so amazed and touched me as China in 1959 . . . Fifteen times I have crossed the Atlantic and once the Pacific. I have seen the world. But never so vast and glorious a miracle as China. This monster is a nation with a dark-tinted billion born at the beginning of time, and facing its end; this struggle from starved degradation and murder and suffering to the triumph of that Long March to world leadership. Oh beautiful, patient, self-sacrificing

China, despised and unforgettable, victorious and forgiving, cruci-
fied and risen from the dead.''[9]

And finally, the move to Ghana, there to work until death parted
breath from work and left Du Bois in peace in the laterite of his
spiritual homeland.

For a man whose salary hovered at five thousand dollars for
much of his professional life, the amount of travel was closer to
extraordinary than to unusual. He wanted to know, and his student
days had taught him the delight of knowing firsthand. He liked
good food and wine. He enjoyed the camaraderie of bright people.
He welcomed the respite from routine insult in America, his elegant
manner and command of German and French making him different
from other American tourists—different and esteemed, not different
and demeaned.

The foreign portions of his travel were the highlights, not the
total. From the earliest days in Atlanta through his *Crisis* years and
beyond, Du Bois was ever on the go across and around the United
States. During his heyday he was a favorite of the young on college
campuses. Among older people there was a generation that could
remember that Du Bois had challenged, outlived, and eventually
vanquished B. T. W. and his program, and their reverence was a
tonic for doubts or despair. After Du Bois's indictment in early 1951
for failure to register as the agent of a foreign principal, he was on
the trail again, raising money to defend himself and scorning what
he regarded as the Truman administration's attempt to stifle his
''determination to think and speak freely on the economic foundation of the wars and the frustration of the 20th century.''[10] After the
trial he was off to tour again, triumph and poverty making a heady
pair of engines. Only when he reached Accra in 1961 did the
pace—ninety-three-year-olds being what they are—slacken.

Beyond travel was study, that is, vicarious travel into other
men's minds, reflection on both kinds of experience, and then
perhaps a new synthesis, sometimes a dramatic new synthesis. His
perception of World War I in 1915 showed this process of synthe-
sizing in a highly dramatic way. The young Du Bois had traveled
widely in Europe; his summaries for the *New York Age* were detailed travelogues of a conventional character; something to write
home about, perhaps, but nothing requiring preservation into per-

petuity. Then after his return home, his research and study focused on domestic topics. Along the way, the Negro part of his two-ness noted that the problem of the twentieth century is the problem of the color line. His own research and agitation led him to the writings of American socialists—Spargo, Riis, Ely—and maybe, directly or indirectly, to L. T. Hobhouse. From his combined experience—travel, study, racial insight—his judgment on the war had an integrity of its own. He loathed the Belgians, whose conduct in the Congo deserved retribution. He had a sentimental tie to England and France, whose treatment of darker people was fairer than most. He knew of no color line in Russia, and he rejoiced in Japan's rise to power in the war of 1904-5. Germany simply exalted race prejudice, and its victory would make necessary a world war of races. Six months later Du Bois added a socialist variation to his analysis: in "The African Roots of War," he worked through an analysis of a new "democratic despotism"—an alliance of exploiting capitalists and skilled and unskilled labor that divided up the spoils created by colonial labor forces, largely dark colonial peoples. He used all his ways of knowing, and his judgment went beyond what he could prove statistically to what he knew intuitively, or at least to what he could appraise from his own experience. [11]

Du Bois had more than one way to summarize his experience, and he refined his judgments in poetry and short stories as well as in sociological accounts. *The Quest of the Silver Fleece* (1911) is a thinly coated tract on the crop lien system and its profits for Northern capital and Southern planters. *Dark Princess* (1928) is a mad romance about the conspiracy of the whole colored world for mastery. If the first work was Dreiser, the second was unmatched Hergesheimer. Yet, in fact, both were Du Bois just as *The Philadelphia Negro* and "The Litany of Atlanta" were Du Bois. All were ways to extend his experience, both his personal experience and his vicarious experience, that then provided a rich lode from which he could draw by whatever device best served the need at hand. His classic work, *The Souls of Black Folk,* showed his versatility—sketches of people, bits of autobiography (including the meditation on the death of his infant son), some sociology adapted for the *Atlantic Monthly,* short stories, a trenchant but respectful polemic against Booker Washington. Its central argument challenged accommodation as a social policy and set the tone for the next era—protest and resistance, manhood and full citizenship.

Freedom from Institutional Bonds

Insight into the black and white worlds—a gain in depth—and experience and study that made him at home all over the world—a gain in breadth—could have lost their thrust if Du Bois had found himself confined by institutional obligations. A need for caution at this moment, a consuming committee assignment at that, a call for unity at a moment of peril, a sense of ruin if security were sacrificed to what at any moment seemed to be principle—the hundred cares to which talent may feel vulnerable—these things narrow options, suggest compromises, invite conformity. But they had little effect on Du Bois: in a long life he resisted ties that would confine him. He paid the price, to be sure: abrupt changes of jobs, financial insecurity beyond what even his close friends realized, isolation at times when institutions might have provided support. Yet he regarded his own independence from institutional bonds as more important than the price.

Du Bois's life is a parade of situations in which he guarded his independence, none more vivid than his relations with the NAACP. During Du Bois's first term of employment there, as editor of *The Crisis* from 1910 through 1934, the outside world, to the extent that it cared at all, viewed the NAACP and its lively editor as one. News of the association was carried in the columns of *The Crisis*, its victories in the Supreme Court were recorded and applauded there. But Du Bois's voice was the one most often heard; the editor was the most active perambulating speaker at association conventions and regional functions. Within the organization during those twenty-five years, only James Weldon Johnson, appointed executive secretary in 1920, was in Du Bois's league; Johnson's predecessors were inconspicuous, and his successor, Walter White, however talented, conspicuously lacked the stature of either Du Bois or Johnson. So completely did the world outside view Du Bois and the NAACP as one, that his departure in 1934 came as an incomprehensible thunderbolt. The master was denouncing his apprentices. The heart was renouncing the body.

Reality was more complex, as reality is wont to be. For the first ten years of its life, the NAACP had largely white leadership—the phrase "new abolition society" was applied to it more than once. The board of directors was dominated by white leadership—Moorfield Storey, Spingarn, Villard, Ovington—and even the executive secretary was white in the early years. This group had a common program to remove discrimination, especially segregation, from all aspects of American life: it planned to educate the American people to the scandal of their abuse of Negro rights, to initiate action in courts and legislatures to remove existing obstacles to Negro progress, and to organize in a single large pressure group Americans black and white who knew that the color line undermined democratic values.

Du Bois did not quarrel with this program, though he found himself more ready than his upper-class white liberal associates to become explicit in denouncing the "oppression of shrewd capitalists" and the "shackles on social intercourse from the President and the so-called church of Christ down to bootblacks." But theirs was not his program, and *The Crisis* sang an independent tune. The white board sought to remove barriers. Du Bois called upon Negroes to work out their own projects: "Conscious self-realization and self-direction is the watchword of modern man, and the first article in the program of any group that will survive must be the great aim, equality and power among men." He called for Negro unity—in cooperatives for production and distribution, in art and literature, in politics, in Negro organizations (including the NAACP) unswervingly committed to "our objects, our aims, our ideals."[12]

The tension between Du Bois and his white associates erupted in board meeting after board meeting, so much so that Villard, Du Bois's main adversary, finally withdrew to a passive position. Du Bois could have his way, in part because the board knew, Du Bois knew, and each knew that the other knew, that no one could really replace him, and in part because the success of *The Crisis* (at one point in 1919 it was selling 104,000 copies a month) gave Du Bois an independent power base. He might agree that his editorials should never drop to a "level of petty irritation, insulting personalities or vulgar recriminations"[13] (imagine not agreeing to such a proposition!), but he never let the association set his priorities. In fact, when he set about organizing his Pan-African congresses from 1919 to 1927, he cajoled partial support for his expenses from the NAACP board, even though the members of the board were skeptical of or hostile to the whole project.

The institutional tie continued on Du Bois's terms. The association understood that its truculent employee brought it distinction. Du Bois recognized the value of his institutional base: it gave him a well-established podium that left him time and freedom to travel, to study, and to write, without any more hindrance than an occasional explosion in board meetings. He was accustomed to explosions, both as victim and as incendiary. He usually emerged without a scratch.

The depression that began in 1929 changed the rules, for it deprived *The Crisis* of financial independence. Walter White, as executive secretary of the NAACP, sought to use fiscal control as a way of bringing *The Crisis* to heel, closer to the institutional priorities expressed by the NAACP itself, especially the continued struggle against segregation. Du Bois responded by developing his ideas on Negro separatism into a fully elaborated program for a totally autonomous Negro community, in which artists and colleges, capitalists and workers, politicians and churches, served complementary roles in achieving black security in a collapsing white capitalist world. As for the NAACP's now traditional stand against segregation, Du Bois said bluntly that the Negro people could not base their salvation upon the empty reiteration of a slogan. The board, rejecting his position, made clear that it would not tolerate his use of *The Crisis* to argue against the association's position. Du Bois, who for just under twenty-five years had never accepted that kind of editorial dictation, was, at the age of sixty-six, not willing to turn his independence over to anyone, least of all to Walter White. He left—with scarcely a backward look.

The long episode at the NAACP—for the historian, if not for the sociologist, the most significant portion of Du Bois's life—is both instructive and typical. *The Crisis*'s success allowed Du Bois to keep his own counsel; until the very end he was an employee only in the sense that the NAACP paid his salary. The institutional cord was conspicuous, serving both his purposes and the NAACP's, but slack enough to leave him unhampered. When the cord grew tight, he broke it, reasserting the independence that he had always required. In Great Barrington, high school had been for learning—no more. He may have thrown himself unequivocally into his new life at Fisk, but when he got to Harvard, he held aloof from the institution as anything but a classroom, a sentiment that Harvard reciprocated fully until very recently. At Wilberforce and Pennsylvania, his first jobs after Europe, he recalls himself as the visiting German-trained scholar, complete with gloves and cane. Even his dozen years at Atlanta never committed him fully to the life of the place—"I did not know my students as human beings; they were to me apt to be intellects and not souls."[14] He was ever the demanding, austere professor of sociology whose interests ranged far beyond the university. The Pan-African congresses, as his own creation, imposed only institutional ties that he defined and controlled. His reprises at Atlanta (1934-44) and at the NAACP (1944-48) repeated earlier patterns in a striking way, Du Bois's independence in each case reinforced by the added dignity of his years. He went into the Socialist party as a favor to Miss Ovington, and out again when he sensed the danger of limitation. He joined the Communist party when he was in his nineties, past the time when institutional restraints could touch him.

The lifelong pattern had its price—he never managed to put aside enough money to take care of tomorrow—but it left him the riches that he wanted, the freedom to write and speak as his vision of the world commanded him.

A Mission to Tell

That vision commanded him imperiously from his earliest years. He developed a sturdy pride during his high school years, partly the heritage from the strength of his mother, to whom he was very close; partly the product of his success in school, known and applauded by the neighbors in Great Barrington; partly the result of the special status as judge and spur that his weekly columns in the *Age* conferred upon him.

An undirected sense of impending greatness grew within him. At every stage of his development, he could look around and say: who has done better? The answer was invariably reassuring. The lad who at the age of fifteen had already begun to save and annotate his collected papers assured his fellows at Fisk that he had not come South to pose as a critic "but to join hands with this, my people." When quips from his sharp tongue threatened to get him a fist in the teeth from his heftier classmates, he learned prudence. But on the important matters, he knew how to speak out. He made himself a close student of politics in Tennessee. He learned about the conditions of blacks in that and surrounding states. He caught a vision of white aristocrats in the South working with educated Negroes to lead the masses in both races, and he urged his own generation of college students to cast off the race's grateful thralldom to the Republican party so that Negroes could bargain effectively, perhaps even making their strength the balance of power between the two old major parties. At graduation he delivered an encomium on Bismarck: Bismarck, as Du Bois recalls in his *Autobiography,* "had made a nation out of a mass of bickering people." Would Du Bois do likewise, not with subtle diplomacy and conquering armies, but with the power of truth—the true "mission of the black orator of the 20th century"?

At Harvard the dream seemed plausible. The black community of Boston and Cambridge, hospitable, impressed, gave him and his schoolmate William Monroe Trotter the deference due to Harvard men. His professors treated him seriously, not casually (which would have been discouraging), nor ebulliently (which would have been patronizing), but seriously, professionally, recognizing talent that needed training rather than genius that need coddling. The young Du Bois took their counsel in the spirit of shared professionalism in which it was given. His interests turned from the natural sciences through philosophy to history, where Hart could encourage him both to success and to a career. Schmoller, with an oblique assist from Adolph Wagner, took him the next step into sociology.

In Germany, on his twenty-fifth birthday, he played with alternatives for his next quarter-century. Would he seek to raise an empire in Africa through England, France, or Germany? Would he make his name in science or in literature? If such a life was doomed to hopelessness, he mused, at least there was grandeur in that hopelessness, and perhaps at some future time he would live to strive again. "I am glad I am living, I rejoice as a strong man to run a race, and I am strong—is it egoism is it assurance—or is it the silent call of the world spirit that makes me feel that I am royal and that beneath my sceptre a world of kings shall bow. The hot dark blood of that black forefather born king of men—is beating at my heart, and I know that I am either a genius or a fool... Heaven nor Hell, God nor Devil shall turn me from my purpose till I die....I therefore take the work that the Unknown lays in my hands and work for the rise of the Negro people, taking for granted that their best development means the best development of the world." [15] Later that same year—it was 1893—he made his specific commitment: to build a department of sociology at a Negro university— Howard was his first choice—there "scientifically to study the Negro question past and present with a view to its best solution." [16] *The Philadelphia Negro* showed a close match between his ambition and his talent, and his appointment to Atlanta University in 1897 set him off on what he had always called his "real life work."

Du Bois's keen sense of his own individuality and of his mission became something of a legend during his lifetime. Bruised egos in every group that he touched were a continuing reminder that the easy cordiality of institutional politicking invariably took second place, a very low second place, to the pressing business of getting on with a job for which there were, and are, always too few talented innovators. Characteristically—indeed it was characteristic of both of them—Du Bois never got along with Monroe Trotter. From his desk at *The Crisis*, Du Bois needled black editors and black ministers, the two groups of leaders whose local contact with large groups of people provided the surest conduit of influence for him and his ideas.

Within the NAACP, he tangled with everyone who was not a subordinate—with the staff, with the board of directors, with branches all over the country. Professor Spingarn warned him against magnifying personal differences into issues of principle; even Du Bois's close friends at the NAACP and in the whole colored world, Spingarn said, felt "mingled affection and resentment." When Du Bois left the NAACP, even Miss Ovington, his friend for more than thirty years, greeted with relief the departure of the "octopus" that had been draining the strength of the organization.[17]

Du Bois never hankered after people who could not keep up with him: "I often discount human facts in comparison with divine thoughts," he once said.[18] He had a clear sense of who he was, of his function at the cutting edge of racial progress, of the unlikelihood that he could combine popularity with truth as he knew it. It was not his mission to be lovable, or comfortable as an old shoe. It was his mission, he thought, to know the race, the nation, and the world, and to tell each what they needed to know about the other two.

Flexible Responses to a Changing World

In his long life Du Bois found himself advocating a whole range of positions. He looked to scholarly research as a way of convincing white America of its obligation to racial justice, and he made himself the professional activist for reform. He worked for integration into white America, and he defended the necessity and the virtue of separate black development. He recognized the reality of the Negro's status as one person in ten in a predominantly non-Negro society, but in isolated moments his despair led him to cry out for violence as the response to violence. He focused on America, and he viewed the rising tide of color throughout the world as the context for the struggle in America. He accepted the reality of capitalism, and he looked to socialism as the reality of the future. He had an enduring commitment to peace; yet he supported, somewhat belatedly, America's entry into World War I.

With an intellectual's affection for consistency, Du Bois liked to reconcile his position today with his position yesterday. The complexity of his changing positions allowed him to write what historians sometimes call "lawyer's history" in making a case. To give lawyers their due, lawyer's history is not without its own legitimate claims. But in a swiftly changing historical context, consistency is a dubious virtue; only an astonishingly static and rigid person can bridge decades without new thoughts. In fact, Du Bois had the resources to change in response to context, and his ninety-five years covered an astonishingly changeable context. His insights into worlds both black and white; his experience, both personal and vicarious; his independence from structural or institutional commitments; his intense sense of his own individuality and mission—all let him deal with changing reality and kept him as vibrant in his closing years as he had been in his prime and in his youth.

At twenty-seven, Du Bois could plausibly endorse Booker Washington's emphasis on an economic base for Negro progress at the expense of political activity and social acceptance. The generation since the Civil War had brought deep trauma to the South, both white South and black South, and a variety of political alignments, probed on a trial-and-error basis, had led not to the emergence of white and black men of education leading the masses of both races or to the emergence of an effective Negro voting force serving as the balance of power between old white parties—both patterns that Du Bois had projected at Fisk—but to the gradual exclusion of Negro voting that started dramatically in Mississippi in 1890 and was to be completed in Georgia eighteen years later. The dreams of Frederick Douglass had never come true. Washington's speech at Atlanta was a plausible stopgap in a deteriorating situation: create the solid base of economic security, and all else would follow in good time. Du Bois gave his approval conditionally: the South must open doors of economic activity. It must respond to "political sympathy" that Negroes would extend.

But the stopgap became a dead end. Disfranchisement spread like the plague, legal discrimination followed, and violence became endemic. Du Bois would tolerate educational and property qualifications for voting as long as they applied equally to both races; but the Hardwick bill in Georgia in 1899 promised no such evenhanded treatment. Du Bois acknowledged the importance of industrial training even as he argued for the training of college-bred leaders as the cutting edge of the race and for the foundation of fact that would guide future policy. But he found no reciprocal support from Tuskegee when he approached Northern wealth to which Washington held the key. Furthermore, he grew doubtful that Tuskegee was in fact providing the economic base that was the only justification for the Atlanta Compromise: Tuskegee was preparing for a handicraft age when the present, to say nothing of the future, lay with a mechanized society. And, in any case, how many graduates of Tuskegee went on to the economic roles for which their education supposedly prepared them?

Looking at his own work, Du Bois could detect little impact from his research. *The Philadelphia Negro* was not on everyone's lips, even within the scholarly world. The Atlanta Publications won scholarly praise but no substantial support; the profession itself, Du Bois charged to and about Walter F. Willcox of Cornell, preferred judgments based on chance observations from the window of a railroad car. The magazines of general circulation—*Dial*, *Harper's Weekly*, *Atlantic*, *Outlook*, *McClure's*—were losing interest in the Negro.

The context changed. Du Bois changed. *The Souls of Black Folk* pointed the direction, "The Litany of Atlanta" indicated its intensity, and the program of the Niagara Movement proclaimed its range. When the Progressive movement spilled over into a concern for racial justice, the NAACP gave Du Bois his base for a brilliant quarter of a century.

The Great Depression eroded that base, and once again Du Bois moved on. Once again his own growth interacted with the changed world in which he lived. Living in New York and traveling extensively outside the South, he developed a perception of politics that gave him some of the most penetrating columns in *The Crisis*. His concern for Negro labor led to a solid understanding of the nature of trade unions in an industrial capitalist economy—indeed, Du Bois, almost alone, was spared the barbs of a younger generation of Negro intellectuals in 1933 who condemned their elders for ignorance of the economic roots of Negro degradation. He worked out a sense of relation between black and white that spared only Spingarn from mistrust. These new perceptions within Du Bois were occurring as the whole of American society was changing. Negroes migrated North in dramatic droves, and urban America joined the rural South as home for the black population. A new generation of problems grew up in the new setting: the huddled groups in cities had their impact on residential patterns, on employment (blacks being the new immigrants now that the European flow had slowed to a trickle), on politics, on the growth of a substantial middle class, on social interaction within the black community and with the surrounding white neighbors. A campaign like Marcus Garvey's back-to-Africa movement had a marketable product because it now had a clearly defined market.

Through the twenties Du Bois chronicled the development of this new world—its resources, its potential. *The Crisis* monitored colleges. It encouraged new writers. It observed banks and businesses. It recorded, and stimulated, racial pride. It warned against excesses: Du Bois gave Garvey sufferance for two years, then denounced his movement for its "spiritual bankruptcy and futility." When the deep poverty of the depression blotted out all hope for the future, Du Bois urged the race to turn inward to its own resources and to build a world it could call its own. Having lived a long time, more than sixty years, and having faced the need for a segregated facility when nothing else was conceivable—a colored YMCA, a separate officers' training camp in World War I, *The Crisis* itself as "capitalized race prejudice"—Du Bois had no difficulty in arguing that an autonomous Negro community, stretching across state and class lines, was consistent with what he had always believed. The "Negro Renaissance" brought attention to a lively generation of new writers, and in drama and the arts new talents emerged. Negro colleges, especially their students, struggled to free themselves from white control by trustees and administrations. Blacks as a separate political force became a real possibility when segments of the 12 million Negroes became concentrated in small geographical areas. Business and the professions developed in the same context. Despairing of white America, because of its prejudice and because of the bankruptcy of its economic system, Du Bois turned to an autonomous black community as the true way to the light. He did not shudder to call the movement "segregation," and when the NAACP and Walter White threatened his job, he handed it to them.

The Negro press viewed his new policy as a massive retreat. Was Booker Washington right after all? the *Chicago Defender* asked sadly. In fact, the resemblance between Du Bois's position and Washington's position was superficial, for Du Bois made the race master in its own house on a basis more easily understood in 1972 than in 1934. That people could not see was, for Du Bois, more a function of their myopia than of his miscalculation.

Withdrawing to Atlanta for a decade, 1934-44, Du Bois never regained stage center. Even before his eclipse, leadership had passed to functional areas—trade unions, newspapers, business, churches, politics, literature—and, until Martin Luther King, Jr., no one took Du Bois's charismatic place. Yet, ironically, his final years are in many ways his most characteristic, for they gave him a stage worthy of his talents. His decade in Atlanta was only a remarkable reprise of his earlier stay; many of the same scholarly enterprises engaged his attention, and at some points he consciously modeled his work on earlier tasks. But when he reemerged in 1944, first at the NAACP, then at the Council on African Affairs, then on his own, his attention ranged over the emerging colonial nations and his public controversies centered on socialism and peace. All these topics were deeply rooted in his own past.

In a sense the world, at least the world of America, finally caught up with him. He had become aware of colonial frictions while he was abroad as a graduate student, and he had formed his judgment of European nations to some extent on his view of their dealings with their colonial subjects—a high rating for France and England, a low rating for Belgium and Germany. In 1915 his remarkable essay on "The African Roots of the War" had called Americans' attention to topics remote from their perception of the German menace. After the war, the Pan-African congresses, the first in 1919, the fourth and last in 1927, had been his vehicle for unifying the voices of the oppressed in Africa under American Negro leadership to encourage the colonies' freedom from their imperial masters. He had watched India's restiveness under British rule with mounting hope, and he had made a sorrowful chronicle of Ethiopia's subjection by the Italians. World War II blew the old world apart. Du Bois understood: *The World and Africa* and *Color and Democracy: Colonies and Peace* were useful handbooks that caught the worldwide mood of emancipation.

He stayed abreast of the spread of socialism. As early as 1907, he had told readers of his magazine, *The Horizon*: "In the socialist trend ... lies the one great hope of the Negro American." He had welcomed the Bolshevik revolution and, after his trip to Russia, in 1926, he had identified himself with it, however little good he had to say about the American Communist party. Until World War II, other topics had muted this one, but he never forgot the socialist tune.

American policy after World War II brought many of his long-held ideas into focus. In the 1920s, Pan-Africanism was only a dream, its resolutions for colonial liberation the stuff of scarcely noted rallies. But in 1945, the restless colonial people were making their voices heard. Du Bois, referred to as the "soul" of Pan-African congresses by a European newspaper in the earlier era, issued the call once again when the guns were barely cool. Sixty nations and colonies were represented in London in October 1945, the Gold Coast by Kwame Nkrumah, later the first president of Ghana. Du Bois returned from the conference ebullient and encouraged— and also miffed, for the movement had enough vitality to become wary of an American voice, even Du Bois's, as its spokesman. From Du Bois's point of view, freedom was triumphing everywhere; so much that he had perceived from his early years was coming to pass before his eyes, so many judgments ratified, so many causes triumphing. Russia, no longer the pariah, now emerged as the second of the great powers, a master to command, not a suppliant to petition. In China the victory of the Communists was not far in the future. The old colonial powers, except the United States, were in collapse: India would throw off England peacefully; France would lose Indochina in a snarling war.

In Du Bois's view, only the United Sates, rattling its armies and its wealth and its atomic and hydrogen bombs, stood in the way of the new order. So he took up the cause against the United States in the name of peace and for the triumph of socialism. When black Americans gave faint response to his plea for help at the time of his trial, he traveled abroad to draw his plaudits from the colored and socialist world. Humboldt University in Berlin, Charles University in Prague, Lomonosov State in Moscow named him "Doctor," and China gave national notice to his birthday.[19] In his move to Ghana at the end, he turned his back on his native land, giving up at last the American half of the "two-ness" that had molded him since his youth, and looked for continuing rest in the continent of the future. He had sensed the future, and he had told of it. Now it had come to meet him.

From the beginning and all along the way Du Bois's career had a central thrust—equal justice for all men, especially for men of color for whom the experience would be so novel. He never ceased to enrich his experience, looking to both the white and the colored worlds. He never tied himself into an inflexible position that would restrain him in his prophetic mission. Along the way, as times dictated, he went this way or that. But tactical versatility never gave him pause. Indeed, he never paused.

Notes

1   W. E. B. Du Bois, *The Autobiography of W. E. B. Du Bois* (New York: International Publishers, 1968).

2   Du Bois, "My Evolving Program for Negro Freedom," in Rayford W. Logan, ed., *What the Negro Wants* (Chapel Hill, 1944), p. 32.

3   Ibid., p. 36.

4   "Harvard and Democracy," typescript of speech, n.d., W. E. B. Du Bois Papers.

5   "Comments on My Life," typescript, ca. 1943, Du Bois Papers.

6   *The Souls of Black Folk* (Chicago, 1903), p. 3.

7   *Autobiography*, pp. 154-82.

8   *The Crisis* 32 (November 1926): 8.

9   *Autobiography*, pp. 47, 53.

10   Ibid., p. 377; Du Bois, *In Battle for Peace* (New York, 1952), passim.

11   *The Crisis* 9 (November 1914): 28-30; Du Bois, "The African Roots of War," *Atlantic Monthly* 115 (May 1915): 707-14.

12   "The Immediate Program of the American Negro," *The Crisis* 9 (April 1915): 310-12.

13   Minutes of the board of directors of the National Association for the Advancement of Colored People, January 3, 1916.

14   *Autobiography,* p. 283.

15   Quoted in Francis L. Broderick, *W. E. B. Du Bois: Negro Leader in a Time of Crisis* (Stanford, 1959), pp. 28-29.

16   Du Bois to Slater Fund Trustees, ca. April 1893, Du Bois Papers.

17   Joel Spingarn to Du Bois, October 24, 1914, James Weldon Johnson Collection, Yale University; Mary White Ovington to Oswald Garrison Villard, July 22, 1934, Oswald Garrison Villard Papers, Harvard University.

18   *The Crisis* 35 (July 1928): 388.

19   *Autobiography,* pp. 23, 25, 32, 405.

2

Elliott Rudwick

W. E. B. DU BOIS AS SOCIOLOGIST

The works of several of the most prominent black sociologists—E. Franklin Frazier, St. Clair Drake, and Horace Cayton—
reveal their indebtedness to W. E. B. Du Bois. Frazier, for example,
dedicated *The Negro in the United States* to Du Bois and said his
efforts were "the first attempt to study in a scientific spirit the
problems of the Negro in American life" (Frazier 1957, p. 503).
Drake and Cayton, in their classic *Black Metropolis* (1954) noted
that Du Bois's *The Philadelphia Negro*—written nearly a half-
century earlier—was the "first important sociological study of a
Negro community in the United States" (Drake and Cayton 1945,
p. 787). Ironically, their teachers, the influential Robert Park and
Ernest Burgess, were aware of Du Bois's writings and cited him in
their texts; they did not mention his *Philadelphia Negro*, while they
did cite sources such as Charles Booth's *Life and Labour of the
People in London* (1889, 1891), *Hull House Maps and Papers*
(1895), plus other social surveys (Park 1929, pp. 4-7; Burgess
1916, p. 493).

Du Bois, in fact, is best known as the most prominent propagandist of the Negro protest during the first half of the twentieth
century, largely because he was one of the principal founders of the
National Association for the Advancement of Colored People and for
almost twenty-five years editor of the NAACP's official publication,
The Crisis. Yet from the time he received his Ph.D. from Harvard in

An editors' note presenting additional data and alternative conclusions to some of
Elliott Rudwick's formulations appears on page 50.

1895 until shortly before World War I, Du Bois was responsible for impressive pioneering research on black Americans. In both his training and the quality of his published scholarship, Du Bois compares favorably with other sociologists.

At the turn of the century, sociology was just emerging as an academic discipline from the more generalized field of "social science" that included political economy, government, social problems, and even history (Bernard and Bernard 1943, pp. 559-644). The first formal department of sociology was organized in 1892 at the University of Chicago, the second at Columbia in 1894 (Bernard and Bernard 1943, p. 657; Barnes and Becker 1938, pp. 976-79). Moreover, the American Sociological Society was not founded until 1905, when sociologists separated from the American Economic Association (Bernard and Bernard 1943, p. 559).

Thus, in the 1890s, sociology, economics, the study of social problems, and the field of social ethics were closely intertwined and often not distinguished. Many scholars were interested in using social science to improve human society. Much of their work was imbued with a reformist spirit more akin to the study of social ethics than to scientific sociology. We should emphasize that the concern of these scholars with problems of the criminal and the poor did not involve a belief that society needed fundamental change. Their interest was reformist rather than radical and was closely related to the developing field of social work. In fact, during the early twentieth century the most important studies of American blacks, done by contemporaries of Du Bois like John Daniels (1914), Mary White Ovington (1911), and George Edmund Haynes (1912), were all explicitly directed toward providing knowledge for social work programs.

Reflecting this faith of an important segment of America's social scientists that knowledge would lead to the solution of social problems, Du Bois, during his early career, passionately believed that research could supply the basis for achieving a racially equalitarian society. He contended that race prejudice was caused by ignorance and that social science would provide the knowledge to defeat injustice. Sociology was not recognized as a separate discipline at Harvard when he studied there; Du Bois took his Ph.D. in history, but also earned many credits in the social sciences. He recalled that "my course of study would have been called sociology" (Du Bois 1940, p. 39). Among the courses he took was Ethics of Social Reform, taught by F. G. Peabody, who in the 1880s had been one of the pioneers in teaching academic courses in "social science." Peabody was interested in applying knowledge of society to the treatment of its ills (Bernard and Bernard 1943, pp. 614-16). From his advisor, Albert Bushnell Hart, Du Bois imbibed an emphasis on careful empirical research. Du Bois himself largely credited Hart's research methods with having "turned me back from the lovely but sterile land of philosophic speculation, to the social sciences as the field for gathering and interpreting that body of fact which would apply to my program for [advancing] the Negro" (Du Bois 1968, p. 148).

In 1892, during his graduate work at Harvard, Du Bois went to the University of Berlin for a more concentrated program in the social sciences. He examined Prussian state reform under Rudolph von Gneist and "Industrialism and Society" under Adolph Wagner. For Gustav von Schmoller's seminar, Du Bois wrote on "The Plantation and Peasant Proprietorship System of Agriculture in the Southern United States." Probably more than any other professor under whom Du Bois had studied, Schmoller stressed the value of a hard-nosed empiricism and the faith that a systematic body of knowledge could be used to shape national policy (Broderick 1958, p. 16).

With his zeal for collecting "facts," Du Bois had only impatience for the armchair generalizing of such social theorists as Herbert Spencer or Franklin H. Giddings. He commented: "The biological analogy, the vast generalizations, were striking, but actual scientific accomplishment lagged. For me an opportunity seemed to present itself. I could not lull my mind to hypnosis by regarding a phrase like 'consciousness of kind' as a scientific law. . . . I determined to put science into sociology through a study of the condition and problems of my own group. I was going to study the facts, any and all facts, concerning the American Negro and his plight, and by measurement and comparison and research, work up to any valid generalization which I could" (Du Bois 1940, p. 51).

Du Bois's opportunity came in 1896, when municipal reformers in the Philadelphia settlement-house movement invited him to describe and analyze black participation in local politics and other social institutions. Familiar with Booth's *Life and Labour of the People in London* as well as with the *Hull House Maps and Papers*, Du Bois and his sponsors believed that a painstaking study of Philadelphia's Negroes could provide a guideline for improving their social conditions (Du Bois 1899, p. x; Davis 1967, p. 96). Accordingly, in addition to writing a rigorous empirical monograph, Du Bois set forth specific proposals for racial advancement. In *The Philadelphia Negro*, which Gunnar Myrdal described as a model "of what a study of a Negro community should be" (1944, p. 1132), Du Bois enthusiastically played his dual role of social scientist and social reformer.

Philadelphia in the mid-1890s had over 45,000 blacks, the largest Negro population of any city in the North. For over a year Du Bois was a participant-observer in the Seventh Ward, "the historic centre of Negro settlement in the City," where about one-fifth of the community's blacks lived (Du Bois 1899, p. 58). His study area was appropriate not only because the Seventh Ward contained the largest concentration of Negroes in Philadelphia but also because it was the chief locus of black community institutions such as the church and, as Du Bois put it, because all social classes, with their "varying conditions of life," were represented there. Using a lengthy questionnaire, he did a house-to-house survey of all the black families in the ward. He compiled voluminous data on patterns of migration into and within the city, family structure, income, occupations, property holdings, social stratification, black community institutions, politics, pauperism. The data gave a dismal portrait of unemployment, job discrimination by both employers and trade unions, wretched housing, family breakdowns, substantial criminality, and widespread health and hygienic problems. On the other hand, Du Bois's monograph was a brilliant description of the contours and functioning of the black community, its institutions, and its mechanisms for racial survival and advancement.

His interviews revealed that three-fourths of the black working-men of the Seventh Ward were "laborers and servants" and that about the same proportion of the women were employed as "day laborers and domestic servants." The color bar in Philadelphia's many manufacturing plants was especially striking—about 8 percent of the blacks had factory jobs (Du Bois 1899, pp. 101–2, 108). Du Bois commented that, in the Seventh Ward, "the mass of Negroes are in the economic world purveyors to the rich—working in private houses, in hotels, large stores, etc." (Du Bois 1899, p. 296). Most blacks were thus engaged in low-paying jobs, and many could obtain only irregular work. "Stevedores, hod-carriers and day-laborers are especially liable to irregular employment, which makes life hard for them sometimes.... The mass of men ... meet their greatest difficulty in securing work. The competition in ordinary laboring work is severe in so crowded a city. The women day-laborers are, on the whole, poorly paid, and meet fierce competition in laundry work and cleaning" (Du Bois 1899, p. 133).

However, about one-fourth of the men were employed in skilled trades, in the professions, and as small businessmen, providing the economic base for what Du Bois termed the city's small black "aristocracy." Yet even the most successful black entrepreneurs—the barbers and caterers—labored under serious difficulties. Barbering had once been "an almost exclusively Negro calling" but, by the end of the century, competition by white immigrants was driving blacks out of the lucrative white market. Changes in fashion and "the application of large capital to the catering business" had destroyed the position of the nationally famous black caterers who had dominated this business in Philadelphia throughout much of the nineteenth century. Du Bois noted: "If the Negro caterers of Philadelphia had been white, some of them would have been put in charge of a large hotel, or would have become co-partners in some large restaurant business, for which capitalists furnished funds" (Du Bois 1899, p. 120).

The black man's economic plight was, of course, reflected in the various "social problems"—illiteracy, "pauperism," crime, and family disorganization—which had initially prompted the white philanthropists and social workers to ask Du Bois to undertake his study. *The Philadelphia Negro* includes trenchant descriptions of the overcrowded squalor in which the city's black poor were forced to live. It discusses extensively how such poverty, exacerbated by the new influx of many penniless and illiterate Southerners and by the serious economic depression of the 1890s, accounted for black criminality. More important for long-range sociological interests, however, was Du Bois's pioneering examination of black family life.

Du Bois described the direct connection between economic status and family structure. He contrasted the conventional middle-class family life of the "well-to-do," a group that E. Franklin Frazier later termed the "Black Puritans," with the temporary cohabitation and common-law marriages among the very poor. Du Bois noted the difficulties of sustaining a cohesive family life, even for workers with regular employment. He was the first sociologist to indicate the disproportionately numerous female-headed households among the black poor. The substantial number of women describing themselves as "widowed and separated indicates widespread and early breaking up of family life. . . . The number of deserted wives . . . of unmarried mothers . . . is astoundingly large and presents many intricate problems" (Du Bois 1899, pp. 66-68). The situation, he explained, resulted partly from the heritage of slavery and even more from harsh economic realities in the cities. As he observed, "economic difficulties arise continually among young waiters and servant girls"; having married, they "soon find that the husband's income cannot alone support a family; then comes a struggle which generally results in the wife's turning laundress, but often results in desertion or voluntary separation" (Du Bois 1899, p. 67). The role of the black woman as breadwinner, both when the husband was absent and when he was present, was revealed in the statistics: where 16 percent of the native white women were employed, 43 percent of the black women were breadwinners. Thus, even among the "great mass of the Negro population" characterized by households headed by men with regular employment, the minimal income of these men, combined with the relatively high rents families had to pay, often involved serious problems. "The low wages of men make it necessary for mothers to work and in numbers of cases to work away from home several days in the week. This leaves the children without guidance or restraint for the better part of the day" (Du Bois 1899, pp. 113-14). Forced to rent part of their dwellings to lodgers in order to pay the landlords, "38 percent of the homes of the Seventh Ward have unknown strangers admitted freely into their doors. The result is, on the whole, pernicious, especially where there are growing children. . . . The lodgers are often waiters, who are at home . . . at the very hours when the housewife is off at work, and growing daughters are thus left unprotected. . . . In such ways, the privacy and intimacy of home life is destroyed, and elements of danger and demoralization admitted" (Du Bois 1899, pp. 193-94).

Du Bois identified three factors responsible for this "pressing series of social problems": slavery, which left so many of its victims untrained, uneducated, and impoverished; the enduring prejudice of white Americans; and the influx of migrants from the South. In slavery, with its "attendant phenomena of ignorance, lack of discipline, and moral weakness," and in migration, with its increased competition, lay two basic causes of the urban blacks' condition. "To this must be added a third as great—and possibly greater influence than the other two, namely the environment in which a Negro finds himself—the world of custom and thought in which he must live and work, the physical surroundings of house and home and ward, the moral encouragements and discouragements which he encounters" (Du Bois 1899, p. 284). Though *The Philadelphia Negro* was written in scholarly tones and during an era of widespread accommodation to white supremacy, Du Bois's indictment of white prejudice was unmistakable. He stressed that blacks lived in a different environment from whites, that the basis of the difference was "the widespread feeling all over the land, in Philadelphia as well as in Boston and New Orleans, that the Negro is something less than an American and ought not to be much more than what he is" (Du Bois 1899, p. 284).

He found discrimination pervasive, but devoted his attention particularly to the barriers in the way of the black man's economic development. Regardless of ability, a black man did not have the same opportunity to work as a white man. "There is no doubt that in Philadelphia the centre and kernel of the Negro problem so far as the white people are concerned is the narrow opportunities afforded Negroes for earning a decent living" (Du Bois 1899, p. 394). His examples ranged from the school system, which refused to appoint black graduates of its own normal school to positions outside the few all-black schools, to the trade unions, whose policies of exclusion drove blacks from the foothold they once had in the building trades. Not only were caterers and barbers losing their white customers, Negro shopkeepers were unable to attract white patronage. Black pharmacists, clerks, and unskilled workers of all kinds found it difficult to get employment in the fields for which they were training. Even butlers, coachmen, and janitors were being displaced by whites (Du Bois 1899, pp. 89, 128, 326-32). Blacks were forced into poverty, and the black paupers became objects of philanthropic assistance. Even though many charitable institutions were discriminating against blacks, Du Bois concluded ironically, "the class of Negroes which the prejudices of the city have distinctly encouraged is that of the criminal, the lazy and the shiftless; for them the city teems with institutions and charities ... for them, Philadelphians are thinking and planning; but for the educated and industrious young colored man who wants work and not platitudes, wages and not alms, just rewards and not sermons—for such colored men Philadelphia apparently has no use" (Du Bois 1899, p. 352).

Du Bois also emphasized the impact of discrimination on the personalities and aspirations of black men and women and their children. Foreshadowing the interest of scholars like Frazier, Charles S. Johnson, and Allison Davis, who in the early 1940s would explore the impact of segregation and discrimination on blacks, and especially on Negro youth, Du Bois observed: "when one group of people suffer all these little differences of treatment and discriminations and insults continually, the result is either discouragement, or bitterness, or over-sensitiveness, or recklessness.... The Negro finds it extremely difficult to rear children in such an atmosphere and not have them either cringing or impudent: if he impresses upon them patience with their lot, they may grow up satisfied with their condition; if he inspires them with ambition to rise, they may grow up to despise their own people, hate the whites and become embittered with the world" (Du Bois 1899, pp. 324-25).

In stressing the importance of migration, Du Bois also prefigured a subject that would interest later sociologists studying black urban communities. The "Great Migration" began during

World War I, nearly two decades after Du Bois did the research for *The Philadelphia Negro*, yet throughout his book he displayed a keen awareness of the significance for urban Negro life of the movement of Southern blacks to the cities. Like Johnson, Frazier, and the others to come, Du Bois emphasized the fact that the desire to escape from oppression in the South motivated the migration. He reported that most of the blacks in the Seventh Ward were migrants, the majority having arrived during the preceding decade. Only one-third were born in Philadelphia; more than half had been born in the South (Du Bois 1899, pp. 74-79). These young, impoverished, often illiterate Southerners settle "in pretty well-defined localities in or near the slums, and thus get the worst possible introduction to city life." Constantly, Du Bois related the problems of urban Negroes to their Southern rural and small-town origins— whether in examining literacy, pauperism, crime, or family life. For example, in discussing criminality, he observed that while arrests among blacks "after the war . . . decreased until the middle of the seventies," after that, "coincident with the new Negro immigration to cities," they rose steadily (Du Bois 1899, pp. 81-243). This migration, he explained, accounted for "much that is paradoxical about the Negro slums," which had long remained at the same locations. "Many people wonder that the mission and [reform] agencies at work there for so many years have so little to show by way of results." In large part the reason was "that this work has new material continually to work upon," as those who moved up economically moved away and left the poor behind (Du Bois 1899, p. 306).

Du Bois's generalizations about social problems later became standard in sociology. But when *The Philadelphia Negro* was written, they contrasted strongly with the racist assumptions held by most sociologists and by the general public. Du Bois rejected explanations based on biological differences or inherent inferiority, emphasizing instead the critical importance of historical and environmental factors. In describing his method of studying black Philadelphians, Du Bois stated that the student of the social problems affecting ethnic minorities must go beyond the group itself. He "must specially notice the environment: the physical environment

of city, sections and houses, the far mightier social environment—
the surrounding world of custom, wish, whim, and thought which
envelops this group and powerfully influences its social development" (Du Bois 1899, p. 5). Discounting notions of innate differences between classes and peoples, he observed: "We rather
hasten to forget that once the courtiers of English kings looked upon
the ancestors of most Americans with far greater contempt than
these Americans look upon Negroes—and perhaps, indeed, had
more cause. We forget that once French peasants were the 'Niggers'
of France, and that German princelings once discussed with doubt
the brains and humanity of the *bauer*" (Du Bois 1899, p. 386).

But *The Philadelphia Negro* would scarcely be an important
contribution to sociology if it had been confined to describing social
problems and discussing their causes. This book lives because it is a
well-rounded study of a local black community—its social strata, its
institutions, and its varying life styles. It was thus a forerunner of
the holistic community case studies that culminated in Drake and
Cayton's *Black Metropolis*.

Especially important was Du Bois's emphasis on the complexity
and variety in the black community, most notably in the differentiation among the social classes and their varying life styles. This was
directed partly at countering white stereotypes of blacks. More
important, his discussion of social class was functional in terms of
understanding the black community. Finally, his class analysis was
at the heart of his proposals for race advancement.

Du Bois observed, "There is always a strong tendency ... to
consider the Negroes as composing one practically homogeneous
mass. This view has of course a certain justification: the people of
Negro descent in this land have had a common history, suffer to-day
common disabilities, and contribute to one general set of social
problems." Yet, if the numerous statistics supplied in the volume
"have emphasized any one fact it is that wide variations in ante-
cedents, wealth, intelligence, and general efficiency have already
been differentiated within this group" (Du Bois 1899, p. 309).

Du Bois's analysis of social stratification in Philadelphia's black
community reflected the moral standards of the social reformers of
that period. While his conceptualization was not so refined as that

employed by social scientists today, he used criteria that included income, occupation, and life style. He described four general social "grades" or classes. At the top, constituting about one-tenth of the population, was an upper class or "aristocracy," "families of undoubted respectability earning sufficient income to live well; not engaged in menial service of any kind; the wife engaged in no occupation save that of housewife . . . the children not compelled to be bread-winners, but found in schools; the family living in a well-kept home." Primarily entrepreneurs and professional people, they were largely Philadelphia-born, often descended from domestic servants, and included many mulattoes. This was the class most assimilated to American middle-class culture. Its members usually felt compelled, as the elite of the race, to spend more than their white neighbors on clothes and entertainment.

The next group, about half of the whole, was "the respectable working class; in comfortable circumstances, with a good home, and having steady, remunerative work, the younger children in school." This group consisted of "the mass of the servant class, the porters and waiters, and the best of the laborers." Ambitious and anxious to rise in the world, they were hard-working and beginning to accumulate property. While they usually had lodgers and their wages were low compared to those of whites, they had neatly furnished homes. "The best expression of the life of this group is the Negro church where their social life centers." Their greatest difficulty was finding suitable careers for their children; the lack of "congenial occupation, especially among the young," produced widespread disappointment and discouragement.

Below this group of strivers came "the poor; persons not earning enough to keep them at all times above want; honest, although not always energetic or thrifty, and with no touch of gross immorality or crime." About one-third of the population, they were "the poor and unfortunate and the casual laborers"; many lived in slums or on back streets. "They include immigrants who cannot get steady work; . . . unreliable and shiftless persons who cannot keep work or spend their earnings thoughtfully; those who have suffered accident and misfortune . . . many widows and orphans and deserted wives. . . . Some correspond to the 'worthy poor' of most charitable organizations and some fall a little below that class." The children of the very poor tended to go to school irregularly and, through poverty and sometimes parental neglect, became "the feeders of the criminal classes."

At the bottom of Du Bois's classification was the group with criminal records—about 6 percent, which loomed large in the eyes of white Philadelphians (Du Bois 1899, pp. 311-18).

As in *Black Metropolis* and other works of the Warner school, the theme of social class was used in *The Philadelphia Negro* as an integrating device, although not so explicitly as later scholars like Allison Davis and Drake and Cayton would use it. Yet, as Drake and Cayton have noted, "All serious students of Negro communities since Du Bois have been concerned with the nature of social stratification" (Drake and Cayton 1945, p. 787). In *The Philadelphia Negro*, occupation, property-holding, literacy, and income, on the one hand, and style of family life, on the other, are all related to social class. Similarly, the institutional structure of the black community—notably the church—was clearly integrated with the class structure. The well-to-do mostly attended either St. Thomas Episcopal Church, representing the most educated and economically secure of the black Philadelphians, or the Central Presbyterian Church, representing "the older, simpler set of respectable Philadelphians." Their style of worship was formal and reserved; the aristocracy "shrink from the free and easy worship of most of the Negro churches." The great mass of "respectable" working-class people attended the large African Methodist Episcopal and Baptist churches. Thus at Mother Bethel AME Church, one found "the best of the great laboring class—steady honest people," while at Union Baptist "one may look for the Virginia servant girls and their young men." The very poor largely did not have a church, but some tended to fill "a host of noisy missions" (Du Bois 1899, pp. 172, 177, 198, 203-4, 220).

Du Bois emphasized that the church performed a number of important social functions, some latent, that served as an integrative force in the black community. Black Philadelphia churches were the center of social life "to a degree unknown in white churches." They also offered opportunities for status, recognition, and office-holding that made them "almost political." Their forums, lyceums, and musical events were important in the community's cultural life. Their publishing houses and newspapers gave them a significant place in the black economy of the city. Finally, "all movements for social betterment are apt to centre in the churches" (Du Bois 1899, pp. 201-3, 207). Many beneficial societies, building and loan associations, and secret societies were organized in churches. Ministers frequently served as employment agents; and considerable charitable work was conducted by churches.

Du Bois stressed the importance and integrative functions of the secret and beneficial societies and of other forms of cooperative endeavor—ranging from building and loan associations, through organizations of waiters, coachmen, and barbers, to social welfare institutions such as the Home for Aged and Infirmed Colored Persons and the Frederick Douglass Hospital and Training School. These organizations showed "how intimately bound together the Negroes of Philadelphia are" (Du Bois 1899, p. 227).

Another important contribution in *The Philadelphia Negro* was Du Bois's implicitly functional analysis of black participation in city politics. At the time, Philadelphia was one of the most notoriously corrupt American cities, dominated by a powerful Republican machine. In Du Bois's words, most blacks were the machine's "willing tools." While personally critical of its venality, Du Bois attempted to show the machine's functions for blacks. In that era Negroes, of course, were traditionally loyal to the Republican party because of its role in the Civil War and Emancipation and because the Irish, the blacks' chief competitors and antagonists in the labor market, were Democrats. In fact, Du Bois demonstrated that the Republican machine functioned for blacks as the Democratic party did for the Irish. On a very practical level, the machine offered protection to those engaged in vice and minor crime and to a larger body of noncriminal migrants harassed by the police. It provided clubhouses where the poor could come for drinking, gambling, and sociability. City Hall, although dispensing only token jobs as schoolteachers, policemen, and clerks, was nonetheless the largest employer of blacks in nonmenial positions in Philadelphia. Given the highly limited economic opportunities for blacks, these few white-collar jobs were extremely important and were ordinarily filled by well-qualified blacks of high ability and education.

Du Bois made the earliest analysis of the relationship of turn-of-the-century municipal "good government" movements to the Negro population, in an illuminating discussion of "The Paradox of Reform." The reform movement promised "efficiency" and "honesty" in government and condemned the corrupt machine's relationships to poor immigrants and blacks, but it failed to recognize the important needs that the machine filled for the minority communities. A few economically secure Negroes did support the reformers but, as Du Bois perceived, their victory was likely to be dysfunctional for blacks, depriving them of the few benefits they received from political participation (Du Bois 1899, pp. 372-84; 1905, pp. 31-35).

The Philadelphia Negro was a conscientious and perceptive sociological study. But Du Bois undertook the research as more than description and analysis. In the final section of his monograph, Du Bois the social scientist and fact-gatherer became the social reformer recommending solution for the problems he had highlighted. He criticized whites for offering platitudes and sermons rather than providing jobs and extensive financial aid for racial advancement. Discrimination, which Du Bois called "morally wrong, politically dangerous, industrially wasteful and socially silly," was to be eliminated by the whites: "It is the duty of the whites to stop it" (Du Bois 1899, p. 394). "A radical change in public opinion" was needed to give blacks equal opportunity to forge ahead. Such a change "would inspire the young to try harder; it would stimulate the idle and discouraged, and it would take away from this race the omnipresent excuse for failure: prejudice. Such a moral change would work a revolution in the criminal rate during the next ten years" (Du Bois 1899, p. 395).

However, Du Bois insisted that much of the responsibility for the race's advancement lay with blacks themselves. "That the Negro race has an appalling work of social reform before it need hardly be said," he observed. Despite the history of oppression and discrimination, Du Bois contended that modern society had the right to demand "that as far as possible and as rapidly as possible the Negro bend his energy to the solving of his own social problems." Blacks had the "right to demand freedom for self-development" and substantial aid from whites for schools, relief, and preventive agencies, "but the bulk of the raising [of] the Negro must be done by the Negro himself. . . . Against prejudice, injustice and wrong the Negro ought to protest energetically and continuously, but he must never forget that he protests because those things hinder his own efforts, and that those efforts are the key to his future" (Du Bois 1899, pp. 389-90).

Du Bois believed that this key required the development of the cooperative economic and social endeavor which he had described. Economically, while advancement must come largely from a change in white attitudes and behavior, cooperation among Philadelphia's blacks would provide many job opportunities in black-owned establishments. The hope of blacks was in "the mastery of the art of social organized life." In pushing the race forward, the black "aristocracy" would play the crucial role, but it was the duty of whites to support their efforts. In a foreshadowing of Frazier's *Black Bourgeoisie,* Du Bois unhappily reported that the black upper class felt considerable alienation from the masses and had a pronounced tendency to remain aloof. Fearing that they might be mistaken for the masses, many of the elite isolated themselves and rationalized their not acting as race leaders by arguing that they refused to draw "the color line against which they protest." Although the rise of Philadelphia's tiny number of business and professional black men had been so difficult that "they fear to fall if now they stoop to lend a hand to their fellows," Du Bois reiterated their "duty toward the masses." They should establish more social services, such as day nurseries and sewing schools. They should develop more building and loan associations, newspapers, labor unions, and industrial enterprises. In short, foreshadowing his famous theory of the "Talented Tenth," Du Bois preached an ideology of Negro self-help and solidarity, a program of racial self-elevation under the leadership of an educated black elite (Du Bois 1899, pp. 233, 389-96).

Du Bois conceived of *The Philadelphia Negro* as the start of a larger research program in which Negroes in other key American cities and in selected rural areas would be similarly studied. Discovering that many black Philadelphians had migrated from rural Virginia, he went there in the summer of 1897 and gathered material for a social study that the United States Bureau of Labor published as *The Negroes of Farmville, Virginia*. That autumn, he returned to Philadelphia to address the American Academy of Political and Social Science, where he urged support for his ideas about an extensive program of research among blacks. From the standpoints of pure science and of practical social need, he argued, the study of more than eight million Americans of African descent should be a matter of the highest priority. Unfortunately, the research thus far done had been "lamentably unsystematic and fragmentary" and, "most unfortunate of all," had been superficial and racially biased. "The most baneful cause of uncritical study of the Negro is the manifest and far-reaching bias of writers. . . . When such men come to write on the subject, without technical training, without breadth of view, and in some cases without a deep sense of the sanctity of scientific truth, their testimony, however interesting as opinion, must of necessity be worthless as science" (Du Bois 1898a, p. 22). Du Bois maintained that, because Negroes were readily identifiable and segregated, they provided especially valuable subjects for historical, anthropological, and sociological inquiry that would contribute substantially to the advancement of human knowledge. At the same time, the importance of scientific knowledge as a prerequisite for social understanding and the solution of social problems remained an important consideration: "The sole aim of any society is to settle its problems in accordance with its highest ideals, and the only rational method of accomplishing this is to study those problems in the light of the best scientific research" (Du Bois 1898a, p. 16). Accordingly, he proposed a research plan far more ambitious than merely encouraging small-scale studies by independent, individual scholars. The necessary work would be difficult and expensive and would require decades to complete. Only a venture involving cooperation between a black college and the major universities would be sufficient to carry it out. "The first effective step toward the solving of the Negro question will be the endowment of a Negro college which is not merely a teaching body, but a centre of sociological research, in close connection and cooperation with Harvard, Columbia, Johns Hopkins, and the University of Pennsylvania" (Du Bois 1898a, p. 22).

There was no interest in his appeal, and Du Bois attempted to implement the proposal on his own. He accepted a teaching position at Atlanta University in 1897. There, building on a modest research program already inaugurated by President Horace Bumstead and trustee George Bradford (Du Bois 1903a, p. 436), Du Bois unveiled a grandiose one-hundred-year plan for a comprehensive investigation of various aspects of black community life, such as business, education, the church, welfare organizations, family life, and criminality. He envisioned "ten-year cycles" in which data on each topic were to be published. During each decade, such research projects were to be continued simultaneously. After a century, enough would be known about Negro life to be of inestimable benefit to the entire society (Du Bois 1903a, pp. 435-39). As he explained, "The method employed is to divide the various aspects of his [the black American's] social condition into ten great subjects. To treat one of these subjects each year as carefully and exhaustively as means will allow until the cycle is completed. To begin then again on the same cycle for a second ten years. So that in the course of a century, if the work is well done we shall have a continuous record on the condition and development of a group of 10 to 20 millions of men—a body of sociological material unsurpassed in human annals" (Du Bois 1904, p. 88). In presenting this program, Du Bois used arguments similar to those used at the American Academy of Political and Social Science. Sociology had to move from the broad abstractions and unsystematic fact-gathering that "have neither permanently increased the amount of our own knowledge nor introduced in the maze of fact any illuminating system or satisfying interpretation" to "the minute study of limited fields of human action, where observation and accurate measurement are possible and where real illuminating knowledge can be had. The careful exhaustive study of the isolated group, then, is the ideal of the sociologist of the 20th century—from that may come . . . at last careful, cautious generalization and formulation" (Du Bois 1904, p. 85). A study of American blacks provided "a peculiar opportunity . . . never in the history of the modern world has there been presented . . . so rare an opportunity to observe and measure and study the evolution of a great branch of the human race as is given to Americans in the study of the American Negro. Here is a crucial test on a scale that is

astounding and under circumstances peculiarly fortunate. By reason of color and color prejudice the group is isolated—by reason of
incentive to change, the changes are rapid and kaleidoscopic; by
reason of the peculiar environment, the action and reaction of social
forces are seen and can be measured with more than usual ease."
Denouncing the racist bias of contemporaries, he called for a dispassionate, scientific attitude: "We urge and invite all men of
science into the field, but we plead for men of science—not for ...
men with theories to sustain or prejudices to strengthen. We sincerely
regret that there has been a tendency for so many men without
adequate scientific knowledge and without conscientious study to
pronounce public opinions and put gratuitous slurs on me and my
people which were as insulting to us as they were to their own
scientific reputations" (Du Bois 1904, pp. 86, 89).

Since Atlanta University was a struggling and impoverished
institution that could not afford to support Du Bois's research
adequately for one year—much less for a decade or a century—it is
a tribute to his determination that he actually supervised the preparation of sixteen Atlanta University sociological monographs between 1897 and 1914. Obliged to use only unpaid part-time investigators, Du Bois was limited in the breadth and extensiveness of the
study projects. He has described the method he was forced to use:
"work in sociology was inaugurated with the thought that a university is primarily a seat of learning and that Atlanta University, being
in the midst of the Negro problems, ought to become a centre of
such a systematic and thoroughgoing study of those problems....
It goes without saying that our ideals in this respect are far from
being realized. Although our researches have cost less than $500 a
year, yet we find it difficult and sometimes impossible to raise that
meagre sum. We lack proper appliances for statistical work and
proper clerical aid; notwithstanding this, something has been done.
The plan of work is this: a subject is chosen; it is always a definite,
limited subject covering some phase of the general Negro problem;
schedules are then prepared, and these with letters are sent to the
voluntary correspondents, mostly graduates of this and other Negro
institutions of higher training. They, by means of local inquiry, fill
out and return the schedules; then other sources of information,

depending on the question under discussion, are tried, until after six or eight months' work a body of material is gathered" (Du Bois 1903b, p. 162).

Considering the limited resources at Du Bois's disposal, it is not surprising that the Atlanta monographs do not compare with *The Philadelphia Negro* as a contribution to sociology. They were uneven in quality, planning, methods, and content. At the less successful end of the spectrum were *Some Efforts of Negroes for Their Own Social Betterment,* done in 1898 and repeated in 1909, and *Economic Cooperation among Negro Americans,* produced in 1907 and dealing partly with the same kind of material found in the other two monographs. "Mathematical accuracy in these studies is impossible; the sources of information are of varying degree of accuracy and the pictures are woefully incomplete" (Du Bois 1909, pp. 5-6). In attempting to examine the charitable work of churches, secret societies, and other organizations that blacks were establishing for themselves, Du Bois in 1898 selected several Southern cities. The college graduates who collected the data were asked to record "typical examples." He was fortunate to obtain the services of these interviewers, but he gave them few instructions beyond telling them to submit limited descriptions of some benevolent organizations within their own communities. Du Bois recognized that he could not check the material he would receive for reliability or validity. He succeeded in amassing an encyclopedic array of facts, often having little connection to each other, and he simply added them up where he could. There is list after list of services and societies, with little or no comment except an indication of what could be accomplished through greater collective action. The local church questionnaire, for example, included such items as: number of enrolled members, number of active members, value of real-estate indebtness, number of religious meetings weekly; entertainments per year, lectures and literary programs per year; suppers and socials per year; concerts and fairs per year; number of literary and benevolent and missionary societies; annual income, annual budget, disbursements for charity, number of poor helped, and so on. Du Bois considered his presentation as a significant "scientific" contribution which demonstrated that Negroes were not "one vast unorganized, homogeneous mass." However, race prejudice had isolated the group and caused the accelerated formation of racial institutions for which no adequate preparation had been made. He believed that more inquiries like his would establish the extent of white aid which the race required (Du Bois 1898b).

This Atlanta monograph, and all the others as well, offered Du Bois considerable opportunity to play the role of social reformer. At the conclusion of each year's project, he and Atlanta University hosted a conference that brought educated Negroes and a sprinkling of sympathetic whites to the campus for a discussion of the relevance of the research topic to the future advancement of the Negro. Du Bois usually served on the resolutions committees of these conclaves and was influential in composing exhortations and admonitions about ways to improve living conditions among blacks. The resolutions printed in the annual monographs generally did not grow out of the inductive studies and typically failed to suggest specific techniques to accomplish the desired ends. Thus in 1898 Du Bois's resolutions committee urged black churches to cut their operating expenses and use the money to increase charitable work. Funerals were criticized as too extravagant—blacks were urged to make them simple and inexpensive, and to eliminate tawdry display. Similarly, black secret societies were told to "be careful not to give undue prominence to ritual, regalia, and parade" (Du Bois 1898b, pp. 47-48). Obviously, Du Bois and his fellow counselors of austerity failed to appreciate the integrative and status functions of expensive rituals here. In this, of course, they were imbued with the Puritan ethic of reform that characterized much of sociology in the progressive era.

The 1907 *Economic Cooperation among Negro Americans* was to be "a continuation and enlargement" of the 1898 account. In his treatment of the black church in 1907, Du Bois did not use the 1898 material on individual churches. Instead, he discussed the income, expenses, mission work, and many other details of the larger religious denominations. In this later study, he did not refer to his handling of the beneficial and insurance societies in 1898. The 1898 monograph had contained a catalogue of various local secret societies, giving the usual data on membership, income, and expenses.

The 1908 work included the history and purposes of some of the larger societies, such as the Masons. The two treatments were not related to each other. The 1898 monograph had mentioned several cooperative businesses and described a few in some detail. One, a North Carolina cotton mill called the Coleman Manufacturing Company, was also discussed in 1907, but no connection was made between these examinations of the same company. Nothing was said about its development in the intervening nine years. Du Bois mentioned that the founder had died "and a white company bought the mill and is running it with white help." An excellent opportunity for a case study of how a race enterprise failed—but not enough data had been gathered and related.

The 1907 conference resolutions committee, in urging more cooperative effort among blacks, noted a "crisis." The Negro race was "at the crossroads—one way leading to the old trodden ways of grasping individualistic competition, where the shrewd, cunning, skilled and rich among them will prey upon the ignorance and simplicity of the mass of the race and get wealth at the expense of the general well being; the other way leading to co-operation in capital and labor, the massing of small savings, the wide distribution of capital and a more general equality of wealth and comfort" (Du Bois, 1907: p. 4). This conclusion was not developed from the data presented in the monograph. Two years later *Efforts for Social Betterment among Negro Americans* was published, and it too presented a cornucopia of facts without making any connections to material in the earlier volumes.

The best monographs in the series were two dealing with *The Negro Artisan* (1902 and 1912) which made a more thorough and ordered contribution to our knowledge of blacks. Du Bois realized that he faced a "peculiar difficulty," since much of his data came from "interested persons," although to some extent part of the material could be checked by "third parties." For instance, in some cases the word of the workers was validated by making inquiries of their fellow workers and their employers. The 1902 research was based upon many sources. A questionnaire was distributed to hundreds of black artisans, most residing in Georgia, who described their work experiences in comparison with those of white artisans in the same occupations. Another was sent to "correspondents" in many states, who surveyed skilled workers in their own communities. One man described the trades Negroes entered in Memphis and whether they belonged to the same labor unions as whites. Independent unions and those affiliated with the American Federation of Labor received a questionnaire on the black worker. Another was distributed to the central labor bodies in a number of cities. Inquiries were also made of state federations.

Du Bois was thus able to determine which unions admitted Negroes and the relative proportions of blacks to the total membership. He could pinpoint the trades in which Negoes encountered hostility. He appended the views of labor leaders on race relations in industry. Industrial schools submitted information on their courses of study. Educational leaders in all Southern states were asked about the kinds of manual training included in their curricula and requested to comment upon the results. Employers in various parts of the South were asked to appraise Negro efficiency in relation to that of whites. Comparative data were secured on the wages paid to blacks and whites in various trades. In the 1912 survey, similar questionnaires were sent to some of the same groups. Comparisons of census data for the two periods were made, to estimate whether blacks were holding their own in the various trades.

Although the Atlanta University studies clearly had their limitations, their value and importance should not be ignored. At a time when serious study of the black community was otherwise absent, Du Bois amassed a body of data that not only compared quite favorably with the social survey research being done at the time but has provided a valuable storehouse of information to his successors. Du Bois himself modestly evaluated the significance of his worth: "When we at Atlanta University say that we are the only institution in the United States that is making any serious study of the race problems . . . we make no great boast because it is not that we are doing so much, but rather that the rest of the nation is doing nothing" (Du Bois 1908, pp. 835-36). In short, the real importance of the Atlanta University monographs lies in the fact that, in them and in *The Philadelphia Negro*, Du Bois single-handedly initiated serious empirical research on blacks in America.

Despite the depth of Du Bois's commitment to sociology, he was in the main ignored by the elite in the profession. It is interesting that Albion W. Small, a founder of America's first department of sociology in 1892, of the *American Journal of Sociology* in 1895, and of the American Sociological Society a decade later, had, like Du Bois, been trained in Germany by Schmoller (Barnes 1948, pp. 766-92). In spite of this similarity in professional background and although the *American Journal of Sociology,* in addition to publishing theoretical articles, devoted many pages to social welfare problems, Small clearly considered Du Bois's work of minor importance. Yet books by known racists were reviewed and often warmly praised. In 1906, Thomas Nelson Page's *The Negro: The Southerner's Problem* was glowingly lauded by Charles Ellwood, who had been Small's graduate student (*American Journal of Sociology* 11 [1905-6: 698-99]; Barnes 1948, pp. 853-55). In another review, Ellwood gratuitously commented,"it is only through the full recognition that the average negro is still a savage child of nature that the North and the South can be brought to unite in work to uplift the race" (*American Journal of Sociology* 12 [1906-7]: 275).

The *American Journal of Sociology* never published a single one of Du Bois's many articles on the Negro. On one occasion, however, the *Journal* included his remarks at a 1908 symposium on "Is Race Friction between Blacks and Whites in the United States Growing and Inevitable?" In this address he restated his "dream . . . that we could . . . begin at a small Negro college a movement for the scientific study of race differences and likenesses which should in time revolutionize the knowledge of the world. . . . As I have said [whether blacks are an inferior race] is primarily a scientific question, a matter of scientific measurement and observation; and yet the data upon which the mass of men, and even intelligent men, are basing their conclusions today, the basis which they are putting back of their treatment of the Negro, is a most ludicrous and harmful conglomeration of myth, falsehood, and desire. It would certainly be a most commendable thing if [the American Sociological Society] and other learned societies would put themselves on record as favoring a most thorough and unbiased scientific study of the race problem in America" (Du Bois 1908, pp. 835-36).

Under Small's editorship, though the *American Journal of Sociology* included such articles as "Has Illinois the Best Laws in the Country for the Protection of Children?" "A Decade of Official Poor Relief in Indiana," "Boston's Experience with Municipal Baths," and "Sanitation and Social Progress," articles about black Americans were relatively few. It is true that the *Journal* did carry articles by a man like W. I. Thomas, who criticized racist theories, but other items displayed the racial biases of their authors. The September 1903 issue included an article by H. E. Berlin entitled "The Civil War as Seen through Southern Glasses," in which the author described slavery as "the most humane and the most practical method ever devised for 'bearing the white man's burden' " (Berlin [1903]: 266). In 1908 the *Journal* carried a piece by the same author on "A Southern View of Slavery" (Berlin [1908]: 513-22). The publication of such views in the *American Journal of Sociology* reflected theories about race held in the profession at the time. Sociological theory on race prevalent before World War I generally stressed the biological superiority of the white race and the "primitiveness" of the "inferior" black's "racial temperament," which predisposed him toward "shiftlessness and sensuality," rendering him basically unassimilable.

As Frazier has described the situation, the "general point of view" of the first sociologists to study the black man was that "the Negro is an inferior race because of either biological or social heredity or both; that the Negro because of his physical characteristics could not be assimilated; and that physical amalgamation was bad and therefore undesirable." These conclusions were generally supported by the marshalling of a vast amount of statistical data on the pathological aspects of Negro life. In short, "The sociological theories which were implicit in the writings on the Negro problem were merely rationalizations of the existing racial situation" (Frazier 1949, p. 2; 1947, p. 268).

Thus, ironically, Du Bois, who by training and research orientation toward both empiricism and reform was part of the mainstream of American sociology as it evolved at the turn of the century, found himself relegated to the periphery of his profession.

The Chicago school of urban sociology that began about the

time of World War I did not consider Du Bois's work significant, even though its leader, Robert Park, was deeply interested in the study of race relations. The social survey movement sensitized sociologists to the importance of studying the urban community and urban problems (Short 1971, p. xvi; Burgess and Bogue 1964, p. 3). Indeed, Park and his colleagues recognized the value of Booth's internationally famous research on London, Chicago's *Hull House Maps and Papers*, and the noted Pittsburgh Survey of 1909-12. Yet they and almost every commentator since, while mentioning these and other case studies of communities, failed to include *The Philadelphia Negro*. (For some examples, see Elmer [1914], Taylor [1919], Steiner [1934]). Among those who have written of the origins of modern sociology and social research, only Nathan Glazer appears to have recognized *The Philadelphia Negro*'s contribution (Glazer 1959, p. 64). As Frazier said, "It appears that there was a feeling, perhaps unconscious and therefore all the more significant, that since the Negro occupied a low status and did not play an important role in American society, studies of the Negro were of less significance from the standpoint of social science" (Frazier 1949, p. 2). The neglect of Du Bois's work appears all the more remarkable when his work is compared with other products of the social survey movement. *The Philadelphia Negro* was, in fact, one of the finest monographs inspired by Booth's study of London. It was superior to *Hull House Maps and Papers* and antedated by ten years the elaborate and influential Pittsburgh Survey. But in the United States of the early twentieth century, white sociologists were not likely to recognize the contribution made by a study of a black community.

Yet times would change and the *American Journal of Sociology* would soon be publishing many serious articles on the Negro. Under Park's leadership, the University of Chicago's sociology department became a major center for the study of race relations in America (Rose 1968, p. 3). Blacks like Charles S. Johnson and E. Franklin Frazier became students in sociology at Chicago and began producing work that owed much to Du Bois's influence. But by then Du Bois had ceased to think of himself primarily as a sociologist. He had become deeply aware of the seething and often erupting anti-Negro forces in America. After being confronted with situations, like lynchings, that "called—shrieked—for action," he concluded that social research was futile (Du Bois 1920, pp. 21-22). Almost completely in vain, he had made public appeals for money to finance the annual Atlanta studies. In despair, he remarked, "If Negroes were lost in Africa, money would be available to measure their heads, but $500 a year is hard to raise for Atlanta" (Du Bois 1903b, p. 162; 1904, pp. 85-90). He had become less sure that social science could seriously effect social reform. Increasingly, he turned his attention to writing propaganda that aggressively and unconditionally demanded the same civil rights for blacks that other Americans enjoyed—a theme absent from the Atlanta studies. In 1909 he became a founder of the National Association for the Advancement of Colored People. In 1910 he left Atlanta University to work for the new organization. For a brief period he continued the Atlanta studies, but his basic interests now lay elsewhere.

Although Du Bois himself thus left the field of sociology, his influence on students of the black community was profound. His was more than the obvious model for the surveys of Negroes in New York and Boston by Ovington, Haynes, and Daniels in the period before World War I. His pioneering work also bears important similarities to such later studies as Johnson's *The Negro in Chicago*, Frazier's *Negro Youth at the Crossways*, Davis and Gardner's *Deep South*, and Drake and Cayton's *Black Metropolis*. In their holistic approach to the study of black urban communities, in their attention to the importance of social class, and in their painstaking scholarship and quest for scientific knowledge, their likeness to Du Bois is evident. Like Du Bois, they clearly showed the social problems arising from white oppression and discrimination and at the same time described the richness and diversity of black life and the inventiveness which Negroes displayed in creating institutions and life styles that enabled them to cope and survive. Finally, like Du Bois, they all hoped that their research and published works, by reaching an influential white audience, would promote beneficial changes for blacks in American society.

Editors' Note. On the question of the treatment of Du Bois by the *American Journal of Sociology*, the *Journal* did in actuality, in its volume 62, publish a full abstract of Du Bois's article "The Study of the Negro Problem," which had appeared in the *Annals* in 1898 and which drew on his *Philadelphia Negro*. It is of course not possible to present an adequate overview of Du Bois's treatment without reference to the basic focus of attention of the *Journal* during those years. The *American Journal of Sociology* reflected the concern of its editors with issues of socialism and government control of business. It was relatively localistic in orientation. Interestingly enough, the actual space devoted to Du Bois equalled that allocated to Ferdinand Toennies, whose theoretical writings had moved into the center of sociological debate. It should be noted that the *Journal*, in its January 1896 issue, had an article by W. I. Thomas, entitled "The Scope and Method of Folk Psychology," which included the statement, "There is no occasion at present to modify the important expression of Sir Henry Maine that race theories appear to have little merit except that the facility which they give for building on them inferences is tremendously out of proportion to the mental labor which they cost the builder" (p. 439).

Systematic content analysis rather than specific and selective excerpts are required to describe the focus of attention of the *American Journal of Sociology*. Such a content analysis remains to be carried out. No one would suggest that reference to two articles by one author and one book review would suffice for an analysis of the treatment of race relations in the *American Journal of Sociology* during its first decade of existence, in which it published over five hundred pages each year. Even a sheer listing of the articles and references dealing with race topics confirms the point of view presented by some scholars at the national conference on black sociologists that, within sociology, there developed a consistent critique of popular notions of racism. In fact, the degree of imbalance in this direction was so pervasive that, given the state of popular public opinion, the editors of the *Journal* must have deliberately labored to implement their own orientation. During the first five years of the *Journal*'s existence, there was not a single reference which could have been inserted into the racist content category. During these years there were at least fifteen to twenty references to race, depending on the unit of analysis, a most noteworthy finding. In addition to the classic article by W. I. Thomas in the first volume, there was also the famed analysis by Charles E. Cooley on "Genius, Fame and the Comparisons of Race," and, of special interest, the critical article by Antonio Llano, "The Race Preservation Dogma." During the next five years, in which the three racist references were found, the number of articles and references to blacks increased, so that the imbalance remained overwhelming.

With respect to Frazier's writings, the record shows that he also stated, "During this period there began to emerge a sociological theory of race relations that was formulated independent of existing public opinion and current attitudes. As early as 1904, W. I. Thomas presented in an article entitled "The Psychology of Race Relations' in the Journal [*American Journal of Sociology*], a systematic theory of race relations." In fact, W. I. Thomas's first article critical of biological racism was published in 1896 in the *American Journal of Sociology*. Thomas's approach was based on a critique of biological determinism and offered, instead, a sociological and social psychology orientation which served as a cornerstone for subsequent sociological analysis. "Thomas assumed that race prejudice could be destroyed and he did not assume that people of divergent racial stocks must inevitably remain apart or could only live together in the community where a caste system existed" (Frazier 1947).

Nevertheless, Du Bois was attracted to sociology because he saw in it an intellectual basis for the redefinition of the issues of race relations. He saw in sociology more than a method for collecting information about black people. He was powerfully attracted by the modes of reasoning and analysis in sociology. Sociology helped to fashion his outlook on society even as he made his contribution to the development of the discipline. In this double sense, Du Bois was and remains part of the sociological tradition.

References

Barnes, Harry Elmer, ed.
  1948   *An introduction to the history of sociology.* Chicago: University of Chicago Press.
Barnes, Harry Elmer, and Becker, Howard.
  1938   *Social thought from lore to science.* Vol. 2 Boston: Heath.

Berlin, H. E.
   1908   A Southern view of slavery. *American Journal of Sociology* 13
            (January): 513-22.
   1903   The South as seen through southern glasses. *American Journal
            of Sociology* 9 (September): 259-67.
Bernard, L. L., and Bernard, Jessie.
   1943   *Origins of American Sociology.* New York: Crowell.
Broderick, Francis L.
   1958   The academic training of W. E. B. Du Bois. *Journal of Negro
            Education* 27 (Winter): 10-16.
Burgess, Ernest.
   1916   The social survey, a field for constructive service by departments
            of sociology. *American Journal of Sociology* 21 (January):
            492-500.
Burgess, Ernest, and Bogue, Donald.
   1964   *Contributions to urban sociology.* Chicago: University of Chi-
            cago Press.
Daniels, John.
   1914   *In freedom's birthplace: A study of the Boston Negroes.* Boston:
            Houghton Mifflin.
Davis, Allen F.
   1967   *Spearheads for reform.* New York: Oxford.
Drake, St. Clair, and Cayton, Horace.
   1945   *Black Metropolis.* New York: Harcourt, Brace.
Du Bois, W. E. B.
   1968   *The autobiography of W. E. B. Du Bois.* New York: International
            Publishers.
   1940   *Dusk of Dawn.* New York: Harcourt, Brace.
   1920   *Darkwater.* New York: Harcourt, Brace, and Howe.
   1912   *The Negro-American artisan.* Atlanta: Atlanta University Press.
   1909   *Efforts for social betterment among Negro Americans.* Atlanta:
            Atlanta University Press.
   1908   Race friction between black and white. *American Journal of Soci-
            ology* 13 (May): 834-38.
   1907   *Economic cooperation among Negro Americans.* Atlanta: Atlanta
            University Press.
   1905   The black vote of Philadelphia, *Charities* 15 (October 7): 619-22.
   1904   The Atlanta conferences. *Voice of the Negro* 1 (March): 85-90.
   1903a   The Atlanta University conferences. *Charities* 10 (May 2):
            435-39.
   1903b   The laboratory in sociology at Atlanta University. *Annals of the*

American Academy of Political and Social Science 21 (May): 160-63.

1902 *The Negro artisan.* Atlanta: Atlanta University Press.

1899 *The Philadelphia Negro: a social study.* Philadelphia: University of Pennsylvania.

1898a The study of the Negro problems. *Annals of the American Academy of Political and Social Science* 11 (January): 1-23.

1898b *Some efforts of American Negroes for their own social betterment.* Atlanta: Atlanta University Press.

Elmer, Manuel C.

1914 *Social surveys of urban communities.* Menasha, Wisconsin.

Frazier, E. Franklin.

1957 *The Negro in the United States.* Rev. ed. New York: Macmillan.

1949 Race contacts and the social structure. *American Sociological Review* 14 (February): 1-11.

1947 Sociological theory and race relations. *American Sociological Review* 12 (June): 265-71.

Glazer, Nathan.

1959 The Rise of social research in Europe. In Daniel Lerner, ed. *The human meaning of the social sciences.* Cleveland: World.

Haynes, George Edmund.

1912 *The Negro at work in New York City: a study in economic progress.* New York: Longmans, Green.

Myrdal, Gunnar.

1944 *An American dilemma.* New York: Harper.

Ovington, Mary White.

1911 *Half a man; the status of the Negro in New York.* New York: Longmans, Green.

Park, Robert.

1929 The city as a social laboratory. In T. V. Smith and Leonard D. White, eds. *Chicago, An experiment in social science research.* Chicago: University of Chicago Press.

Rose, Peter I.

1968 *The subject is race.* New York: Oxford.

Short, James F., Jr.

1971 *The social fabric of the metropolis.* Chicago: University of Chicago Press.

Steiner, J. F.

1934 The sources and methods of community study. In L. L. Bernard, ed. *The field and methods of sociology.* New York: Long and Smith.

Taylor, Carl C.
  1919   *The social survey, its history and methods.* Columbia, Missouri.

3

Richard Robbins

CHARLES S. JOHNSON

Scholarship, Advocacy, and Role Balance

In the 1940s, Everett Hughes, the most creative and perceptive of the second-generation sociologists of the Chicago school,
wrote a seminal essay on "dilemmas and contradictions of status."
He argued that when "new kinds of people in established [pro-
fessional] positions" are assessed by others, that assessment of
their statuses and the role activity associated with them is likely
to be made not only on the basis of universally accented technical
criteria but also in terms of "auxiliary" characteristics carried
over from such other social contexts as race and sex. Not surprisingly, he chose for an illustrative centerpiece the status of
the Negro physician in America in the forties—white patients
perceived "race" where they should have been thinking "professional standing." However, the most apposite case could have
been that of the black scholar in the social sciences and humanities.
For when we concede the prejudices of the white patient toward
the black doctor, of the male client toward the female lawyer,
there has to be, on both sides in the last analysis, reliance on
technical, universalistic criteria—the surgeon's skill with the
knife, the lawyer's with the brief. Whereas, for the social sciences
and the humanities, the "race problem" penetrates the very work
itself, and there is no way out of the dilemma save to fuse into the
work itself one's commitment to one's people and one's commitment
to the "objective truth" of scholarship and the "objective standards" of enduring art.

Given the depth and pervasiveness of racism in the United States, if a man or woman is a historian and black, a sociologist and black, then he or she is compelled to work out a distinctive role-balance between scholarship and advocacy, between creativity and commitment.

No one has written more insightfully on this subject than John Hope Franklin. The most elemental point he makes is a ground-clearing one. Whatever the gross unfairness of the racial pressures on the black playwright or essayist, the work itself must still come first and stand on its own; it is almost inevitably (though not necessarily) "about race," yet it cannot be exclusively assessed "according to race." So Ralph Ellison has to draw on the classical as well as the folk and the blues tradition in music—no matter the segregation in the Alabama libraries. He does not have to be reminded of the facts of race in America; neither does he have to conform to someone else's definition of "the Negro protest novel." Franklin puts the matter even more strongly: "when his work is recognized it is usually pointed to as the work of a Negro. He is a competent *Negro* sociologist, an able *Negro* economist, an outstanding *Negro* historian [his italics]. Such recognition is as much the product of the racist mentality as the Negro restrooms in the Montgomery airport."[2] Yet the problem is more complex than this.

Judgment of the work itself—implied in such phrases as "a competent sociologist," "an able economist"—would constitute the essential standard if other things were equal, that is, if the society in general had been guaranteeing a rough equality of access to scholars and writers irrespective of skin color. Since that has not been the case, and still is not, despite rapid changes in the direction of equality of opportunity, the racial designations are going to be applied by the dominant group in any case, whether from motives of discrimination, condescension, patronage, mechanical liberalism, or whatever. Therefore, the black social scientist owes it to himself and the black community to fashion his own sense of balance *inside the work itself*—objective, scholarly analysis of the racial situation, its history and its structure, *and* passionate advocacy of freedom, justice, and group identity.

The effort at balance might mean, as it did for Charles S.

Johnson, a primary dedication to sociological research always coupled with a determination to marshall the fruits of research in the interest of baring the depths of racial injustice. In this effort Johnson maintained a consistent balanced liberalism, the grim tidings of "patterns of segregation" set against the prospects of Negro movement "into the mainstream" and the good news of emerging "best practices in race relations in the South."

Whatever the balance achieved, precarious or seemingly serene, the inner costs exacted have often been high for a black scholar. Even near the time when Everett C. Hughes was compiling his "contradictions and dilemmas," John Hope Franklin, on a research mission in North Carolina, found himself defined by a white woman in the archives department as that "Harvard nigger." And in the mid-thirties, Charles S. Johnson, attending a convention of the American Sociological Association, was told to use the back entrance.

Johnson, who, for the most part, maintained a remarkably controlled orchestration of the two roles, and who devoted his career primarily to demonstrating that the damning indictment of a racist society could be powerfully drawn from the objective data of social science itself, could not always hold professionalism and protest in creative tension. He often worked with white social scientists who were men of reasonably good will but who were extremely obtuse; who did careful research in the same style as Johnson's but who never questioned *au fond* the ideology of racial segregation, or even if they questioned it privately kept a discreet silence in public about its devastating consequences. St. Clair Drake remarks on the severe migraine headaches suffered by Johnson when he attended those endless conferences on "interracial cooperation" in the midst of a rigidly segregated society.[3] Nevertheless, Johnson recognized realistically that even in the face of this crippling situation, where a different reality intruded as soon as the black professor left the campus library and boarded the back of the bus to go downtown, that the research commitment and the research role had to be maintained, indeed expanded.

Charles S. Johnson, playing a multiplicity of roles—scholar, writer, editor, administrator, foundation executive, advisor to countless commissions, research director, university president—forged his own role integration as social scientist and advocate. He lasted, and he got his work done.

Life and Work: Virginia, Chicago, New York, Nashville

He was born in Bristol, Virginia, on July 24, 1893, the son of a minister who was an emancipated slave. Johnson's father was tutored by his master along with the master's own son. The father went on to obtain his B.D. degree from Richmond Institute and preached in Bristol, a rail community. As a small boy, Johnson read avidly, even as he worked in a barber shop and at other odd jobs. There was no high school for blacks in Bristol, so he was sent to Wayland Academy in Richmond, the high school attached to Virginia Union University. Moving up through the Virginia school system, he took an A.B. degree at Virginia Union, a private denominational institution for Negroes which, over the years, sent out a considerable number of distinguished teachers, ministers, and other professionals. It was still shaped then, in large part, by white philanthropy and had, as did so many other Negro colleges, a white president. (Johnson himself became the first Negro president of Fisk in 1947.) After graduation (in three years, with honors), he moved to Chicago in 1917. It was a vital time for both the city and the University of Chicago, where he commenced graduate studies. The war had accelerated the movement of blacks from the rural and small-town South. The demand for black labor had, paradoxically, both opened up black economic opportunity and intensified racial tensions as whites moved against potential Negro competition and set severe restrictions on employment, housing, and access to public facilities. In the summer of 1919 Chicago was the scene of the worst race riot in the nation's history.

At the same time, within the university, Johnson became associated with a stimulating group of scholars, most notably Robert E. Park, who remained a lifelong mentor, as well as W.I. Thomas, Albion Small, and G.H. Mead (though Mead's influence was indirect). Johnson, whom Ernest W. Burgess has described as an excellent student of "unusual ability, energy and originality," recognized that the Chicago group had not been taken in by pseudoscientific doctrines of racial determinism; on the contrary, they argued that "racial" differences were actually rooted in differential social experience.⁴ These men were ahead of their time, even if a sociology textbook like Park's and Burgess's still retained some archaic ideas about Negro life. The Chicago group also demonstrated to Johnson the value of the synthesis of sociological theory—especially theory of the cycles of social change—and comprehensive research—especially research combining the statistical survey and the personal document. Thereafter, Johnson's best work reflected that perspective, the statistics providing the solid base for generalization, the personal portraits bringing the data vividly to life. The effect in his books, as the poet John Crowe Ransom noted, is often "more like that of an art than of a science." Oral history of the kind later employed by Oscar Lewis in anthropology and by Studs Terkel in his portraits of urban folk in the Depression is foreshadowed in Johnson's work.

With brief time-out for army service overseas in France, Johnson moved directly into research and action. As research director for the Chicago Urban League (Park was president), he was the logical candidate to direct the work of the Chicago Commission on Race Relations, formed in the wake of the disastrous riots. But role definitions being what they were, the executive position went to a white educator, Graham Taylor, who was charged with responsibility for the report; Johnson had the post of "associated executive secretary" charged with undertaking the basic research. The Commission Report, *The Negro In Chicago; a Study of Race Relations and a Race Riot* was a striking document for its time, whatever the criticism of its caution in coming to terms with the part played by the white power structure in sustaining discrimination. And Johnson's distinctive stamp is on it in various places. The report still makes illuminating reading.⁵

Launched on what Lewis W. Jones describes as his life work, "client-organized research," Johnson did not need a degree beyond the B.A. Leaving Chicago for New York, he took the post of director of research for the National Urban League and editor of its review, *Opportunity*, from 1923 to 1928. (The poet Countee Cullen was assistant editor.) As an editor Johnson was concerned with bringing social science research to a general Negro readership. At the same time, with his continued interest in style and his sensitivity to creative work (though he would not attempt it himself), he was able to make the pages of *Opportunity* a forum for black writers, poets, and artists engaged in Harlem in what Alain Locke called affectionately "our little Renaissance." The Harlem Renaissance of the twenties was a significant and exciting, if small-scale, movement. Its importance lay not only in refuting absurd white stereotypes about "primitive" Negro work but also in giving voice to a wide range of talents at a time when it was extraordinarily difficult for the creative black writer and artist to find a source of support. Yet its base was fragile. Its problems were complicated through the exploitation of "exotic" aspects by well-meaning but insensitive whites outside the community. How could a band of gifted writers create freely when all around them the economic and social conditions of Harlem pressed in? The Great Depression shattered the movement. Alain Locke, writing in the thirties of "the new Negro" and "our little Renaissance," addressed himself now to "the Harlem that the social worker knew all along but had not been able to dramatize. . . . There is no cure or saving magic in poetry and art for. . . precarious marginal employment, high mortality rates, civic neglect."[6] Few writers were able, like Langston Hughes, to weave the "weary blues" into a form of expression, the poem, that was at once particular and universal.

Nevertheless, while it lasted, the Harlem Renaissance did provide élan and lift in New York black life. And Johnson, as editor, played a quiet but strategic part in publishing the material of social scientists, established writers (mostly black, but some white), and the stories and poems of young students from the Negro colleges in the South. A representative sampling can be found in his collection *Ebony and Topaz*, where sociological contributions from Frazier, Faris, and Reuter are found side by side with creative work from Arna Bontemps, Countee Cullen, James Weldon Johnson, Rudolph Fisher, Claude McKay, Zora Neale Hurston (whose remarkable life and work has still not received the attention it deserves), Ira De A. Reid, and many others. Johnson, with his understanding of social movements, his perspective, his quiet, edged humor, could make the fairest statement: "The most that will be claimed for this collection is that it is a fairly faithful reflection of current interests and observations on Negro life."[7] Moreover, when he took on the role of critic, as in his comments on the poet Jean Toomer, he showed how the sociologist is not impeded from getting inside the work itself simply because he is primarily concerned with context.[8] Johnson's own sociological essays display in their taut style, tightly controlled anger, and sharp insight the qualities which would mark his later work. For example, in "After Garvey—What?" he is more than willing to concede Garvey's flamboyance and eccentricity, but he notes that these were the very factors which made him the tough, electrifying leader he was. Moreover, Johnson is well aware of the way in which whites would like to concentrate exclusively on the personality of Garvey in order to turn away from the real issue, how Garvey the black leader symbolized "the hopes and aspirations of a million Negroes."[9]

Although the years with *Opportunity* were a valuable experience for Johnson, social science was to prove a stronger force than involvement in the Harlem Renaissance. He returned to the South and to research. For the next twenty years—until 1947 and the Fisk presidency—he directed the Department of Social Science at Fisk University. In research projects, in books, in monographs, in papers delivered on all sorts of occasions and in memoranda which he submitted to many foundations and conferences, he made a major contribution to the understanding of the South as a region, the economic foundation of race relations, and the racial problem itself. The organizational work alone at Fisk commands great respect: the search for funding, the sponsorship of studies, the publication of Fisk University Press monographs, the graduate programs, the coup in bringing Robert Park to the staff in 1936 (the new Fisk social science building was dedicated to Park in 1955), and the numerous conferences. The catalytic administrative role in research is vitally necessary to the research role itself.

But there is more to the Fisk years. From the first, during the period with the Chicago Commission, Johnson had to think through the relation of social science research to public policy. No area required this more than that of race relations, where there was still much to learn but even more to accomplish, if the appalling burden of racial discrimination and segregation was to be lifted. As Kenneth Clark has noted sardonically, from the time of the Chicago Commission report in the early twenties to the Kerner Commission report in the late sixties, there has been a surrealistic, Alice-in-Wonderland quality about such studies. All of them have found massive inequalities in race relations, all have resulted in recommendations, and nearly all the recommendations have been neglected ... until the next study. Given the gulf between the measured prose of the reports and the reality of conditions in the urban ghetto, it is not surprising that some black people, black community organizers, and black scholars have reached the point of crying "enough" on this material; or at least have insisted that a new kind of research, not very clearly specified but more "relevant" and "closer to the community," replace the conventional kind.

Johnson would have readily understood this new debate, and would have been deeply sympathetic to the effort of younger black sociologists to structure a different kind of role, with scholarship more firmly tied to community needs, and with a much more militant advocacy in the areas of public policy and social action. Still, his whole professional career and life style would have moved him to insist that his type of research was just as relevant as the new and, indeed, as much related to the need for decisive change in public policy in race relations. Solid fact and solid generalization, by the sheer weight of the argument, he assumed, would have to make an impact. Even if it made less of an impact than one hoped, a black social scientist concerned with race relations had no other recourse but to continue the work essential to him and to anticipate that, when social change came, it would be more effective if advocacy were also sustained by dependable research. With the wisdom of hindsight (remembering that only a decade or so after the Supreme Court school-segregation decision of 1954 came Watts, Newark, and Detroit), it is easy to argue against Johnson's kind of indirect commitment. Lewis Jones writes, "This indirection is regarded by many who read his work as being evasion, certainly understatement."[10] This "indirection" did not spring from any kind of timidity but from disciplined belief, from conviction. When a time came for advocacy, Johnson did not hold back. He was the sole Negro college president to come publicly to the defense of Du Bois in 1951 when, in an episode that disgraced the American government, Du Bois was indicted technically for alleged subversion.

These comments are necessary as prelude to the recording of the astonishing range of Johnson's involvement with commissions and foundations concerned with public policy, from the Chicago period to post-World War II service with President Truman's commission for the reorganization of education in Japan. In 1930 he was a member of the League of Nations commission to investigate forced labor in Liberia. Johnson wrote an account of this situation, *Bitter Canaan,* which was never published, possibly because Johnson felt that his criticisms of Liberia would be highlighted at the expense of his sympathetic portrayal of the Liberian and other African people exploited by white imperialism—a far more serious problem. In 1931 he coordinated President Hoover's special commission on Negro housing and home building. During the New Deal period there was other advisory and research work for the Tennessee Valley Authority, the Southern Commission on the Study of Lynching, and the Southern Regional Council. Other commission responsibilities concerned farm tenancy, national health priorities, and national manpower needs. He served as well on the advisory board for the National Youth Administration (NYA) in Tennessee in the early forties and, in the same period, participated actively in the White House Conference for Children. *Growing Up in the Black Belt* was prepared from the research he directed as head of the Southern Rural Division, Negro Youth Study, for the American Youth Commission and the Council of Education. After World War II he was involved in work with the United States Education Commission for Japan. He served as a member of the first delegation to UNESCO in Paris and on the United States Commission for UNESCO. During this period, Johnson maintained close ties with the Urban League, the Rosenwald Fund, the Fund for the Advancement of Education (Ford Foundation), and other private agencies and foundations sponsoring research and action programs.[11] And he participated extensively in research sponsorship by the Board of Foreign Scholarship (Fulbright) and the Social Science Research Council. Finally, mention should be made of Johnson's ties to Christianity in general and the Negro denominational groups in particular. He was active in the social action programs of the Congregational Christian Church. This summary is only suggestive and far from exhaustive but it does convey the scope of Johnson's contribution—if only by "indirection"—to policy bodies and action agencies.[12]

To research and applied sociology should be added his activity on Fisk's campus itself. With his accession to the presidency, and with his many other commitments to national groups, Johnson's role in the Department of Social Science tended to diminish somewhat from the late forties to his death in 1956. Even before that time, a number of colleagues and students who knew him agreed that classroom teaching was not his forte. He was too busy with other projects, other demands. Few students came to know him well in the undergraduate setting.[13] His strength lay in making Fisk the intellectual center for sociological study of the socioeconomic and racial structure of the South and in providing a resource base not only for fellow scholars but for many community groups involved in intergroup relations. (Agencies and organizations made very effective use, for example, of the newsletters on race relations circulated in the forties and of the "community self-survey of race relations," both of which he developed.) These constituted striking achievements, especially when one considers how much less the large "white" state universities of the Deep South accomplished with so much more in the way of resources. His conference at Fisk, bringing together many scholars and community specialists with different points of view, was from all accounts, a signal event.

In the end, however, what counted most decisively and what still counts today is the published work—by one bibliographical enumeration, seventeen books or monographs for which Johnson was author or coauthor, fourteen others to which he contributed chapters, and more than sixty major articles.[14] A rough sorting-out is required.

Black Belts, Plantation Counties, Industrial Society . . . and Race

It is hard to generalize about so diverse a body of work. On the whole, the studies which still attract our interest, those which

will endure as classic models of the research enterprise, are the ones
in which the sociological—and the ethical—conclusions are anchored to concrete, specific circumstances (in this, Johnson following Park). Here the body of fact and the interspersed personal
portraits build up a full and coherent picture of the implications of
socioeconomic and racial injustice. Theory, drawn from the Chicago
school, is present but only in the interest of advancing the argument
empirically.

Shadow of the Plantation and *Growing Up in the Black Belt* are
taken rightly as the best in this genre. The attention given to these
books, however, has obscured to some degree the same strength and
incisiveness in the shorter studies. Without apparently having any
real interest in Marxist theory, either to defend it or oppose it,
Johnson nonetheless arrived pragmatically at a very close understanding of the way in which powerful agrarian and industrial
interests shaped the "human relations" of race and racism. If the
position stemmed from the data rather than from ideological dis-
position, that gave it just as much conviction. An instance is the
essay written in the mid-thirties on the tobacco industry. Johnson
had readily seen that for Negroes the Great Depression was two-
edged; "Race relations have improved under an economic distress
which was common to all groups, and . . . manifestations of racial
friction have increased through the competition for fewer jobs." [15]
But this semihopeful generalization applied more to the urban-
industrial North. In the South, in the tobacco industry, racial discrimination simply compounded economic exploitation. In tobacco,
racial segregation of jobs reinforced the peculiar, and highly discriminatory, triangular relationship among employers, white workers, and black workers. The employer wanted to expand Negro labor
since that could mean lower costs; still he could not move too far in
this direction for he would then have to challenge a social system
under which whites operated the machinery and got paid more,
"niggers handled the dirty work" and got paid less.[16] Again, in his
rigorous study of the collapse of cotton tenancy in the South, in his
analysis of the economic processes maintaining racially restrictive
covenants in housing (written with Herman Long), and even in the
prosaic compilation of a statistical atlas of Southern counties (work-

ed out with the assistance of Lewis Jones, Buford Junker, Eli Marks, and Preston Valien), Johnson demonstrated again and again the disturbing economic consequences of racial discrimination.[17] In the last volume mentioned one had only to turn to the per capita expenditures for white and Negro pupils in such-and-such a county to recognize the pervasiveness of the color barrier in the thirties.

It is worth noting in this connection, for the benefit of many historians of the New Deal period who continue to emphasize the dramatic socioeconomic changes effected by the New Deal, that Johnson understood, as did many other black social scientists, how tightly the national subsidies and economic supports conformed to a grossly unjust system of racial segregation; to a "striking and indefensible inequality," in Johnson's words, between white and black farm communities. Under Roosevelt, federal intervention in the South, mediated through the politically conservative wing of the Democratic party, perpetuated racial exploitation as it ameliorated economic exploitation. There were a few notable exceptions—TVA and the CCC, for example, where there was a rough distributive justice by race—but we are still paying today for this policy of abdication in the 1930s. The voices of Johnson and other black social scientists went largely unheeded. Secretary of Agriculture Henry Wallace was not available to see the black leader Mary Mc-Leod Bethune when she came to Washington to inform him of the implications in the South of official sponsorship of "separate and unequal."[18]

Johnson's conception of his own role balance, his advocacy that was made more effective by scholarship, the case for a more insistent struggle against racial injustice strengthened by the sheer weight of the empirical evidence of socioeconomic and racial exploitation, were most powerfully put in *Shadow of the Plantation*. It is one of those terrible ironies, properly belonging to the pages of Ralph Ellison's *Invisible Man,* that the study was in part possible because the U.S. Public Health Service, with support from the Rosenwald Fund, had already prepared the way by setting up in the early thirties, in Macon County, a system of clinics for treating venereal disease among black people, At the same time, the system provided basic sociological information on the black population in the Tuskegee area. A base for research and a sample were available. Only recently have we learned the true nature of the Tuskegee medical study. Incredibly, for purposes of "controlled" research more than four hundred Macon County blacks were deliberately denied treatment, which was available, for syphilis! How many died unnecessarily, how many had their life spans shortened, how many were needlessly crippled—all in the name of "research"—we do not know.

Shadow of the Plantation, published in 1934, is based on research on six hundred black families in Macon County. The book was written with the assistance of Lewis W. Jones and others on the staff of the Tuskegee Social Science Department. Its historic importance is that it took on a racial myth, the conception of the easygoing plantation life and the happy Negro, and replaced the myth with the objective truth: Macon County was a twentieth-century form of feudalism based on cotton cultivation. At the outset, in the "folk" material, there are traces in Johnson's approach of that defensiveness, that accommodation to white definitions of "the Negro problem," which marked some of the social science research of the time. It was still the thirties and Tuskegee, Macon County, still reflected the politics of accommodation to whites. Johnson seems somewhat apologetic for patterns of black "folk culture"— the looser network of extended family, the question of illegitimacy, the emotionality of traditional Negro religion. But as he plunges more deeply into the basic problem, the consequences of the decline of the slave economy and its successor, the economy of tenantry, as he fills in the details of the ethnography of the black social heritage, Johnson arrives at a factual, objectively described indictment of an enormously exploitative social system. The indictment is the more devastating because of the understatement, the ordering of the data in the language of social science: "It is of course impossible to determine the extent of exploitation of these Negro farmers, so long as the books are kept by the landlord, the sale price of cotton known only by him, and the cost and interest on rations advanced in his hands."[19] Every index supported the picture of a dual society. For example, of 460 male heads of black families only 27 had more than eight years of schooling. About 25 percent of the male heads were illiterate; another 50 percent were barely literate. As in his other work, Johnson inserts into the text personal portraits and the words of black men and women themselves. A farmer says, "What kills us here is that we jest can't make it cause they pay us nothing for what we give to them, and they charge us double price when they sell it back to us." Johnson recognized the source of the "backwardness" of the black rural people in Macon County; it was due to nothing less than "a fatal heritage of the system itself." [20] The system is documented thoroughly in the data and the descriptive materials. Yet what comes through, what gives the book its unity, in a sense, is not simply "the problem" but the extraordinary resilience, richness, and complexity of black community life, in spite of "the problem." This sense is conveyed almost entirely through the moving personal accounts. Johnson carried through the Chicago school mandate, or perhaps more exactly the Parkean mandate, to combine the extensiveness of empirical data with the intensiveness of the personal document.

Growing Up in the Black Belt, the eight-county study of Negro youth in the South, is in some ways more ambitious than the Macon County research, although it employs the same integration of such research techniques as questionnaires, open-ended interviews, and personality profiles. Late in the Depression era the American Council on Education sponsored the American Youth Commission's research project, an exploration of the problems of young people in a changing society. In particular, the focus was to be on the impact of both economic crisis and minority group status on personality development in the black community. Allison Davis and John Dollard (*Children of Bondage*), E. Franklin Frazier (*Negro Youth at the Crossways*), and W. Lloyd Warner and associates (*Color and Human Nature*) wrote on related aspects of this problem, but the work of Johnson and his collaborators on the sample counties seems the most resourceful in the group of studies and the most likely to endure. It is, methodologically, the most sophisticated of his works. More important, it succeeds. Through the personality profiles, the explanations from the young people and their parents, and the descriptions of youth enmeshed in a variety of social structures, the study shows black adolescence to be at once a product of the omnipresent color system and of the socialization process as it works out in any complex society where there are differences among young people in age, sex, class, urban or rural background. As Johnson says, one lives "a normal routine with its problems and tensions," in growing up black in the South's rural and small-town areas, yet one cannot escape, all the same, "the shadow of the white world" over one's life.[21]

How, then, can the young black adolescent escape what Harry Stack Sullivan describes, in a special appendix to Johnson's book, as a possible "warping" influence on personality, given the destructive character of "the prevailing white view of the Negro"?[22] The answer is implied in the psychological tone of the personality profiles and made explicit in the sociological observations of Johnson on "the caste system" in the final chapter. With regard to the first consideration, there is no doubt of the enormous pressure, brought about by race, on the Negro boy or girl growing up in the South of three decades ago. In one of the personality profiles Essie Mae sums it all up: "they [the whites] think they are better than the colored and try to keep colored people down." Nevertheless, Essie Mae is not standing alone, altogether vulnerable. There is a strong buffer in Essie Mae's socialization, in the "normal routine" of family structure, school (even if segregated), church, peer group, black community. Sociologically, Essie Mae's situation would be desperate only if a condition of racial "caste" fully obtained, one that froze her hope, and her children's, for change. Johnson explicitly argues that "the southern race system does not ... appear to meet fully the description of a caste system."[23] The very necessity to enforce color caste by law, the very struggle by whites to shore it up and by blacks to resist it, means whites do not take it for granted as given in custom and blacks do not accept it with resignation. Thus change, and not the static condition of caste, is the key to the prospects for better race relations and personality integration, under circumstances of "normal routine" for Essie Mae's children ... or grandchildren.

A belief, then, in accelerated social change informs Johnson's view of growing up in the Black Belt. In no sense did he underestimate the scope and depth of racist institutions. But the last sentence of his book reads: "In general the Negro continues to occupy a subordinate position, but the fact that he is struggling against this status rather than accepting it, and that the white group is constantly redefining its own status in relation to the Negro, indicates that in the future, if one cannot safely predict progress in race relations, he can at least predict change."[24] Today we may well find the faith in social change as thin a reed as the faith in social science. These were, however, the twin elements in Johnson's outlook. Our confidence in them has been severely battered—but not sunk.

There is a final, and critical, point to make about the other, perhaps lesser, books which Johnson wrote. In this context we are back to the difficult problem, sketched in the first section, of role integration among black scholars in the social sciences and humanities. We have seen that so long as Johnson anchored his sociology in specific research projects, in empirical data, his work had power and force; the very understatement in the language of social science made the indictment of racial injustice even more evident, the plea for more rapid social change even more keenly felt. When Johnson says at the end of *Shadow of the Plantation* that the fate of the black tenant and the Southern farmer generally "awaits a comprehensive planning, which affects not merely the South but the nation," we believe him, because the data have shown us that nothing less than comprehensive planning (by the federal government) will be required to lift the terrible pressures on the black people of Macon County.[25] When at the end of *The Negro College Graduate* Johnson calls for a greater degree of "control and self-correction" on the part of Negroes "in anticipation of broad institutional changes in progress or impending," we recognize that this is not a Booker T. Washington-like argument for passive acquiescence in white domination but an appeal to blacks to maintain the spirit and resilience that have enabled them in the past to be tested so sorely and yet stand fast.[26] And we accept such an interpretation because in the preceding pages Johnson has shown in great historical detail, as well as in interviews with living graduates, just how difficult it was for Negroes to get to college and to move ahead from there. At the outbreak of the Civil War in 1860 there were exactly twenty-eight

Negro college graduates in the country. It took Harvard 200 years and Yale 125 years to graduate their first Negro students.[27] When, in *Patterns of Segregation*, Johnson concludes with a demand (in 1943) for far stronger civil rights legislation, "as mandatory as those [regulations] imposed on ... economic life," we see that it is a necessary and right conclusion because in the preceding pages he has demonstrated that "the unequal treatment of theoretical equals" is so deeply rooted only enforceable law can effect change. The evidence of segregation has been piled up, not only in the strategic institutions of economics and politics but also in the nuances and subtleties of interpersonal relationships ("caste etiquette"). Johnson gives a classical example of caste etiquette: "Where public courtesy is demanded, any Negro of status who cannot be addressed by his first name without giving great offense is called professor." [28]

In the general works, however, where Johnson is not anchoring his analysis to a specific research mandate—in *The Negro in American Civilisation, Race Relations* (written with Willis D. Weatherford), *A Preface to Racial Understanding, To Stem This Tide, Into the Mainstream, Education and the Culture Process*—there is a loss of momentum, a tendency to resort to broad, often vague declarations in behalf of progress or the reformulation of values, a reiteration of the faith in social change but without focus on specific institutions such as cotton tenancy or higher education.[29] To be sure, this work was aimed at a different kind of readership, under circumstances different from those attending the research mandate. Nonetheless, one wonders why Johnson did not take advantage of the opportunity, in writing for a more general audience, to move on from the scholarly role to a more militant, or at least more insistent, role of advocacy, directing attention away from "the Negro problem" toward the far larger issue of the white-dominated system of power and the need for a far greater assault by black counterpower.

There are any number of explanations. These general books were written in the thirties and forties, and we should not try to read them from the perspective of the civil rights revolution of the sixties. It may also be argued that, starting with the collaboration with Park, whose essential conservatism on change was paradoxically linked with an enlightened view on race, as Madge, Myrdal, and others have shown,[30] Johnson continued to work so closely with the white philanthropic and governmental establishment over so many years that he could not bring himself to a dramatic challenge in print against the real white power structure that sanctioned the whole system of discrimination and segregation. But this seems to be an ungenerous view. It may be, too, that the years of service on the research coalitions, the foundation boards, the governmental commissions, convinced him that persuasion in the Urban League style, based on research, would work best for him. Jones's term, "indirection," is apt. It appears that Johnson firmly believed in the capacity of the scholarly role as a kind of powerful instrument of advocacy in itself; the more thorough the work on the scope and extent of lynching, the more the white community would be stirred to anger, outrage, and—what counted most—action. As he said to Lewis Jones, when Jones was student editor of the Fisk paper: "This piece says you are angry; that is not what you are after; you want to make other people angry." The impact of *Shadow of the Plantation, Growing Up in the Black Belt,* and *Patterns of Segregation* is in the anger they provoke in us, not in any anger in the texts themselves. Johnson's dedication to social science, his humanism, his balanced humor, his understanding of the white community (even at its most bigoted) could not have produced any other than that perspective. "Indirection" carries its own strategy.

Yet a price was paid in tension for that resolution of role balance for the black scholar in the thirties and forties. That can be seen most readily, perhaps, in the race relations textbook he wrote in the mid-thirties in collaboration with a white scholar, W.D. Weatherford, a "Professor of Applied Anthropology, YMCA Graduate School." The authors note with some pride, "no textbook in sociology has heretofore been undertaken by a white man and a Negro as joint authors," and the labor is about evenly divided, each chapter separately initialed.[31] In content, however, there are odd aspects. Although Weatherford contributes significantly in his discussion of the richness of African culture from an anthropological point of view, it is hard to see why he, rather than Johnson, was assigned the chapters on Negro politics, Negro literature, Negro leadership, and "the solution or the amelioration" of the race problem. His material, when he ventures forth from description and analysis, projects a rather sunny optimism, with many references to emergent "harmony," "more friendly" race relations, "unquenchable good will" that are wholly out of keeping with the depression reality. He is open and enlightened himself but shows no awareness of the economic and political system which underwrites prejudice. The concepts of "power" and "conflict" make no appearance, either in the text or the index. Johnson's contribution is far better as social science analysis, particularly in his assessment of the Negro worker and in his commentary on the economic and social costs of discriminatory health care. But, in contrast with the research books, there is frequently an appeal to the white community, to "the best element in the South" and so on, to foster attitudinal change—this in place of a tough-minded analysis of the conditions for structural change. (In the chapter on black labor Johnson does recognize, however, that white workers are likely to hold tenaciously to racial privilege and that Negro workers must achieve change largely "by some effort of their own.") Johnson falls in with the majority-group invocation of "mutual tolerance" and concludes with the philosophical African proverb he employed in subsequent books and articles: "If you know well the beginning, the end will not trouble you much."

All this is marginal criticism, especially when delivered from the perspective of the seventies, *after* the changes prophesied by Johnson have taken place. I make it only to draw a line between the research work and books like *Race Relations* and *Into the Mainstream* where Johnson is drawn from scholarship to advocacy, but in a curiously muted way. At the least, Johnson's resolution of the "dilemmas and contradictions" implicit in the status of black leaders of the era from 1930 to 1950 can be seen as far more forceful than that of the white liberals of the South during the same period. Why does it so often happen, Johnson reflects, in *Into the Mainstream,* published in 1947, "that the intellectual liberals who know what should be done are torn between their private convictions and their public caution."[32] At all events, Johnson was a sociologist, a black sociologist of great energy and ability, before he was a "race leader," and we can return, finally, to a summary of the contribution in and to social science which he and his associates made during the more than quarter-century, from the twenties to the fifties, when their work was accomplished. Three important themes emerge.[33]

First, the work demonstrates the principle of continuity and growth in sociological research. Johnson's studies are dated in time but not in value. One of the difficulties in developing and strengthening the new black and Afro-American studies is the skepticism of many young black people about the work that was done and the people who did it in the era before Black Power and Malcolm X. That distorts the balance between Johnson's scholarly role and the more ambiguous, if marginal, advocacy role of "indirection." We need to assert again that from the research of Du Bois at the turn of the century down to the work of Frazier, Johnson, Cayton, Drake, Locke, Hansberry, and many others in the thirties, forties, and fifties, there was achieved, against great odds, a solid body of sociological and historical inquiry which stands the test of time. Black social scientists, in sum, have a long, not a short, tradition. Those, in particular, who came out of the Chicago school, provided an indispensable base for research today, no matter that the term "Negro" was used interchangeably with "black." Charles S. Johnson was central in that number. We are in his debt.

Second, Johnson's research underlines the importance of the ethnographic and case study approach in American sociology. Just as W. L. Warner turned to New England and *Yankee City,* as the Lynds turned to the Midwest and *Middletown,* so Johnson was bound to turn to the South, to the county units of the black belt, in order to show the microstructure inside the macrosocial structure. Objectively, yet with full awareness of the deep injustices inflicted by the class-color system in the South, Johnson and his associates gave us enduring portraits of Macon County, Alabama, of Johnson County in North Carolina, of Greene in Georgia, of Davidson in Tennessee, of Madison in Alabama, of Boliver and Coahoma in Mississippi. All were, are, part of the South. But there was diversity too—cotton counties (differing from each other for all the common monoculture), an urban type, counties with diversified farming. Moreover, within each of these areas the distinctive blend of techniques was applied: the survey, the psychological tests, the personality profiles, the self-portraits. The material used in this way to study Negro youth in the South was employed more broadly in *Patterns of Segregation*, where characteristic counties were regrouped by region: The rural South, the urban South, the border area, the urban North. In the urban South category, for example, comparisons were drawn among Birmingham, Nashville, Richmond, Atlanta, Houston. It is now a commonplace to assert there is not a South but many Souths. The Johnson research spelled out theme and variation. In the brief introduction to *The Statistical Atlas of Southern Counties* compiled by the Johnson group, Johnson sought to give life to the columns of figures and to dispel the sense of a "single region," evoking "the bayou dwellers of Louisiana and the bristling, aggressive farmers of North Carolina ... the Southern highlanders who live in the lower reaches of the Appalachians and the Texas farmers who flourish in the black waxy land that is the new hope for cotton." Black and white cut across regions, subregions, economic areas.

So, in the mid-thirties, Du Bois's dream of ample resources applied to sustain comprehensive research in the South came to be at least partially realized. The ethnographic detail was pulled together by Johnson and others to contribute to a rounded social anthropology; the methodological techniques were used in clusters to develop sociological generalization on the fading plantation system and on the role dilemmas of young black people in the segregated South. Sociological research added to conventional history and supplemented the written record with reports of living witnesses.

Third, the research of black social scientists in this era gave a resounding answer to bigoted whites, laymen and scholars alike, who argued that "racial inferiority" in general among blacks had to mean "scholarly inferiority" when blacks came to study their own social structure. It is difficult to credit this absurd argument today. But one has only to reread some of the social science literature on race and on immigration written in the thirties to realize that race prejudice went deep in the academy and in the library, as in the society. What were "Harvard niggers" doing in the archives?

Such wildly erroneous ideas should have been laid to rest decades before. After all, Du Bois was writing his classic study of the Philadelphia Negro at the turn of the century. Still, preconceptions die hard. *Shadow of the Plantation, Growing Up in the Black Belt, The Negro Family in the United States, Black Metropolis* and scores of other studies, demonstrated, if it had to be demonstrated at all, the fallaciousness of a double standard of evaluation for the work of social scientists. In the process, too, there was built up in both the social sciences and the humanities a resounding answer to the white assertion, equally wrongheaded, that the black community could be analyzed *only* in terms of discrimination, family disorganization, and personal crisis. On the contrary, those who peopled Johnson's books, the many thousands gone now and the many still living, were portrayed not simply as "victims" but as many-sided people, struggling as all of us do to hold fast and to work through. If there was despair in Macon in the Depression, there was also in full measure, in the black community, resiliency, endurance, cultural strength, a sense of community. Especially in the moving quotations from the rural folk of Macon and the young adolescents of the Black Belt, Johnson succeeds in breaking out from the confining mandate that everything in the South must be fitted to the two abstractions "the white problem" and "the Negro problem." Macon County and Essie Mae were not abstractions.

These three contributions—the strengthening of the social science tradition by black social scientists, the development of the county case-study comparative method in the rural South, and the implicit rebuke to white racist mythology about the Negro scholar and "the Negro problem"—were made by Johnson and his colleagues and students as ends in themselves, as efforts to advance an objective social science to which black and white scholars alike could repair. Nevertheless, there were never far from Johnson's mind profound questions of value concerning the injustice of the racial system. Johnson wavered on strategy from time to time, but not on his sovereign assumption: the "separate but equal" doctrine could not be other than a bankrupt ideology. To that degree, advocacy was informed by scholarship; one role gave direction to the other.

The Shadow of Macon County

We have seen that for Charles S. Johnson what held professionalism and protest in creative tension—at a personal price paid—was not only a faith in social science research but a faith in the acceleration of social change. His most important work occurred in the grim end-of-the-Depression years and at the beginning of the war boom. As he noted, the war years brought some economic relief to young black people, particularly those who continued the great northern migration to the cities. But economic change, as he also noted, in other ways tightened the noose around the bottom racial groups during the Depression. Nor could much be seen of really militant protest movements through the thirties and into the war, apart from such special events as the 1941 March on Washington, organized by A. Philip Randolph, which induced President Roosevelt to establish the Fair Employment Practices Commission. The courts were still enmeshed in trying to make "separate but equal" a little more equal, an impossible mandate. The New Deal's socioeconomic measures aided the black man only in a very indirect way, as previously noted.[34] The breakthroughs of the fifties and sixties could hardly be imagined. And yet, *the seeds of change, as Johnson knew, were there.* The adult blacks of the South in the thirties and forties were no less conscious than their children of the weight of racial oppression: denial of franchise, police brutality, exclusion from job opportunity, mob violence against blacks, separate and unequal public accommodations. What they lacked was the power to organize effectively, that is, politically, legally, economically against an entrenched white power structure. Even so, what they could communicate as family heads to their children, as professors to their students, was the urgent necessity for far greater change. At the same time, they exerted what limited power they could command as a kind of holding action in a very constricting situation. In this way the next generation of black people was, so to say, socialized into change.

As inflexible as the system looked in 1940, those younger people who listened to Johnson were given hope that it could be cracked by 1960—or however long it might take. Some who came to maturity in the late fifties and sixties found their vehicle for the new militancy in the civil rights movement; others went on from there to black community organization, to black power, separatist and integrationist in varying degree. Whatever the ultimate strategy, the acceleration of change began to be evident even in the Eisenhower years. Johnson lived long enough to witness the initial stages—the landmark Supreme Court decision of 1954 striking down segregation by race in the public schools, the landmark experiment in nonviolent direct action—Martin Luther King's boycott of the segregated bus system in Montgomery, Alabama, in 1955. That these events, in turn, only a decade later, came to be interpreted as too gradualist in the light of the crisis of the cities underlines the increased speed of change. It is true, as well, that Johnson lived long enough to witness the intensification of white resistance and white terror directed against black voters and families, an old story continued. Change is an uneven process.

If he were alive today it seems possible that the first question Charles S. Johnson would direct to us would be whether there has been extensive and accelerated change in Macon County—and the rest of Alabama. Research subsequently carried out by Tuskegee Institute social scientists and by other scholars would show an improved but still mixed picture in terms of black-white comparison on occupational, income, health, educational, and other comparable statistical indices. There might be cited, additionally, the rising black vote in Alabama, black political control of Greene County, the election of a black sheriff in Macon County itself, black mayors in Tuskegee and in Pritchard. Against that would be placed an account of persistent restrictions on blacks in political, economic, and social institutions, the whole presided over by a governor, George Wallace, symbol of white supremacy. The "Southern liberal" defending his Senate seat in the 1972 election would be John Sparkman, Democratic candidate for vice president twenty years before, but now, in the face of a conservative resurgence, scuttling back toward a racist position.

In broader terms, in the context of the advocacy as well as the scholarly role, how would we respond to a question about the achievement of justice as well as the acceleration of social change in

Alabama? Probably along symbolic lines. There were, at last count, more than three hundred black students at the University of Alabama, and no doubt one of them is a potential writer, is reading Hemingway, and is, like James Baldwin, hoping to last and get his work done. The "white man's school or movie house" has been opened to the next generation after Ralph Ellison's, but there are still good reasons for a young black student to choose Tuskegee, very much changed itself, in his search for music or literature or chemistry. If a replication of the Johnson study were attempted four decades after the original, "the system itself" would appear to have demonstrated accelerated change and yet marked resistance to change. In the end, if we were to search for a linkage between the rural Alabama of the thirties and the rural and small town Alabama of the sixties, we might do best to consider Johnson's own research technique, the interplay of survey data with personal document, and conclude with two personal accounts, the one touching on despair, the other hope.

In *Shadow of the Plantation* Johnson explains "the system" in the thirties under which many white landlords would pay low in buying cotton from their black tenants and charge high in extending credit to them. In such circumstances "hopelessness crystalizes itself at times into despair.... Henry Robinson had been living in the same place for nineteen years, paying $105 a year rent for his land. He raises three bales of cotton a year, turns it all over, and continues to go deeper in debt. He said:

> I know we been beat out of money direct and indirect. You see, they got a chance to do it all right, 'cause they can overcharge us and I know it being done. I made three bales last year. He said I owed $400 at the beginning of the year. Now you can't dispute his word. When I said "Suh?" he said "Don't you dispute my word; the book says so. When the book says so and so you better pay it, too, or they will say "So, I'm a liar, eh?" You better take to the bushes too if you dispute him, for he will string you up for that.[35]

Much remains to be done to change "the system" in Alabama. But now, at least, the very places Johnson wrote about in 1932 ring with a new resonance, the result of The Movement of the sixties. Selma, Montgomery, Birmingham, Damascus Baptist Church—

these connote resistance to racial exploitation as they once connoted, in Johnson's study, accommodation of what he called "black peasantry" to the economic situation: *A fatal heritage of the system itself.* There is a little-known footnote to the celebrated march on Selma, to the story of the confrontation, the conflict, the disputes between the older black leaders in the SCLC and the younger, more militant leaders of SNCC. In the midst of all this, Martin Luther King had come over from Selma to Gee's Bend, Alabama, population seven hundred, all-black, still terribly poor. He said:

> "I came over here to Gee's Bend to tell you, you are *somebody*.... you are as good as any white person in Wilcox County."

The old ladies [in the church] with head scarves knotted in front nodded, and said, "It's so. It's so."[36]

Macon County, Alabama, 1932, and Gee's Bend, Alabama, 1963, are part of the same story.

Notes

1   Everett Hughes, "Dilemmas and Contradictions of Status," *American Journal of Sociology* (March 1945), pp. 353-57.

2   John Hope Franklin, "The Dilemma of the Negro American Scholar," in Herbert Hill, ed., *Soon One Morning: New Writing by American Negroes* (New York: Alfred A. Knopf, 1966), p. 61.

3   St. Clair Drake, introduction to the 1967 paperback reissue of Charles S. Johnson, *Growing Up in the Black Belt* (New York: Schocken Books, 1967), p. xviii (original ed.: Washington, D.C.: American Council on Education, 1941.)

4   Ernest W. Burgess, "Charles S. Johnson: Social Scientist and Race Relations," *Phylon* (Fourth Quarter, 1956), p. 317.

5   *The Negro in Chicago: A Study of Race Relations and a Race Riot* Report of the Chicago Commission on Race Relations (Chicago: University of Chicago Press, 1922). For background on the commission see Patrick Malley, "Three Early Commissions in American Sociology" (Ph.D. diss., University of Chicago, June, 1971).

6   Quoted in Gilbert Osofsky, *Harlem: The Making of a Ghetto—Negro New York, 1890-1930* (New York: Harper & Row, Torchbook, 1968), p. 187.

7   Charles S. Johnson, ed., *Ebony and Topaz.* Selections from *Opportunity,* a Journal of Negro Life. (New York: National Urban League, 1927).

8   Toomer, poet and novelist, author of *Cane,* was an elusive and enigmatic man of great talent who could not work through the problem of role balance and identity. Johnson, as critic, says of him, "More than artist, he was

an experimentalist, and this last quality has carried him away from what was, perhaps, the most astonishingly brilliant beginning of any Negro writer of this generation." Johnson is quoted in Arna Bontemps' Introduction to Jean Toomer, *Cane* (New York: Harper & Row, Perennial Classic, 1969), p. vii. *Cane* was originally published in 1923.

9   Charles S. Johnson, "After Garvey—What?" *Opportunity* (August 1923).

10   Lewis W. Jones, "The Sociology of Charles S. Johnson," draft notes for a paper, p. 8.

11   On Johnson's role in this respect see Clarence Faust, "Charles S. Johnson: Educational Statesman, and Philanthropic Enterprises," *Phylon*, (Fourth Quarter 1956).

12   The record of these multiple activities may be consulted in Preston Valien, "Sociological Contributions of Charles S. Johnson," *Sociology & Social Research* (March-April 1958).

13   Cf. Charles U. Smith, "Contributions of Charles S. Johnson to the Field of Sociology," *Journal of the Social and Behavioral Sciences* (Spring 1972), p. 30.

14   Valien, "Johnson."

15   Charles S. Johnson, "Incidence Upon the Negroes," *American Journal of Sociology* (May 1935), p. 744.

16   Charles S. Johnson, "The Conflict of Caste and Class in an American Industry," *American Journal of Sociology* (July 1936).

17   Charles S. Johnson and Herman H. Long, *People Versus Property: Race Restrictive Covenants in Housing* (Nashville: Fisk University Press, 1947). Charles S. Johnson et al., *Statistical Index of 1,104 Southern Counties* (Chapel Hill: University of North Carolina Press, 1941).

18   Lewis W. Jones has written that "according to the Johnson legend" Johnson's account of the grim conditions of Southern tenant life and the failure of the Agricultural Adjustment Act (AAA) to provide relief (see Charles S. Johnson, Edwin R. Embree, and W. W. Alexander, *The Collapse of Cotton Tenancy* [Chapel Hill: University of North Carolina Press, 1935]) was instrumental in the passage of the Bankhead-Jones Act and the establishment of the exceedingly important New Deal agency, the Farm Security Administration. That would be a significant instance, certainly, of the force of Johnson's advocacy role through "indirection," but I have not been able to find any documentation of this relationship of scholarly work to policy in the literature on the New Deal. Cf. Lewis W. Jones, "Charles S. Johnson," p. 9.

19   Johnson, *Shadow of the Plantation,* (Chicago: University of Chicago Press, Phoenix Edition, 1966), p. 120. This reprint is by the same press that published the original edition in 1934, with an introduction by Robert E. Park.

20   Ibid., p. 212.

21   Charles S. Johnson, *Growing Up in the Black Belt,* 1967 edition.

22   Ibid., p. 332.

23   Ibid., p. 325.

24   Ibid., p. 327.

25   *Shadow of the Plantation*, p. 212.

26   Johnson did not accept Washington's accommodative acquiescence in white domination. But as a sociologist he understood Washington's strategy of role playing. By telling the white establishment what it wanted to hear about "good" and "industrious" Negroes, Washington was able to manipulate the white community, was able to wring more concessions from whites in situations where they had a virtual monopoly on power and blacks were virtually powerless. See Charles S. Johnson, "The Social Philosophy of Booker T. Washington," unpublished MS, 1940, cited in August Meier, *Negro Thought in America, 1880-1915* (Ann Arbor: University of Michigan Press, 1963). Johnson's anger at racism and racial injustice did not, of course, have to be concealed, like Washington's. It could come through, but in the work itself, in the power of the recital of the facts. H. L. Moon, reviewing *Patterns of Segregation,* writes, "Whatever fury the author, himself a Negro, may have experienced in the preparation of this volume, he has effectively sublimated in his writing. The result is a coldly logical documentation of race relations in America today" (*New Republic*, March 8, 1943).

27   Charles S. Johnson, *The Negro College Graduate* (College Park, Md.: McGrath Publishing Co., reprint, 1969), p. 366. The original edition, published by University of North Carolina Press, appeared in 1938. From 1826 to 1936 there was a total of known graduates of only 40,000. There were only some 2,300 graduates by 1900! There were as many Negro college graduates recorded in the eight years from 1924 to 1932 as in the century from 1826 to 1934.

28   Charles S. Johnson, *Patterns of Negro Segregation* (New York: Harper, 1943), p. 324.

29   Charles S. Johnson, *The Negro in American Civilization* (New York: Henry Holt, 1930); *Race Relations* (with W. D. Weatherford) (New York: D. C. Heath, 1934); *A Preface to Racial Understanding* (New York: Friendship Press, 1936); *To Stem This Tide,* New York: Pilgrim Press, 1943); *Into the Mainstream* (in association with Ely Allen, Horace M. Bond, Margaret McCulloch, Alma Forest Polk) (Chapel Hill: University of North Carolina Press, 1947); *Education and the Cultural Process* (New York: Macmillan, 1951).

30   On the critique of Park's sociology and view of race relations as essentially conservative, see Gunnar Myrdal, *An American Dilemma* (New York: Harper, 1944), Appendix 2, pp. 1049-50; and John Madge, *The Origins of Scientific Sociology* (New York: Free Press, 1962), p. 125.

31   *Race Relations,* p. viii.

32   *Into the Mainstream,* p. xii.

33   This section on the three themes is drawn, in revised form, from Richard Robbins, "Shadow of Macon County," *Journal of Social and Behavioral Sciences* (Fall-Winter 1971-72).

34   Charles S. Johnson, "The Negro," *American Journal of Sociology* (May 1942). In spite of the way in which both the New Deal and the war effort maintained forms of racial discrimination within the thrust of economic change,

Johnson argued here that, on the whole, both developments would contribute ultimately to accelerated social change.

35   *Shadow of the Plantation,* pp. 126-27.

36   Quoted from Pat Watters and Reese Claghorn, *Climbing Jacob's Ladder* (New York: Harcourt, Brace & World, 1967), p. 161. On the mood of hope in the Freedom Movement, see Richard Robbins ''Negro Politics in the South,'' *Dissent* (January-February 1968).

4

G. Franklin Edwards

E. FRANKLIN FRAZIER

When E. Franklin Frazier was elected president of the American Sociological Society (now the American Sociological Association) in 1948, it marked the first time in the history of this country that a black person was chosen as the head of a national professional association. This recognition by his peers came as a result of a record of solid achievement in scholarship embodied in seven books and more than one hundred scholarly journal articles and chapters in books.[1] This voluminous body of writing centered around two major subjects, the Negro family and race relations, to both of which he made distinctive contributions. As conceived by Frazier, these two major areas were related because, as he expressed it, "the most fruitful approach to the study of race and culture contacts, especially those aspects as regards acculturation and assimilation, was through the study of the family."[2]

As the titles of his articles suggest, it would be possible to classify Frazier's intellectual and research concerns under a variety of fields: urbanization, stratification, human ecology, social organization. In essence, however, his involvement in the subject matter of each of these specialized areas was primarily for the contribution that theories in these areas made to a further understanding of the family and race relations. His concern with urbanization, for example, was basically with the manner in which this process produced changes in Negro life, primarily in family life, and greater social differentiation and stratification; secondarily, he was interested in the effects on individual behavior. The urbanization of the Negro population, moreover, changed the character of race relations from an accommodation based upon a castelike order which characterized the period in which the Negro population was predominantly Southern and rural to an order which promised the prospect of greater integration into American life.[3] It was the influence of the larger societal and community forces upon the institutions of Negro life, and, reciprocally, the impact of the Negro presence upon the larger society, that constituted the major framework for Frazier's research interests. This held true whether the investigation related to family behavior or race relations in the United States, the Caribbean, Latin America, or Africa. Although Frazier was not engaged primarily in the development of stratification theory, the science of human ecology, personality theory, or a general theory of urbanization, to the extent that his research findings documented or modified existing theories in these areas it may be asserted that he made a contribution to them.

In later sections of this paper we shall give attention in some detail to what we regard as Frazier's major contributions, as represented in *The Negro Family in the United States,* which received the Ainsfield Award as the volume which made the greatest contribution to race relations in the year of its publication (1939); *Black Bourgeoisie,* for which Frazier received the MacIver Lectureship Award of the American Sociological Association in 1956; and *Race and Culture Contacts in the Modern World* (1957), which best expresses Frazier's ideas regarding race relations in the modern world and advances a framework for the study of such relationships.

It remains to be pointed out in this introductory section that Frazier was, in the best sense of the term, an academic man. He fully understood the role of the scholar in social life and the discipline required for intellectual achievement. He was sensitive to the contributions professional associations made to the advancement of the individual scholar and to the discipline. He was a founding member of the District of Columbia Sociological Society and served a term as its president; he actively participated in the Eastern Sociological Society and served for two terms as its president. His association with the American Sociological Association covered a period of forty years, and, as mentioned earlier, he served a term as its president. In addition, he held membership and participated in the work of the International Sociological Association and the African Studies Association.

Frazier devoted most of his energies to teaching and research. He thought that the primary contribution of the scholar to social change was through the production of knowledge, although he was aware that it usually took a considerable period for ideas to become diffused in the marketplace and to become accepted, especially when they challenged existing structures and authority. He did envisage a more direct role for the scholar in the relationship between state and society when opportunities arose for the scholar to apply his expertise to problems for which some solution or remedy was sought. It was in line with this conviction that he undertook two major nonacademic assignments. He served as research director of the Mayor's Commission on Conditions in Harlem following the Harlem riot of 1935 and as chief of the Division of Applied Social Sciences of the United Nations Educational, Scientific, and Cultural Organization (1951-53). Those who read the Harlem Report[4] will be impressed with his analysis of social and economic discrimination as factors responsible for the unrest which resulted in the riot and, even more, with the recommendations directed to the government's responsibility for improvement of living conditions of the Negro population and for elimination of racial inequities.

Although Frazier, as a scholar, always sought to be objective in his research analyses, he was a person who held firm political beliefs. As pointed out in the following sections, he early espoused a belief in democratic socialism as a viable political system. One student referred to the fact that, upon his return from study abroad as a young student, Frazier was a "maverick Neo-Marxist."[5] He was not, however, a practicing politician, for he regarded this as inconsistent with his role as a scholar. That his political orientations influenced his interpretations is evident, however, in his assessment of government's responsibility for the maintenance of adequate living standards for all elements of the population. In large part, the disorganization observed in Negro family life as it adjusted to various conditions was owing not so much to a failure of Negroes as persons but to the untoward circumstances they encountered in the American environment. This latter point is not always appreciated by Frazier's contemporary critics. Given Frazier's racial identification, high intelligence, sensitive nature, and the fact that his major personal socialization and academic training occurred in a period characterized by sharp racial discrimination and segregation, it appears inevitable that he would develop strong political views. This aspect of Frazier's life is discussed in the following section.

The Making of a Sociologist

The major forces which shaped Franklin Frazier's decision to become a sociologist are known to us only in a general way. His personal papers are not yet available for systematic study, and he was not given to extended discourses on his personal, familial, and educational experiences. Although it was my good fortune to be associated with Professor Frazier for more than a score of years as a student and colleague, it is fair to state that, despite his zest for conversation and social commentary, he was an extremely reserved and private person. I doubt that he ever considered seriously the writing of an autobiography, although he fully understood that such a document would have great value for its revelations of the experiences of a Negro intellectual and for its evaluation of conditions affecting Negro life during the period it would cover.

Franklin Frazier was born in Baltimore, in 1894, one of five children of James Frazier, a hard-working and extremely race-conscious bank messenger. Frazier's father took a great interest in his family and was a patriarch in the best sense of the term. From available evidence, it is clear that he spent a great deal of time with his children. Although he was a man of limited education, he read to his children about current events and insisted that they discuss the subject matter of the readings with him. His interest in contemporary affairs, particularly in discrimination against Negroes and in the achievements of individual Negroes, are reflected in notebooks in which he assembled newspaper clippings. On the notebook covers he wrote: "From James Frazier to his Children."

Although we know little of the family dynamics beyond what is mentioned above, it is reasonable to infer from this limited information that the Frazier family was a stable, well-integrated unit which provided achievement motivations for its children. Three of the boys became professional men: our subject an academician, one brother a lawyer, and another a physician. The other brother became a small-businessman, and the girl in the family became a housewife.

While we are not concerned with psychological reductionism, this fragment of Frazier's early family life is mentioned because we can reasonably infer that it had some relationship to questions in which he later became interested: his own race consciousness, his strong interest and drive for achievement in intellectual life, and his awareness of the meaning of social mobility among Negroes.

The record indicates that Frazier was an extremely bright student whose performance led his teachers in the Baltimore High School to recommend him for scholarship aid which permitted him to enroll at Howard University, from which he was graduated cum laude in 1916. At Howard he took the classical curriculum which provided courses in languages, literature, natural sciences, and some social sciences. From the language options Frazier took Latin, Greek, French, and German. He took numerous courses in English and American literature, and in the science group he concentrated on mathematics. These courses were offered by competent teachers whom Frazier came to admire, and provided the credentials for his later teaching experiences at the high school level: first at Tuskegee (1916-17) where he taught mathematics; at Saint Paul's Normal and Industrial School, Lawrenceville, Virginia (1917-18) where he taught English and French; and at the Baltimore High School (1918-19) where he taught French and mathematics. It should be observed that Frazier, in common with many others of his generation who later became professional sociologists, did not take formal courses in sociology while an undergraduate, although Kelly Miller had begun to teach courses in the subject at Howard as early as 1903. (Miller organized a department of sociology at a later time and was its chairman until 1934, when Frazier assumed the leadership of the department.) While at Howard Frazier read Giddings's *Principles of Sociology*, a book which fascinated him because of the manner of subject-matter presentation; but he was more interested in a wide range of social problems. He became a member of the

Intercollegiate Socialist Society and served as president of the Political Science Club.[6]

After leaving college, his interest in socialism continued. But during his experience at Tuskegee, he began to take an intense interest in the Negro problem. "I was militant in my opposition to the existing race relations," he writes, "and urged young Negroes to assume a militant attitude toward discrimination and oppression. . . . I resented being drafted in a war which, in my opinion, was a conflict between imperialistic powers and in view of the treatment of the Negro in the United States the avowed aim, to make the world safe for democracy, represented hypocrisy on the part of America."[7] So strongly did Frazier feel about the war as a contest of imperialist powers, that he wrote a tract entitled "God and War," which he had privately printed and distributed.

It was during this same period, however, that he attests to nourishing an ambition to take graduate work in sociology because it appealed to him as the social science which most nearly provided an explanation and understanding of race and class conflicts. "As I look back now," he wrote, "it appears to me that during this period I was developing an objective outlook on racial and other social problems which was divorced in a sense from my reaction to these problems as a person and as a member of society."[8]

This ambition to study sociology formally was realized when he received a scholarship for graduate study at Clark University, Worcester, Massachusetts, during the academic year 1919-20. At Clark he came under the influence of Professor Frank H. Hankins, whose theory courses he credits with opening up to him the possibility of sociological analysis uncontaminated by such matters of expediency as interracial policies in the United States. In general, he regarded the intellectual discipline he received at Clark as having a marked influence on his development as a sociologist. It is interesting to note in this connection that, despite his acknowledgment of Hankins's influence, he was quick to add that he did not always agree with Hankins's position on race and other social problems. Frazier was awarded the Master of Arts degree from Clark at the end of the school term, writing a thesis on "New Currents of Thought Among the Colored People of America."

After the year at Clark, Frazier became a research fellow at the New York School of Social Work, where he began a study of Negro longshoremen of New York City. This study, later completed under a grant from the Russell Sage Foundation and published in the *Howard Review* under the title "A Negro Industrial Group," was Frazier's first empirical investigation.[9] This early effort is of interest because it is related to Frazier's later concern with the effects of the urban community upon an essentially migrant group. Frazier found that the Negro longshoremen were, in overwhelming numbers, Southern migrants to New York City who experienced problems in housing and in their family and recreational life. Their adjustment was affected not only by those problems, but by their failure to understand the nature of union organization in the industry. In line with Frazier's studies in social work, and doubtless the interest of his sponsors, the study made a number of recommendations for improvement of the living and working conditions of this new urban industrial group. Significantly enough, the recommendations urged municipal intervention as the proper lever for some of the transformations regarded as necessary.

The final year of what may be regarded as Frazier's protracted *Wanderjahren* (1916-22) was spent in Denmark as a fellow of the American Scandinavian Foundation. There he studied the folk high school of that nation and the school's role in the cooperative movement. Upon his return to this country, he became professor of sociology at Morehouse College, Atlanta. In his first year at Morehouse he helped to set up the Atlanta School of Social Work and, following its organization, served as its director.

The Atlanta years provided an exposure to the problems of Negroes in a Southern city, problems related in large part to the movement of Negroes from rural areas to the metropolis. Many of the problem conditions had a deleterious effect on race relations as they reinforced the conceptions whites held of Negroes as a defective, dependent, and delinquent group. The need to remedy these problem conditions through social casework methods brought the Negro family unit into focus. It was during this period that Frazier began his writings on the family under such titles as "Three Scourges of the Negro Family"[10] and "Is the Negro Family a

Unique Sociological Unit?"[11]   The three scourges to which Frazier referred were social disorganization, poverty, and sickness.

The article which raises the question of whether the Negro family is a unique sociological unit deserves more extended comment, for it reveals the extent to which his analysis of the Negro family had advanced and his conclusion that empirical study of many of the questions suggested by his formulations was required. In a revealing passage, he wrote:

The first fact that makes the Negro family the subject of special sociological study is the incomplete assimilation of western culture by the Negro masses. Generally when two different cultures come into contact, each modifies the other. *But in the case of the Negro in America it meant the total destruction of the African social heritage.* Therefore in the case of the family group the Negro has not introduced new patterns of behavior, but has failed to conform to patterns about him. The degree of conformity is determined by educational and economic factors as well as by social isolation.[12] (Emphasis added.)

This passage, which is meaningful for an understanding of Frazier's later work, was written prior to his study at Chicago and the educational influences there. The conception of the destruction of the African heritage, the influence of social isolation on Negro behavior, and, in a later passage, the view of broader forces making for both integration and disintegration (behavior as a result of the social process) were all present in his thinking. He concluded the article by stating that "the Negro family is not unique in being based upon attitudes foreign to the American family, but because of the influences given above, it requires special study as a sociological unit."[13]

There is one further aspect of Frazier's work during the Atlanta University period which should be observed. Frazier had begun to take account of the process of differentiation in the Negro group, as expressed in his article on "Durham: Capital of the Black Middle Class."[14] He extolled the virtues of Negro entrepreneurs, many of whose enterprises had lasted for at least two generations; these men showed many of the puritan virtues which characterized white entrepreneurs and managers in larger enterprises. A reading of this article, in the context of his other articles, however, suggests that the concern with business as an avenue of Negro development was an epiphenomenon. A year before the Durham article, Frazier had published an article on "Some Aspects of Negro Business"[15] in which he pointed out the limitations of business enterprise among Negroes. Negroes were consumers rather than producers, he wrote, and could not amass the required capital to engage in large-scale business enterprise. In other writings of this period he indicated that, in his judgment, cooperatives were more relevant as a form of business organization than the small enterprises which Negroes operated.[16] Viewed in this context, Frazier's concern with the Negro businessmen of Durham was more with the stable family lives and disciplined habits of individuals discussed than with the promises of Negro business. This group offered a sharp contrast to the disorganized family life about which he had written and which was a central concern of his work as director of the Atlanta School of Social Work.

The Atlanta years brought together many of Frazier's concerns both as a person and as a professional. He had begun to see clearly that more highly integrated Negro family life was of importance both for the Negro and for the improvement of race relations. Equally important, in his thinking, was the importance of the South's developing adequate social welfare institutions to administer to many of the problems of the Negro group. As a person he reacted sharply to the treatment accorded Negroes, both the masses and educated persons such as himself. It was against the background of these experiences that he wrote "The Pathology of Race Prejudice,"[17] which discussed the irrationality of prejudice as a phenomenon and the mechanisms which operated in the prejudiced person. The article provoked such strong reactions among whites in the Atlanta community that Frazier's life was threatened, and he was forced to leave the community almost simultaneously with the appearance on the newsstand of the magazine in which the article was published. Thus ended Frazier's Atlanta years. He now decided to resume study as a graduate student at the University of Chicago.

The Negro Family in the United States: Its Contributions and Its Critics

As pointed out earlier, Frazier's interest in the family developed from his observations of Negro life and his professional identification with social work. When serving as a research fellow at the University of Chicago, he took occasion to analyze the data on the Chicago community available in the department's research laboratory. He was curious as to whether the gradient patterns Burgess had discovered for the city of Chicago also held for the Chicago Negro community. Upon discovering this to be the case, he pursued the idea and made it the subject of his doctoral dissertation, which was later published as *The Negro Family in Chicago.*[18] The late Professor Ernest W. Burgess characterized this study as the first community investigation to combine effectively the case study method with the method of human ecology. Following completion of this work, Frazier was encouraged to undertake a larger study of the Negro family, which he began under a subvention from the Social Science Research Council, while serving, first, as research professor and, later, as professor of sociology at Fisk University, 1929-34. All of the basic data for *The Negro Family in the United States* had been gathered by the time Frazier left Fisk in 1934 to become chairman of the Department of Sociology at Howard University. The delay of the volume's writing and publication (in 1939) resulted from the pressures of adjusting to his new position and having to spend a year (1935-36) as director of the mayor's commission to investigate conditions in Harlem following the Harlem riot of 1935.

The significance of this work, which Burgess characterized as the most important contribution to the literature of the family since the publication of the *Polish Peasant,*[19] lies in its conception of the "natural history" of the Negro family as it developed under varying conditions. The basic assumption was that, lacking a patterned form as a result of the break with the African background and because of exigent conditions in the American environment, first under slavery, then in the plantation South after freedom, and later in the cities of both South and North, the Negro family underwent many structural changes and was characterized by behavioral patterns which sharply distinguished it from many normative patterns associated with the American family. Some of these patterns were the important role of females in the Negro family, as indicated by the larger number of female-headed households; a larger percentage of common law marriages and illegitimate children; higher incidences of desertions and divorces, poverty, crime, delinquency, and other variations, including distortions in class identification and values. The behavioral forms resulted in the main from the impact of slavery, the continuous social isolation in which Negroes lived, and the disorganizing influence of urban life, for which the masses of Negro migrants were inadequately prepared and to which prejudice and discrimination by whites contributed heavily.

The Negro Family in the United States, however, does not deal only with variations of Negro family life from conventional norms. Attention is also given to stable and conforming family units, as suggested by such chapter headings as "Sons of the Free" and "Black Puritans." Alongside its value in tracing out the structural and behavioral changes of the Negro family as conditioned by the American environment, the work may be taken as a severe indictment of American civilization for what it had done to Negroes in this country. The definition of Negroes as biologically inferior, immoral, and incapable of adjusting to American life, a conception to which American sociologists contributed,[20] resulted in prejudice and discriminatory practices which further exacerbated the conditions under which Negroes lived. Perhaps the most incisive evaluation of the work as a corrective of the stereotyped thinking of the period and of its contribution to the sociological literature is furnished in the following passages from the preface to the work by Professor Burgess:

all persons concerned with the Negro whether engaged in research or involved in practical problems, will find this volume indispensable. It explodes completely, and it may be hoped once and for all, the popular misconception of the uniformity of behavior among Negroes. It shows dramatically the wide variations in conduct and in family life by social classes and the still wider differences between individuals in attitudes, interests, ideas and ideals. The first prerequisite in understanding the Negro, his family life and his problems is the recognition of the basic fact that the Negro in America is a cultural and only secondarily a biological group and that his culture with all of its variations is American and a product of his life in the United States.

... an important contribution of this volume is that it provides a *Gestalt* in which the problems of the Negro family, both for research and for practical action, take on new perspective and meaning. For this reason, if for no other, the work is both a necessary background and a starting point for further research upon the problems of the Negro family in America.[21]

During the past generation this work has remained the single most important study of the Negro family and continues to be regarded as a sociological classic. In recent years, however, it and its author have become the objects of criticism as a result of a number of conditions, chief among which were the growing concern with the problems of lower-class life and poverty in this country and changes in the life conditions of Negroes resulting from the civil rights movement and the development of black consciousness. These changing conditions are not unrelated. To these may be added certain changes in sociological and anthropological modes of analysis.

The civil rights movement brought to national consciousness the glaring inequities of the society. At first the movement's targets were those areas which showed differentials in personal and group rights—school attendance and public accommodations. As success in removing the legal bases of these differentials was attained, the targets became those legal barriers which contributed to social, economic, and political inequalities. Governmental intervention was regarded as a necessary force for corrective action in the areas of housing, employment, education, and voting rights. It was against this background that Michael Harrington's *The Other America* dramatized the poverty of blacks, the aged, and Appalachian whites, so that poverty, though not actually greater than in previous years, became a matter to which public attention was directed. [22] The war against poverty was a campaign to improve the lot of the economically disadvantaged; it thus connected with the legislative concern to remove political, economic, and social disabilities affecting blacks.

To the ferment of these developments, which affected the consciousness of blacks regarding their status in the society, may be added the Moynihan report on the Negro family, a United States Labor Department document which carries the publication date of

March, 1965, though, in fact, it was not made available to the public until several months later.[23] The *Report* pointed to increases over time in the indicators of Negro family disorganization as a result of a "tangle of pathology," which included such elements as the large number of female-headed households, male unemployment, youth problems, delinquency and crime, and alienation. The condition created by these forces was capable of perpetuating itself, so that a national effort must be directed, the *Report* argued, to the question of family structure if improvement in the status of Negroes was to be achieved. The objective of such a national effort should be to strengthen the Negro family.

The *Report* served as the basis of President Lyndon Johnson's highly-praised commencement address at Howard University in June, 1965, and encountered no serious criticism until the Watts riot of August, 1965.[24] When President Johnson mentioned in the course of the speech that he intended to call a White House conference under the title "To Fulfill These Rights," civil rights leaders became concerned that, by focusing on the Negro family as the major problem area, the conference's deliberations would be deflected from what they considered the proper targets—employment, education, housing, and voting rights. Watts had demonstrated that the problems to be attacked were the broader social and economic conditions affecting life in the ghetto—not the family. As planning for the White House conference proceeded, the Moynihan *Report* came to be viewed as an attack upon the Negro family and its author was widely criticized for his views. The fact that much of the subject matter treated in the *Report* had been addressed by Frazier in *The Negro Family in the United States,* coupled with Moynihan's frequent citation of the volume, established a linkage between the two works. One critic, Charles A. Valentine, stated that "the document [the *Report*] contains very little more than an updated rehash of Frazier."[25]

Professor Valentine, a social anthropologist, has proved to be Frazier's severest critic. In his volume *Culture and Poverty: Critique and Counterproposals*, he accuses Frazier of having established a pejorative tradition by concluding that the Negro masses do not live by any coherent cultural patterns, and that the "existence of the modern Negro poor is an immoral chaos brought about by the disintegration of the black folk culture under the impact of urbanization." Frazier's conception of disorganization among Negroes in cities, he asserts, is based upon four kinds of statistical data: "official Census data, statistical reports of social service agencies, records from the police and the courts, and case histories from social workers." Each of these sources has built-in biases, regarding which Frazier shows little awareness. The conceptions of Negro lower-class life as deviant betrays Frazier's personal commitment to middle-class values and mainstream sociology. The essence of Valentine's indictment is captured in the following passage:

An essential element in Frazier's reasoning is one that is perpetuated by later thinkers. This is a direct logical leap from social statistics, which are deviant in terms of middle class norms, to a model of disorder and instability. Such reasoning effectively eliminates consideration of possible cultural forms that, in spite of differing from Frazier's assumed standard, might have their own order and function.[26]

It should be pointed out, as Nathan Glazer has done,[27] that the notion of cultural relativism has contributed to the upsurge of criticism of what Valentine calls Frazier's pejorative view of the disorganized lower-class life. Indeed, there has been a shift in research emphasis during the 1960s away from the macrosociology which attempted to analyze general social and economic conditions as they affected the black family to analyses which attempt to discover order and meaning in the behavior of the lower class. This general line of research has generated scores of investigations into the culture of povery, about which there have been conflicting views. However one lines up on the question of whether there is a "culture of poverty," the objective of investigations in this general area is to examine the behavioral practices, sentiments, and values of the lower class in terms of the functions they serve in the adaptations of individuals and family units. Professor Robert Staples has stated this viewpoint clearly in the following passage:

If we were to look at Black family life styles objectively, we would find that its culture is not a poor imitation of its white counterpart but a fully developed life style of its own. Whether its distinctive cultural patterns are due to its African past, alienation from white society, or economic deprivation is not important. What matters is how it is integrated into

Black family life and whether it is related to the Black condition in American society. This writer submits that Black family culture and social achievement are largely independent of one another.[28]

Frazier died in 1962, when the civil rights movement was being stepped up and concern with poverty and studies of lower-class behavior were being initiated. It is a matter of conjecture as to how he would have reacted to his critics. It is my belief that he would have applauded this line of investigation for the knowledge it provides on the adaptations lower-class families are forced to make and the attenuations produced in other institutions by their life circumstances. This approach was not inconsistent with his natural history approach to the study of the family. He would have agreed, I am certain, with the conclusions reached by Hylan Lewis's study of child-rearing practices among low-income families and the insights they furnish into lower-class family behavior, particularly the conclusion that lower-class families subscribe to general American values, with failures to conform in overt behavior resulting from a lack of money, a diminution of the will to conform, and a lessened confidence in parents of their own, and especially of their children's, life chances.[29] The same may be said of other conclusions; to wit, lower-class parents, with few exceptions, do not approve of the circumstances in which they now live and in which they must rear their children. He would have objected to the notion that there was a "culture of poverty" which implied closure, in the sense that the behavior examined represented a distinctive way of life that was blandly accepted.

It remains to be pointed out that Frazier's approach to the study of Negro family life is not inconsistent with that of contemporary researchers whose interests lie in discerning the life styles and "cultural configurations" of lower-class black families. To a large extent the two approaches are complementary. Both admit of the untoward circumstances under which members of the lower class live. But the different premises which guide the two research frameworks and influence the interpretations have created the apparent conflict. Frazier's basic assumption was that there was little of the African past which influences the Negro American experience; the Negro's basic orientations and values are American. Proceeding within such a framework, departures from American norms were interpreted as deviant behavior, the underlying causes of which were to be found in the conditions under which Negroes have lived in this country. The more recent social anthropological investigations have proceeded on the assumption that there are elements of Negro life which were distinctly Negro; these elements are not in accord with basic American middle-class values but have their own functional importance.

The conflict between Frazier and his critics has emerged mainly from Frazier's use of the concept "disorganization" to apply to the deviant forms of behavior he observed. What is patently absent from the evaluations of his critics is the recognition that Frazier viewed disorganization as a part of a social process which led to reorganization. There is abundant evidence of this approach in Frazier's writings, but nowhere is it more clearly stated than in the final paragraph of *The Negro Family in Chicago,* in which he wrote:

The widespread disorganization of Negro family life must be regarded as an aspect of the civilizational process in the Negro group. It is not merely a pathological phenomenon. The stability of family relations which one finds among the isolated peasant groups in the rural communities of the South is not the same kind of stability which is achieved by the families in the areas of the Negro community in Chicago. In the latter case the Negro has learned to live in a more complex world. As the Negro is brought into contact with a larger world through increasing communication and mobility, disorganization is a natural result. The extent of the disorganization will depend on the fund of social traditions which form the basis for the reorganization of life on a more intelligent and efficient basis.... Unless artificial barriers are raised to nullify the influence of efficiency in the competitive process, increased efficiency will mean greater participation in the communal life. This greater participation will bring the Negro, as we have seen in the case of Chicago, ever-widening conceptions of life which will become embodied in common traditions and aims and purposes of his group.[30]

A fuller appreciation of Frazier's framework of analysis can be gained if one understands its intellectual source. The concepts of social disorganization and social reorganization as related aspects of a process were first used by W. I. Thomas and Florian Znaniecki in the *Polish Peasant* to analyze the problems encountered by peasant communities as their contacts with the wider community increased in number, variety, and intensity.[31] A period of disorganization, defined "as a decrease in the influence of social rules upon individual members of the group," is followed by a period of social reorganization or social reconstruction, in which new rules and institutions, better adapted to the needs of the group, are fashioned from preexisting elements of the peasant culture.

A second major source of criticism, not unrelated to that mentioned in the foregoing paragraphs, is that Frazier espoused the conception, first advanced by Robert E. Park, of a race relations cycle, the end product of which was assimilation. The sequential stages—contact, competition, conflict, accommodation, and assimilation—were considered irreversible. As stated by McWorter, this represented a white, liberal ideology and accounts for Frazier's view that Negro family patterns should conform to those observed among whites.[32] What was needed, in McWorter's judgment, was a social theory connected with a revolutionary black ideology. This view is held by contemporary black activists and those who espouse theories of racial separatism. The imputation to Frazier of a conservative ideological position on race relations has come from other quarters as well.[33]

There is a fundamental misunderstanding on the part of those who hold that Park's conception of assimilation envisaged the disappearance of all differences between interacting groups. According to Ralph H. Turner, "Park explicitly repudiates the view that assimilation means becoming alike."[34] Moreover, there is a common failure to recognize that Park's major preoccupation with race relations lay in the movement between accommodation and conflict.[35] Frazier credits Park with changing the framework for study of race relations from one which conceived of Negro-white relations as a biracial, parallel order based upon accommodation, to one which envisaged the Negro as a minority group, a conception which implies a conflict with the majority for an improvement of the minority's status.[36]

There is also an erroneous impression that Frazier accepted the race relations cycle ending in assimilation as a uniform and irreversible process. He indicated, in one of his articles, that the different stages of the cycle may exist simultaneously, and that they did not represent a "unilinear evolutionary process." [37]

With regard to the assimilationist doctrine, Frazier was more concerned with integration than with assimilation. He had been identified with the Negro Renaissance of the 1920s, was deeply concerned with the preservation and development of traditions as a basis of strengthening the Negro family and enhancing Negro self-esteem, and, in general, believed in a cultural pluralism rather than assimilation. His criticism of Negro intellectuals was directed to the failure of this group to develop ideas and knowledge that would contribute to racial self-respect.[38] In advancing the pluralistic idea, he took as a model the Jews, who insisted upon sharing in the economic, political, and social privileges, as well as the burdens, of the larger society but maintained a sense of group identity. Unfortunately, American society had so brutalized blacks through subordination and isolation that, for Frazier's period at least, the ideal he envisaged was not realizable.

These recent criticisms have led to challenges to the attention he gave to the matriarchate. The conception that such households are dysfunctional in all instances for the discharge of family roles, particularly the rearing of children, is a distortion of his viewpoint.[39] While he did point to the untoward economic and socialization consequences of the absence of the male, he did not regard these families as all deviant and dysfunctional. Nor should he be accused of indicating that such families are typical of Negro family organization.[40] There is, indeed, a warm and humanistic recognition of the strengths of the Negro female in those chapters of *The Negro Family in the United States* which deal with them.

The works of recent scholars have extended our knowledge of the causes of family breakdown, especially our knowledge of the underlying reasons for the absence of the male. It was not only the lack of a tradition but the pressures of contemporary social life that have contributed heavily to the absence of the father. Jackson has pointed to the higher death rate, at earlier ages, of Negro males, as compared with white males, which makes a heavy contribution to the low sex ratio among Negroes and to the number of female-headed families.[41] Liebow has provided additional evidence of the forces of contemporary life which result in Negro males' leaving their families.[42] As indicated previously, Frazier would have recognized the contribution of these scholars, for he regarded his work only as a resumption of scholarship on the black family after the long period intervening between Du Bois's early study and his own works on the subject.

The current concern with Pan-Africanism as an expression of black consciousness has led to renewed efforts to discover African survivals in the art, music, and family life of Negroes. This is as much a political and rhetorical matter as it is social and scientific. A renewed interest is expressed, therefore, in the Herskovits-Frazier controversy over African survivals in the experience of American Negroes.[43] Regarding this, Frazier would suggest that the burden of establishing continuities between the African background and the experiences of American Negroes is on the researcher and would indicate, as he did earlier, that parallels in behavior do not imply common origins. It is necessary to state again that he was not critical of such investigations when they were carried out in an objective manner with the sharpened tools of contemporary sociology and anthropology.

Other Areas of Intellectual Concern

Race Relations. While the Negro-family studies represent Frazier's major contribution to the sociological literature, his work in this area is closely related to his interest in race relations. This is why, in the latter part of the previous section, though it is primarily concerned with the family, his views on race relations were discussed. The interrelation between race relations and the family is seen also in his study of the Negro family in Brazil. There he calls attention to the high degree of intermarriage and the presence of large number of mixed bloods in the Brazilian population as contributing to a different pattern of race relations than that which exists in the United States.[44] But the differences in family relationships were the products of variations in historical and cultural conditions existing in the two countries. In Brazil, for example, plantations were larger and more self-sufficient than in the United States, and Brazil remained a more rural country. Although slavery existed in Brazil until 1888, its abolition was not followed by a period of intense competition in the towns between poor whites and emancipated blacks, and a castelike system did not develop. The greater degree of acculturation of Negroes in Brazilian society, as compared with the relative isolation of Negroes in the United States, resulted not only from the more tolerant racial attitudes of the Portuguese settlers (as compared with the English), but from variations in the social and economic framework in which Negro-white relations in the two countries were conducted.[45]

For Frazier, patterns of race relations and racial attitudes became meaningful only when analyzed in a social organization framework; it was for this reason that his writings in this area take account mainly of the structural, rather than attitudinal, aspects of behavior. The view is expressed fully in "Race Contacts and the Social Structure," his presidential address to the American Sociological Society.[46] This view occupies a central position in his analysis of desegregation in two articles on the subject in which he stated that an understanding of the process must consider the meaning of desegregation for the institutions of Negro life and the role of class-related values as well as the impact it is likely to make upon white institutions and values.[47] The study of desegregation and other aspects of race relations by means of attitude measures, social distance scales, and other quantifiable instruments was likely to miss the social reality. In any event, attitudinal and other social psychological aspects of race relations become meaningful only when they are analyzed in the social context in which they are formed.

A further demonstration of Frazier's conception of and empirical approach to the study of race relations and related social psychological aspects is furnished in his work *Negro Youth at the Crossways: Their Personality Development in the Middle States.*[48] The study on which the volume was based was conducted as a part of a larger investigation sponsored by the American Council on Education into the personality development of Negro youth in several community settings. The Frazier study used the border cities of

Washington, D.C., and Louisville, Kentucky, as research sites. In examining the socialization of Negro youth and the forces affecting their personality development, he had his subjects respond to a number of themes and examined the socialization influences of the family, neighborhood contacts, the school and church, and, in addition, elicited their views regarding employment and their reactions to social movements and ideologies. This was carried out on a social class basis. In this connection it is important to observe that the research took account of the social organization of the Negro community which had been shaped in large part by its relationship to the dominant white community.

Following his return to his teaching position after serving in Paris for two years (1951-53) as chief of the Division of Applied Social Science at the United Nations Educational, Scientific and Cultural Organization, he broadened his writing on the subject by publication of *Race and Culture Contacts in the Modern World.* The volume doubtless was stimulated by his experiences at UNESCO. He thoroughly disagreed with the psychological approach to interethnic relations in terms of attitudes, and to conflicts between nations in terms of tensions. The approach he adopted was a broad framework which employed the findings of all of the social sciences—human geography, anthropology, economics, political science, and sociology. This resulted from the fact that the geographic environment and technological development of people and variations in their economic and political institutions were factors to be considered as well as differences in race and other aspects of their culture. In stating what he regarded as the proper sociological approach to the problem, he indicated:

it is not difficult to show that the character of race and culture contacts in the modern world is determined by the spatial distribution of people, their method of gaining a livelihood and the distribution of economic power. Moreover, the traditions and culture of people with different racial backgrounds shape their attitudes toward each other. Finally, the existing political structures, the distribution of political power, and the laws regulating the relations of people with divergent racial and cultural backgrounds are all determinants of the kind of group contacts and interpersonal relations which exist at any moment in history.[49]

This is not an original approach to the study of race relations. Those familiar with the writings of Robert Park on the subject will readily discern that Frazier's framework is basically Park's.[50] It should be observed, however, that Frazier went beyond Park in giving greater emphasis to the role of political power in the determination of race relations patterns; in his scheme, Park placed greater emphasis upon symbiotic and economically competitive relations. It remained for Everett C. Hughes, himself a Park disciple and a distinguished student of race and culture, to point out that:

Park himself never wrote a book in which he put his scheme for study of race and culture contacts together. It is greatly to Frazier's credit that, late in his career, he took the time and trouble to give us a book which does it; it is Frazier's book, however, not Park's, the mature work of a disciple who valued, but bettered, the Master's instruction—a disciple who had himself become Master.[51]

Urbanization and Stratification: Black Bourgeoisie

Elsewhere we have discussed Frazier's analysis of the deleterious consequences of urbanization for Negro family life. He was interested in urbanization for the differentiation produced in the black community by the broadened economic opportunity for work in clerical and professional occupations. With the growth in community size as a result of the great migrations, the black urban community was capable of supporting a substantial number of black professionals. Frazier thus describes the emergence of two basic classes in the Negro community—a black proletariat and a brown middle class—both of which lacked the stability of the peasant of the plantation South and the gentlemen of the older middle class. The new emergent classes in cities are rootless; whereas the black proletarian masses experience various problem conditions following migration (crime, delinquency, broken families, and others), the brown middle class experiences a distortion of values. It lacks a strong entrepreneural group, the usual backbone of middle classes, but persists in its belief in "making it" in the business world. Its preoccupation with society and status is an imitation of the white upper class, leading Frazier to conclude that it was interested in "status without substance."

The above views are expanded upon in *Black Bourgeoisie*, which appeared first in France in 1955.[52] Besides having feelings of inferiority and frustrations that led to the black bourgeoisie's delusions regarding business and its preoccupation with conspicuous consumption, this class failed to provide leadership for the Negro masses. Its fixation on imitation of white upper-class values resulted, in fact, in its deserting the masses. In a trenchant paragraph, Frazier stated:

When the opportunity has been present the black bourgeoisie has exploited the Negro masses as ruthlessly as have whites. As the intellectual leaders in the Negro community, they have never dared think beyond a narrow opportunistic philosophy that provided a rationalization for its own advantages. Although the black bourgeoisie exercise considerable influence on the values of the Negroes, they do not occupy a dignified position in the Negro community. The masses regard the black bourgeoisie as simply those who have been "lucky in getting money which enables them to engage in conspicuous consumption." When this class pretends to represent the best manners or morals of the Negro, the masses regard such claims as hypocrisy.[53]

This behavior Frazier attributed not only to rapid social mobility, but also to the separate black community with its isolation and the oppression of Negroes by whites. Middle-class behavior, however objectionable to him, was regarded as a compensatory form for the failure of this class to be accepted by the American society. In another connection he had discussed the vested interest of this class in the maintenance of segregation.[54]

One of the sharpest criticisms of the class is its failure to perform the functions of a responsible elite in a minority group: "the black bourgeoisie," he wrote, "has shown no interest in the 'liberation' of black people except as it has affected their own status or acceptance by the white community. They viewed with scorn the Garvey Movement with its nationalistic aims. They showed practically no interest in the Negro Renaissance.... Therefore, they have become, as has been observed, 'exaggerated' Americans."[55]

The intellectual members of this class among Negroes stand in sharp contrast to the intellectuals among Africans. Although African social organization is undergoing marked changes as cities develop, with a breakup of previous kinship ties and the emergence of new mutual aid organizations, the African intellectuals are playing a quite different role in the "liberation" of African people and the development of a national consciousness than the Negro intellectual is doing in this country.

The intellectual leaders who represent the mentality of the new cities of Africa are creating the new ideologies and the new culture of the nations which are coming into existence in Africa. They are the men who are creating the new literature of Africa. They are the men who are writing the history of a people who have long been called by Europeans a people without a history. Some of the ideologies which they are creating [are a] response to a need to rationalize and justify the political awakening in Africa and the new political organization which is taking form.[56]

Black Bourgeoisie produced strong, conflicting reactions in the black and wider scholarly communities. Members of the middle class regarded it as a polemic. Others attacked it as an exposure of the Negro group, and still others attacked it on methodological grounds. Frazier took occasion to answer these critics in his Preface to the paperback edition of the work. Regarding the exposure of the class, he quotes from a reviewer who stated: "A sad truth is better than a merry lie."[57] In answer to the methodological criticism, Frazier reacted by stating that he was not interested in "adequate" samplings of middle-class Negroes with respect to attributes that can be treated statistically. "In my cases, as a participant observer, I collected case materials in the same manner as an anthropologist gathers materials for studies."[58]

As *Black Bourgeoisie* was being read during the period in which the civil rights movement was developing, it found a sympathetic audience among those who regarded the lack of unity within the black community as a major problem the movement faced. The conception that the middle class had deserted the black masses appealed to many of the younger civil rights leaders and protesters. Included in the latter group were many of the leaders of the college sit-ins who, Frazier observed, did not have their social origins in the middle class he discussed.[59]

Whatever one's views of *Black Bourgeoisie* and Frazier's defense of it, it polarized opinions regarding the role and style of life of the black middle class. At best, it is a profile of the class and its values as a product of rapid social mobility, isolation, and oppression. It does not give attention to many stable elements among the class. But the most important observation on the book is that it helps one to assess more accurately Frazier's views of what should be the relationship of Negroes to American society. It should be clear that he was not an assimilationist, as his critics have asserted, but that he strongly opposed segregation and believed in integration. There were strong "nationalist" elements in his thinking, if by "nationalist" we mean a consciousness of group identity and racial self-respect. [60]

The Negro Church. As a student of social organization, Frazier recognized the important role of religion in the experiences of the Negro and the social forces which made the Negro church the single most important institution in the Negro community. This analysis of religion and the Negro church is furnished in *The Negro Church in America,* a posthumous publication based upon the Sir James Frazer Lectures which Frazier gave at the University of Liverpool in 1953. [61] The church served as a refuge for the slave and the folk Negro, but with the urbanization of the Negro population it has become more secular and exercises less control on the lives of the middle and upper classes. As the Baptist and Methodist churches, denominations with which the masses of Negroes are identified, became larger in size and less fundamentalist in theology and outlook, large numbers of lower-class persons have become identified with sects and cults. The middle and upper classes, in substantial numbers, have become identified with the Congregational, Presbyterian, and Episcopal churches. Most members of these classes, however, remain identified with the Baptist and Methodist churches for status reasons as much as for religious values.

Frazier regarded the folk tradition, of which religion is such a fundamental part, as the most vital tradition in the experience of the Negro. It is for this reason that the church has been the most powerful political and economic institution in the Negro community, and Negro clergymen the most important functionaries, until the present at least, in leadership roles in Negro life. These historical facts—the folk tradition and the role of the clergy—help explain the significant contribution of the church and its leaders in the civil rights movement. But despite the role of the Negro church in the mobilization of the masses for social change, Frazier concluded that it would be the institution most resistant to desegregation and integration, mainly because of the meaning it gave to the lives of the masses as a result of their heavy identification with it.

Conclusion

The contributions and style of work of Franklin Frazier enumerated in the preceding pages are the products of his formal training in sociology, mainly at the University of Chicago, and his own robust intellectual propensities. The crystallization of his basic sociological views occurred during the period when a distinctive Chicago approach was being fashioned, chiefly by W. I. Thomas, Robert E. Park, and Ernest W. Burgess, but to which others, including Ellsworth Faris and William Ogburn, made distinctive contributions.[62] Although misinterpreted by others as the Chicago Ecological School, the approach was more concerned with the study of social organization and cultural relationships, to which the understanding of human ecology made a substantial contribution. In assessing the research approach employed in *The Negro Family in Chicago*, for example, Frazier stated that hypotheses tested may be narrowly defined as follows: "Family disorganization among Negroes was an aspect of the selective and segregative process of the urban community. The ecological approach to this study provided an adequate test of this hypothesis. However, the frame of reference of the study was much broader.... The sociological problem is essentially the problem of social organization."[63]

In addition to the influence of this basic Chicago approach, more specific linkages may be pointed out. As previously mentioned, the conceptual framework of W. I. Thomas had a great influence upon Frazier; not only did he make use of the concepts of social disorganization and reorganization, but his use of the concept "social isolation" and "definition of the situation" Frazier attributed to Thomas. From Burgess he borrowed the gradient concept and applied it in the analysis of the Chicago Negro community. He expanded upon the concept, however, in his study of the Negro Harlem community by demonstrating that gradient patterns may be found within a racial community as well as within the city as a whole. [64]

To Park, Frazier's indebtedness appears rather more considerable. He credits Park with changing the study of race relations from a social problems approach to a sociological approach which made for a more objective analysis of behavior in this area. His framework for the study of race and culture contacts is taken over from Park, although, again, with some modification; and his natural history approach to the Negro family and the concepts of the lack of influence of the African background on Negro American experience owe much to Park. It must be noted, however, that it was Frazier, and not Park, who adduced empirical evidence in support of the position and who became the more visible exponent in the sociological debate over the issue.[65] He borrowed Park's concept of a biracial order but expanded it in his analysis of the influence of urbanization upon the differentiation of the Negro population and his delineation of the class or status structure of the Negro community.

Frazier did not make any significant contribution to the methodology of sociology. In his empirical studies he employed the techniques of human ecology and the case study method. In response to one of his critics, he stated:

It is not difficult to explain the scientific outlook of the Negro scholar and the conceptual tools he utilizes. If ... the Negro scholar has arrived, he has become only a competent thinker and craftsman. The techniques and conceptual tools which he utilizes have been acquired during the course of his education. Doubtless, he has made some worthwhile contributions in the various fields, but so far he has not broadened our own intellectual vistas or forged new conceptual tools.[66]

Frazier fully expected that future generations of Negro scholars would make methodological as well as larger substantive contributions to sociology and to other areas. In sociology he thought Negro scholars should make substantial contributions to our knowledge of race relations and of Negro institutions and behavior. These were respectable areas of study which deserved the attention and energies of competent scholars. He argued that as members of the group Negro investigators had a particular advantage as insiders, but he recognized the value which other sociologists, as outsiders, might make to studies in this area.

That Negroes had not made more substantial contributions to sociological knowledge—and to the knowledge base in other areas— he attributed in part to the institutional conditions under which they worked following completion of their formal training. The careers of members of his generation were spent in Negro institutions of higher learning and/or in the Negro community, neither of which was supportive of intellectual activities. There did not exist in Negro colleges and universities a climate which encouraged intellectual exchange among colleagues, nor were there the necessary facilities and freedom for the conduct of research. On the contrary, the atmosphere in these institutions was restrictive and repressive, a fact to which Frazier was fully sensitive, as he had taught not only in a variety of Negro institutions but on a part-time or visiting basis at a number of white institutions, including New York University, The New York School of Social Work, The New School for Social Research, Carleton College, and the University of California at Berkeley.

It is to his credit that he overcame many of these handicaps to produce what he did, works for which the University of Edinburgh and the Morgan State College, Baltimore, Maryland, conferred honorary degrees upon him. But he was saddened by the fact that at the university with which he was identified for more than a quarter of a century it was not possible to develop an ongoing program of sociological research for the training of sociologists and the production of sociological knowledge on the Negro.

When he left Fisk University in 1934 to join the Howard University faculty he was sanguine in his belief that through his association with other scholars at that institution who also were interested in the study of Negro life—Alain Locke, Ralphe Bunche, and Abraham Harris—Howard could and would become a major center for research on the Negro community. This hope did not materialize for a number of reasons, including the administration's failure to grasp the concept of the necessity to expand research activities as a basis for graduate study.

To some extent Frazier shared the failure of Negro educational institutions to support Du Bois's studies of the Negro with Du Bois. In the early 1940s Du Bois was hopeful of resuming the early Atlanta University studies on the Negro, but on an expanded basis. He presented a plan for cooperative research to the presidents of the Negro land-grant colleges in 1941. The research proposal was accepted in 1942, and conferences were held in 1943 and 1944. Before the project was fully funded, Du Bois was asked, quite unexpectedly to him, to retire from Atlanta University because of age. He had expected to continue in the service of the university, with direction of the cooperative project as one of his duties. He negotiated the transfer of the project to Howard University in 1944, and Frazier became its director. But, as Du Bois writes, "Frazier was not given funds for continuing the project and the land grant colleges gradually ceased to cooperate." [67] The project was abandoned within two years of its transfer.

It was Frazier's tough-mindedness which permitted him to react vigorously to race prejudice and discrimination and to develop a feeling of kinship with other Negro intellectuals with similar characteristics. He was a great admirer of Du Bois, to whom, along with Robert Park, he dedicated *The Negro in the United States* for Du Bois's pioneering studies of the Negro. But the basis of Frazier's admiration was broader than respect for Du Bois's scholarly achievement in this area. Du Bois was a foremost example of a strong Negro male who challenged the racial system for its oppressive characteristics. An indication of Frazier's loyalty to and respect for Du Bois may be gained from an event which threatened to humiliate Du Bois. Plans for a celebration of Du Bois's eighty-third birthday by a distinguished group of Negro and white sponsors were threatened with cancellation because a downtown New York City hotel had denied the use of its facilities for the event, following Du Bois's indictment by the U.S. Department of Justice for his work with the Peace Information Center, which the Department contended was an agency of a foreign government. Many of the original sponsors, including the scheduled speakers, withdrew their support. But, as Du Bois wrote of the circumstances, "Franklin Frazier, the chairman, stood firm. He said the dinner must and would go on." [68] The celebration was held on schedule at a Harlem site; Frazier presided and served as one of the speakers.

The tough-mindedness of which we write was only one aspect of Frazier's personality. He was also a compassionate human being, a keen observer of the human condition in both its comic and tragic manifestations. The respect and admiration of confreres in this country and abroad were responses to this aspect of his personality as well as to his scholarly achievements. His students were quick to recognize the warmth and tenderness which lay beneath his apparent toughness and distance. His wife of forty years, the former Marie Brown, is wont to talk of his deep concern for others.

For Negro scholars of the present generation, Frazier leaves a rich legacy. He will be remembered as a devout believer in the possibility the science of man holds for the production of useful knowledge. Beyond this, he stands as an important symbol of the art of the possible, having overcome the handicap of race and lowly social origin to attain distinction.

Notes

1   Frazier's bibliography is included in G. Franklin Edwards, ed., *E. Franklin Frazier on Race Relations* (Chicago: University of Chicago Press, 1968), pp. 325-31.

2   Howard W. Odum, *American Sociology: The Story of Sociology in the United States through 1950* (New York: Longman's, 1951), p. 238.

3   This point is made in many of Frazier's articles, but nowhere more clearly than in "The Racial Issue," in Robert MacIver, ed., *Unity and Difference in American Life* (New York: Harper and Brothers, 1947), pp. 43-59.

4   The unpublished report entitled "The Negro in Harlem: A Report on the Social and Economic Conditions Responsible for the Outbreak of March 19, 1935" may be found in the New York Municipal Archives. Chapters 1 and 9 are reproduced in Anthony M. Platt, *The Politics of Riot Commissions, 1917-1970* (New York: Collier Books, 1971), pp. 165-82.

5   E. Franklin Frazier, *Negro Youth at the Crossways* (New York: Schocken Books, 1967), p. ix.

6   Odum, *American Sociology*, p. 234.

7   Ibid.

8   Ibid.

9   Frazier, "A Negro Industrial Group," 1 (June 1924): 196-211.

10   *Opportunity* Magazine, 4 (July 1926): 210-13; 234.

11   *Opportunity,* 5 (June 1927): 165-68.

12   Ibid., p. 166.

13   Ibid.

14   In Alain L. Locke, ed., *The New Negro* (New York: A. and C. Boni, 1925), pp. 333-40.

15   *Opportunity,* 2 (October 1924): 293-97.

16   "Cooperatives: The Next Step in the Negro's Development," *Southern Workman,* 53 (November 1924): 505-9.

17   *Forum,* 70 (June 1927): 856-62.

18   (Chicago: The University of Chicago Press, 1932).

19   In Frazier, *The Negro Family in the United States* (Chicago: The University of Chicago Press, 1939), p. ix.

20   See Frazier's "Sociological Theory and Race Relations," *American Sociological Review,* 12 (June 1949): 265-71.

21   Frazier, *The Negro Family in the United States,* pp. xvi-xvii.

22   Michael Harrington, *The Other America: Poverty in the United States* (New York: The Macmillan Co., 1962).

23   *The Negro Family: The Case for National Action* (Office of Policy Planning and Research, United States Department of Labor: Washington, D.C., March, 1965).

24   This point is discussed at length in Lee Rainwater and William Yancey, *The Moynihan Report and the Politics of Controversy* (Cambridge, Mass.: The Massachusetts Institute of Technology Press, 1967), pp. 194-215.

25   Valentine, *Culture and Poverty: Critique and Counter-Proposals* (Chicago: The University of Chicago Press, 1968), p. 29.

26   Ibid., pp. 20, 22, 23.

27   See Glazer's Foreword to *The Negro Family in the United States,* revised and abridged edition (Chicago: The University of Chicago Press, 1966), pp. ix-xi.

28   Robert Staples, "Toward a Sociology of the Black Family: A Theoretical and Methodological Assessment," *Journal of Marriage and Family Living,* February 1971, p. 134.

29   Hylan G. Lewis, "Culture, Class and Family Life Among Low Income Urban Negroes," in Arthur Ross and Herbert Hill, eds., *Employment, Race and Poverty* (New York: Harcourt, Brace and World, 1967), pp. 149-72.

30   *The Negro Family in Chicago,* p. 252.

31   W. I. Thomas and Florian Znaniecki, *The Polish Peasant in Europe and America* (New York: Alfred A. Knopf, 1927), 2:1304. For a fuller discussion of these concepts, see pp. 1127-33 and 1304-6 in the same work. These pages are reproduced in Morris Janowitz, ed., *W. I. Thomas on Social Organization and Social Personality* (Chicago: The University of Chicago Press, 1966), pp. 3-10.

32   Gerald McWorter, "The Ideology of Black Social Science," *The Black Scholar,* December 1969, p. 30.

33   See, for example, L. Paul Metzger, "American Sociology and Black Assimilation: Conflicting Perspectives," *American Journal of Sociology* 70 (January 1971): 631-32. See also Pierre van den Berghe's reference to Frazier as the darling of the white liberals in *American Sociologist* 6 (August 1971): 257; and Oliver C. Cox's criticism in his Introduction to Nathan Hare, *The Black Anglo-Saxons* (New York: Marzani and Munsell, 1965), p. 13, in which he states: "His professional career had to be contrived on the tight rope set up by the associational establishment."

34   Turner, *Robert E. Park on Social Control and Collective Behavior* (Chicago: The University of Chicago Press, 1967), p. xxxiii.

35   Ibid., p. xxxiv.

36   Frazier, "Race Contacts and the Social Structure," *American Sociological Review* 14 (February 1949): 2.

37   Frazier, "Race Problems in World Society," in J. Masuoka and Preston Valien, eds., *Race Problems in World Society* (Chapel Hill: The University of North Carolina Press, 1961), p. 40.

38   Frazier, "The Failure of the Negro Intellectual," *Negro Digest*, February 1962, pp. 26-36.

39   Jacquelyne J. Jackson, "But Where Are the Men?", *The Black Scholar*, December 1971, p. 36n.

40   Ibid.

41   Ibid.

42   Elliot Liebow, *Tally's Corner: A Study of Negro Streetcorner Men* (Boston: Little, Brown, 1966).

43   For a discussion of the Frazier-Herskovits controversy, see Frazier, *The Negro Family in the United States*, pp. 3-22; and Frazier, *The Negro in the United States* (New York: The Macmillan Company, 1949), pp. 3-21. See also Frazier's rejoinder to Herskovits's criticism of his "The Negro Family in Bahia, Brazil," *American Sociological Review* 8 (August 1943): 402-4.

44   Frazier, "The Negro Family in Bahia, Brazil," *American Sociological Review* 7 (August 1942), pp. 468-78.

45   Frazier, "A Comparison of Negro-white Relations in Brazil and in the United States," *Transactions of the New York Academy of Science* 6 (May 1944): 251-69.

46   *American Sociological Review* 14 (February 1949): 1-11.

47   "The Middle Class and Desegregation," *Social Problems* 4 (April 1957): 291-301; and "Desegregation as an Object of Sociological Study," in Arnold Rose, ed., *Human Behavior and Sociological Processes* (Boston: Houghton-Mifflin, 1961), pp. 608-24.

48   (Washington, D.C.: The American Council on Education, 1940).

49   *Race and Culture Contacts in the Modern World* (New York: Alfred A. Knopf, 1957), pp. 31-32.

50   See, especially, "The Nature of Race Relations" and "Race Relations and Certain Frontiers," chaps. 7 and 8 in Robert E. Park, *Race and Culture* (Glencoe, Ill.: The Free Press, 1950).

51   From "Frazier as Sociologist," remarks of Everett C. Hughes on the occasion of the Memorial Service for Frazier, Howard University, Washington, D.C., October 19, 1962.

52   Frazier, *Black Bourgeoisie* (Glencoe, Ill.: The Free Press, 1957).

53   Ibid., p. 236.

54   "Human, All too Human: The Negro's Vested Interest in Segregation," *Survey Graphic* 36 (January 1947): 74-75, 99-100.

55   *Black Bourgeoisie*, p. 235.

56   "Urbanization and Its Effects Upon the Task of Nation-Building in Africa South of the Sahara," *Journal of Negro Education* 30 (Summer 1961): 221-22.

57   *Black Bourgeoisie* (New York: Collier Books, 1962), p. 14.

58   Ibid., pp. 12-13.

59   Ibid., p. 12.

60   Frazier's nationalist view (as defined in the text) is given attention in "The Thought of E. Franklin Frazier: Nationalist Assumptions and Implications," a paper presented by John Bracey at the fifty-third Annual Meeting of the Association for the Study of Negro Life and History, New York City, October, 1968.

61   Frazier, *The Negro Church in America* (New York: Schocken Books, 1963).

62   Robert E. L. Faris, *Chicago Sociology, 1920-1932* (San Francisco: The Chandler Publishing Company, 1967).

63   In Ernest W. Burgess and Donald Bogue, eds., *Contributions to Urban Sociology* (Chicago: The University of Chicago Press, 1964), p. 416.

64   Frazier, "Negro Harlem: An Ecological Study," *American Journal of Sociology* 43 (July 1937): 72-88.

65   See note 45 above.

66   From Frazier's Rejoinder to William T. Fontaine, "Social Determination in the Writings of Negro Scholars," *American Journal of Sociology* 49 (January 1944): 313-15.

67   W. E. B. Du Bois, *The Autobiography of W. E. B. Du Bois* (New York: International Publishers Co., 1968), p. 324.

68   Ibid., p. 368.

II. Black Sociologists in a
Segregated Society

5

Butler A. Jones

THE TRADITION OF SOCIOLOGY
TEACHING IN BLACK
COLLEGES: THE UNHERALDED
PROFESSIONALS

The research findings of a professional sociologist and a journalist's commentary serve as a fitting prologue to this paper, which was initially intended to be a review of the lives and works of the many black teachers of sociology who in divers ways directly or indirectly helped the discipline to grow. These are the "Unheralded Professionals" of its subtitle. Westie reported that 19 of the 63 presidents of the American Sociological Association were unknown by work and name to over half of the 198 nonrandomly selected graduate faculty sociologists who returned his mail questionnaire.[1] When the responses were categorized by age, he found that 10 of the first 20 presidents were unknown by name or work to "more than 90 percent of the youngest group of respondents." Jacquelyn Hall has commented on the apparent paucity of materials in the files of the *Atlanta Constitution* which made it difficult for that distinguished newspaper to give more than a few lines to the death of a woman whose early and continuing crusade against lynching contributed significantly to the drastic decline in that particular form of bestiality in the decade of the thirties.[2] Jessie Daniel Ames founded the Association of Southern Women for the Prevention of Lynching and was for a decade and a half the activist arm of the old Southern Commission on Interracial Cooperation headquartered in Atlanta. Her activities were regularly chronicled (and sometimes roundly condemned) in the public press of the South. She was the person to whom the communication media in Atlanta frequently turned for commentary on happenings on the race relations scene. Yet, as Mrs. Hall remarks, at the time of her death the record of Jessie Daniel Ames's life lay so deeply buried that the task of exhumation was too time-consuming for obituary editors faced with a publication deadline. If, as sociologist and commentator indicate, the name and work of men and women once so much in the limelight can be so easily lost to recall among those active in the profession, then it becomes almost axiomatic that until someone does have the time and necessary funding to enable him at least to spend time in the libraries at Atlanta, Fisk, Dillard, and Howard, many of the pioneer black sociologists will remain unheralded, their identities lost in a collection of college catalogs and their research and writing preserved only in the sarcophagi of fugitive materials.

But the reconstruction of the academic and cultural milieu in which these pioneer teachers of sociology to black youth were compelled to operate is an elusive goal. This paper is intended to focus on that issue.

Sociology has a long and honored tradition in the curricula of black colleges. In privately supported black institutions the sociology tradition dates from 1897, when Du Bois began his Atlanta University studies of the Negro in that city. In the publicly financed colleges it begins with the first efforts to mount a collegiate program. In both types of black institutions, sociology appeared as a separate discipline before it did in a host of colleges and universities which now claim distinguished departments in the subject.

Explanations for sociology's early emergence and continued survival in the curricula of public and private colleges for blacks apply also, with some notable exceptions, to the many white institutions where the subject gained an early foothold in the curriculum. However, these reasons take on a special significance in the case of black colleges. Among the more compelling of these reasons were: (1) the relatively low cost of carrying on instruction in sociology;[3] (2) the discipline's early image as the "science" of social amelioration if not wholesale social reform; (3) the very considerable ease with which a faculty could establish a reasonable claim to competence in the field; and (4) the apparent compatibility between the claims of sociology and those associated with prevailing political and religious dogmas.

In the early days of the development of black colleges, the low cost of instruction in sociology made it especially appealing to administration and faculty on the dual grounds of budget and curriculum. To add sociology to the curriculum meant one more "college level" course and another step in the transformation of the institution into one of genuinely collegiate grade. Since the add-on budget cost would be minimal, this addition to the curriculum was quite defensible economically. The major concern of many white philanthropists, also shared by some black college adminstrators, was social amelioration. Wherever their support so dictated, new courses in sociology reflected this interest, as did the proliferation of courses in social pathology or social problems. One consequence was an enduring perception of "social problems" as the basic subject matter of sociology.[4] Note that the early academic and public image of sociology was reformistic and problem oriented. Little more appeared to be required of its earliest teachers than a deep concern about the moral fabric of society and some knowledge of the conditions of the downtrodden.

In these early years the faculties of black colleges overflowed with concerned men and women who also had a theological education that was thought to give them a special competence to deal with ethical questions. They also had practical experience with black-white interaction. Therefore it was assumed that with a little added effort a faculty member could acquaint himself with the relevant literature and by his own efforts acquire as much knowledge in the subject matter as that possessed by all but the select few at the great centers of sociological learning. Even under these favorable circumstances sociology might not have been added to the curriculum of the black college during this period if its concentration on the significance of external factors for individual and group behavior had not sparked the hope among some administrators that sociology might provide some further intellectual support for their belief in the perfectibility of man. In more specific terms, at least to some of the white adminstrators and faculty of black colleges sociology appeared to be the academic route to validation of their belief that, though blacks were possessed of the same potential as whites, socially generated forces operated to blunt that potential. To include sociology in the curriculum was to widen the opportunities for students to learn of "the scientifically discovered causes" of social pathologies including prejudice and discrimination. When, decades later, the publicly supported black colleges moved in the direction of college-grade work, except for a shift in emphasis from sociology as a reformistic science to sociology as an ameliorative discipline, essentially the same factors operated to induce its inclusion in their curricula.

Given the long history of sociology teaching in black colleges, one is constrained to ask why so few black sociologists achieved high professional visibility before 1960. A partial answer is that much time was needed for blacks to acquire even the most minimal preparation for assuming the scholar-teacher role. Some indication of the amount of time required may be gleaned from the fact that as late as 1915 there were only 195 schools (67 public and 128 private) providing even a semblance of secondary education for the nearly 10 million blacks living in the Southern states. Nowhere in the region was the quality of secondary education on a par with recommended standards. Of thirty-three black institutions giving some semblance of college work in 1915, only three were deemed to be truly post-secondary. Consequently, with the notable exception of Du Bois at Atlanta (an institution which in 1915 had only forty-four college-level students), the teaching of sociology and other nonindustrial or "literary subjects" was, until the end of the second decade of the twentieth century, the almost exclusive preserve of whites on the faculties of the black colleges. The size of the student body and perhaps the lack of formal training in the discipline precluded a wide range of course offerings in sociology. This in turn meant less than adequate training and thus the need for more time before the black sociologist could complete requirements of rigorous graduate study. In short, historical circumstances dictated the delayed advent of black sociologists in meaningful numbers until long after the teaching of sociology in black colleges had begun.

A second partial answer to the question of why so few black sociologists have achieved high professional visibility is to be found in the opportunity structure available to them. Upon graduation from college, the aspiring black sociologist was required to further his education in a graduate institution outside the region. Here the dual factors of cost and competition militated against him. While his white counterpart could be selective in choosing from a wide array of graduate schools in which he might seek admission, the range of choices available to the black were especially narrow and limited. Many black students not only faced disabilities of poor academic preparation but serious financial deprivations. Necessarily, many were forced to seek financial aid in order to do graduate study.[6] If the aid was granted, they had to struggle for academic survival in such highly competitive sociology centers as Columbia, Chicago, Wisconsin, Michigan, and Ohio State. It is perhaps far less remarkable that some were able to overcome the obstacles than that so many were foolhardy enough to try. But even for those who met the challenge and emerged with the M.A. and subsequently with the Ph.D. the opportunities were limited and the economic rewards minimal. Neither industry nor government was favorably inclined to their employment. Social service agencies (another principal source of employment for professional sociologists) that were receptive suffered only slightly less acutely from the same endemic ailment as the black colleges—too little money.

It would be a healthy boost to black pride if it could be shown or even reasonably argued that despite the deterrents of miniscule financial rewards and a limited opportunity structure it was the compelling urge to learn that alone inspired the early Ph.D.-seekers among blacks to persevere. But among blacks as among others motivation is always mixed, varied and multiple. Beyond a doubt there were some among the pioneer black Ph.D.-seekers whose motivation was primarily intellectual. There were, however, other propellants. The status rewards conferred upon advanced-degree holders by the black community, coupled with the individual's need for a particular kind of ego satisfaction attendant upon completion of a Ph.D., were of no little consequence. Status rewards included recognition as a quasi-folk hero, deference from other blacks (especially from his academic colleagues) and legitimation of his prerogative to fashion a particular popular image of himself by choosing one among several highly esteemed roles in the black community. These varied from the radical (man ahead of his time) to the iconoclast, from race leader of Solomonic wisdom to scholarly ge-

TABLE I
Operating Budgets, Colleges and Universities for Negroes, 1935-1936

Institutions	Status	Total Operating Budget
Agricultural & Mechanical Normal College	Public	$ 194,053
Alcorn Agricultural and Mechanical College	Public	170,218
Allen University	Private	55,745
Atlanta School of Social Work	Private	24,270
Atlanta University	Private	250,235
Bennett College for Women	Private	107,128
Bishop College	Private	108,276
Bishop Payne Divinity School	Private	13,492
Clark University	Private	66,221
Colored Agricultural and Normal University	Public	181,320
Dillard University	Private	106,519
Fisk University	Private	352,901
Florida Agricultural and Mechanical College	Public	393,094
Gammon Theological Seminary	Private	33,135
Georgia State College	Public	145,979
Hampton Institute	Private	1,189,161
Houston College for Negroes	Public	21,062
Howard University	Private	1,042,374
Jackson College	Private	14,513
Johnson C. Smith University	Private	130,064
Kentucky State Industrial College	Public	148,396
Knoxville College	Private	84,093
Lane College	Private	46,500
Leland College	Private	30,551
Lincoln University	Private	199,989
Lincoln University	Public	350,575
Livingstone College	Private	55,318
Meharry Medical College	Private	246,082
Miles Memorial College	Private	30,276
Morehouse College	Private	142,299
Morgan College	Private	129,595
Morris Brown University	Private	96,730
Negro Agricultural and Technical College	Public	152,324
North Carolina College for Negroes	Public	71,032
Paine College	Private	73,337
Prairie View State College	Public	444,020
Rust College	Private	31,205
Selma University	Private	24,407
Shaw University	Private	145,304
Spelman College	Private	209,027
Southern University and Agricultural and Mechanical College	Public	191,910

State College for Colored Students	Public	98,510
State Colored Normal Industrial, Agricultural, and Mechanical College	Public	163,836
Talledega College	Private	181,343
Tennessee Agricultural and Industrial State Teachers College	Public	315,209
Texas College	Private	77,315
Tillotson College	Private	61,090
Tougaloo College	Private	71,801
Virginia State College for Negroes	Public	685,219
Virginia Union University	Private	142,820
West Virginia State College	Public	289,957
Wilberforce University	Private	432,620
Wiley College	Private	144,458
Xavier University	Private	172,298

Taken from Earl J. McGrath, *The Predominantly Negro Colleges and Universities in Transition* (New York: Teachers College Press, Columbia University, 1965), p. 23.

nius martyred by the prejudice of his white coprofessionals. Among the ego satisfactions was some assuagement of the individual's persistent inner doubts as to the validity of his prior assessment of his own capabilities. He could now point to the fact that he had entered one of the great and prestigious centers of learning, had done intellectual battle with other graduate students under rules that denied him almost every advantage, and had emerged with the ultimate prize: the university's imprimatur on a sheepskin document designating him a Doctor of Philosophy and proclaiming him entitled to "all the rights, responsibilities and privileges appertaining thereto." The fact remains that black sociologists were forced to turn to black institutions for employment.

An examination of the chronic state of near financial bankruptcy which characterized black colleges suggests another reason why black sociologists lacked real visibility before the 1960s. Even without the refinement of a breakdown by categories of faculty salaries paid, research and library allocations, equipment expenditures, travel funds, and the like, the data in table 1 illuminate conditions in 1935. For black colleges as a group it is a uniform picture of low faculty salaries, excessive teaching loads, minimal library allocations, negligible research support, and no faculty travel funds.[7] Nor is there marked variation when one ignores the run-of-the-mill institutions and examines only the "elites" among black colleges, for example, Atlanta University (in 1935 exclusively devoted to graduate work and once again the academic domicile of W. E. B. Du Bois), Fisk, Morehouse, Talladega, Lincoln (Pa.), and Howard, with its several professional schools and graduate program.

The need for money in each of the black colleges imposed a special obligation upon the president to husband its scarce resources. The expenditure of even small sums had to be made according to some general definition of priorities. Money spent for travel should come back in the form of funds raised on the trip. Under these constraints, and independently of other motivating influences, the president of the black college felt compelled to give priority to a one hundred dollar expenditure to defray the cost of a male quartet tour over a faculty member's request for a twenty-five dollar subsidy to attend a professional meeting—even a meeting of the American Sociological Society. Consequently, the black sociologist was denied the opportunity even to acquire that degree of professional visibility which derived from mere attendance at professional meetings. Finally, the steady state of near insolvency which engulfed the black colleges precluded institutional investment in faculty research and severely limited library acquisition of basic research data materials. [8]

The low visibility of black sociologists is further understood by the stance of black presidents of black colleges toward their black faculty colleagues and peers. Throughout their tenure, with rare but quite notable exceptions, [9] the white presidents of black colleges exhibited a sacrificial mien but adopted a paternalistic stance toward their black charges. They were frequently determined that none among the permanent black faculty should achieve more than limited outside recognition lest it foment jealousies, discontent, and restiveness among the others. To this end the white presidents constantly emphasized the teaching function. Research and publication are important, it was said, but these are the province of the university scholar. Here we teach! Thus the white president of the black college often succeeded in convincing the black faculty member that his contribution to the uplift of the race could best come from teaching—not from research and publication. The black president of the black college most commonly found his role model in the white presidents of black colleges. Thus his attitude toward his black faculty members who sought travel and research funds served to maximize the importance of "true dedication to teaching" and to minimize scholarly research.

For the black president, however, there was an added dimension. It was his own sense of insecurity. This often caused the black president to see the emergent black scholar on his faculty as a potential, if not actual, rival for his job. Though proud of the black faculty member who earned a higher degree or who achieved some recognition in his field of specialty, the black president nonetheless felt it to be his advantage to insure low visibility for his peers, particularly off-campus where he (the president) could not apply counterpressures.[10] Inasmuch as the scarcity of college funds for essential operations was a matter of general knowledge, the black college president used financial exigence as an excuse for the denial of financial support for travel to professional meetings for those faculty who might seek it. The end result of the policies and practices of both the white and the black presidents of black colleges was to further impede the black scholar's efforts to achieve recognition in his field through research, publication, or attendance at professional meetings.

The explanations offered so far can never provide more than a partial answer to the question of why black sociologists did not earlier achieve high professional visibility. Because it reveals without obscuring and is independently capable of accounting for the historic fact, "white racism" provides a more definitive answer to the question.

By "white racism," is meant the whole complex of attitudes and behaviors toward blacks exhibited by the dominant white population in the United States. In range, these attitudes extended from outright hatred of particular blacks and insensitivity to blacks as a group to genuine affection for individual blacks and a highly sensitized response to black aspirations. In behaviors, the continuum moved from the lynchings of individuals and quasi-pogroms to the personal care of a favored black and vigorously active support of all efforts to upgrade the status of the entire black population. It was almost inevitable that some white sociologists would reflect in their behaviors towards blacks some of the attitudes current in the dominant white community.

Some of the most revered pioneers of American sociology are indeed best remembered among older blacks trained in sociology both for the venom of their classroom comments about the alleged intellectual and moral shortcomings of blacks and for their acts of outright discrimination against black graduate students. Some are remembered for their expressions of concern for the plight of black students in the context of the particular university setting and for their personal efforts on behalf of black graduate students. Still others are remembered for their studied efforts to achieve impartiality and to see students simply as students. In later years many of these latter came to be among the most admired and respected by their former black students. The basic reason for this is obvious. Only those in this category of white sociologists were, in fact, prepared to accept and deal with black students as persons in their individual capacities; for the distinguishing characteristic shared by the other white sociologists (those who were openly hostile to blacks and discriminatory in their behaviors toward them and those who were liberally oriented and supportive of black aspirations) was the very inability to see blacks as persons in their individual capacities. These two groups might polarize on the issue of the blacks' intellectual potential, but they tended to be as one on the black need for external direction. One behavioral consequence of this belief among white sociologists about the black need for external direction (commonly disguised as friendly advice and counsel in the determination of appropriate strategies and tactics for movement forward) was the denial of support to those blacks who wished to move to the beat of another drummer. Since many of these same white sociologists served as gatekeepers to professional recognition and acceptance, the prospect that this behavior might be evoked served silently to coerce blacks to accept the white determination of the "proper" or "correct" analytic scheme, goal priority, or action tactic and strategy. On the larger national scene the refusal of blacks to listen to the "experts" occasioned a generally negative response to any recalcitrants. It should be kept in mind that racism tended to equate expertness with skin color. The label "expert" was applied only to those blacks who were white certified.

Myrdal observed in 1939 that white expectations of black professionals and intellectuals of all kinds were so narrowly focused and uniformly the same that he could appropriately treat them as a single "expectancy." "This expectancy," he wrote, "is entrenched in all institutions in American society, including universities, learned societies and foundations." As a result of this "tyrannic expectancy of society" he concluded that "the Negro genius is imprisoned in the Negro problem."[11] White racism among academic professional sociologists in the United States contributed significantly to this enslavement of the black scholar in the black problem. For by responding to this "tyrannic expectancy" and urging black graduate students to focus their specialized professional interests on race relations, they restricted further the development of a wider range of academic and professional interests—and in doing so tended to lessen the probability that the black sociologist would achieve high visibility in the profession.

Of all reported Ph.D. dissertations done by black graduate students in the years prior to 1955, fewer than 10 percent dealt with a facet of sociology not directly related to race (basically black-white) relations. These statistics belie any real freedom of choice for the black graduate student in the selection of his area of specialty and the selection of his dissertation. Despite the almost hourly intrusion of race upon his life, mere chance would have produced a greater variation of academic interest among aspiring black sociologists than is here represented. Nor is there denial of the simple fact that many black graduate students freely chose race and ethnic relations as a specialty and dissertation area. Some have openly admitted its use as part of an academic "hustle." But the folklore of older black male sociologists abounds with stories relating how each, on some occasion, got around Professor X, Y, or Z's insistence that he do his term paper on some facet of black-white interaction. Sometimes this bordered on the ridiculous, as when one professor suggested to a black graduate student that he do one of his exercises in statistics on data relating to black attendance at minstrel shows.

To repeat, the point of emphasis here is that this insistence that blacks confine themselves essentially to the study of race and race-related issues did not come from a mere unwillingness to have them do otherwise. It stemmed instead from: (1) an *inability* among

many white sociologists to perceive blacks as capable in other substantive areas of the discipline and (2) a static conception of social
life which assumed that race relations in the United States would
stabilize under the then existing patterns, with black sociologists
permanently and essentially confined to the black academic community. Much is implicit in the perspective of the permanent exclusion of black sociologists from the academic mainstream and the
notion of a strong probability of very slow change in the overall
condition of the black population. For example, the white academic
may very well have assumed that he was making a distinct contribution to the future elevation of blacks by directing his black graduate
students into a deeper study of race relations rather than into some
of the more esoteric and less relevant specialties within the discipline. The inability to accept the fact of the black sociology student's capabilities in a wide range of course areas often persisted
even in the face of a record of exceptionally high grades in theory,
statistics, stratification, and so on. A frequent reaction to performance at this level was to write off the particular black student as
exceptional. Given his skin color (or racial identification) and the
fact that many of his class assignments were focused on race, the
black graduate student frequently came to be looked upon by his
graduate-student peers as having competence only in that area. In
later years, he was able to be remembered as the person who wrote
very informative papers on blacks. (The bull sessions on theory,
statistics, and social change in which that same black had exhibited
the same high levels of performance would be conveniently forgotten.) Since it was often from among these graduate-student
peers that the subsequent leadership of the profession came, the
long-range effects of this labeling process are apparent. The black
sociologist came to be regarded as having competence in only one
area: black-white relations in the United States.

It is somewhat paradoxical that the expertise in race relations
which blacks presumably developed either by personal choice or
from academic coercion did not result in commensurate rewards.
Black sociologists were denied all but a residual share of the money
and prestige rewards which later flowed from government and foundation coffers in support of a wide range of research and action

programs relating to blacks. With a few exceptions it was white sociologists who, particularly in the postdepression years prior to 1950, achieved prominence on the basis of some government-sponsored or foundation-financed survey-research activity. One reason for this was the lack of continuing professional contact between black and white sociology professionals. Under normal circumstances these contacts would have brought many black sociologists into personal acquaintance with their white counterparts. In the absence of extensive personal acquaintance among black sociologists, white sociologists were frequently called to conduct research or to designate research directors for projects dealing with black-white relations in the United States. In almost every instance, regardless of the scope of the study, white sociologists either recommended or appointed other whites. Admittedly, the black sociologist was occasionally used and listed among the research assistants. But only as research assistants graduate to research or project directors do they tend to acquire real professional visibility.

It is no mere happenstance that, exclusive of Du Bois, the black sociologists who achieved the highest professional visibility during this period came to prominence first as directors of Urban League, or nonuniversity or foundation-sponsored, research projects. Even in those instances where the germ of the idea for further and detailed researches into the black community came from the blacks (as in the numerous Du Bois proposals to various foundations and agencies), the proposals, when implemented, were supervised and directed by whites. Schrieke and Myrdal, sponsored by the Rosenwald Fund and the Carnegie Corporation, respectively, are cases in point. Only the desensitized antennae of white academic sociologists could have failed to pick up the shock waves of deeply felt disappointment and hurt which emanated from black sociologists upon announcement of Gunnar Myrdal's selection of the young Arnold Rose as his principal research assistant. Without in any sense diluting the importance of Rose's own personal qualities, or his scholarly attributes and performance, as factors in his rise to eminence in the profession, the fact remains that this rise was almost meteoric after completion and publication of *An American Dilemma*. In the context of this discussion, therefore, it is not entirely inappropriate to raise for consideration the question of what might have happened to the professional visibility of blacks in sociology had one of the several young black sociologists then at Howard, Fisk, or Atlanta been chosen instead of Rose, or, alternatively, had one of the *already* mature black sociologists (Frazier, Reid, Johnson, Moses, Roberts) been given the job.[12]

It would, of course, be arrant nonsense to suggest that the radical shift in tenor, method, and focus which accompanied the coming of age of American sociology in the 1920s was conditioned by racist considerations. It was but a long overdue attempt to divest the subject of its ethical content and reformistic urge. The objective was to better fix the discipline's parameters and to reorient it as a value-free science dependent upon empirically validated experience for proof of its generalizations. Competition, cooperation, conflict, and accommodation became key words in the guidelines to the new sociology, and a host of excellent social ethnographies were produced by those being educated in the new wisdom. But the black sociologists remained imprisoned in the black problem, and, as indicated above, white academic sociologists were among his jailers.

Journal editors were not effectively interested in the findings of the black sociologist and so refused him the accolade of professional recognition—publication in a scholarly journal. Only four blacks are included among the approximately 750 contributors to the first forty volumes of the *American Journal of Sociology*. Only one was included among the contributors to *Sociology and Social Research* between 1916 (the date it began) and 1940. Nor were blacks used in any more representative numbers as book reviewers or book-note writers in these two journals. Of the more than five thousand signed book notes or reviews published in these two magazines prior to 1940, fewer than twenty are by blacks. As might be expected of a journal oriented primarily to the regional problems of the South between 1925 (the date it began) and 1940, *Social Forces* had a slightly better record (and in a shorter period).

Since comparatively few sociologists have or are likely to publish in the scholarly journals, it may be argued that the low representation of blacks among journal contributors in these early years did no more to enshroud black sociologists than other nonpublished individuals. This argument ignores the realities of the day. Because they were already set apart and otherwise kept out of the mainstream of academic and intellectual life in the United States, black sociologists were more desperately in need of the exposure to be derived from publication in one of these journals than were their white counterparts. Even if exiled to one of the poorer white colleges or to one of the less affluent social welfare agencies, the white sociologist did not entirely lose his advantage. There were still many avenues (a network of friends and acquaintances in the profession, contacts made in social gatherings) open to him that were closed to blacks. The pioneer black sociologists might well have survived their relative exclusion from the scholarly journals and achieved professional recognition through articles written for and printed in the popular journals of the day had leaders of academic sociology not seized upon these as proof positive that the black sociologist-authors were not scholar-professionals but propagandists.[13] It was a mixture of motives, undoubtedly including some with racial overtones, that led white academics to see so frequently some significant sociological content in, for example, Sumner's popular journal articles but only special pleading in those written by Du Bois. Nonetheless, the distinction was made and the generalization established: black sociologists are propagandists whose writings do not warrant professional consideration. Since there was no room for the propagandist among the practitioners and devotees of the new sociology, to so categorize the black sociologist-writer was, in effect, to put him permanently outside the pale. It is true, of course, that some of the principal academic spokesmen for the new science were then busily sounding the alarm against "the yellow peril," chronicling the performance of mulattoes and deducing therefrom proof of the superiority of whites and the genetic depravity of blacks. But this was not propaganda. These were scientific truths, objectively arrived at and impartially presented! Only propagandists and special pleaders were in dissent!

By providing moral justification for and motivating the adoption of surrogate control over black sociologists, white racism functioned again to cloud the visibility of these sociologists. Surrogate control is a plantation or colonial mechanism firmly rooted in the proposition that power over a subject group is maximized when control is surrogated to a member or members of the subject group. In order for the mechanism to function effectively, it is imperative that those in power identify the person or persons in the subordinate group with whom they will establish and maintain communication for purposes of contact with the subject peoples. As applied to the situation of contact between the white sociology establishment and black applicants for admission to the guild, effective operation of the mechanism required the selection and appointment of a black sociologist "overseer" to screen and regulate the flow of other blacks. At least four easily recognizable circumstances operated to give the University of Chicago the leadership opportunity for this task. First, Chicago was then the undisputed center of sociological training in the world and therefore the home base of most of the sociology establishment. Second, the Julius Rosenwald Fund, the largest and most influential philanthropic foundation in the United States devoted almost wholly, if not exclusively, to race relations, was headquartered in Chicago on the university doorstep. Third, because of the ties which had developed between them and the major sources of financial support for social action or research, some members of the Chicago sociology faculty were in a favorable position to exercise significant influence upon the directors and administrators of potential foundation support for work in race relations. Fourth, at least one member (Robert E. Park) of the inner circle at Chicago had extensive contacts in the Negro community and acceptable (if not impeccable in the eyes of certain black intellectuals) credentials for assuming within the inner circles of the power elite the role of spokesman for blacks in sociology.

The black initially chosen at Chicago for anointment as the "prime mover," "overseer," or "establishment nigger" in sociology was Charles S. Johnson. His duties at first limited to those of research-collaborator and communication link with social agencies principally concerned with blacks, Johnson gained the respect and confidence of the entire white leadership of the profession and was eventually granted control over the entire province of black sociology. He was the new Booker T. Washington, exercising suzerainty over a more limited and specialized territory but within it possessed of a freedom of action never accorded Washington. Just as Washington in an earlier period had been the black to see if one wanted certain kinds of favors for blacks from whites, so Johnson now became "the black" for other blacks to see in matters relating to financial support for, or in some instances, academic recognition of social science research.

Johnson in time came to be supplied with a veritable arsenal of organizational affiliations and personal and institutional contacts. He was from the beginning, of course, a protégé of Robert E. Park. He became a confidante of Edwin R. Embree, Director of the Rosenwald Fund; John Hay Whitney, multimillionaire donor of the Whitney Opportunity Fellowship, gave him a key to his New York City apartment; and he was in constant and close contact with W. W. Alexander, Southern spokesman for many Eastern philanthropies and director of several small foundations. The list of Johnson's acquaintances and personal contacts is as impressive as it is long. Nor is the organizational list any less impressive. He was, for example, variously an adviser to or member of the General Education Board, the Carnegie Corporation, the Whitney Opportunity Fellowship Program, the Rosenwald Fund, the American Missionary Association, the Southern Commission on Interracial Relations, and many others.

Johnson has been deservedly praised for the quality and quantity of his research. It was by all reasonable standards particularly well-organized and generally reflected acceptable levels of execution. Further, the community of black sociologists has freely admitted its indebtedness to him for his work in maintaining at Fisk a center for the education and training of blacks in the intricacies of sociological research. It was an especially productive outpost, for out of it came many of those who should now be designated middle-generation (not all of them middle-aged, however) black sociologists. Johnson and the "Fisk machine" were functional for the development of black sociologists.

But there were also dysfunctional elements. Johnson's preeminence (that is, greater acceptance by whites) led to professional jealousies and feuding among the relatively small number of leaders who were emerging among black sociologists.[14] One consequence of this was the inability to assemble from among them a faculty of the strength and diversity needed to create a first-rate center for graduate training in sociology. Johnson's control over, or relatively exclusive access to, research and other support funds available to blacks tended to force all research by black sociologists in a direction favored or at least not opposed by him. This control or access position made it difficult for black sociologists with different interests to get unbiased evaluation of their research support proposals. Johnson's use of his favored position to concentrate fellowship-funded research and other forms of financial aid for students and faculty made it more difficult for other centers of graduate study for blacks to secure much-needed funds for the same purposes. Consequently, the strengthening and growth of these centers were inhibited.

Nothing so far said in this paper should suggest a conspiracy among white sociologists to deny visibility to black sociologists. In nonsociological terms, the extremist interpretation of the foregoing is that, in consequence of a comedy of errors of good intentions towards black sociologists, certain tragic consequences (for the black academic community) emerged. In more prosaic sociological terminology, the detailed explanations offered here of the manner in which white racism served to block the professional growth of black sociologists do little more than illustrate the manner in which unintended consequences frustrate intended ends. I have little doubt, for example, that the intent of the sociology establishment at Chicago in lending effective support to Johnson was to accelerate, not retard, the professional growth and exposure of black sociologists. That the effort was only a partial failure is at least a compliment to the good intentions of its supporters.

Although the identity of a host of pioneer black sociologists has been obscured by time, the list of those who are known by name and career history is a long and impressive one. Since there probably exists no scheme satisfactory to all critics for choosing those who most deserve detailed attention, all that can be said about the choices here made is that I regard them as in many ways representative of the group under consideration.

George Edmund Haynes (1880-1960)

For nearly twenty years after Du Bois first articulated it, the need for an objective, multidisciplinary approach to the study of social issues of race relations in the United States went unheeded. Then, in 1910, the trustees of Fisk University voted to establish at Fisk a department of social science geared to serving this specific need. The president of Fisk was instructed to select and appoint an appropriately qualified person to organize and head the new department. Beore the summer ended he had made his choice and received word of acceptance from the appointee. The year 1910 is important for it not only clearly established the seniority of the social science department at Fisk over those at other institutions in the South. It also highlights the fact that, among colleges in the South, it was a black institution which first officially recognized the need for and organized an academic program to utilize a cross-disciplinary approach for the study of problems of social disjunction.

By every index then used to determine such matters, the individual initially chosen to organize and head the Fisk Department of Social Science, George Edmund Haynes, was one of the most highly qualified among the nation's new breed of social scientists. Born in Pine Bluff, Arkansas, in 1880, Haynes was a 1903 graduate of Fisk. From Fisk he had gone to Yale, from which he received an M.A. in 1904. During the summers of 1906 and 1907 he had studied sociology at the University of Chicago. From 1908 until 1910 he had been a fellow of the New York Bureau of Social Research. Just a few weeks before his appointment at Fisk, he had graduated (the first of his race) from the New York School of Philanthropy (now called the New York School of Social Work). Two years later he was to achieve another "first" for blacks when Columbia awarded him the Ph.D. Between 1908 and 1910, as a fellow of the Bureau of Social Research, he had done studies on Negro migration and the condition of Negroes in the urban North. Out of these studies had already come several preliminary published reports. These in turn had attracted the attention of Mrs. William Henry Baldwin, who just before his departure for Fisk had joined with Haynes in cofounding (1910) the

National League on Urban Conditions Among Negroes (since re-
named the National Urban League).

In addition to his academic credentials and research capabilities Haynes brought to his new job at Fisk a wide practical acquaintance with the black academic, professional, intellectual, and religious communities in the South. This acquaintance he had acquired
during his three-year (1905-8) stint as travelling student secretary
for the International Committee of the YMCA. The job had taken
him to at least two churches in each of the major cities in the South
and to the campus of every one of the important Negro colleges in
the region. This was no small accomplishment, given the relative
absence of automobiles capable of extended travel, the conditions of
jim-crow train travel, the almost total absence of hotel facilities
available to blacks in even the major cities of the South, and the
chronic threat to life and limb which white Southerners directed
toward "dressed-up niggers who been up North and got spoiled."
These conditions suggest as a relevant question not how Haynes
managed to find the time for his multiple activities but how he
survived in the South during these years.

Pride of recognition that frequently motivates academics to return to their undergraduate alma maters as teachers may help to
explain Haynes's decision to return to Fisk. Other motives were
more important. Haynes was inspired to return to Fisk and assume
the task of organizing and directing its new Department of Social
Science by what he perceived to be the probability of achieving
certain objectives. One such objective was to insure a continuing
program of research on the history and condition of blacks in the
United States. His own experience in securing funds for more limited research efforts had convinced him that the manpower and other
cost factors in research were such that the prospects for long-term
private support on the scale needed were near zero. He believed that
by making such a continuing research program part of the college
budget the prospects for permanence were greatly enhanced. By
accepting the appointment at Fisk and orienting its research program to the goal of continuity, he reasoned, he would achieve this
particular objective.

Another objective was to provide for a continuing increment to the supply of fully qualified blacks capable of carrying out research and of training others. An important added incentive to acceptance of the appointment was, of course, the fact that Fisk's location in the South, where the bulk of the potential trainees lived, its lower tuition costs and less rigid admission and retention standards substantially increased the likelihood of a significant enrollment. This in turn heightened the probability that the objective of continued gains in the number of blacks qualified to do the needed research would be reached.

A third objective was to find a relatively low-cost means of meeting the particular research needs of the newly formed National Urban League. As executive director of the league, Haynes was particularly sensitive to its need for research focused particularly on the condition of blacks in the urban North. Then, as now, a detailed research report on the status of blacks in a given community was an absolute prerequisite to consideration of that community's need for an Urban League branch. The national league, however, was a shoestring operation that could not afford to absorb the cost of such surveys even in those cities where the most casual surface observation tended clearly to indicate the need for a league branch. As director of the department of social science he would have access to the needed manpower in the person of student enrollees and could therefore legitimately undertake much of this research as part of the training program. Consequently, this objective would be advanced.

A fourth objective which motivated Haynes to accept the position was his firm conviction that there was a need to establish a national repository of source materials and research data on blacks which would be useful not only for immediate purposes but to future scholars. As director of social science at Fisk he would have available to him funds, however limited, to begin the task of collecting such materials and would have the physical facilities for their storage and safekeeping.

A lesser but additional motivating factor was Hayne's deeply felt need for a center of objective research, in a black institution of higher learning, on the history, characteristics, and condition of blacks. Studies undertaken there would serve to put into perspective, if not to counterbalance, particularly those then emanating from the faculty of political science at Columbia. In order to clearly understand this special motivation one must keep in mind the fact that the center of historical research in the Civil War and Reconstruction period had shifted at the turn of the century from Harvard to Columbia. By 1910 the consequences of this shift were proving to be subversive of the aspirations of blacks in the South and in the nation at large. Although Albert Bushnell Hart and his Harvard colleagues, because of their New England bias, might have been too harsh in their historical judgments of the motivations and behavior of the white South during the Civil War-Reconstruction periods, they had nonetheless been relatively free of negative personal bias against blacks as a group. Consequently, their histories of these periods had tended to emphasize the moral and political issues at stake. In this perspective blacks were viewed either as victims or pawns in the struggle.[15]

At Columbia, however, historical studies of the periods tended to emphasize the clash of economic and political interests as causative agents and specifically to deny the importance of moral considerations. Instead of pawns or victims, blacks, along with Northern industrial interests were portrayed as the only real beneficiaries of the system of slavery. Convinced of the innate inferiority of blacks, Burgess and Dunning, the two major forces in history and political science at Columbia, undertook the task of directing a complete rewriting of the history of Reconstruction. To this end, they and numerous graduate students under their tutelage had in 1910 already begun to produce a seemingly endless series of historical exposés of the Reconstruction era. From these, an entirely new image of blacks as subhumans emerged. Titillated by the persuasiveness of the historical evidence produced under the Columbia imprimatur and influenced, of course, by the writings of certain Europeans, scholars in disciplines other than history began to raise questions about these behaviors among blacks. The response was largely an elaboration of the Burgess-Dunning theme of the innate inferiority of blacks.

In his eleven years (1910–21) at Fisk, Haynes moved steadily toward the achievement of the various objectives enumerated above. He began the systematic collection of the masses of source materials which today make Fisk a major library resource for the study of blacks in the United States. He was a founding member of the Association for the Study of Negro Life and History. He organized and taught the first systematic courses in black history to be given in American colleges. He attracted to the department young black historians who subsequently produced historical works that put the Reconstruction experience in a perspective at variance with that of Burgess and Dunning. As executive director (until 1916) of the National Urban League he was frequently made acutely aware of the information gap relating to Negro life and conditions in particular cities. As head of the social science department he proceeded to direct his students in the research needed to fill these gaps. Between 1911 and 1914 he undertook preliminary studies on the conditions of life among blacks in Nashville, Pittsburgh, Philadelphia, and Newark. In 1917 *The Negro Newcomer to Detroit, Michigan* was published. During his tenure at Fisk, Haynes was in great demand as a consultant to industrial, religious, and welfare groups that evinced an interest in race relations. Finally, in 1918 he took leave of absence from Fisk to serve the federal government in the dual capacities of special assistant to the Secretary of Labor and specialist in Negro economic life. In this latter role he became also a special consultant to the Children's Bureau in its fight to curtail child labor. Out of these government years came *Negroes at Work During World War I and Reconstruction* (1921), the first comprehensive government report on economic conditions among Negroes.

Following his government service, Haynes returned only briefly to Fisk. It was from Fisk that he launched a major survey of Negro religious life. Commissioned and paid for by the Interchurch World Movement, the 1920-21 survey of Negro churches and religious life was the first systematic attempt to gather detailed data on the membership, organization, ministry, beliefs, and practices among a nationwide representative sample of Negro congregations. Before the survey was completed, Haynes accepted appointment as executive secretary of the Department of Race Relations of the Federal Council of Churches of Christ in America. He remained in that post until his retirement in 1947.

A contrast of the recognition accorded George Edmund Haynes

by the sociological fraternity with that given Howard Odum serves to illustrate the manner in which the race *dicta* operant in the United States served to mute the voice of black sociologists as professionals without regard to their relative qualifications and professional accomplishments.

Odum and Haynes had much in common. They were contemporaries, having been born only four years apart. Their research interests throughout their careers tended to focus on the same core. They were for years actively involved together in at least one of the same "causes" (the Southern Commission on Interracial Cooperation). Each was born and reared in the Deep South. Each received his A.B. degree from what can only be described as aspiring church-related postsecondary schools, with Odum perhaps getting the better of the bargain. Each attended graduate school in the North (Haynes, Yale; Odum, Clark) before going on to Columbia. At Columbia each took a common core of courses under the same teachers. At Columbia each was looked upon as a student of superior intellect and, as was the custom of the day, each had his dissertation published by the Columbia University Press. Each returned to the Deep South to begin a teaching career in 1910. There were, however, some significant differences in career development even at this time. In 1908 Haynes had begun his active research career, and in 1908-9 had published portions of his research findings, with the results already noted. In the interval between 1910 and 1921 these career differences became more marked. Aside from his dissertation, Haynes published during this period two major research reports and in 1922 yet a third; Odum, nothing.

After 1921 the two careers veered sharply. Odum's star was in the ascendancy. A white man, possessed of two earned Ph.D.'s and holding an endowed chair as senior professor in his discipline at an expanding and awakening university, Odum was over the next thirty years to write twenty books and more than a hundred and fifty articles and editorials; to found and edit for nearly all that time a scholarly journal; to direct a school of public welfare; to establish at his institution (fourteen years after Fisk) and to direct for the entire period an Institute for Research in Social Science; to serve as an assistant director on the (U.S.) President's Commission on Recent

Social Trends and as chief of the Social Science Division at a world's fair (the Century of Progress, Chicago, 1933); to be invited as visiting professor to some of the nation's best-known universities; to be awarded honorary degrees by Harvard, Clark, Emory, and a host of lesser institutions; to take on periodically and temporarily a wide variety of public and private welfare or other humanitarian programs; to be elected president of the Southern Commission on Interracial Cooperation and its successor-organization, the Southern Regional Council; and finally, to be elected president of the American Sociological Society. Somewhere along this energetic career he was to pause long enough to repudiate the findings and the method of the research (but not the men who directed him) that earned him a Ph.D. at Columbia. Despite this early flaw, the overall record is almost overpowering in its impressiveness.

In the same thirty-year period, George Edmund Haynes, black, possessed of an M.A. from Yale, a certificate from the New York School of Social Work, and a Ph.D. from Columbia, was to publish four books and write more than one hundred and fifty articles and commentaries; to serve on two presidential commissions; to participate in three White House conferences; to succeed in getting nationwide church observance of Race Relations Sunday and subsequently to expand this to Negro History (later Brotherhood) Week and during each of the years in the thirty-year span to prepare an outline for a suggested program of observance; to direct and supervise more than two hundred small-scale research projects relating to the role of the church in social action; to organize and direct interracial clinics as a means of coping with racial tensions in more than thirty cities; to plan and direct two major surveys in Africa; to serve as co-executive of the Southern Commission on Interracial Cooperation; to periodically and temporarily serve as person-in-charge of special projects with humanitarian objectives; to receive honorary degrees from such lesser-known institutions as Fisk and Dillard; to serve as an organizing trustee for the merger into one of two previously independent colleges for blacks; to plan and administer a program for making an annual award for distinguished achievement among Negroes; to write the articles on "Negroes" for the 1929 and 1939 editions of *Encyclopaedia Britannica*, its 1938 and 1939 yearbooks, and the 1935 and 1939 editions of the *Social Work Yearbook*; to direct two major surveys of cotton-growing communities in Arkansas and Alabama; to serve as a consultant or board member for a score or more philanthropic or eleemosynary agencies and a half-dozen specialized state agencies; to occupy a place on the governing board of a major state university system; and to attend frequently the annual meetings of the American Sociological Society. And nowhere along the busy way was he impelled either by his conscience, the embarrassed references of his scholarly colleagues, or by new discoveries in the field to repudiate either the findings or the method of investigation used in the research which earned him the Ph.D. On the surface and to the uninitiated the record is certainly far less impressive than that of his contemporary Howard Odum, but was it really so bad that he should have been forever excluded from recognition by the members of the sociological profession? For his efforts he was not to be granted even the most lowly of organizational rewards: membership in an appointed ad hoc committee.

Kelly Miller (1863-1939)

If George Edmund Haynes and W. E. B. Du Bois are to be described as the calm voice of objectivity and academic research scholarship among the pioneer black sociologists, Kelly Miller must be labeled the inflammable catalyst who constantly sought to kindle the alleged spark of "Christial Love" lodged in the white man's breast. Born in 1863, the son of a slave mother and a "free man of color," Miller's first school was the creature of the post-Civil War "carpetbag" government of South Carolina. Demonstrating early a real flair for mathematics, Miller was transferred from his local public school to Fairfield Institute, a mission school founded by the northern Presbyterian church. Leaving the institute in 1880, he went to Washington where he found a job in the United States Pension Office and entered the college preparatory school at Howard. Six years later he graduated from Howard University with honors in mathematics. While continuing in his job at the Pension Office throughout 1887, he studied mathematics, physics, and astronomy under Simon Newcomb, the distinguished senior astronomer at the Naval Observatory. From September 1887 until June 1889, he was a full-time enrollee in the graduate school at Johns Hopkins with concentration in these same subjects. For one year (1889-90) he taught mathematics at the Dunbar High School in Washington. In 1890 he became professor of mathematics at Howard University, where he remained until his retirement in 1934. In addition to his teaching duties in mathematics he served as dean of the College of Arts and Sciences from 1905 to 1918. But as the years passed he derived less and less satisfaction from his mathematics teaching and more and more from the courses in sociology which he had introduced as early as 1912. In 1918, when he was relieved of the deanship, he turned exclusively to the teaching of sociology. Later, he organized the Department of Sociology and headed it until the return of his pupil and successor, E. Franklin Frazier.

Through his lectures and his popular discourses in the leading magazines of the day, Miller sought to delineate the basic issues of the race-relations controversy. Though generally devoid of elaborate statistical tables, Miller's essays were nonetheless marked by rational observations derived from his careful study of the raw data. In one telling piece, by comparing the figures on criminal behavior among whites in Mississippi with those on whites in Massachusetts, he illustrated the pitfalls of a naive reliance upon the gross statistics when linking crime with race.[16] The gross statistical results clearly indicated that the whites of Mississippi were racially superior to the whites of Massachusetts. As Kelly pointed out, the conclusion was obviously devoid of other than gross statistical support. In like fashion he argued that many of the conclusions relating crime to blacks were equally false and based on a similar misuse of statistics producing equally erroneous conclusions.

But Miller's competence as a professional sociologist goes beyond the content of his fifty-odd essays. It was rather impressively demonstrated in a brief article ("Enumeration Errors in Negro Population") published in *Scientific Monthly* in 1922. Utilizing his expert knowledge and skill in mathematics and statistics, he showed how the Census Bureau had compounded some relatively minor initial errors into a serious undercount of the black population in the 1920 census. Aside from its careful marshalling of facts and figures from the raw data submitted by local public school officials and state education agencies in the South, Miller's monograph-length chapter on "The Education of the Negro" (*United States Bureau of Education Report 1900-01*) is a penetrating sociological analysis of the socialization of black children through the manipulation by whites of the formal educative process. His treatment of the stratagems used by black teachers to counteract the process and to promote race consciousness among black children is suggestive of the work that was to come years later from Dollard (*Caste and Class in Southerntown*) and Davis, Gardner, and Gardner (*Deep South*).

Walter R. Chivers (1896-1969)

Of the pioneers among black sociologists, perhaps none is less well-known than Walter R. Chivers. He wrote no books and only a few articles. He never received a Ph.D. nor could he boast of ever having spent any prolonged period of time at the University of Chicago, as so many of the early and later black sociologists could. Almost all of his academic professional life was spent on a single undergraduate campus. (In no one of the more than fifty years that he taught did his teaching load ever drop below twelve semester hours per week.) Except for year-long periods of leave for "further study," he rarely left the home stand. When he did leave, it was usually for a short stint at a sister institution. Exceptions came during the depression when, as several of his colleagues did, he accepted a government post at the behest of the college president in order to permit the latter to pare and, it was hoped, meet the faculty payroll. Only occasionally did he submit a paper for presentation at the regional social science association meeting. When he did, the paper was usually accepted and generally well received. In his later, less financially pressed, years, he was in regular attendance at the ASA meetings. Despite all the apparent meagerness of this record, it is doubtful that any black sociologist has had a more seminal influence upon the development of black sociologists. For over fifty years, Chivers sent a steady stream of young blacks to the centers of graduate sociology study in the East and Midwest. In the early years, for financial reasons, the M.A. degree was terminal for most of these students. In the late 1940s and the 1950s, however, as money for scholarships and other forms of aid became more available, his students tended to stay on and finish the Ph.D. degree. Between 1930 and 1965, nine of his students went on to completion of the Ph.D. in sociology, three more took their Ph.D. in social science or social work, and a host of others went on for the M.A.

Walter Richard Chivers was born in Montgomery, Alabama, just as the populist movement in the South entered its final death twitches. As was required by law, he attended the local segregated schools. In 1915 he entered Morehouse College and was one of a total of three who graduated four years later. In 1922 he went to New York City for work and further education. In 1924 he was graduated from the New York School of Social Work. President John Hope of Morehouse College was at the time much interested in the establishment of a school of social work in Atlanta. He therefore invited Chivers to join the Morehouse faculty as instructor in sociology, hoping thereby to add to the pool (which included E. Franklin Frazier) of qualified persons to launch the new school. Chivers accepted and so returned to Atlanta and Morehouse, where he remained until retirement in 1968.

In addition to his role as one of the organizing and early faculty members of the social work school, Chivers's career at Morehouse was highlighted by the successful launchings of an Annual Institute of Successful Marriage and Family Life and the Visiting Lectureship Program in Sociology. Begun in 1946 and modeled after the Groves Institute, the annual institute focused on the black family. Its origins were grounded in Chivers's deep concern for family life, dating back to his fieldwork days as a student at the New York School for Social Work. He frequently referred to that experience and the conviction derived from it—that the key to comprehending the behaviors of blacks and to effecting significant change in their status could be fashioned only out of a keener appreciation of the characteristics of black family organization and in strengthened family organization.

Unlike Moynihan, however, he did not regard that family structure as abnormal or pathologically deficient. Quite the contrary! He insisted that part of the problem stemmed from efforts by blacks to mold their family structure to the conditions of life as it existed for whites in the United States rather than in response to the realities of life for blacks. He believed that if the traditional (the historically and ideally typical) structure of the black family were systematically examined, one would find there, rather than in the white family system, the constructive elements required to fashion a new model, one that would be molded to fit the black experience. He saw the annual institute as the vehicle for exploring that possibility. It was a matter of some disappointment to him that the many distinguished and well-known persons brought to the campus for the annual institute never seemed to get to this issue, though several made gingerly approaches to it. In at least two other respects, however, the institute served its purposes well. It did bring to the campus and expose to sociology and other students plus interested members of the black community some outstanding personalities in the field of the family with whom they otherwise would probably never have had the opportunity for direct contact. It served also as a stimulant and a model for other black institutions. The Visiting Lectureship Program in Sociology was aimed more directly at providing a stimulant to sociology majors at Morehouse. Students and Morehouse graduates who had earned the Ph.D. and were now in positions of merit were brought to the campus, plus leading figures in the discipline from a variety of institutions. The object was twofold: to showcase the Morehouse graduates and let the sociology majors hear from them of their graduate-school experiences, research interests and activities, as well as of some of the special problems faced in getting ahead in the profession; and to give students an opportunity to have a direct exchange with some of the "big names" in the field and thus strengthen their identity with it. The format of the lectureship called basically for a two-day stay on campus with a formal public lecture and informal contacts with students during the period. The lectureship program was designed to be informative and inspirational. Student response to the program remained high until the late 1960s, when the demand for "speaker relevance" to the black cause forced its modification by curtailing the range of acceptable choices. Although sympathetic from the start to many of the student demands, Chivers was disappointed with the turn of events, which allowed some students, on race grounds, to blunt attempts at intellectual endeavor and thus partly defeat the objectives of this program.

Although his bibliography is a short one, Chivers was not entirely disengaged from research. Instead, he was frequently involved in gathering and analyzing data for government agencies, usually one attached to the Department of Agriculture. The refined data were sent to Washinton where they were at best frequently included in a sociologically meaningless form in some pamphlet circulated to the farm population. In the depression years (1930-37) there was much of this kind of research, the object of which, essentially, was the employment and preservation of research skills rather than the research itself. Consequently, many of the research projects that engaged the scholars' attention were never completed. Local representatives of government funding agencies were chosen from the local population. They tended to reflect the established pattern of placing whites in charge and so rarely made direct grants to the urban Negro scholar to direct and conduct the research. The task was most commonly assigned to a white sociologist as principal investigator, who, if he chose, might share a part of the job with a black. Under these circumstances it was an equally common practice for the white sociologist to take full credit for the effort or at best to give footnote recognition to assistance by the black sociologist. In this way the black sociologist was again exploited and denied professional recognition. Because he needed the added cash income and because he saw in such projects the opportunity to involve his students in research activity, Chivers was himself a frequent investigator under these circumstances.

In the years between 1925 and 1935, when lynching was still a fairly frequent occurrence in the South, Chivers was often the black investigator dispatched by the Commission on Interracial Cooperation to the black community to study and report on the aftermath of the event. These mini-research reports were duly filed in the commission's office and periodically made the basis for later commission summaries. In this way he came to have an almost boundless storehouse of knowledge of the overall conditions of life among the rural and urban blacks in Alabama, Mississippi, and Georgia and an extensive network of acquaintances among blacks at all social levels in these states. From the case histories and personal anecdotes which he told so well, Chivers's students learned of the aspirations and disappointments among the lowly and of the ways in which unlettered blacks resisted, as well as accommodated themselves to, their life conditions.

Charles Goode Gomillion (1901-)

Even if in the future there is some dramatic shift in the writing of the history of the United States which results in texts that give recognition to the constructive activities of blacks, we can be more than reasonably certain of the inclusion of but one of the pioneer black sociologists. There is irony in the certainty that a black sociology Ph.D. will be remembered by the historians of our times for precisely the same reason that almost every school boy remembers the name of an illiterate black slave. He was the plaintiff in a leading Supreme Court case.

Born in rural Enfield County, South Carolina, Charles Goode Gomillion was processed for the future in the unbelievably poor rural schools of his home community. When he completed his schooling in these schools, he took a job teaching in one. In 1928, he graduated cum laude from Paine College in Augusta, Georgia (he received a Ph.D. from Ohio State in 1959). In the fall of 1928 he went to Tuskegee Institute in Macon County (the heart of the Black Belt), Alabama. He stayed there until retirement in 1968. During this forty-year period, he served as dean under three titles (of Men, of the College of Arts and Sciences, of the College of Education), as chairman of the Social Science Division, and in the fifteen years prior to retirement as professor of sociology. Early in his career at Tuskegee he began to assist Monroe Work, the black historian-sociologist, in his efforts to collect and preserve records of the general activities of black persons all over the world but with particular emphasis on the United States. Subsequently, in his various administrative capacities, he provided some budgetary and administrative support for the Tuskegee Bureau of Records and Research which helped to build the bureau into its present eminence as the repository of the most complete record of the day-to-day activities of blacks in the United States. Gomillion was no armchair cogitator. He sought to test in the behavior of men in groups the many sociological principles he daily taught. Consequently, he became active in promoting group cohesiveness and a belief in the prospects for change among the predominantly rural blacks. It was a population that can at best be described as only functionally literate. By dint of much personal energy and the judicious use of well-understood principles of group behavior, Gomillion succeeded at last in achieving his goal.

In 1947 he organized the Tuskegee Civic Association and launched a program of political activism in the local and surrounding rural community which twenty-five years later culminated in control of every elective political office in the city and county. The near miraculous quality of this feat is highlighted by the fact that it occurred in the face of violent opposition from the local white citizenry, in defiance of legislative action at the state level designed to outlaw the movement and stymie its leadership, and over the unrelenting opposition of the governor of the state—a governor who had first achieved national notoriety as an active opponent of voting privileges for blacks and who had since become a major political force in the nation on a platform which, among other things, called for compulsory segregation in the schools, in places of public accommodation, and in housing. It was Gomillion's determination to achieve a real victory by defeating the Alabama state legislature's attempt to nullify black political gains through a gerrymander of the Tuskegee political boundaries. The details of that legal battle (which will insure Gomillion some degree of immortality) and a profile of its leader were first published in a popular magazine with a large circulation among the professional, upper and upper-middle income groups and subsequently in book form. What is important for the pedagogy of sociology is that Gomillion, through the mechanism of political organization, was able to give his students field exercises possessed of a meaningfulness not present in the usual sociology methods courses.

Ira De Augustine Reid (*1901-70*)

Except for the fact that he is the only one of the black triumvirate in American sociology not treated extensively elsewhere in this volume, the inclusion of Ira De A. Reid in a discussion of unheralded professionals would be distinctly out of order. He was neither unheralded nor without significant organizational and scholarly recognition. He was elected president of the Eastern Sociological Society, a member of the council and a vice president of the American Sociological Association at a time when few blacks were either members or especially active in the association as program participants or professionals in attendance. Tall, handsome, impeccably tailored, catholic in his tastes, master of repartee and the bon mot, and possessed of no lingering doubts as to the validity of his claim to equality of treatment, Reid was by all odds the most self-assured and psychologically secure of the black triumvirate. Consequently, he moved with such consummate ease among the sociological elite that his racial identity often appeared to have been forgotten.

Born in Virginia, Ira Reid graduated with honors from Morehouse College in 1922. (He was one of the first blacks elected to Phi Beta Kappa when, in 1967, Morehouse was granted a chapter charter.) Subsequently, he enrolled at the University of Pittsburgh but left in 1924 to accept the job of industrial relations secretary of the New York Urban League. In 1928 he moved up to the National Urban League, succeeding Charles S. Johnson as director of research. In 1934 he left the National Urban League to accept the post of chairman and professor of sociology at the Atlanta University graduate school. Upon Du Bois's forced departure from that institution, he succeeded him as editor of *Phylon*, the race-relations journal founded by Du Bois in 1939. From Atlanta University he went (1946) to New York University as visiting professor and from there, in 1947, to Haverford College as chairman and professor of sociology. Except for periodic leaves, he stayed at Haverford until his retirement in 1968. During the time he was at Atlanta, Reid served variously as director of special projects or adviser-consultant to the United States Departments of Commerce and Labor, the

Social Security Administration, and a host of private agencies and research organizations. At Haverford, he continued to function in like capacities for public and private agencies. In addition, he spent a year each at the University of Ibadan (as Danforth Distinguished Professor of Sociology) and Tokyo Christian University (as visiting professor) and taught in summer sessions at Harvard and Pennsylvania State.

Reid was a prodigious worker, an effective organizer, and a prolific writer who managed always to appear unharried. He carried this ease of personal style over into his writings, which are lucid and readable. His summary study of the social characteristics of Negro youth, *In A Minor Key,* is a classic example of the presentation of masses of statistical information in an easy-to-read and understandable fashion. A like deftness of style and readability is to be found in *The Negro Immigrant* and in Reid's many other works, but it is especially evident in the editorials in *Phylon.* In much of his writing, too, there is a subtle humor which is a delight to the perceptive reader. This is perhaps most evident in his book reviews. But in all of his work, there is the mark of the scholar firmly rooted in his discipline.

Oliver Cromwell Cox (1901-)

As even his name almost suggests, Oliver Cox has from the beginning been an aberrant among black sociologists. Born in Trinidad, the West Indian island long noted for the fierceness in pride of heritage which characterizes its black inhabitants, Cox escaped in his youth those subtleties of socialization which have inevitably produced in blacks born in the United States latent feelings of inferiority. Aware of his relative poverty, Cox (as appears to be generally true among West Indian blacks) was never in doubt as to his status as a free man. He differed also from the other pioneer black sociologists in that he received his undergraduate training in a prestigious Northern, predominantly white institution (Northwestern). Further, physically handicapped, he lacked in some degree the same job mobility and in a much greater degree the physical freedom of movement of his black peers. Without attempting to assay the significance of each of these factors for the subsequent direction of his scholarly interests, I would nonetheless hazard the proposition that they were of considerable import. Certainly there is some evidence in the relevant literature in milieu psychology to suggest that having been reared in a freer environment than that which obtained for blacks in the United States Cox was psychologically better prepared to escape the bonds which imprisoned the United States black intellectual in the black problem.

Because he alone among them directed his scholarly efforts primarily to an examination of the broader issue of the utility of a particular conceptual framework for the study of social organization, Cox occupies a special niche among pioneer black sociologists. He is the only one in the group with broad-based theoretical concerns. As a black living in the United States, however, he could not escape fully the racist insistence that he act like a black sociologist and write on race relations. But unlike his black brethren whose descriptive and analytic essays on particular features of Negro-white relations were aimed at documenting the failures of the American system or at errors and misconceptions within the sociological fraternity, Cox used the race experience in the United States to document not merely the shortcomings of the country's system but the more fundamental position that the system was incapable of organizing itself to correct the situation. His thinking led him to conclude that American (and to a lesser extent all Western) sociologists had failed to understand stratification and stratification processes partly because they had not fully recognized the meaning of the stratification in the context of overall patterns of social organization. He early determined to provide a meaningful and universally applicable set of guidelines for achieving that understanding.

Since for Cox the major problem was a taxonomic one, he focused his work upon the development of a universally valid taxonomy of stratification. Given his assumptions concerning the inability of the American system to work to provide the needed changes and the taxonomic shortcomings of the current approach to stratification, it was inevitable that Cox would clash with those not yet ready to question either seriously or to abandon the existing definitions. As applied to race relations, this approach means a predetermined and premeditated assault upon the "Negro as caste" school in sociology. As the leading exponents of this school, Park and W. Lloyd Warner were early singled out for attack. Myrdal was added in later years after the appearance of *An American Dilemma*.

Cox launched his attack on the caste school of race relations (and, obversely, on the race school of caste relations) early and has continued it down to the present time. For well over a decade and a half he gave it the appearance of a crusade. Between 1945 and 1959 he published more than a dozen articles and book reviews in which the theme was reiterated. In essence he argued that the caste theorists failed to distinguish clearly among race, class, and caste as analytic concepts. The consequence of this failure he saw as confusion and ultimately a form of mysticism which obfuscated rather than clarified the issues. As illustrative of this lack of definiteness in the use of caste, he points to the various "essences" of caste used by Dollard ("a barrier to legitimate descent"), by Warner ("endogamy"), by Guy B. Johnson ("accommodation"), by Park ("etiquette"). He notes a similar lack of agreement on the meaning of class. Race, he says, seems to defy definition by exponents of the caste school. Prejudice is viewed by members of the school as essentially an attitudinal fix that is subject to change by, among other things, moral suasion. All of this, Cox concludes, blinds the sociologist to the realities. "The race-caste assumption is sterile because it has no way of confronting the real dynamics of race relations." For Cox the reality is that capitalism requires the continuation of an exploitable class in order to preserve itself. He has summarized his position in the language below.

Capitalist, bourgeois society is modern Western society, which, as a social system, is categorically different from any other contemporary or previously existing society.

Capitalism developed in Europe exclusively; in the East it is a cultural adoption.

In order that capitalism might exist it must proletarianize the masses of workers; that is to say, it must "commoditize" their capacity to work.

To "commoditize" the capacity of persons to work is to conceptualize, consciously or unconsciously, as inanimate or subhuman, these human vehicles of labor power and to behave toward them according to the laws of the market; that is to say, according to the fundamental rules of capitalist society....

So far as ideology is concerned, the capitalists proceed in a normal way; that is to say, they develop and exploit ethnocentrism and show by any irrational or logical means available that the working class of their own race or whole peoples of other races, whose labor they are bent upon exploiting, are something apart: (a) not human at all, (b) only part human, (c) inferior humans, and so on. The bourgeoisie in Europe were faced both with the problem of wresting the power from the agricultural landlords and at the same time keeping the workers from snatching any part of that power. Among the peoples of color, however, the Europeans had only the problem of converting virtually the whole group to worker status.[18]

In 1948 Cox published his major work, *Caste, Class, and Race.* Subtitled "a study in social dynamics," the work does more than explicate the author's views on the caste theory of race relations. It offers a restatement of the general principles giving rise to the universal phenomenon of social stratification in human societies. Because it, too, challenges much of the prevailing wisdom in the discipline, this work further marks Cox as a maverick in the profession. By indirection at least, the targets of his critical talents now include such patron saints of sociology as Max Weber, whose treatment of stratification Cox finds weak in many respects. Despite its pioneering status as the first full-length book treatment of the nexus which joins class, status, and race, Cox's work has been much ignored in the literature of race relations and stratification. Rarely does it rise above footnote mention, even though its strictures on the utility of the caste theory of race relations are now widely accepted in the discipline. To suggest that this treatment of Cox's work may not be unrelated to the vigor of his early and sustained attack upon the caste theory of race relations is not to argue a conspiracy theory among professional sociologists.

Summary

Haynes, researcher-scholar-teacher-organizer; Miller, teacher-essayist-polemicist; Chivers, teacher-inspirationalist, curator of lower class values and aspirations; and Gomillion, teacher-editor-activist-leader, are broadly representative of all the pioneer black sociologists. Among many others, the group included a small core of early Ph.D.-holders: Vattel E. Daniel, Henry McGuinn, R. Clyde Miner, Harry Roberts, E. Horace Fitchett, Bertram Doyle, Earl Moses, Eugene S. Richards. But typically, the pioneer black sociologist was a non-Ph.D. who spent the whole of his occupational life within the professionally limiting confines of government or welfare agency employment or on the campuses of black colleges. Some (very few), in the twilight of their careers, were brought into the academic mainstream. (Parrish at Louisville and Bullock at the University of Texas are cases in point.) It may very well be argued that scholarly productivity, in the traditional sense, was not high among this group of black sociologists; one notable exception was the work of Betram Doyle. Nonetheless, it was they who received from their white predecessors and kept alive the tradition of sociology teaching in black colleges. These were the men and women who trained as undergraduates the next generation of black sociologists. These later in turn received the heritage and brought it to fruition.

This second generation of black sociologists also had the spirit of the pioneer. They were in sharp contrast to many of their white counterparts in the profession, who were often afforded the facilities, time, financing, and, perhaps most important of all, continuing access to those who could give advice and help in initiating and carrying through significant research projects. The second-generation black sociologists, on the other hand, had their early professional development blunted by continuing (albeit lessened) racist practices in academia and the society at large. It was generally customary among graduate faculties to retain as colleagues the very best of the new white Ph.D.'s or farm them out to other major departments or prestigious undergraduate colleges for further growth and seasoning. Black Ph.D.'s were never included among those retained or farmed out. This was without regard either to the individual black's performance as a graduate student or promise for future development under reasonably favorable circumstances. Instead, each of these new black Ph.D.'s was initially sent back to black colleges. There, often as a one-man department and almost never as one in a department of more than three, they were required to teach an unduly heavy work-load, graduate students were nonexistent and the press for money seemed only to have diminished on the surface.

Only the liberating push exercised by black students saved many of these second-generation black sociologists from having to repeat the experiences of earlier black sociology teachers. However, the "great awakening" among the nation's white colleges and universities came at the mid-career point for many of these second-generation sociologists. The fact that so many of them have in the years since "liberation" achieved visibility through publication and professional organizational recognition accentuates the tragedy of past denials. Nevertheless, as immediate successors to the black pioneers, they nourished the sociology tradition in the black colleges. There is still time to make amends for past denials to them. Prominent among this group are: John C. Alston, John T. Blue, Tillman Cothran, Sarah Curwood, Joseph Himes, Lewis W. Jones, Charles E. King, Charles R. Lawrence, Hylan Lewis, James Moss, Lionel Newsome, Leonard Robinson, Alvin Rose, Daniel C. Thompson, Preston Valien, Albert Whiting, and Raytha Yokely.

But this is an essay focused on that legion of pioneer black sociologists who kept the tradition of sociology teaching alive in the black colleges in the days "when hope unborn had died." Hidden in the dark recesses of the American intellectual community, their specific identities even now not fully known, forced into a daily struggle to keep their own intellectual spirits alive, these men should not be shunted aside and denied in death, as in life, the recognition they so laboriously earned. Let memories be exhumed, past catalogues be examined, and their names revealed for these are surely the *unheralded professionals.*

Notes

1   Frank R. Westie, "Academic Expectations for Professional Immortality: A Study of Legitimation," *Sociological Focus* 5 (Spring 1972).

2   *South Today*, May 1972.

3   The writer professes no expertness on the question of the relationship between low instructional cost and the inclusion of a particular subject in the curriculum. That cost would be a factor affecting the decision in these particular institutions does seem a reasonable speculation. The point I wish to make is that

the wealthier institutions were less constrained by problems of financial exigence and were therefore freer to choose among the disciplines which they would support.

4   This is in no way intended to disparage the outcomes of instruction in such high-cost areas in the black colleges as physics, chemistry, and biology. While the record clearly establishes that a number of individuals who received their baccalaureate training in the physical and natural sciences in black colleges have gone on to achieve eminence in their chosen field, it is significant that the number varies inversely with the cost of effective undergraduate instruction in these areas. The number in physics (where the cost of undergraduate instruction is high) has been relatively low, in biology (with a lower undergraduate instructional cost) the number has been relatively high. What is suggested here, however, must be regarded as more in the nature of an hypothesis than a conclusion. Any examination of the issue would have to give due consideration to the many operative variables in the total situation.

5   A generalization applicable to white institutions as well, but again one which has special merit for black colleges.

6   In these pre-1960 days, there were no academic scouts from the Ivy League, the Big Ten, or other predominantly white institutions beating the bushes with sizeable scholarship lures for "the disadvantaged." Nor were there NIMH, NDEA, NSF, or other funds.

7   In 1955 the Southern Association of Colleges and Secondary Schools (the regional accrediting agent) defined the normal faculty load for teachers in black colleges as eighteen semester hours. It was fifteen in accredited white institutions. Interestingly enough, the association denied membership to black colleges and refused to accredit them on the grounds that the association constitution limited its accreditation role to member- or membership-eligible institutions. The association did, however, accord to the black institution a special letter category, e.g., A, B, C.

8   For those who would immediately see in this lack of on-campus research materials a feeble excuse for the black sociologist's apparent low productivity, I would remind them that unlike their white counterparts faced also with inadequate library resources, the black sociologist did not have access to local public libraries. For the first half of the twentieth century blacks were almost uniformly barred from the main branch (where research materials are generally kept) of the public library in southern towns and cities. No Negro could have written *Gone With the Wind* for, unlike Margaret Mitchell who was freely permitted to spend long hours in the main branch of the Atlanta Public Library doing the required research, Negroes were barred from the facility until the late 1940s when finally they were admitted under court order.

9   Ware at Atlanta, Jones at Fisk, Gallagher at Talladega.

10   I can personally attest to this ambivalence among black presidents of black colleges with respect to black Ph.D.-holders on their faculties. During the early 1940s I had occasion to be present at a luncheon incident to a meeting of the Association of Colleges and Secondary Schools for Negroes. There were fifteen or sixteen persons present, all black, and with the exception of myself and one other, all college presidents. There was much friendly banter among the presidents concerning the movements of faculty personnel from one campus to the other. A president who had just lured a Ph.D. away from another college spoke gloatingly over his coup while the affected president promised some day to even the score. Individual presidents spoke with pride of the number of Ph.D.'s on their faculties as well as of those beginning or about to complete their Ph.D. work. But interlarded with the boastful comments were negative assertions about Ph.D.'s as a group and about individual Ph.D.-holders. Warnings were given about adding Prof. X to the faculty. He was dubbed a troublemaker. As the conversations and exchanges went on, there were more and more references to specific "faculty troublemakers." Ph.D.-holders were among those most frequently mentioned as persons wishing to upset the apple cart, "to get the students aroused," "to agitate in the faculty." One president lamented that a Ph.D. on a faculty just automatically meant trouble. Several openly assented to this verdict while others spoke of Ph.D.-holders as men unwilling to face the realities of the black college. Black Ph.D.-holders were described as impatient with routine, as "too ambitious," as having been spoiled by prolonged exposure to low teaching loads, expensive and fancy (read modern) equipment, and as more interested in "so-called" research than in teaching.

11   Gunnar Myrdal, with the assistance of Richard Sterner and Arnold Rose, *An American Dilemma: The Negro Problem and Modern Democracy* (New York: Harper, 1944), p. 28.

12   It has been urged that the careers of several black sociologists were "almost decisively fashioned by their association with Myrdal." Without categorically denying the proposition, I report only that I am not able to identify any such individuals. I think it can be reasonably argued that Myrdal spotlighted a pool of available talent in the black community which was subsequently tapped by others.

13   The label was early, and is even now, applied to Du Bois, usually without distinguishing among particular pieces of his work done after 1905. Even such usually sympathetic writers as Rudwick and Meier refer to Du Bois the propagandist when speaking of the post-1910 period. It is as though Du Bois the Harvard and Berlin-trained academic eschewed all the canons of scholarship after some fixed point in time. No such permanent label has been attached to Ellwood (the preacher-moralist of sociology) or Ross (the sociologist-prophet of inundation by the "yellow peril") or William Graham Sumner (the sociologist poet-laureate of the status quo).

14   Almost every black sociologist over forty and possessed of "a Southern exposure" is aware of the long estrangement between Charles S. Johnson and E. Franklin Frazier. So deep was the gulf that Frazier expressed considerable surprise when after many years Johnson finally invited him *as a sociologist* to lecture at Fisk. Although some among Frazier's close associates may now deny it, there are others who, I am sure, will agree with my estimate that Frazier felt

strongly that Johnson had blocked his more rapid rise to prominence in the profession, and that Frazier experienced some bitterness in consequence of it.

Nor is it any secret that neither Frazier nor Ira Reid (Johnson's other principal rival for the limelight) regarded Johnson as his intellectual equal. Frazier in private conversation was frequently quite caustic in his remarks concerning Johnson's scholarly as opposed to his editorial attributes. The urbane Reid was generally more charitable, though, when pressed, he too was more likely to emphasize Johnson's genius for organization and capacity for work than his intellect. Oliver Cox, the theoretician among black sociologists, but never a serious threat to Johnson's status, has at times spoken of Johnson with what can only be judged as contempt.

15   This is not intended to absolve the historians at Harvard of racist behavior or bias (Frederick Jackson Turner was openly pro-Southern). What is here suggested is that the Harvard group (especially those close to Hart) were not committed to the proposition that blacks were innately incapable of rising to the level of civilized (white) men.

16   "Crime Among Negroes," in *Out of Bondage* (1914; reprinted, New York: The Arno Press, 1969).

17   Gomillion v. Lightfoot, 364 U.S. 339 (1960).

18   Oliver Cox, Jr., *Caste, Class, and Race: A Study in Social Dynamics* (New York: Doubleday, 1948), pp. 485-86.

6

Stanley H. Smith

SOCIOLOGICAL RESEARCH AND FISK UNIVERSITY: A CASE STUDY

In the early period of American sociology, the work of black sociologists was done in the main at black institutions. In fact, most of the contributions of these sociologists were made while they were employed at three predominantly black universities: Atlanta, Fisk, and Howard. This was particularly the case for such men as W. E. B. Du Bois, Charles S. Johnson, and E. Franklin Frazier. It is therefore important to analyze the social setting of these institutions as part of the history and development of black sociologists. This is a case-study analysis of one such institution, Fisk University, which became a particularly noteworthy center of social research. The expectation of this study is that it will shed light on problems faced by black colleges and the special conditions that existed at this institution.

For several reasons, Fisk University is used as the prototype for this analysis, which is essentially a case study of a social system.

1. The size and location make it appropriate, as it is small and situated in the South.

2. Fisk University has long been a center for noteworthy contributions in the social sciences in general and, more specifically, for sociology.

3. Relevant data for this case study are accessible in the archives of the Fisk University Library.

4. Many of the outstanding black sociologists, at one time or

An editors' note commenting on the unique situation of Fisk University during the period under discussion in this chapter appears on page 189.

another, had some contact with Fisk. This includes Charles S. Johnson, E. Franklin Frazier, W. E. B. Du Bois, Ira De A. Reid. Many other black sociologists with doctorates took part of their training at Fisk either as undergraduates or as master's-degree students. Among these are Samuel Clifford Adams, Samuel W. Banks II, Florence Beatty Brown, Frank T. Cherry, Joseph Henry Douglas, Gilbert Franklin Edwards, William H. Grayson, Jr., Anna Harvin Grant, Robert Burgette Johnson, Lewis Wade Jones, Charles Ulman Smith, Harry Joseph Walker, Albert N. Whiting, Cecil Eric Lincoln, La Frances R. Rose.

These persons received doctorate degrees at such institutions as the University of Chicago, Ohio State University, Harvard University, Columbia University, Washington State University, Cornell University, Boston University, and Yale University.

Historical Background

Under the administration of President Thomas Elsa Jones, president of Fisk University from 1926 to 1946, the institution began to achieve high educational standards and gain a reputation for academic excellence. Special circumstances led to Jones's selection as president. Foremost among these was the widespread dissension which Fisk experienced in 1925. Student unrest was evident in 1921 but reached its peak in 1925 when the students demanded that Fayette A. McKenzie resign as president of the university.

As a result of conditions which led to McKenzie's departure from Fisk University, a peacemaker who possessed some awareness of the problems of black people was desired. Implications of racism, racial prejudice, and paternalism permeated the charges which students had made about the McKenzie administration. A special effort had to be made to locate and employ black scholars and hold them responsible for developing and achieving academic excellence. A respectable academic program, if developed, would conceivably lead Fisk students toward a more favorable position in American society. Thomas Elsa Jones proved to be the person.

Charles S. Johnson gave a fitting tribute to President Jones on his retirement in 1946:

He came himself to the presidency in 1926 as we would like to feel that we did later, out of the personal conviction that the tradition and mission of Fisk were high enough and important to challenge his complete energies and devotion. It can be said with full truth that he has never sought anything for Fisk that was a whit less than highest standards, in academic excellence and rating, in student achievement and personal development, in faculty competence and scholarship.[1]

A certain kind of faith enabled Jones to fulfill this mission, Johnson states:

The Quaker outlook is based upon a deep faith in human nature which condemns no one, which insists upon recognizing the divinity in every individual and the right of that individual to the fullest opportunity for development and to share in the shaping of our common destiny. Dr. Jones has expressed this democratic and religious faith in his insistence upon academic freedom, and in encouraging initiative and self-expression sometimes even beyond the use which has been made of them. He has expressed this faith also in the extent to which the faculty have been taken into his councils and in the large measure of decision which has been given to the policy-making bodies of the institution. In his relations with the student body, his administration marked a dramatic turning point from a system of wardship with complete faculty control to a system of student self-government which has proved itself. His faith in the capacity of the students to govern themselves could not be shaken though it had to withstand floods of conservative and contrary opinion.[2]

Under his leadership, Fisk University became recognized as an outstanding American college. It was accredited by the Southern Association of Colleges and Secondary Schools and listed among colleges and universities approved by the Association of American Universities.

The accomplishments were attained by attracting to the campus many outstanding teachers and scholars and by reevaluating the educational philosophy and objectives and, as a consequence, the curriculum of the college.

President Jones placed emphasis on research and scientific investigation and therefore opened a graduate school which offered degrees in biology, history, music, mathematics, chemistry, religion, English, education, and sociology. Graduate instruction leading to the master's degree was first established at Fisk Unversity in the academic year 1889-90. It was discontinued shortly thereafter and resumed in 1927-28 because of efforts of President Jones and the faculty he had secured. From the resumption of graduate instruction at Fisk to 1945, some 2,139 students were enrolled in the graduate program. These students came from forty states, the District of Columbia, England, Africa, the Virgin Islands, Panama, and Haiti. Sixty percent of these students received undergraduate degrees from colleges other than Fisk. A total of 260 master's degrees were granted between 1928 and 1945, with the heaviest concentration in the areas of education and sociology. From 1932 to 1956, 199 master's degrees were awarded by the Department of Education and 95 by the Department of Sociology. Charles S. Johnson was chairman of the Department of Sociology from 1928 to 1945.

During this period, the research activities of the faculty complemented and strengthened the graduate program. In addition to strong administrative support given to graduate programs, they were also subsidized by such foundations as the General Education Board and the Rosenwald Fund.

Academic Leadership

The philosophy which permeated Fisk University at this time was that research is not peripheral to the academic world but has a definitive role to play in it. Research—the primary means for the discovery of new knowledge—must be the business of an educational institution. This philosophy allowed for the establishment of a meaningful relationship between teaching and research. At Fisk University, then and now, research is neither divorced nor separated from teaching. The two are closely related and complement each other.

The self-study report of 1968 stated the contribution of President Jones succinctly:

The school year 1926 marked a new era in the history of the Fisk curriculum. Drastic changes were made in administration, overall philosophy, aims and objectives. These changes ushered in the modern Fisk, as it is known today. All auxiliary and sub-college programs were eliminated, along with the Department of Home Economics. Work began on the reorganization and strengthening of the curriculum in accordance with national and regional standards. By 1930, the work of the college had achieved academic status of such proportions as to warrant Class A accreditation by the Southern Association of Colleges and Secondary Schools. In later years, the basic pattern of the present curriculum assumed shape with the organization of the four-year liberal arts curriculum in a lower division devoted to general education, and an upper division devoted to specialized major study in the various academic departments. [3]

The research and scholarly activities at Fisk University during the administration of President Jones and part of the administration of President Johnson meant that between the years 1926 and 1950, seventy-one books and pamphlets were published by Fisk faculty members. These included twelve by Charles S. Johnson and twenty by Arna Bontemps. Faculty members wrote four hundred and three articles published in recognized professional journals. One hundred and forty-six professional and scholarly articles were written by Charles S. Johnson and thirty-five by Arna Bontemps. Contributions in creative areas were made by nationally known faculty members such as John Work, who created and produced fifty musical compositions and arrangements, while Aaron Douglas produced forty paintings, drawings and illustrations. It is of some significance that Johnson, Bontemps, and Douglas, and James Weldon Johnson, all members of the Fisk faculty during this period, made significant contributions to the Harlem Renaissance. In addition, two plays and forty-seven poems were composed and nine short stories written and published.

Charles S. Johnson also collaborated with other scholars in the writing of fourteen additional books. He wrote chapters in seventy-three books, edited seventeen publications, wrote the forewords and/or introductions for ten books, and published book reviews of thirty-three books. During this period, sixteen books and pamphlets were written by other members of the Department of Sociology at Fisk, including eight by Preston Valien. Forty-eight articles were also published by these sociologists, including eighteen by Jitsuichi Masuoka and thirteen by Preston Valien.

Other Fisk faculty who made outstanding contributions to the broad field of behavioral sciences include Edwin Embree, Horace M. Bond, Herman H. Long, Willis Weatherford, Lewis W. Jones, Eli S. Marks, Preston Valien and Ira De A. Reid.

These contributions were made by a faculty of relatively small size. For example, the *1928-29 Catalog of Fisk University* listed only forty faculty members. The catalog for 1928-30 showed an increase to fifty. By 1946, the end of the presidency of Jones, there were fifty-seven faculty members at Fisk, and by 1949-50, the number had increased to eighty.

An examination of the roster for the academic year 1928-29 shows, in addition to Charles S. Johnson, the following well-known personnel:

Alrutheus Ambush Taylor, professor of history and one of the few black experts on the Civil War and Reconstruction.

Bertram W. Doyle, author of one of the sociological classics, *The Etiquette of Race Relations in the South* (Chicago: University of Chicago Press, 1937).

Sterling A. Brown, who brought respectability and gave legitimacy to black literature.

Lorenzo D. Turner, an expert in English literature and an internationally known African scholar and author. He gave leadership to the English Department as its chairman from 1929 to 1946. Dr. Turner made many trips to Africa and in the process accumulated an extensive and valuable African collection. An expert on the African heritage before it became popular, he learned at least twelve West African languages and dialects.

Horace Mann Bond, social scientist, scholar, and author. His book on *The Education of the Negro in the American Social Order* (New York: Prentice-Hall, 1934) is still considered a classic in the sociology of education and on learning theory and the socialization process.

E. Franklin Frazier joined the faculty in 1929-30 as a lecturer in sociology.

James Weldon Johnson joined the faculty as an Adam K. Spence professor of creative literature and writing in 1933.

The great musical composer John W. Work joined the faculty as an instructor in music theory and director of the Jubilee Singers.

Mark Hanna Watkins was employed in 1935 in the Department of Social Sciences and was at that time the only black person with a doctorate in anthropology and with interest and expertise in the anthropology of Africa and the Caribbean.

Horace R. Cayton, an author and social scientist who collaborated with St. Clair Drake on the classic study, *Black Metropolis* (New York: Harcourt Brace, 1945).

Robert E. Park came to Fisk in 1936 as visiting professor of sociology.

John Hope Franklin, who wrote the magnum opus on Afro-American history—*From Slavery to Freedom* (New York: Knopf, 1948)—returned to his alma mater as an instructor in 1937.

In 1938, Aaron Douglas, the internationally known painter, joined the faculty as an assistant professor of art education.

Donald Pierson, an authority on race and culture contacts in Brazil, was added to the faculty in 1939 as an assistant professor of sociology.

Kenneth Boulding, the economist, joined the faculty in 1943.

Edward B. Reuter was appointed professor of sociology in 1945.

The presence of such men between the years 1926 and 1946 stimulated a concern at Fisk University for academic excellence and effective research. Under the leadership of Thomas Elsa Jones and Charles S. Johnson, Fisk created a nucleus of scholars who established an intellectual climate which permeated the university and contributed significant scholarly achievements in many areas.

It should be noted that a number of social forces and conditions existed in the decades of the twenties, thirties, and forties which led many to look to the social sciences, especially sociology, as sources for solutions to societal problems. Any assessment of conditions in this period should include an examination of: the Depression and its aftermath; the impact of a rapid rate of industrialization and urbanization in the South; the increased rate of migration of blacks from the rural areas of the South to the North, with all of the attendant social and personal problems; the role of the federal government under the leadership of Franklin Delano Roosevelt; the latter's social philosophy and interest in the scientific method and social planning as mechanisms for exerting some control on the rate and direction of social change. It is significant that Fisk had the leadership and the trained and highly motivated personnel to begin the launching of academically oriented programs that were sensitive to these issues.

In the thirties and forties the Julius Rosenwald Foundation, the American Council on Education, the General Education Board, Sears Roebuck, and the American Missionary Association expressed through major financial outlays their interest in the kinds of programs being launched by Fisk and its department of sociology. These funds contributed to the intellectual and scholarly growth of the academic community at Fisk. A major portion of these funds went to the sociology department for the development of diverse programmatic enterprises.

A typical example of these projects is highlighted in a column published in *The Philadelphia Tribune* of September 1, 1945, by Theodore O. Yoder, Director of Public Relations at Fisk University. Entitled "Better Racial Relations, Goal of Fisk University," the article pointed out the traditional involvement of Fisk through its Department of Social Sciences in examining the spectrum of black-white relations and the pragmatic focus which these programs had.

The work which Fisk has been doing for years to improve relations between colored and white people of America was greatly augmented in 1942 when the American Missionary Association decided to concentrate its efforts in the same area and selected the Fisk Institute of Social Sciences as the hub from which the various activities were to be conducted.

The Department of Social Sciences of Fisk University was chosen by the American Missionary Association because of the department's noteworthy achievements in the areas of human and race relations. The column continues:

Through this cooperative setup, the educational program of the Institute of Social Sciences has been extended into the community with representatives travelling between Nashville and numerous small towns throughout the country.

The well-known Annual Institute of Race Relations was a definite outgrowth of this cooperation. The first of these institutes was held in July of 1944. The duration of the institute was three weeks, during which time community leaders of both races made concerted efforts to study, discuss, and deliberate on race and culture, and to devise methods for dealing with racial situations. The program, supported by the Julius Rosenwald Fund, emphasized in its broad aspects fieldwork as a means for testing the relevance or applicability of certain theoretical concepts. This merger of theory and practice was one of the unique features of sociology at Fisk University.

Another item appearing in the same issue of the *Philadelphia Tribune* underscores the importance which President Jones attached to social science and sociology at Fisk. It is called *An Explanation.*

Until Fisk succeeds in raising enough money for a new dormitory for women and a new classroom and laboratory building for the Department of Social Science, Fisk's enrollment must be limited to 700 students. More than 300 students who applied for admission in September 1945 had to be turned away for lack of living accommodations. We hope this situation will be improved during the coming year.

The importance of financial support from the Julius Rosenwald Fund cannot be lightly stressed. The fund contributed heavily to the growth and development of programs in sociology and the Department of Social Sciences. Chartered in 1917 with an endowment of twenty million dollars, the fund has concentrated on equalization of opportunities for minority and disadvantaged groups with the general objective of improving human relations. As a consequence, it has funded programs in black education, the health of blacks, and fellowships for black and white Southerners. The fund has also been instrumental in the publication of books and pamphlets in the field of race relations. One unique feature of this foundation was the stipulation by its founder that it should phase itself out within a generation by spending all of its principal as well as the income. By July, 1947, the fund had already expended approximately twenty-two million dollars and was set to conclude its activities by June 30, 1948.

It was fortunate for the university that Edwin R. Embree was one of the chief administrators of the Julius Rosenwald Fund. Educated at Yale University in philosophy and cultural anthropology, he was favorably disposed towards the humanities and social sciences. Embree saw the future viability of American society as inextricably woven into race and race relations. Its survival was, therefore, contingent on its ability to solve these problems. Johnson writes of Embree's philosophy:

The central theme of Embree's social philosophy with respect to race and race relations was that the problems were not a minority problem, but demonstrably national problems, to be corrected in the interest of the entire nation, as its best chance of survival as a democracy, or even as a state.

Through the Julius Rosenwald Fund, Embree was instrumental in attracting scholars and in bringing about significant improvements in teaching and research throughout the university.

The high regard which Embree had for black scholars and their important roles in black colleges is further highlighted in the same correspondence.

In general, I think at present one can get a higher type of Negro than of White teacher, for almost any given post in a Negro college. For example, I think the Negro members of your faculty outrank their White colleagues. Charles Johnson, James Weldon Johnson and St. Elmo Brady to name only a few are, I believe, unequaled by any of their paler associates.

The Role of a University Press

A university derives a certain degree of visibility and gains some academic respectability through the quality of its publications. A university press, is, therefore, helpful in giving coverage necessary to enhance not only the academic prestige but also the intellectual growth and development of the university.

Fisk University Press served such a purpose and was in operation during the presidency of Thomas Elsa Jones. Among outstanding sociological books published by Fisk University Press was *The Free Negro Family* (1932), written by E. Franklin Frazier while he was a professor of sociology at Fisk. According to Frazier: "The materials presented in this study form part of a comprehensive study of the Negro family which is being carried on as one of the major projects of the Social Science Department of Fisk University" (Preface).

A continuation of this research led to the publication of *The*

Negro Family in Chicago (Chicago: University of Chicago Press, 1932). In this latter study, analysis of data consistently suggested that certain Negro families experienced relative stability despite rapid social adjustments to which they were exposed. As Frazier stated in the previous work: "Those families with a heritage of traditions and economic competency extending back before the Civil War have constantly played a stabilizing role in the population as the Negro has been compelled to make adjustments to our changing civilization" (Preface).

The translation and publication of *A History of Ancient Mexico* was undertaken as a part of the Fisk University Social Science Series.[6] The focus of this volume was to assess the impact of the expansion of Europe on the indigenous culture of Mexico.

In 1933, Fisk University Press published a pamphlet compiled by Charles S. Johnson entitled *The Economic Status of Negroes.* This study consisted of an analysis and summary of materials presented at a conference held in Washington, D.C. on May 11-31, 1933, under the sponsorship of the Julius Rosenwald Fund.

The last title to be published by Fisk University Press was *People vs. Property: Race Restrictive Covenants in Housing* by Herman H. Long and Charles S. Johnson in 1947. This volume addressed itself to inadequate housing, discrimination against minority groups and their relationship to racial segregation. The study grew out of a three-year program of action research on race restrictive covenants. The book was rushed into publication with the expressed purpose of affecting policy. Race restrictive covenants in housing were being argued before the Supreme Court.

The Social Science Institute of Fisk University published five social science documents, all edited by Johnson, during 1945 and 1946: *The Unwritten History of Slavery* (1945), an autobiographical account of Negro ex-slaves; *God Struck Me Dead* (1945), which dealt with the religious conversion experience and autobiographies of Negro ex-slaves; *Racial Attitudes* (1946), an analysis based on interviews which revealed the attitudes toward Negroes of Southern and Northern white persons of a wide range of educational and occupational levels; *Orientals and Their Cultural Adjustments* (1946), consisting of life histories, interviews, and social adjustment experiences of Japanese and Chinese of different backgrounds and varying lengths of residence in the United States; *The Social World of Negro Youth* (1946), in which data and analyses were based on interviews with Southern Negro youth about personal, social, and racial adjustment experiences.

The institute also published, in 1951, *The Sociology of the South* by Preston Valien and June Borders. This was a bibliography of 223 doctoral dissertations and master's theses written in the South, and primarily about the South, between 1938 and 1948.

The American Council on Education and Sociological Contributions

Johnson's *The Shadow of the Plantation* (Chicago: University of Chicago Press, 1934) was the book which first brought Fisk University, Johnson, and the Department of Social Sciences widespread and favorable publicity. *Growing Up in the Black Belt* may be regarded, however, as an even more important contribution. Its research design included extensive and intensive documentation supplied by in-depth, verbatim interviews. It was one of six studies sponsored by the American Council on Education between 1935 and 1940. Four books were the result of data collected from field research sponsored by the American Youth Commission, which was established by the American Council on Education in 1935.[7]

The fifth volume was a compilation, description and summary of previously available knowledge about Negro youth in the United States.[8] The sixth book consisted of a summary of findings of the four field-studies, with recommendations for action.[9]

The American Council on Education was a federation of national educational associations and agencies such as colleges, technological schools, universities, private secondary schools, state departments of education, and city school-systems.

The American Youth Commission was established to:

1. Consider all the needs of youth and appraise the facilities and resources for serving those needs.
2. Plan experiments and programs which will be most helpful in solving the problems of youth.

3. Popularize and promote desirable plans of action through publications, conferences and demonstrations.[11]

Homer P. Rainey was director of the Negro Youth Study Project, assisted by Robert Sutherland, who became the associate director. Basic assumptions were made that needs of Negro youth were different. There were differences in essential facilities which serve the needs of Negro youth, and priorities and courses of action must, therefore, be different.[11] In other words, the study of Negro youth had two rationales. First, there were problems incident to the minority status of the Negro which might not affect American youth generally, certainly not to the same extent or degree. Second, since Negro youth lived in an abnormal environment, any attempt to apply remedial measures based upon norms for American youth in general would be difficult, if not impossible.[12]

The four studies undertaken addressed themselves to the question, "To what extent does minority status of Negro youth affect their personality development?"[13]

Black behavioral scientists expressed their concern about the execution of studies on Negro youth and indicated to Rainey and Sutherland their strong feelings that they should do the "actual directing of these studies as Regional Directors." Those most active in expressing such concerns were Ira De A. Reid, Allison Davis, E. Franklin Frazier, and Charles S. Johnson, all of whom were eventually involved in an aspect of the study and had some responsibility for the final four books.[14]

On December 18, 1937, Homer P. Rainey wrote Charles S. Johnson that a grant had been secured and that the project was approved by the General Education Board. He sought nine or ten persons "who are thoroughly acquainted with this field to help us direct this work"[15] and requested him to be a member. Other potential members of this committee whose services he sought were: W. W. Alexander, W. Lloyd Warner, Robert S. Lynd, Fred McCuistion, Robert L. Sutherland, Charles H. Thompson, Ira De A. Reid, and Robert Weaver.[16] Among the problems to be investigated were the following:

1. The influence of race mores on the character and personality of Negro youth.

2. Segregation and isolation.

3. Feelings of social inadequacy as reflected in loss of interest in school.

4. Lack of incentive.

5. Frustration.

The volumes of this series were based on elaborate methodological techniques and in varying degrees contributed to the development of the literature on socialization and personality development. However, the personality perspective was and remains a controversial subject. Moreover, the outbreak of World War II, with its massive social changes, diverted attention temporarily away from such scholarly undertakings.

The main thrust of *Children of Bondage* was an in-depth analysis of the life experiences of eight Southern, urban Negro adolescents. Two behavioral scientists, one black and the other white, collaborated in this study.

Negro Youth at the Crossways concentrated on analysis of life experiences and personality development of Negro youth in the middle states, more specifically in Washington, D.C., and Louisville, Kentucky. The object was to see if these differences were significant when compared with the urban or rural Deep South.

Chicago was chosen as the city in *Color and Human Nature,* in an attempt to assess the impact of a Northern city on the personality development of Negro youth. According to Robert L. Sutherland: "This book represents a systematic study in which the effects of color discrimination upon personality are examined for every shade of Negroidness and for every type of social position within Negro society. Negro youth of low and high estate within their own society react in many different ways to the castelike limitations which the White world has placed upon them." Walter Adams, one of the authors and a black psychiatrist, brought his skills as a psychiatrist to the analysis of personality data. The significance attached to color is certainly one of the important findings of this study. According to the authors:

Such traits as skin color, hair texture, and Negroid features have an exaggerated importance in determining social or vocational success, both within the caste and in relation to white people, and consequently are bound to have far-reaching consequences on the formation of personality (p. 292).

While recognizing the importance of socioeconomic factors, sex, education, and regional background, the authors nevertheless state that:

Inasmuch as color is the badge of racial separateness as well as, in very large measure, the basis of high or low position in the Negro society hierarchy, this factor is the most important single element that determines for better or for worse the development of Negro character (pp. 292-93).

Growing Up in the Black Belt

Johnson's *Growing Up in the Black Belt* was also concerned with the personality development of Negro youth. However, its primary emphasis was on the rural areas of the Deep South—the cotton plantation Deep South. Preparation for the research leading to the publication of this work lends evidence to our theme that Fisk University provided an environment that was highly favorable for scholarly endeavor. Sound, published research, involving a team, is usually a consequence of competent leadership and an imaginative staff. Charles S. Johnson assembled an effective team. It included Lewis Wade Jones, an outstanding sociologist with significant experience in survey design; Joseph Douglas, who worked at top levels of the federal government; E. Nelson Palmer, who was highly respected for his skills in research methodology; and Eli S. Marks, who had experience with studies of attitudes towards race, international issues, and imperialism; he was fully cognizant of the problems of race and class-biased tests, especially in their applicability to Negro children from the rural South.

Recognizing the importance of measuring and assessing personality development and racial factors affecting or influencing this, Johnson saw a need to draw upon the psychoanalytic approach. Hortense Powdermaker, a well-known anthropologist with fieldwork experience in the Deep South, who was personally involved in this study, highly recommended Harry Stack Sullivan, a psychoanalyst.[17]

Sullivan was engaged as a consultant for this particular study and was available to assist E. Franklin Frazier in his study. [18] Sullivan spent some time in Greenville, Mississippi, and other places, interviewing Negro youth and collecting information on psychiatric aspects of the study. Both Frazier and Johnson had difficulties in obtaining final reports from Sullivan after his field visits. This probably explains why Sullivan's observations could not be incorporated into the text of *Growing Up in the Black Belt* and had to be placed in Appendix A, under the title of "Memorandum on a Psychiatric Reconnaissance" (pp. 328-33).

Such in-depth analysis of major forces affecting the development of personality among black youth reinforces respect for the overall quality of the project. The methodology, described in Appendix B of the study, underscores the importance of this contribution; the methodological approach was thorough, extensive, and innovative. Five new tests were constructed for the study by Eli S. Marks in collaboration with Lily Brunschwig of the Department of Education at Fisk University. [19]

When one considers the high quality and scholarly character of this project, one is surprised that this work is relatively ignored among sociologists and that it failed to gain the recognition such a work would normally receive.

Two additional books by Charles S. Johnson attest to his scholarship as well as his ability to draw upon other resources available at Fisk. *Backgrounds to Patterns of Negro Segregation* (New York: Harper, 1943) was the result of a larger study of the Negro in the United States. This study led finally to Gunnar Myrdal's classic work, *An American Dilemma* (New York: Harper, 1944). Charles S. Johnson was one of twenty scholars of Negro life in the United States who was asked to prepare a memorandum for that work. It was agreed that, after the main report was published, each contributor was free to use his own material. *Patterns of Negro Segregation* was extracted from extensive data which Charles S. Johnson and his team collected in the field, in part from ongoing research in the Department of Social Sciences.

This study documented the existence of variations in traditions, customs, mores, and folkways connected with interracial practices, behavior, and expectations. It warned against overgeneralization about racial customs and practices in the South. It also pointed to adjustment problems blacks would normally experience in moving from one locality to another, and to their need to quickly "size up" social situations and behave accordingly.

This book further elaborated upon the theme of race and culture contacts. Again, prominent black and white scholars formed an interracial research team. This pattern was becoming institutionalized in the Department of Social Sciences.

Lewis Wade Jones, Harry J. Walker, and Joseph T. Taylor, black scholars who later distinguished themselves in the field of sociology, were among the field staff who had responsibility for the interviewing and reporting. Bingham Dai was helpful in the psychiatric interpretations. Basic responsibility for ordering and classification of field data was in the hands of Preston Valien and G. Franklin Edwards. Both subsequently became chairmen of departments of sociology at two outstanding, predominantly black institutions, where they made even more significant contributions to sociology. The former succeeded Johnson as chairman of the Department of Sociology and Anthropology at Fisk University and the latter was chairman at Howard University.

Others involved included Louis Wirth, Donald Young, Eli S. Marks, and Mark Hanna Watkins. Robert E. Park was a consultant at large and Bonita H. Valien effectively coordinated the logistical and physical dimensions of the whole project.

The *Statistical Atlas of Southern Counties* (Chapel Hill: The University of North Carolina Press, 1941) is another example of broad involvement in a published work which contributed to sociological theory and methodology. It was developed as a result of concerns of the Council on Rural Education to improve rural education, especially in the South. This council was funded in part by the Julius Rosenwald Fund. In the process of exploring rural schools and analyzing their data, social scientists observed that certain patterns emerged among groups of counties. For example, a cotton plantation county in one state would show the same uniformities present in other cotton plantation counties in other states.

In addition to Johnson, this study also involved a number of prominent social scientists, including W. Lloyd Warner and Edwin R.

Embree. They formed a special committee of the council, drew up the research design, interpreted the findings, and began the outline for specific information on Southern counties. In the final analysis, primary responsibility was given to Johnson, who in turn delegated it to Lewis W. Jones, Eli S. Marks, Buford Junker, and Preston Valien. Much of the hard data used came from previous data collected in the department on other research assignments.

The study concerned itself with an analysis of 1,104 counties in thirteen Southern states. The statistical breakdown in each county was by occupational distribution, ratio by race, density of population, types of farms and major crops, school attendance, proportion of mortgaged farms, comparative expenditure for education by race, proportion of illiteracy by race, and so on. On the basis of these categories, the South was divided into certain sociocultural types. Each county was classified in terms of two broad categories: agricultural, with a delineation of the major crops and degree of economic diversification; and industrial and urban, categorized in terms of extent of urbanization and of industrial or commerical activity.

This volume is invaluable for its classified data. The classification is so well constructed that it remains a reservoir of useful knowledge. The work had tremendous implications for sociological theory, particularly for what was to become popularized as social system and structure-function analysis.

The research efforts at Fisk were an important ingredient in the teaching program. Charles S. Johnson's coming to Fisk heralded the formal establishment of the Department of Social Sciences in 1928. This made possible a coordination of anthropology, economics and business administration, sociology, and history in an administrative unit with the expressed purpose of establishing an interdisciplinary focus. The specific aims of the department, according to the *Fisk University Bulletin* of 1928–1929, were to:

effect a productive working relationship between the teaching and research activities in the social science field; to stimulate and support research projects which offer promise of contributing to the store of useful knowledge in the social sciences; to provide a field of training for students in active social practice; to seek out and encourage productive scholarship; to assist, through its inductive handling of social materials, in converting social theories into a basis for social action. The interests and work of the department are thus related directly to the community.

The aim of the department was that its activities should be functional and that sociological knowledge, specifically, should serve as a basis for social action. This emphasis was quickly seen in the course offerings in sociology, where the major focus was in the area of race and culture, both in research and teaching. Courses were offered on the Negro in America, Culture Conflicts, Personality and Culture, and, in methodology, the Social Survey and Methods of Social Research. Additionally, there was a graduate seminar on Race and Culture with emphasis on the expansion of European civilization and its results. In order to underscore these principles, a specific course was offered entitled the Expansion of Europe, which was a survey of racial and cultural consequences of migration of peoples in the modern world.

Closely related, was a course on Race Differences. This was interdisciplinary and addressed itself to psychological, sociological, and anthropological aspects of race differences. Basic emphasis was on critical evaluation of the literature, taking cognizance of what is becoming more and more relevant today—methodological procedures and implicit assumptions.

The same objectives as Race and Culture and Expansion of Europe were sought when, in 1943, a course on geopolitics was offered. This course, as described in the *Fisk University Bulletin, 1942-43*, dealt with an analysis of the interrelationships between:

political events and geographical environment, to the end of providing a more realistic understanding of the forces that are operating upon a rapidly changing world. Topics included are: the arrangement of the continents; history and methods of geopolitics, the theory of geopolitical fields; the problem of frontiers; America's strategy in world politics; rise and fall of colonialism; cycles of assimilation and acculturation; racial and cultural contacts and conflicts in major world regions, especially in the Caribbean and in the Near East; the participation of colored peoples in post-war reconstruction and world order.

Courses were offered on Rural Social Organization and Field

Course and Seminar in Problems of Negro Rural Communities which relied heavily on data collected by the department in its field studies for the *Deep South* volume. This graduate course exposed its students to direct experience in dealing with problems prevalent in black rural communities, such as recreation, community organization, and education.

Community Organization and Community Education were courses also related to these efforts. The university bulletin for 1948 describes the former as:

A study of techniques, procedures, and skills used by functional groups and agencies in meeting social needs within a community. Special emphasis will be given to problems affecting the general welfare and integration of minorities.

The latter was a more direct outgrowth of Charles S. Johnson's work with UNESCO, and concerned itself with:

A sociological investigation of the objectives and methods of community education in terms of changing social needs and cultural contexts in urban and rural areas, with special reference to UNESCO's concept of Fundamental Education. The course will include studies in the media of communication and in group dynamics, and members will be expected to engage in experimental research projects.

The importance of social psychiatric factors in personality development was examined in Personality Problems. This was the natural outcome of emphasis on psychiatric factors related to personality development in the study which led to the publication of *Growing Up in the Black Belt*.

A further development of this emphasis was seen in Social Psychiatry, offered in 1944, and dealing with:

An analysis of the pathology of the mind in relation to culture. Chief emphasis is placed upon (a) structure of the personality; (b) the natural history of its development; (c) psychoses, neuroses, and behavior problems; and (d) the problem of juvenile delinquency in American culture.

Essentially, many courses grew out of department research investigations. This is again illustrated in the undergraduate and graduate course, Principles and Problems of Housing, which developed from a research project on housing in Nashville, in which the department was engaged at the request of the Nashville Housing Authority.

Curriculum on Africa and the Caribbean

As indicated, the department saw Africa and other nonwhite frontiers as laboratories to explore the themes presented in Race and Culture Contacts. From 1928 on, there was a gradual steady increase in the number of courses offered which dealt with those ecological frontiers where the meeting of different races and ethnic groups took place. While the primary emphases were on Africa and the Caribbean, other areas such as Peru and Mexico were also studied. Most of these courses were offered in anthropology; a few were also offered in economics and the interdisciplinary thrust was maintained in the Interdepartmental Curriculum in African Studies, offered in 1944.

One of the earliest courses on Africa was Civilization of Aboriginal Africa. Other courses in anthropology which were offered on Africa included: Elementary Ethnology of Africa, Research Work in African Linguistics, Introduction to African Studies, African Cultures and Institutions, A Study of an African Vernacular, Native Peoples and Culture of Africa, and European Contacts and Culture in Africa. Lorenzo D. Turner and Mark Hanna Watkins, two internationally known experts on Africa with considerable research field-experience in Africa, were members of the faculty at Fisk University and were responsible for developing this work.

The interest in Mexico as a racial and cultural frontier was manifested by the publication of the translation of Sahagun's *Ancient Mexico* by Bandelier. This interest was continued in at least two courses offered in this area, Native Peoples and Cultures of Mexico and Mexican Folk Cultures. The anthropologists made an important contribution toward the understanding of black-white relations in the United States and on other frontiers, as these could be developed within the framework of Race and Culture Contacts.

Three specialized teaching programs expressed Fisk's basic philosophy. These were the Southern Rural Life Curriculum, the Curriculum in Race and Culture and the Interdepartmental Curriculum in African Studies.

The primary purpose of the Southern Rural Life Curriculum was to prepare persons for effective social and educational leadership in the rural South and to provide a medium through which the resources of the university could be appropriately utilized in dealing with persistent problems of Southern rural communities. There were concerns about the quality of education for blacks, improvement of their standard of living, improvement of social institutions such as the church, and with providing improved health and recreational services. Leaders were trained by means of seminars and courses relevant to rural life. Field studies, demonstrations, research, and experimentation formed integral parts of this curriculum. The areas of economics, education, religion, and sociology were directly involved.

Closely related to this curriculum was a program operated in conjunction with the Department of Social Sciences of Fisk University, Tuskegee Institute, and the Farm Security Administration. This program was partially funded by Sears, Roebuck and was established to train agricultural specialists and rural community workers. Courses offered by the Department of Social Sciences at Fisk were structured to give a broad orientation to students to assist them in developing understanding of rural people and the problems of rural communities. This was the liberal arts dimension. Tuskegee Institute concentrated on agriculture as a vocation and offered technical experience. Outreach experience was provided by the Farm Security Administration, which gave students internship opportunities under its supervision.

Basic courses taken in the Department of Social Sciences were a seminar in rural problems and a course on the rural survey, in which training was given in techniques and methods for studying the rural community. Other available courses included Rural Sociology, The Family, Modern Labor Problems, The Cooperative Movement, Personality and Culture, and Business Organization and Management.[20]

Most students involved in this program were able to secure employment either with the Farm Security Administration or with one of the state educational institutions in the South.

In 1944, an interdepartmental Curriculum in African Studies was introduced. The three objectives in the university bulletin are of contemporary significance:

Firstly, it forms part of the University's purpose to widen the student's social and intellectual horizon by introducing him into a world inhabited by people who differ from himself in custom and belief. Africa is in the main historical background of the Fisk student's life and, therefore, should be of peculiar interest to him. Secondly, the aim is to provide experience in the scientific investigation of cultural, psychological and biological data for which Africa offers so rich a field. Thirdly, the vocational aspects of these studies must be emphasized. Opportunities will be increasingly offered for American Negroes to share with Africans in Africa those advantages which they have gained in the United States. Medical men and women, social workers, agriculturists, teachers, missionaries—there is room for all of these in Africa. All such workers need, in addition to professional qualifications, specific training in African Sociology, Economics, Linguistics and Religion if they are to fit into the African environment and render effective service.

Haiti was the special area of emphasis in the Caribbean. In addition to field research in Haiti, some Haitian students came to study social science at Fisk University.

The Curriculum in Race and Culture, established in 1943, resulted from the rising expectations of the nonwhite peoples of the world who had experienced colonial status and who now, because of sociopolitical changes, were striving toward liberation. The specific focus was on blacks in the United States, but repercussions in other parts of the world and their impact on blacks in the United States were examined, with special attention to Africa. The 1943 bulletin description of this special curriculum succinctly stated: "The sweep of new cultural and economic forces, the awakening consciousness of members of the darker races in many parts of the world and the many problems of relief and reconstruction call for careful study, experienced leadership and competent workers."

The establishment and operation of the Fisk University Social Center was an outstanding example of an effort to further implement their basic philosophy of merging theory and practice or of using theory as a basis for certain kinds of social action. The Social Center was a settlement located in a transition area in Nashville inhabited largely be low-income black families. In addition to providing social programs for the community, the center also served as a "social laboratory" for graduate students interested in social problems by providing them with experience with real-life situations.

The social program of the center was significant in its anticipation of contemporary concerns. It included the following:

A People's College. An experiment in adult education which attempts to work out educational procedures, taking into account cultural factors influencing the learning processes. In addition to a regular schedule at the Center, decentralized classes of one or more persons are conducted in various homes in the Center community.

Children's Institute. A kindergarten for the pre-school age children aims to provide careful training in habit formation at the most urgent age.

Health Clinics. For examinations, consultations, guidance and follow-up work.

A Community Library and Reading Room. For stimulating reading habits in children and adults and promoting effective literacy.

Recreation Programs. Which include boys' and girls' clubs, gymnasium and playground activities (*Fisk University Bulletin, 1939,* pp. 91-92).

Much of the value of this project rested on the controlled character of its programs, the careful measurement of trends and results, and the planning of its programs by persons from the fields of sociology, anthropology, psychology, education, public health, and social work.

Conclusion

This case study points to some social-psychological and sociological factors which appear to have been conducive to major contributions in sociology by black sociologists.

The administration of a university must be interested in intellectual pursuits and must be able to attract and keep scholars. Academic freedom must, therefore, permeate the whole structure.

Significant sociological contributions will, seemingly, be made in an environment in which important contributions in other academic areas are also made. Scholars must be in a position to stimulate each other intellectually.

Fisk University during this period was a veritable mecca for scholars, particularly black scholars. (The roster included the following: Charles S. Johnson, James Weldon Johnson, Mark Hanna Watkins, Lorenzo Turner, Sterling Brown, E. Franklin Frazier, John Hope Franklin, Horace Cayton, Horace Mann Bond.) These were supported by a cadre of white scholars who established very close contacts with the university and were directly involved in many of its academic activities. (Among these were Robert E. Park, E. B. Reuter, Edwin Embree, Robert Sutherland, Harry Stack Sullivan, Hortense Powdermaker, Louis Wirth.) They came to Fisk because it had carved out a special academic area of emphasis to which it contributed greatly. This area was related to the black experience throughout the university as a whole. More specifically, in the Department of Sociology at Fisk University, the emphasis was in the area of race and culture contacts. Schools and departments, then, must develop competence in specific areas.

Both teaching and research activities revolved around this main focus. Scholarly activities in the Department of Sociology were, in turn, supplemented by the high-quality work which attracted promising black students from the whole nation and abroad. These students, both graduates and undergraduates, were not only involved in generating new data, but were constantly analyzing and interpreting data in seminars and other classroom experiences. Research projects were generally followed by new courses and/or seminars structured to make knowledge more functional. In the final analysis, however, the contributions of Fisk University in sociology and in the social sciences generally can, to a large extent, be attributed to the highly developed organizing and planning abilities of Thomas Elsa Jones and Charles S. Johnson. They set the stage for the unfolding of this memorable sociological experience.

Editors' Note. From 1920 onwards sociology and social research developed continually in the universities and the colleges of the United States under relatively favorable circumstances. Staffs were assembled, funds were made available, and, in varying degrees, university administrators came to support the efforts of the academic sociologists. That was the case in white institutions. At black colleges and universities, the bulk of which were located in the South, black sociologists had to work under the most difficult circumstances and with very limited and meager resources at best.

The social environment of the surrounding communities, for the most part, was hardly conducive to scholarship. Often black presidents husbanded already limited resources for their own special uses which, not infrequently, did not include support for the sociological research by black faculty. Research facilities, including access to "public" libraries, were either minimal or unavailable. A commitment to scholarly research was difficult to sustain under such conditions. Many black colleges and universities came to institutionalize "teaching" as their primary function; they therefore effectively relegated scholarship to a minor role in academic life.

One important exception was Fisk University. Stanley H. Smith presents a case-study account of the accomplishments of sociologists under the very special conditions that came to prevail at that black university and which resulted in a body of outstanding research accomplishments. The factors that account for this record include: the outstanding administrative leadership of President Thomas Elsa Jones, from 1926 to 1946, and the energetic research and administrative leadership of Charles S. Johnson, who later became president of Fisk University; the support of the Julius Rosenwald Foundation and other such groups; the spirit and intellectual bravery of both student body and the faculty. Nevertheless, this case study should be viewed as an exception to the modal pattern which prevailed in predominantly black institutions. Butler Jones's discussion is a closer approximation of the conditions under which most aspiring black scholars worked during the period covered by Stanley Smith's presentation. The achievements at Fisk University are particularly noteworthy as they demonstrate the immense potential for scholarly contributions when support is available.

Notes

1   Charles S. Johnson Papers, "Tribute to Dr. Thomas Elsa Jones on Behalf of the Faculty of Fisk University." Fisk University Library Archives, Box 175, Folder 21.

2   Ibid.

3   George N. Redd, ed., *A Self-Study Report: Fisk University at the End of a Century* (February 1968), p. 85.

4   Johnson Papers, "The Social Philosophy of Edwin R. Embree," Fisk University Library Archives, Box 173, Folder 31.

5   The Julius Rosenwald Papers, "Letter Written by President Jones on January 2, 1934 to Edwin Embree," Fisk University Library Archives, Box 198, Folder 6.

6   Fray Bernardini de Sahagun, *A History of Ancient Mexico: 1547-1577,* translated by Fanny R. Bandelier from the Spanish version of Carlos Maria de Bustamente (Nashville: Fisk University Press, 1932).

7   See the following: Allison Davis and John Dollard, *Children of Bondage: The Personality Development of Negro Youth in the Urban South* (1940); E. Franklin Frazier, *Negro Youth at the Crossways: Their Personality Development in the Middle States* (1940); Charles S. Johnson, *Growing Up in the Black Belt: Negro Youth in the Rural South* (1941); W. Lloyd Warner, Buford Junker, and Walter A. Adams, *Color and Human Nature: Negro Personality Development in a Northern City* (1941).

9   Ira De A. Reid, *In a Minor Key: Negro Youth in Story and Fact* (1940).

10   Robert L. Sutherland, *Color, Class and Personality* (1940).

11   See the Foreword by Floyd Reeves to the four field-studies of the series.

12   Johnson Papers, "American Youth Commission," Fisk University Library Archives, Box 16, Folder 8.

13   Johnson Papers, "The Proposal of a Special Study on Negro Youth," Fisk University Library Archives, Box 16, Folder 8.

14   Ibid.

15   Ibid.

16   Johnson Papers, "Letter to Charles S. Johnson from Homer P. Rainey," Fisk University Library Archives, Box 16, Folder 15.

17   Ibid., Box 17, Folder 16.

18   Johnson Papers, "Letters to Charles Johnson from Hortense Powdermaker," Fisk University Library Archives, Box 17, Folder 8.

19   Johnson Papers, "Letters to and from Charles S. Johnson and E. Franklin Frazier about the Involvement of H. S. Sullivan," Fisk University Library Archives, Box 16, Folder 12.

20   The tests included personal attitude (one for each sex), color rating, personal values, occupation rating, and race attitude (pp. 338-52).

21   Johnson Papers, Fisk University Library Archives, Box 24, Folder 29.

7

Charles U. Smith and Lewis Killian

BLACK SOCIOLOGISTS AND
SOCIAL PROTEST

"What does it mean to be black and a sociologist?" Since sociology has so long been associated in the minds of both its practitioners and the public with criticism of the existing racial order, it might be concluded that the sociological enterprise is a form of social protest. Early in his career, the first black sociologist, W. E. B. Du Bois, certainly saw scientific social inquiry as an essential and long-absent first step in the elimination of racial discrimination. He declared in 1898, "The sole aim of any society is to settle its problems in accordance with its highest ideals, and the only rational method of accomplishing this is to study these problems in the light of the best scientific research."[1] From this premise, it would follow that to be a sociologist would enhance, and provide an outlet for, the protest motives of a black or a member of any other oppressed minority. To be a sociologist is to be a revolutionary!

Of late, radical criticism of sociology has brought this premise into question. The radical critique suggests that sociologists, through their assumptions, their methods, and their theories, have been oriented to adjustment and reform of the social system, not to protest against its basic values and established structure. In seeking to remedy the dysfunctions and remove the sources of discontent, sociology, it is charged, has served to sustain an oppressive system which, when finally unmasked, has proved to be a welfare-warfare state. From this premise, it would follow that to become a sociologist would not be likely to enhance the protest tendencies of a member of the black minority.

Examination of the historical relationship of black sociologists to social protest may contribute to the resolution of this problem in the sociology of sociology. This inquiry is, then, an exercise in the sociology of knowledge.

To be black in America has meant, and still means, to be a member of an oppressed minority. That some black men and women have been filled with rage and emboldened to engage in dangerous acts of social protest is not surprising. What cries out for explanation is why more blacks have not protested more often. On the other hand, to be a sociologist has meant traditionally to be committed to the rules of logic and the test of empirical verification. Skepticism, detachment, suspension of judgment have been exalted as scientific virtues. How, then, can the sociologist *qua* scientist forsake these cherished attitudes to commit himself wholeheartedly to social protest? Can he be, at the most, any more than an ideologist of protest, willing to allow his research to serve the cause of social action when it may?

Minority and Profession as Perspectives

If the old notion of the compartmentalization of the roles of scientist and citizen were accepted as feasible, then the black sociologist would have faced only a problem of role management. If the black minority and the sociological profession are conceived as separate social worlds providing perspectives which interpenetrate each other in both the theory and the action of the black sociologist, a different sort of question is suggested. The roles themselves have not been static, for the perspectives provided by these reference groups have undergone dramatic revision.

While blacks have long been oppressed in the United States, the analysis of the causes of the oppression has undergone successive transformations. The transitions from the era of accommodation to the decade of the civil rights movement, and then to the season of black power, each brought changes in the constraints on blacks to actively resist injustice, as well as in the very definition of what constitutes social protest. The connotations of the term "militant" are different in 1972 from what they were in 1960, and even earlier, in 1950, when a plaintiff in a test case brought by the NAACP might have been classified as a "black militant."

The decade of the 1890s saw the legalization of segregation by the Supreme Court in the case of *Plessy* v. *Ferguson*. Just four years before this decision, the first department of sociology in the United States was established, in 1892, at the University of Chicago. In view of the significance of social science research for the subsequent reversal of the legal principle of "separate but equal," it is interesting to note that the 1896 decision went unchallenged by the early sociologists. In retrospect, it has been easy to see how much they were men of their times. Many of them accepted popular assumptions of innate racial differences and instinctive racial antipathies. This is not to say that there was a uniform, unquestioned racism in the sociological community. As early as 1897 Charles H. Cooley had challenged the concept of innate inferiority in this article "Genius, Fame and the Comparison of Races."[2] Yet there was not present the sort of united front of condemnation of racist ideas such as greeted the works of Arthur Jensen and William B. Shockley seventy years later. Most of these early sociologists displayed strong humanitarian sentiments, but their goal was to establish an objective, value-free sociology, practiced by scientists who would study, but not attack or defend, the prevailing social system. Over half a century later, sociologists who have assiduously pursued this goal, reassuring themselves that they were detached and uninvolved, found themselves under attack for retaining unacknowledged "establishment" biases. Others who thought they were putting their scientific skills to the service of social reform were forced to ask whether they were really being coopted by a system of entrenched privilege, adept at diverting social protest into rituals of nonrevolutionary adjustment. What it means to be a sociologist is very unclear today, just as what it means to be a black militant is unclear.

W. E. B. Du Bois and the Sociological Community

The question, then, is not merely how the black sociologist has reconciled conflicting roles, but how two separate but related worlds of experience have interacted and changed each other. Analysis of the interpretation of these two social worlds must begin with that early dramatic symbol of protest, W. E. B. Du Bois. Belatedly, he has been recognized as the first black sociologist, yet it can be said that during his lifetime he was, at best, marginal to the profession.[3] This may seem to demean the work of a scholar whose very first major publication, *The Philadelphia Negro* (Philadelphia: The University of Pennsylvania, 1899) compared most favorably to the work being done by the "founding fathers" of American sociology. While Small, Ward, Ross, and Sumner were still attempting to develop global interpretive schemes in the manner of Comte and Spencer, Du Bois was executing what must now be acknowledged as the first survey research project done by an American sociologist. Whatever its deficiencies, *The Philadelphia Negro* approximated what would later become the most widely accepted model of empirical sociological research. Furthermore, Du Bois brought to his first sociological venture impeccable credentials. Not only had he studied under outstanding scholars in psychology, philosophy, economics, and history, but he had been exposed to the ideas of Max Weber. He started his career with the conviction that the amassing of knowledge through social science research was an indispensable first step to social reform.

If being a sociologist is viewed merely as a form of intellectual activity, Du Bois was for his day a sociologist par excellence. Being a professional sociologist may be viewed in another way, however; a profession is fundamentally a community. The historical evidence shows that during the period when Du Bois placed greatest weight on playing the role of the social scientist he was excluded from the sociological community. When he went to Atlanta in 1897, Du Bois would find no chapter of the new sociological fraternity with which to interact. Of course, during this period race would have been an insuperable barrier to such interaction had there been any white sociologists in the region. But the neglect of Du Bois's work in the early volumes of the *American Journal of Sociology* suggests that outside the South he might have encountered intellectual barriers as formidable as the legal and social barriers of Southern-style segregation. True, the values of the nascent sociological community at the turn of the century were humanitarian and philanthropic as much as they were scientific. The assumptions about race and race relations reflected, however, the notions of an innate black inferiority prevalent in popular thought. Such notions, according to Fred H. Matthews, are found in the humanitarian progressivism of this time:

Most of the Progressive politicians and sociologists were born in the 1860's and their maturing years were influenced by the disillusionment resulting from the failure of the Reconstruction Period "experiments." Many sociologists saw the Negro as permanently inferior, unable to adapt to the white cultural norm, advancing as far as he did only through the intermixture of white blood.[4]

Du Bois, intensely conscious of his socially defined blackness, despite his mixed ancestry, could accept no such assumption. Sociologists did not cling to it for long. In 1914 Robert E. Park joined the community of sociologists when he went to Chicago. In the next ten years, he, W. I. Thomas, Herbert Miller, and others of the Chicago School played a major role in transforming the ethos of sociology as it concerned race. But by 1910, Du Bois had left Atlanta, abandoning his dream of making it the center of a comprehensive research enterprise. He had become director of publication and research for the newly formed NAACP. Propaganda and social action, not research, had become the first steps to social reform for him. Du Bois the sociologist had become Du Bois the ideologist of social protest.

Booker T. Washington and Robert E. Park

Is it not ironic that during the very period when the Du Bois-Washington controversy was growing in bitterness, Park was spending those years at Tuskegee of which he later said, "I think I probably learned more about human nature and society, in the South under Booker Washington, than I had learned elsewhere in all my previous studies."[5] Although he laid no claim to being a sociologist, Washington, the great apostle of accommodation, may have exerted far more influence on the sociological tradition and on black sociologists than did Du Bois, the ideologist of protest. The first blacks to be fully incorporated into the sociological community, Charles S. Johnson and E. Franklin Frazier, were students of Park, not of Du Bois. Ernest Burgess said of Park's expressed admiration for the Tuskegean, "He referred particularly, I think, to Washington's consummate ability in the strategy and tactics of social action."[6] Certain of the salient themes of the Chicago School must be examined, therefore, in their implications both for theory of race relations and for social protest.

If we view social protest as direct action or as ideological exhortation, the history of black protest, at least up to the 1950s, is marked by the low profile of black sociologists. As scholars oriented toward applied research and social reform, their activity was more obvious as they described vividly the plight of blacks in the United States in both rural and urban areas. This pattern of subdued protest represented not only the generalized and largely assimilationist approach of the majority of black leaders but also reflected the thinking of the sociological community as epitomized by Park. With the exception of W. E. B. Du Bois, black sociologists were not manifestly involved in frontal attacks on white racism and institutionalized discrimination.

The research of black sociologists as academics, beginning with George E. Haynes's *The Negro at Work in New York City: A Study in Economic Progress* (New York: Columbia University Press, 1912) certainly delineated the plight of blacks as an oppressed minority. About this time, some black sociologists left academia, permanently or temporarily, to put their research skills at the service of interracial organizations. Haynes worked for the National Urban League while teaching at Fisk, then went permanently with the staff of the Federal Council of Churches. Ira De A. Reid worked for the Urban League for ten years; Charles S. Johnson edited that organization's magazine, *Opportunity*, from 1923 to 1929. The style of these organizations was that of social work and social reform rather than of direct protest. Du Bois, thundering out his polemics in the pages of *The Crisis*, the magazine of the NAACP, was the emerging symbol of the separation of the worlds of science and protest. In the fast-growing community of sociologists, including now an increasing number of blacks, this separation was becoming normative.

The Empiricist Tradition

Ralph Turner has asserted, "Probably no other man has so deeply influenced the direction taken by American empirical sociology as Robert E. Park."[7] Another tradition, more theoretically oriented, was developing in the East under the influence of Robert MacIver and Robert S. Lynd, but the Chicago School was preeminent in the study of racial and ethnic relations. This field of study was strongly influenced, then, by the conception of the role of the sociologist symbolized by Park. This view was essentially the same as that espoused by Du Bois at the beginning of his career, but abandoned when he became the "propagandist of the Negro protest" as Rudwick describes him.[8] Harking back to his early experience as a journalist, Park wrote:

My interest in the newspaper had grown out of the discovery that a reporter who has the facts was a more effective reformer than an editorial writer who merely thundered from his pulpit, no matter how eloquently.

According to my earliest conception of a sociologist he was to be a kind of super-reporter, like the men who write for *Fortune*.[9]

Park's sociology, like that of most of his contemporaries, had a reformist thrust, but not of the sort that would encourage his students, even the black ones, to become activists or propagandists. In fact, according to Ernest Burgess, he explicity discouraged their involvement in social protest:

Park told them flatly that the world was full of crusaders. Their role instead was to be that of the calm, detached scientist who investigates race relations with the same objectivity and detachment with which the zoologist dissects the potato bug.[10]

Numerous generations of sociologists were trained in accord with this spirit. Until this conception of the role of the social scientist came under attack, socialization into the community of sociologists was not usually a process which encouraged manifest engagement in social protest. If there were pressures from the social world of the black minority for the black sociologist to become an activist, identification with the social world of sociology produced, for most, countervailing pressures. The persistence of this perspective over succeeding generations of sociologists is revealed in the observation of Charles S. Johnson's younger colleague and biographer, Preston Valien:

> In view of the nature of his training at Chicago, it is not surprising that one of Johnson's major sociological contributions was his demonstration that the emotion-ridden subject of race relations could be studied by sociologists from an objective and scientific point of view.[11]

It should never be forgotten that the "objective and scientific" studies of Johnson, Frazier, and Bertram Doyle, all students of Park, and studies by their students in turn, did produce data which constituted a powerful critique of segregation, discrimination, racism, and the effects of these practices on black people. In many instances the ethnographic descriptions and penetrating analyses seemed to go far beyond Park's admonition of cold objectivity. (This fact may be related to the now popular hypothesis that no white can truly identify with the "black experience" and that no black can truly escape it in his attempt at scientific objectivity.)

In the case of Charles S. Johnson many regard his poignant description of the life of the black cotton tenant in *Shadow of the Plantation* as the best of all his publications and a dramatic indictment of (institutionalized) racism and poverty in the rural South. Though Johnson could be dispassionate in his research, his abiding concern for ameliorative programs caused Valien to note in an earlier publication "his unusual ability to marshal facts for practical application in the solution of concrete problems."[12] Ernest Burgess pointed out Johnson's ability to apply his findings to social problems.[13] The development of his community self-survey techniques attests to his desire for social action. The publication of the *Monthly Summary of Events and Trends in Race Relations* while he was chairman of the Department of Social Sciences at Fisk University documents his concern for improvement in race relations.

Similarly, E. Franklin Frazier's research and writings on the Negro family reflected his social consciousness and deep awareness of the victimization of blacks. His tenure at the Atlanta University

School of Social Work and his subsequent service as director of Applied Social Sciences for UNESCO showed his commitment to social action.[14]

Likewise, Bertram Doyle's *Etiquette of Race Relations in the South* was a strong but low-keyed protest against racial segregation. Johnson's *Growing Up in the Black Belt,* Frazier's *Negro Youth at the Crossways* and Ira De A. Reid's (not a student of Park) *In a Minor Key* were written explicitly to focus attention on problems of the Negro and, it was hoped, to generate positive change. They did not, however, generate the sort of radical attack on white American civilization and its values that is associated with black nationalism, cultural and revolutionary. On the other hand, the title of one of Johnson's major volumes, *Into the Mainstream,* symbolizes the assimilationist theme which for so long dominated the sociological study of race relations.

The Assimilationist Tradition

In this connection, we may speculate again about the influence that Washington may have had on Park and, in turn, on succeeding generations of sociologists. Park's famous, and now much-maligned, theory of the race relations cycle was realistic in its "conception of the social order as a pattern maintained by accommodation."[15] In its time it was a particularly apt characterization of the state of black-white relations in the United States and especially in the South. Turner has pointed out that Park was not what would today be called a "consensus" theorist, observing that to him, "the 'natural' state of society is not one of peace derived from unanimity but a working adjustment to differences."[16] Neither, however, was he a "conflict theorist," nor was he a sociological pessimist. That part of his theory is exceedingly optimistic which portrays slow but inevitable assimilation as the process taking place during the stage of accommodation.

While the theory of the race relations cycle was started in a specific and definitive form only after Park's studies in Hawaii, there is a significant parallel between his theory and Washington's philosophy of social action. It is clear that Washington was not a black separatist. His compromise with segregation is today recognized by all but his most doctrinaire critics as a consequence of his brand of realism. He was a practicing accommodationist. Simultaneously he was an optimist, clinging to the faith that equality and assimilation would eventually be achieved by blacks through self-help and friendliness to whites, without the necessity of abrasive protest and renewal of conflict. Park, the theorist, had turned an earlier sociological view of the black minority around, rejecting the assumption that blacks were an unassimilable mass and inaugurating the comparative approach to ethnic and racial relations. In doing so, he constructed a theory of assimilation which paralleled Washington's program in its major premises of accommodation and assimilation, realism and optimism.

E. Franklin Frazier was the black sociologist among Park's students who attained the highest status in the sociological community, symbolized by his election to the presidency of the American Sociological Association. He, Charles S. Johnson, and Du Bois are the only black sociologists whose biographies are included in the new *International Encyclopedia of the Social Sciences*. Although Du Bois rarely if ever joined in the annual convivium of the profession his name is now coupled with those of Park's two famous students in the Du Bois-Johnson-Frazier Award.

Frazier and Du Bois

If Frazier were, in truth, indirectly influenced by Washington through his training at Chicago, does not the dedication to Du Bois and Park of one of his most important works, *The Negro in the United States* (New York: Macmillan, 1949), constitute a strange juxtaposition of opposites? Not when Du Bois is seen in his roles as sociologist and assimilationist, rather than as propagandist and black nationalist. The Du Bois of whom Frazier writes with approval in the chapter "Social Movements and Race Consciousness," is the Du Bois of the early years of the NAACP. He is the sociologist-lately-turned-ideologist who had challenged Washington's compromise with segregation, not the fiery socialist and Pan-Africanist who had broken with the NAACP over the issue of his black nationalism.

The early Du Bois, it is now recognized, was not as far from Washington ideologically as their antagonism suggested. Lerone Bennet argues that what he condemns as "the Black Establishment" is an intervention of these two radically different men, declaring, "the basic problem in L'affaire Du Bois was not program but style."[17] Bennet attacks the black establishment as an entente between both moderate and militant blacks, on the one hand, and "the better element of whites" and "liberal whites," on the other. Its theme, he contends, is accommodation, not protest. "The Establishment's word, *protest*," he declares, "is a mark for inaction."[18] The NAACP, already deserted by Du Bois, one of its founders, but still highly praised by Frazier in 1949, was seen by Bennet in 1964 as the foremost manifestation of the black establishment. He proposes that it was when Du Bois left this organization that he left the establishment. Before this metamorphosis, however, the first black sociologist had made another transition in his course as the ever more bitter critic of white America. He had removed himself from the community of sociologists, in which, during its formative years, he had received little welcome. The themes of Marxism, black nationalism and anticolonialism which came to dominate his later writings flowered outside the social world of mainstream sociology. It was only after these same themes became popular with later generations within the profession that Du Bois was reclaimed and ceased to be "a forgotten black sociologist."

Not all the scholars who were products of the Chicago School accepted Park's analysis. Oliver C. Cox was one who became a harsh critic. He attacked the theories of both Park and Frazier, and he saw them as part of a single line of development. He wrote, "It was Frazier's lot to be a student at the University of Chicago when three great sociologists, Ellsworth Faris, William F. Ogburn, and Robert E. Park dominated the department. . . . One can discern most clearly the hand of Park on the intellectual life of Frazier."[19] Ironically, this statement was part of an attack on Frazier's *Black Bourgeoisie*. It is in this book that Frazier departs farthest both from the assimilationist model and from Park's admonition not to mix science and moralizing. It reflects the Marxist component in Frazier's background: it has nationalistic overtones in its criticism of the black bourgeoisie for deserting the masses; it is polemic in style to the point of being a caricature of the black middle class. It was one of the first adumbrations of the new radical black sociology which would emerge in the 1960s.

O. C. Cox: Forgotten Sociologist

Oliver C. Cox could, like Du Bois, be described as a "forgotten sociologist." Appearing four years after the publication of Myrdal's *An American Dilemma,* his *Caste, Class and Race* (New York: Doubleday, 1948) was in itself a challenge to, a protest against, the prevailing sociological perspective on race relations. It was, in the end, assimilationist in its thrust, but Cox argued that assimilation could come only as a result of revolutionary action by united black and white proletarians. This explicitly Marxist analysis offered little competition to Myrdal's work, which, for almost two decades, was widely acclaimed as "definitive." Cox received no kudos within the American Sociological Association until 1971, when he was selected for the Du Bois-Johnson-Frazier Award. In *Caste, Class and Race,* he attacked every branch of what he apparently perceived as a sociological establishment in race relations, including many of the prominent black sociologists of the time. Park was attacked for creating a "new orthodoxy" in race relations, and Myrdal was denounced for a mysticism which refused to acknowledge the crucial role of the white ruling class. Cox's third major target was the "Modern Caste School" of W. Lloyd Warner. He denounced as followers of Warner the black sociologists Allison Davis, St. Clair Drake, and Mozell Hill.

Oliver C. Cox's sense of having been excluded from the sociological community, with the accompanying implication that this was because of the "protest" nature of his writings, is most clearly revealed in his ad hominem criticism of Frazier in the introduction to Nathan Hare's *The Black Anglo-Saxons.* He says of Frazier:

His professional career had to be contrived on the tight rope set up by the associational establishment. He won many prizes and honors, but the exigencies of winning involved his soul and his manhood. Sometimes *Black Bourgeoisie* is compared to the *Theory of the Leisure Class* and to *White Collar*. It is, in my opinion, nothing of the sort. Had Frazier assumed the position of Veblen or Mills, he would doubtless have been even more completely consigned to outer darkness to endure in silence the agony of his ways. He hardly confronted even tangentially a real power structure. [20]

Black Protest Before the Civil Rights Movement

Prior to the emergence of the civil rights movement, the work of black sociologists who maintained strong ties with the sociological community did contain a protest motive. It was a protest, however, against the victimization of blacks by personal racism and by segregation, particularly in the South. It did not provide trenchant analyses of institutional racism, nor was it a protest against the American social, political, and economic system. Criticisms of the United States as a capitalist society came chiefly, as we have seen, from two black sociologists who were marginal to the social world of sociology, Cox and Du Bois. The acts of protest of the mainstream black sociologists smacked not at all of black nationalism but sought to push back the barriers to assimilation. Blacks were supported in their objections to segregation by their white colleagues in the American Sociological Society. The all-white council of the society adopted in the early 1930s a policy of not scheduling the annual meetings in the South because of racial segregation in that region. Not until 1965 did the national body meet in a Southern city, and then the site was cosmopolitan Miami Beach.

The Southern Sociological Society had, from its inception in 1936, compromised with regional laws and customs. Black sociologists attended the meetings but their participation was limited to program sessions and the business meetings. Even though Charles S. Johnson was president in 1941, he and black participants could not obtain meals or rooms at the convention hotel. Beginning in 1960, a group of black sociologists in the Southern Society conducted a successful campaign to force the regional association to meet only in facilities (then found only in border states) which would offer unsegregated lodging and dining. No black caucus emerged in either the national or regional associations at this time, however, nor was the structure of the American Sociological Association made a target. These developments were to come only after significant changes in both the black community and the community of sociologists.

Protest During the Civil Rights Movement

Coming between the era of sociological detachment and unquestioned assimilationism and the years of black nationalism was the decade or more of the civil rights movement. During this period black sociologists, as blacks, found themselves part of an aroused community which confronted every individual with the question of whether he should become involved in protest. This protest would consist not in amassing knowledge but in direct action. The goal of assimilation or integration still remained dominant; the justification for scientific detachment and noninvolvement was subjected to grave challenge. The black community called on all of its members to become crusaders.

The period between the death of Booker T. Washington and the ascendancy of Martin Luther King, Jr., has been identified as one in which black leadership was "functional" or "technical." Frazier proposed that there were five types of functional leaders: religious, social welfare, political, labor, and intellectual.[21] The protest motive was manifest in the political maneuverings of Adam Clayton Powell and the March on Washington of A. Philip Randolph, but above all by the legal strategy of the NAACP under the leadership of Walter White, Roy Wilkins, and Thurgood Marshall. Only rarely was protest in the form of direct action used. In some cases, black sociologists, including among others, Frazier and Harry Walker, of Howard University, and Preston and Bonita Valien of Fisk, served the NAACP as consultants or expert witnesses in civil rights cases. The long struggle of the NAACP against segregation reached its zenith in the *Brown* case. The era of functional leadership and protest through litigation was soon overshadowed by the civil rights movement of the 1950s and 1960s.

Charles G. Gomillion: Scholar-Activist

The black sociologist who has enacted the scholar-activist-race man most consistently over the last four decades is Charles G. Gomillion of Tuskegee Institute. From the beginning of his long career at Tuskegee, Gomillion taught the usual sociology courses but inspired his students more significantly through his social and political activities to advance the cause of blacks in the Tuskegee community. Through his individual efforts and work through the Tuskegee Civic Association, which he pioneered, Gomillion fought for the right of blacks to register and vote in a county and at a time when two whites were required to "vouch" for any black who sought to register to vote. If, after this endorsement was obtained, the potential black registrant could "catch" the books open in the Macon County courthouse, he then might be able to get his name on the approved list of voters.

Gomillion's efforts to elevate the political participation of blacks and thereby increase their control over their own destiny reached its pinnacle of success in the case of *Gomillion* v. *Lightfoot* before the United States Supreme Court in 1961.[22] In 1960, the Alabama legislature passed Bill #140 which changed the boundaries of the town of Tuskegee, which formed basically a square, to the shape of twenty-eight-sided polygon. The effect of this gerrymandering was to exclude all but seven blacks from eligibility to vote in the town's elections. Gomillion's successful suit to have this act declared unconstitutional was a high point for him personally and professionally and for Macon County blacks generally. Shortly thereafter, several blacks, including Gomillion, were elected to posts in Tuskegee city government. Though now officially retired from Tuskegee Institute, Gomillion continues his activities as an effective advocate of the cause of blacks. Though perhaps not possessing the traditionally desirable credentials of the sociologist, such as a long publications list, he was nevertheless awarded an honorary doctoral degree from Ohio State University as a recognition of his work. As a sociologist-activist over the past three decades, Gomillion stands alone in the persistence and consistency of his efforts.

Black Sociologists

To ascertain the attitudes and roles of black sociologists with regard to the civil rights movement, the authors undertook a survey of all black sociologists in the United States for whom addresses were available. Combining and cross-matching lists of black sociologists provided by James Conyers, the Caucus of Black Sociologists, and the researchers themselves, a total population of 218 was located to whom mailed questionnaires were sent. By the time it was necessary to analyze the data for the preparation of the paper, a total of 83 usable completed forms had been returned, and this number represents the basic N for the study. While 26 questionnaires were undeliverable because of deaths or incorrect addresses, the 38 percent completed is assumed to be fairly representative of the population.

The analysis that follows is a brief summary of survey findings in regard to three areas of concern about civil rights protests in the 1950s and 1960s: (1) general attitudes toward protest; (2) involvement in protests; (3) feelings about the effectiveness of protests and civil rights leadership. No hypotheses were projected for this study, although the authors tended to feel that there might be meaningful differences in attitudes and involvement for such variables as age, rank, and region.

In general, the findings to be presented here can be succinctly summarized by saying that black sociologists responding to this survey are in strong agreement in their positive evaluation of social protest for the period identified. They also share a high level of involvement in the civil rights protests, both direct and indirect; and display a remarkable consensus that the protests in the last two decades were reasonably effective. The unanimity of their responses indicated that statistical tests of significance were unnecessary and that a descriptive analysis of selected indicators would suffice.

With regard to attitude toward social protest, table 1 shows that over 95 percent of the sample stated that it was either "strongly favorable" or "favorable" to such activities. Tables 2-6 indicate that this consistent positive assessment of civil rights protests generally holds regardless of age, institution of longest employment, rank, region of early childhood socialization, and region of undergraduate education.

Two variations in the pattern of favorable attitudes may be worth noting. First, as shown in table 3, "institutions of longest employment," there is a slight tendency for those whose longest employment has been in public colleges or universities to be less favorable toward social protests than those who have worked longest in private institutions. Second, table 4 indicates that administrators are slightly less favorable toward social protests than faculty members. In both of these instances, such a variation might have been anticipated, but the differences are weak and have very little significance.

Turning to the *involvement* of black sociologists in the civil rights and social protests in the 50s and 60s, respondents were asked about three types—active, indirect, and through publications related to protests. Active involvement was defined on the questionnaire as actual participation in sit-ins, freedom rides, picketing, and demonstrations. Indirect participation included such things as speech writing, assisting with strategies, bail bonds, legal aid, and financing. The findings presented in table 7 show that black sociologists were significantly involved in all three types, with the largest number and percentage in the indirect category and relatively few having published on social protests.

Another indicator of the extent of involvement is the length of time the individuals participated. These results are shown in table 8. Clearly, a majority of these respondents had a lasting commitment to whatever type of involvement they chose. Indeed, 62 percent of those who were actively involved indicated that the duration of their involvement was over a year, as did 65 percent of those who were indirectly involved.

As with attitudes toward social protest, we examined involvement by age, institution of longest employment, rank, region of early childhood socialization, and undergraduate education. These results are shown in tables 9 through 13. No particular pattern of differential involvement emerged relative to any of these variables.

Popular rhetoric from the young today might lead one to hypothesize that there would be a positive linear relation between age and active involvement in social protests by the black sociologists. While the highest percentage of active involvement was in the "under 30" age-group ($N=8$), those black sociologists 60 and over were just as actively involved as those between 30 and 39. Although tables 9 through 13 indicate high involvement of both types (active and indirect), regardless of variables considered, indirect involvement in social protest, with few exceptions, was greater.

The respondents were asked to rate the effectiveness of social protests in the civil rights struggle on a continuum ranging from "highly effective" to "highly ineffective." These findings, including tabulations by the variables previously listed, are presented in tables 14 through 19. Table 14 indicates that, despite assertions by present-day black "militants" that the nonviolent protests of the 50s and 60s were ineffective, a remarkable 98 percent of responding black sociologists thought that such protest were either "effective" or "highly effective."

The remaining tables show virtually no disagreement among the sociologists responding on this issue, although the percentages in the "highly ineffective" column in tables 15–19 seem to indicate otherwise. As the small N's in the categories where "highly ineffective" ratings appear indicate, *only two* respondents are involved. Since these two persons were at such variance with the rest of the sample in their evaluation of the effectiveness of the social protests, we checked some of their characteristics and found that both are young (under 40) and relatively new in their present employment at predominantly white universities. The similarity between them ends here, because one is a female who received her early childhood socialization and undergraduate education in the South, and is now employed in the North. The other is a male who received his early childhood socialization and undergraduate education in the North and is now employed at a private university in the South. The female had no religious preference and was strongly favorable to the social protests of civil rights struggles, indicating active and indirect involvement in them as a leader. Apparently in retrospect, she concluded that they were highly ineffective. The male respondent was a member of the Islamic religion who was indifferent to social protests of the study period and had no involvement with them.

The final indicator of the black sociologists' attitudes toward the social protests in the civil rights struggle of the past two decades to be reported here consists of their responses to a questionnaire item asking them to rank in order of preference twelve prominent civil rights leaders. These results are shown in table 20. Dr. Martin Luther King was the overwhelming favorite, receiving thirty first-choice selections. His nearest competitors, in descending order, were Malcolm X, Roy Wilkins, and Whitney Young. The non-violent, direct-confrontation tactics of King that were regarded as militant and provocative (albeit timorously accepted by many) in the 50s and 60s and are now denigrated by some blacks, remain in high regard by the black sociologists.

The participation of black sociologists in the civil rights movement through direct action constituted a marked departure from the principle of detached, objective noninvolvement advocated by Park. It did not, however, run counter to the assimilationist theme. In fact, the devotion of most sociologists to the promotion of assimilation, beginning with school integration, increased in passion. The reversal of the "separate but equal" doctrine by the Supreme Court suggested that the last phase of the conflict-accommodation cycle of race relations might be under way. As Killian observed in 1968:

> In the mid-fifties it was not enough for the social scientist to affirm his belief that the question of the harmful effects of segregation was not closed in order to escape suspicion of being either senile, bigoted, or mercenary. Even to examine the difficulties of achieving the goals of desegregation and assimilation with any but an optimistic bias was suspect. The proposition that a firm and unequivocal posture on the part of public authorities could overcome resistance to desegregation became almost an article of faith. [23]

It may be added that it seemed unthinkable during the height of the civil rights movement that by 1970 some black social scientists would actually be arguing the merits of black separatism and that Kenneth B. Clark would be angrily denouncing them for "racism-in-reverse." The protest of the civil rights movement involved an alliance of white liberals and blacks. The sociological community had long been in the forefront of white liberalism, at least in its rhetoric. White sociologists joined blacks in direct action; a new generation of sociologists interrupted their graduate studies to take part in COFO in Mississippi. Martin Oppenheimer, a young white sociologist later to become a leader in the Sociology Liberation movement, coauthored *A Manual for Direct Action* in 1965. The civil rights campaign in the South, initiated and sustained by blacks, proved to be a significant training ground for white radicals who subsequently launched the "New Left" movement, including radical sociology.

While the form of protest changed during this momentous decade, the mood of the black community also changed radically. A spirit of aggresiveness and black self-determination grew along with mistrust of white liberal allies. "White racism" was increasingly seen as a basic, pervasive characteristic of American society rather than as an aberration.

The newly developed hostility to the white liberal establishment broke into full view in 1965 when the storm over the Moynihan Report erupted. The disjuncture between the social worlds of blacks and sociologists is well illustrated in the history of this controversy and the minimal role played by black sociologists in it.

Melvin Tumin has proposed that the Moynihan Report marked the end of a hiatus in major race relations research and the beginning of a period during which the federal government would sponsor major, comprehensive studies—*The Negro Family, Racial Isolation,* and *Equality of Education.*[24] Lee Rainwater and William Yancey contend that the Moynihan Report, carefully analyzed, was highly congruent with the nature of social science research in race relations, including that of black sociologists. They declare:

> To sociologists and psychologists with a professional interest in the situation of Negro Americans, the report presented little that was new or startling. Rather, it presented in a dramatic and policy-oriented way a well-established, though not universally supported view of the afflictions of Negro Americans. Indeed, the basic paradigm of Negro life that Moynihan's report reflected had been laid down by the great Negro sociologist, E. Franklin Frazier, over thirty years before.[25]

This reaction was not to prevail for long, for Moynihan's works came to be interpreted as a caricature of, and an attack on, the black family, and many sociologists eventually joined in the criticism. The attack was not started by sociologists, black or white, however. It was launched by black civil rights workers, notably William Ryan, Anna Hedgeman, and Benjamin Payton. Probably the first black sociologist to enter the controversy was Hylan G. Lewis, who after the battle was raging between black leaders and the White House, was brought in as a consultant to the planning staff for the promised conference "To Fulfill These Rights." Lewis was cast in the role of rebutter to Moynihan when he was asked to prepare a position paper with a "non-Moynihan approach" for the planning conference, which had been devised as a compromise solution to what threatened to be a disastrous White House conference.

This planning conference proved to be the occasion when significant black leaders attacked the federal government for insincerity and failure to live up to the promises of civil rights laws and court decisions. The spirit of mistrust of the white liberal establishment and of reliance on black power, not white paternalism, was dominant.

Black Power: The New Protest

Black Protest, whether within the sociological community or in the larger society, is not new; it has a long history. When the theme of "black and white together" was supplanted by "black power" in the mid-sixties, there was an unprecedented shift in the nature of this protest. The backgound for the manifestation of this new spirit within the sociological community involved a brief but significant period of interaction between black sociologists, insurgent white sociologists reflecting the influence of the New Left movement, and the officials of the American Sociological Association. The first confrontation with the alleged "establishment" within the association was precipitated by the self-styled "radical" or "insurgent" sociologists. The black protest did not attain a comparable degree of visibility until two years later. Changes within the community of sociologists combined with changes in the black community to create a milieu in which a black power movement emerged in the American Sociological Association. The community of sociologists was thrown into an era of self-examination by two separate but related questions: "What does it mean to be black and a sociologist?" and "Is it possible to be a radical and a sociologist?"

Radical Sociology and the Black Protest

It was at the San Francisco convention of the American Sociological Association in 1967 that the "radical sociology movement," later dubbed the "Sociology Liberation Movement," began to coalesce. The issue through which the radical sociologists challenged the historic apolitical stance of the professional association was the Vietnam War. "Racism" was mentioned only incidentally, as part of this issue, an issue on which the young new breed and some older sociologists demanded that the association take a moral and political stand. Furthermore, there was no visible presence of a black caucus at these meetings, and the association seemed to remain secure in its belief that deserving black sociologists would receive recognition on the basis of universalistic criteria. A few years later, while protesting what he called the "sociological apartheid" being proposed by the Caucus of Black Sociologists, Pierre van den Berghe offered an apt description of the historical white liberal posture. He wrote:

Radical Black sociologists like O. C. Cox and W. E. B. Du Bois have, of course, been discriminated against, but qua radicals, not qua Blacks. White radical sociologists have not fared any better. Establishment Blacks like Frazier have been lionized, and they still are. [26]

A review of the 1969 ballot of the association reveals that there was no "sociological apartheid" at that time, however. Only two black sociologists appeared on the ballot, and they were nominated for positions on committees. Even though they were not radical blacks, neither was elected. The 1967 ballot had included no black sociologists, but one black had been appointed to the Committee on Nominations.

At the momentous 1968 meetings in Boston, however, there were signs both that black consciousness had been raised and white conscience had been aroused. In the meantime, the radical sociologists had hit their full stride.

The Sociology Liberation movement, with eastern and western branches, had developed a structure and had been alloted space in the convention hotel for their own program. They confronted President Philip Hauser with a threat of disrupting the plenary session in protest against the appearance of Wilbur Cohen, a cabinet officer of the Johnson government. They succeeded in obtaining an agreement for two representatives of the Sociology Liberation movement to comment on Cohen's speech. Neither of the Sociology Liberation movement speakers was black. Whitney Young, Jr., of the National Urban League, who shared the platform with Cohen, was a target for neither black sociologists nor white radicals.

During the meetings, blacks were beginning to caucus, but their incipient movement had no formal structure and no drastic demands. There was a protest by an informal "black caucus" about the under-representation of black presentors in sections devoted to race relations. The all-white Committee on Committees self-consciously sought to anticipate a demand for greater black representation in the association. They asked the ad hoc black caucus to supply a list of black sociologists who might be recommended to the council for committee appointments. Some change did result: seven blacks were appointed to constitutional and standing committees for 1969. One black sociologist showed up on the now-elected Committee on Nominations.

The process of blacks "getting it together" and whites nervously anticipating possible demands continued during the year between the 1968 Boston meeting and the 1969 San Francisco meeting (moved from Chicago on the motion of the Sociology Liberation movement). The report of the president for that year, Ralph H. Turner, reflects these developments. He reported:

Events at the 1968 meeting indicated the concern of so-called radical sociologists and of Black members for a stronger voice at the meetings. Accordingly, we offered program space to representatives of both groups at the 1969 meetings and other forms of cooperation were discussed. Provision was also made for a Women's Caucus. None of these groups is yet certain what form of participation in the ASA their constituencies would prefer.[27]

The ballot of the association for 1970 reflected this new spirit of sensitivity to minority demands for equitable representation. A black was nominated for vice-president, two for council and three for committee memberships. Still, only one secured election, to the Committee on Committees.

By the 1969 meetings the black caucus had finally begun to be reckoned with as a force in the association. It was sufficiently well-organized to compete with the Sociology Liberation movement and the highly efficient women's caucus in introducing resolutions at the business meeting. Participation of young blacks from the San Francisco Bay area, many of them students, gave a militant tone to the emerging black protest. There were program sections on the black experience, organized and presented by blacks. The new spirit of protest and black consciousness was manifest in the symbolic walk-out of a number of black sociologists with the announcement that they would form a separate association.

Yet the overriding point of controversy at the 1969 meetings was still that which had dominated the 1967 meetings—the Vietnam War. The protest activities of even the most aggressive blacks were overshadowed by the disruption of the presidential session by the Sociology Liberation movement. Nevertheless, the meaning of black participation in the community of sociologists had changed. It had become more congruent with the new themes being expressed by the black community. Jan Dizard and David Wellman have described the effects of heightened black consciousness:

The implications of this growing solidarity among Black people are important. The more Blacks act as a group, the less token concessions can satisfy them. Those who benefit from token gains no longer simply view themselves as individual successes. [28]

Applying this to black sociologists and the world of sociology, not even black sociologists who may be "lionized" in the profession are satisfied with their individual successes. In the August 1971 issue of the *American Sociologist,* Joseph S. Himes discussed the changes in the association since 1969. Himes is one of the two black sociologists who has been elected president of the Southern Sociological Society; he has been nominated for vice-president of the national association. Yet he wrote:

Nominating committees have nominated Black members for elective offices. The Black Caucus has continued to press for inclusion and participation. Yet the record of achievement in these two years is discouraging. The table that follows shows the continuing marginal position of Blacks in the structure, power, and process of the Association. These data indicate how desperate the plight of the Black members is and seem to justify the intensity of their efforts for inclusion. [29]

Coincidentally, the bitter letter of Pierre van den Berghe, which appeared in the same issue, revealed how much black sociologists had departed from the "black-and-white together," "we're all liberals and assimilationists" theme which had historically characterized the sociological community. The pluralistic black-power spirit of the black community had finally found its way into this happy family of detached scientists. Van den Berghe protested angrily:

It was, I suppose, predictable that the American Sociological Association would continue to follow every inane twist in the racist convolutions of our sick society, but I feel obliged to protest most strenuously (and, I realize, quixotically) against the obvious piece of racist horse-trading that took place between various ASA committees and the Black Caucus and resulted in the demeaning exercise in racial ticket balancing with which the voting membership was presented at the last elections. [30]

Of James Blackwell's statement calling, like Himes's letter, for intensification of the campaign to increase black participation in the association's affairs, he said:

Essentially it boils down to saying: There is an organized group of Blacks that is going to create trouble and embarrass the association if its demands are not acceded to. [31]

So, by 1971, the evidence of the response it evoked showed that the nature of protest by black sociologists within the profession had changed. In the past, with quick and vigorous support from their white colleagues, they had protested against segregation as a whole or in the convention hotels where they met. Now they had united to make demands on these same white colleagues to give them power within the association, not just protection from bigots outside its boundaries. At the same time, they had begun to explore the theoretical alternative of pluralism and revolutionary nationalism, and had demanded belated recognition for the "forgotten black sociologists," Du Bois and Cox.

It should not be concluded from the foregoing analysis that the new-style black protest would not have emerged within the sociological community in the absence of the Sociology Liberation movement, or that black sociologists had ever been satisfied with the tokenism that white liberalism had endangered. Black revolts were occurring in other professional societies. During the same week that insurgent sociologists seized the microphones at the presidential session in 1969, blacks disrupted a plenary session of the American Psychological Association. A caucus of Negro political scientists presented a series of resolutions at the 1969 convention of the American Political Science Association. There is no reason to doubt that a black revolt would have eventually arisen within sociology even without the interaction with radical sociology that took place. Nevertheless, the radical revolt did precede the black revolt within sociology.

Several reasons for the tardiness of black sociologists in making their discontent more visible may be suggested. One is that certain structural features of the sociological association and of the academic world served to minimize the attendance of black sociologists at the national meetings. While a few well-known black sociologists might be asked by white colleagues to organize sessions or to submit "invited" papers for the programs, the "unknown" black sociologist who submitted a "contributed" paper had to compete with a host of white sociologists for a place in a section. The self-consciously "color-blind" policy of the liberal association meant that his paper might be lost in the shuffle. As black sociologists protested at the Boston meetings, sections devoted to race and ethnic relations often turned out to include no black sociologists, even as discussants. Since participation on the program was often the "ticket" for institutional financing of the trip to the convention, this limited black attendance.

Still, getting on the program was less likely to soften the financial hardship of attendance for the black sociologist than for the white. With so-called desegregated universities outside the South employing black faculty members only rarely, a large proportion of black sociologists found employment in the black universities in the South. Yet because of its opposition to segregation, the American Sociological Association would not meet in the cities most accessible to these black sociologists! Furthermore, the inadequately financed black colleges were the institutions least able to pay the expenses of their faculty members for long trips to professional meetings.

Limited in numbers, those black sociologists who were able to attend the meetings got together privately and informally rather than as a formal power bloc. Not only were they few in number; the whole mood of the national meetings before 1967 was antithetical to the consideration of social issues as matters for action rather than for objective examination. The formation of the Society for the Study of Social Problems in 1951 reflected the dissatisfaction of many sociologists with the traditional value-free stance of the parent society. A number of black sociologists viewed this new organization as a potential forum for social action, but it never freed itself from the influence of the larger body. The Society for the Study of Social Problems has yet to elect a black as its president.

The delayed impact of the civil rights movement in widening the employment opportunities for black sociologists helped to increase black attendance at national meetings. The earliest protests of the emergent black caucus led to conscious efforts to maximize participation by blacks in the program. At the same time, the response of the sociological community to the pressures brought by the Sociology Liberation movement created a climate which was favorable to protest centered on other issues, including institutionalized discrimination within the association. All these developments facilitated the creation of the Caucus of Black Sociologists. Yet the sequence of events, including the priority of the thrust of the radical sociologists, inevitably influenced the nature of the black protest movement within sociology.

Luther P. Gerlach and Virginia H. Hine have proposed that one of the key factors in the dynamics of a social movement is *"real or perceived* opposition from the society at large or from that segment of the established order within which the movement has risen."[32] "Lack of opposition," they suggest, "reduces the risk of participation, obviating the need for deep commitment, thus robbing the movement of its strength."[33] The black protest within the sociological community encountered some opposition but not the degree which Gerlach and Hine characterize as "optimal" opposition, which stops just short of complete repression. Had the black protestors confronted the council of the American Sociological Association before the radical sociologists presented their challenge, the opposition might have been greater and the black caucus quicker to develop its formal structure, rally recruits, and escalate its demands. As it was, the black sociologists encountered an establishment that had already begun to retreat under an attack from another source. Before the 1969 meetings, President Ralph Turner and the council were eagerly seeking to ascertain what demands black sociologists would make even before any had been presented. This could be viewed as a reasonable response to a just cause; it may also be seen as an effort to deradicalize a confrontation which would force the Establishment to mobilize its maximum power resources. This readiness to yield to black demands with a minimum of resistance is fully congruent with the traditional white liberalism of the sociological community. It, with the accompanying threat of cooptation, is the greatest danger that a black-power protest movement within sociology faces.

Radical sociology had roots in the black community because of the civil rights movement. The roots of the black-power revolt within sociology were also in the black community, not within the sociological community. Although attacked by Cox for representing cultural nationalism rather than socialism, and by reviewers for its almost incoherent style, Nathan Hare's *Black Anglo-Saxons,* published in 1965 (New York: Marzani and Munsell), represents one of the first expressions by a black sociologist of the case for black nationalism. It was not this sociological effort by Hare but his leadership of student protest at Howard and at San Francisco State that brought him fame and notoriety. Just as with Du Bois, as Hare's anger and protest have increased, his attachment to the sociological community has diminished. He has not been paired with any other black candidate on a ballot of the American Sociological Association. Nor has another young black who has made headlines with his modern-style protest activities, Harry Edwards, of Olympic games and Cornell University fame. Neither of them is prominent in the structure of the Caucus of Black Sociologists.

Black sociologists have, perforce, always lived in two worlds. Particularly in the early days of sociology, but even until the advent of the civil rights movement, the dictum advanced by the young Du Bois and by Park, that good social science research constituted a form of protest, protected them from the intrinsic tension between these two worlds. As black-power resources have slowly accrued over the years, the pressure for the black sociologist, as a member of the black community, to engage in more direct and less academic forms of protest has grown. While permitting and even commending protest aimed at the symbol of segregation, the sociological reference group has never really encouraged protest by the black sociologist *qua* sociologist. While the black power movement was, after 1965, developing the new themes of black pluralism and the politics of confrontation in the black community, including enclaves of black college students, the sociological community continued on its accustomed course for nearly four more years. It was the Sociology Liberation movement which struck first, challenging the assumptions and disrupting the composure of the profession. A little later, black sociologists brought the new currents from the black world into the community of sociologists, but this was a community already beginning to undertake a searching reevaluation of itself. The style of the sociologist still does not seem to be the style of the black-power advocate, however, and the gulf between the two worlds is at present greater than ever. The Caucus of Black Sociologists may encounter some resistance from white members of the sociological profession who see its activities as "racism-in-reverse." It is likely to feel even stronger pressure from young black sociologists who demand that it become more radical, more aggressive and more "race-conscious" than it now appears.

TABLE 1
Attitude toward Social Protest among Black
Sociologists (percentages) (N = 83)

Strongly Favorable	Favorable	Indifferent	Unfavorable	Strongly Unfavorable	Total
79.3	17.1	2.4	1.2	0.0	100

TABLE 2
Attitude toward Social Protest among Black Sociologists by Age (percentages) (N = 82)

	Attitude Toward Social Protest					
Age	Strongly Favorable	Favorable	Indifferent	Unfavorable	Strongly Unfavorable	Total (N)
Less than 30	87.5	12.5	0.0	0.0	0.0	100.0 (8)
30-39	81.8	9.1	9.1	0.0	0.0	100.0 (22)
40-49	82.6	17.4	0.0	0.0	0.0	100.0 (23)
50-59	70.0	25.0	0.0	5.0	0.0	100.0 (20)
60 and over	77.8	22.2	0.0	0.0	0.0	100.0 (9)

TABLE 3
Attitude toward Social Protest among Black Sociologists by Institution of Longest
Employment (percentages) (N = 83)

	Attitude Toward Social Protest					
Institution of Longest Employment	Strongly Favorable	Favorable	Indifferent	Unfavorable	Strongly Unfavorable	Total (N)
Public college or university	77.6	16.3	4.1	2.0	0.0	100.0 (49)
Private college or university	84.6	15.4	0.0	0.0	0.0	100.0 (26)
Government agency	50.0	50.0	0.0	0.0	0.0	100.0 (4)
Civic agency	100.0	0.0	0.0	0.0	0.0	100.0 (1)
Other	100.0	0.0	0.0	0.0	0.0	100.0 (3)

TABLE 4
Attitude toward Social Protest among Black Sociologists by Rank (percentages) (N = 79)

Rank	Attitude Toward Social Protest					
	Strongly Favorable	Favorable	Indifferent	Unfavorable	Strongly Unfavorable	Total (N)
Administrator	66.7	16.7	8.3	8.3	0.0	100.0 (12)
Professor	78.8	21.2	0.0	0.0	0.0	100.0 (33)
Associate professor	88.9	11.1	0.0	0.0	0.0	100.0 (9)
Assistant professor	78.3	17.4	4.3	0.0	0.0	100.0 (23)
Instructor	100.0	0.0	0.0	0.0	0.0	100.0 (2)

TABLE 5
Attitude toward Social Protest among Black Sociologists by Region of Childhood
Socialization (percentages) (N = 81)

Region of Childhood Socialization	Attitude Toward Social Protest					
	Strongly Favorable	Favorable	Indifferent	Unfavorable	Strongly Unfavorable	Total (N)
North	80.8	7.7	7.7	3.8	0.0	100.0 (26)
South	80.4	19.6	0.0	0.0	0.0	100.0 (51)
West	75.0	25.0	0.0	0.0	0.0	100.0 (4)

TABLE 6
Attitude toward Social Protest among Black Sociologists by Region of
Undergraduate Education (percentages) (N = 82)

Region of Undergraduate Education	Attitude Toward Social Protest					
	Strongly Favorable	Favorable	Indifferent	Unfavorable	Strongly Unfavorable	Total (N)
North	86.2	6.9	6.9	0.0	0.0	100.0 (29)
South	75.0	22.9	0.0	2.1	0.0	100.0 (48)
West	80.0	20.0	0.0	0.0	0.0	100.0 (5)

TABLE 7
Type of Involvement in Social Protest among Black Sociologists (percentages)

| | Type of Involvement | | |
	Active	Indirect	Through Publication*
	74.7	84.8	63.2
(N)	(62)	(67)	(24)

* Includes only those for whom publishing was an applicable activity

TABLE 8
Length of Involvement in Social Protest for Actively Involved and Indirectly Involved Black Sociologists (percentages)

| Type of Involvement | Duration of Involvement | | | | |
	A few weeks	Several months	A year or more	Other	(N)
Active	13.1	21.3	62.3	3.3	(61)
Indirect	12.1	22.7	65.2	0.0	(66)

TABLE 9
Involvement in Social Protest by Age (percentages)

| Age | Type of Involvement | | | |
	Active (N)		Indirect (N)	
Less than 30	100.0	(8)	71.4	(7)
30-39	77.3	(22)	80.0	(20)
40-49	69.6	(23)	90.9	(22)
50-59	65.0	(20)	90.0	(20)
60 and over	77.8	(9)	72.8	(9)

TABLE 10
Involvement in Social Protest by Institution of Longest Employment (percentages)

Institution of Longest Employment	Type of Involvement			
	Active	(N)	Indirect	(N)
Public college or university	71.4	(49)	79.2	(48)
Private college or university	80.8	(26)	100.0	(24)
Government agency	75.0	(4)	66.7	(3)
Civic agency	100.0	(1)	100.0	(1)
Other	66.7	(3)	66.7	(3)

TABLE 11
Involvement in Social Protest by Rank (percentages)

Rank	Type of Involvement			
	Active	(N)	Indirect	(N)
Administrator	66.7	(12)	83.3	(12)
Professor	72.7	(33)	87.9	(33)
Associate Professor	88.7	(9)	71.4	(7)
Assistant Professor	69.6	(23)	85.7	(21)
Instructor	100.0	(2)	50.0	(2)

TABLE 12
Involvement in Social Protest by Region of Childhood Socialization (percentages)

Region of Childhood Socialization	Type of Involvement			
	Active	(N)	Indirect	(N)
North	76.9	(26)	84.6	(26)
South	74.5	(51)	85.4	(48)
West	50.0	(4)	66.7	(3)

TABLE 13
Involvement in Social Protest by Region of Undergraduate Education (percentages)

Region of Under-	Type of Involvement			
graduate Education	Active	(N)	Indirect	(N)
North	79.3	(29)	82.1	(28)
South	68.8	(48)	85.1	(47)
West	100.0	(5)	100.0	(3)

TABLE 14
Rating of Protest Effectiveness among Black Sociologists (percentages) (N=82)

Rating of Protests			
Highly Effective	Effective	Ineffective	Highly Ineffective
35.4	62.2	0.0	2.4

TABLE 15
Rating of Protest Effectiveness by Age (percentages) (N=81)

	Rating of Protests					
Age	Highly Effective	Effective	Ineffective	Highly Ineffective	Total	(N)
Less than 30	37.5	50.0	0.0	12.5	100.0	(8)
30-39	31.8	63.6	0.0	4.5	100.0	(22)
40-49	34.8	65.2	0.0	0.0	100.0	(23)
50-59	40.0	60.0	0.0	0.0	100.0	(20)
60 and over	25.0	75.0	0.0	0.0	100.0	(9)

TABLE 16
Rating of Protest Effectiveness by Rank (percentages) (N = 78)

	Rating of Protests					
Rank	Highly Effective	Effective	Ineffective	Highly Ineffective	Total	(N)
Administrator	41.7	58.3	0.0	0.0	100.0	(12)
Professor	34.4	65.6	0.0	0.0	100.0	(32)
Associate professor	44.4	55.6	0.0	0.0	100.0	(9)
Assistant professor	26.1	65.2	0.0	8.7	100.0	(23)
Instructor	0.0	100.0	0.0	0.0	100.0	(2)

TABLE 17
Rating of Protest Effectiveness by Institution of Longest
Employment (percentages) (N = 82)

	Rating of Protest Effectiveness					
Institution of Longest Employment	Highly Effective	Effective	Ineffective	Highly Ineffective	Total	(N)
Public college or university	35.4	60.4	0.0	4.2	100.0	(48)
Private college or university	38.5	61.5	0.0	0.0	100.0	(26)
Government agency	25.0	75.0	0.0	0.0	100.0	(4)
Civic agency	0.0	100.0	0.0	0.0	100.0	(1)
Other	33.3	66.7	0.0	0.0	100.0	(3)

TABLE 18
Rating of Protest Effectiveness by Region of Childhood
Socialization (percentages) (N=80)

Region of Childhood Socialization	Rating of Protest Effectiveness					
	Highly Effective	Effective	Ineffective	Highly Ineffective	Total	(N)
North	26.9	69.2	0.0	3.8	100.0	(26)
South	40.0	58.0	0.0	2.0	100.0	(50)
West	50.0	50.0	0.0	0.0	100.0	(4)

TABLE 19
Rating of Protest Effectiveness by Region of Undergraduate
Education (percentages) (N=81)

Region of Undergraduate Education	Rating of Protest Effectiveness					
	Highly Effective	Effective	Ineffective	Highly Ineffective	Total	(N)
North	25.0	71.4	0.0	3.6	100.0	(28)
South	43.8	54.2	0.0	2.1	100.0	(48)
West	20.0	80.0	0.0	0.0	100.0	(5)

TABLE 20
Leadership Preference

	1st Choice	2d Choice	3d Choice
Martin Luther King	30	8	8
Whitney Young	8	11	14
Malcolm X	12	12	3
Elijah Muhammed	2	3	1
Roy Wilkins	10	11	8
James Farmer	3	2	6
James Foreman	2	2	3
James Meredith	2	1	
Stokely Carmichael	4	8	5
Rap Brown	3	2	2
Eldridge Cleaver	1	1	5
Huey Newton	2	1	2

Notes

1 John Bracey, August Meier, and Elliott Rudwick, *The Black Sociologists: The First Half-Century* (Belmont, California: Wadsworth, 1971) p. 20.

2 *Annals of the American Academy of Political and Social Sciences* 9 (May 1897): 1-4.

3 See Rudwick, Elliott, "Notes on a Forgotten Black Sociologist: W. E. B. Du Bois and the Sociological Profession," *The American Sociologist* 4 (November 1969): 303-6.

4 Fred H. Matthews, "White Community and 'Yellow Peril'," in Leonard Dennerstein and Frederic C. Jaher, eds., *The Aliens* (New York: Appleton-Century Crofts, 1970), p. 274.

5 Robert E. Park, *Race and Culture*, ed. by Helen Hughes et al. (Glencoe, Illinois: The Free Press, 1950), p. vii.

6 Ernest W. Burgess, "Social Planning and Race Relations," in J. Masuoka and Preston Valien, *Race Relations: Problems and Theory* (Chapel Hill: University of North Carolina Press, 1961), p. 15.

7 Ralph H. Turner, *Robert E. Park on Social Control and Collective Behavior* (Chicago: The University of Chicago Press, 1967), p. ix.

8 Elliott M. Rudwick, *W. E. B. Du Bois: Propagandist of the Negro Protest* (New York: Atheneum, 1969).

9 Park, *Race and Culture*, p. viii.

10 Burgess, in *Race Relations*, p. 17.

11 Preston Valien, "Charles S. Johnson," in *International Encyclopedia of the Social Sciences*, David Sells, ed. (New York: The Macmillan Company and the Free Press, 1968), p. 262.

12 Valien, "Contributions," *Sociology and Social Research* 42, no. 4 (March-April 1958): 43.

13 Ernest Burgess, *Phylon* (1956), p. 321.

14 Bracey, Meier, and Rudwick, *The Black Sociologists*, p. 8.

15 Turner, *Park*, p. xxxii.

16 Ibid.

17 Lerone Bennet, *The Negro Mood* (New York: Ballantine Books, 1964), p. 64.

18 Ibid.

19 Oliver C. Cox, Introduction to Nathan Hare, *The Black Anglo-Saxons* (New York: Marzani and Munsell, 1965), pp. 11-22.

20 Cox, in *The Black Anglo-Saxons*, p. 13.

21 E. Franklin Frazier, *The Negro in the United States*, pp. 547-59.

22 Joseph Tussman, ed., *The Supreme Court on Racial Discrimination* (New York: Oxford University Press, 1963), p. 387.

23 Lewis M. Killian, *The Impossible Revolution?* (New York: Random House, 1968), p. 54.

24 Melvin M. Tumin, "Some Social Consequences of Research on Racial Relations," *The American Sociologist* 3 (May 1968): 118.

25 Lee Rainwater and William L. Yancey, *The Moynihan Report: The Politics of Controversy* (Cambridge: The M.I.T. Press, 1967), p. 7.

26   Pierre van den Berghe, Letter in *The American Sociologist* 6 (August 1971): 257.

27   "Report of the President," *The American Sociologist* 4:345.

28   Jan Dizard and David Wellman, "i love ralph bunche but i can't eat him for lunch," in J. David Colfax and Jack L. Roach, *Radical Sociology* (New York: Basic Books, 1971), p. 265.

29   Joseph S. Himes, Letter in *The American Sociologist* 6 (August 1971): 257.

30   Letter in *The American Sociologist* 6 (August 1971): 257.

31   Ibid.

32   Luther P. Gerlach and Virginia H. Hine, *People, Power, Change* (Indianapolis: The Bobbs-Merrill Company, 1970), p. xvii.

33   Ibid., p. 188.

III. The Contemporary Setting

8

James E. Conyers and Edgar G. Epps

A PROFILE OF BLACK

SOCIOLOGISTS

The sociology of professions and occupations has been one of the focal points of scientific activity for a considerable period of time. It has been only in recent times, however, that the study of various professions has used race as a primary differentiating factor.[1] While a few researchers have reported on the status of blacks in academic and other professions, this remains a relatively unexplored area of investigation.[2]

The paper being presented here is based largely on studies conducted by Conyers and by Epps and Howze.[3] Conyers's study deals almost exclusively with black doctorates in sociology. The survey conducted by Epps and Howze, on the other hand, is a study of black social scientists in America which includes persons with master's degrees as well as doctorates. This study also included a comparison sample of white social scientists.

Impetus for both of these studies can be attributed to a lack of empirical data on black sociologists at a time when white academic institutions, black institutions, and governmental and private agencies began to make a concerted effort to locate and hire "competent" black scholars. It was immediately apparent that the American educational system had failed to recruit and provide graduate training for black Americans. Bryant, in a study funded by the Ford Foundation, reports that "less than one percent of America's earned doctoral degrees are held by Negroes."[4] Similarly, Fred Crossland, in another Ford Foundation report, stated that, while 11.5 percent of the total population in the United States is black, only 0.78 percent of all Ph.D. degrees granted between 1964 and

1968 were awarded to blacks and that only 1.72 percent of graduate students in 1968 were black.[5] These percentages were obtained from 63 reporting universities which provided data about recent black Ph.D. recipients. A total of 105 universities were contacted.

The degree to which blacks are underrepresented in higher education has been recently reported in another work by Crossland in which he determines the relationship between estimated enrollment and estimated population, expressed in percentages, and states that, in order for blacks to achieve proportional representation in higher education, their 1970 enrollment would have had to be increased by 116 percent. The following minority groups would have to be increased even more: Mexican Americans, 330 percent; Puerto Ricans, 225 percent; and American Indians, 650 percent.[6]

Among the social sciences, sociology ranks second to psychology in the number of doctorates awarded to blacks in America. In 1967 Conyers identified 121 doctorates in sociology at the same time that Wispe et al. identified 166 black doctorates in psychology.[7] Since it is unlikely that Ph.D.-granting institutions have produced more than five or six black Ph.D.'s per year since 1967 in these fields, we estimate that there are probably more than 200 black Ph.D.'s in psychology and about 160 in sociology at this writing (1972). Similar patterns exist for other social science areas. The committee on the Status of Blacks in the Profession of the American Political Science Association indicated that "there are probably no more than 80 black political science Ph.D.'s in the United States today."[8] Donald Deskins, Project Director for the Commission on Geography and Afro-America of the Association of American Geographers, has been able to identify only eight black geographers with the doctoral degree.[9] Comparable estimates are not available for other areas of the social sciences, but there is no reason to believe that the pattern would be appreciably different for anthropology, economics, or history. We concur, therefore, with Horace Mann Bond's contention that although blacks constitute about 10 percent (now 11.5 percent) of the population, they constitute perhaps only about 1 percent of scholars in America. Deficiencies in intellect in blacks, as Bond contends, are not responsible for the scarcity of black scholars, but imperfections of a system which wastes a great human asset.[10] The "talented tenth" of which Du Bois has spoken has been, and is, far from realization.

The purpose of this paper is to present some information which will help to provide a general social profile of black sociologists. We have done this by focusing attention upon: (1) demographic and familial characteristics; (2) educational characteristics; (3) employment and career patterns; (4) educationally related considerations; and (5) some political, social, and reputational considerations. We will conclude our paper with a note on the sociocultural, ideological, and manpower implications of our research on black sociologists.

Demographic and Familial Characteristics

In this section we are interested in presenting data on such background characteristics as age, sex, region of birth, education, and employment of parents of black sociologists, and marital status, number of children, number of brothers and sisters, and birth order of black doctorates in sociology.

Age and Sex   In the Epps and Howze study, which included black Ph.D. degree-holders as well as black sociologists without the Ph.D., small differences were found between black sociologists and a comparison sample of white sociologists. The median age was 38 for the black sample and 35 for the comparison sample. Conyers's study, on the other hand, which was based on a 70 percent return of black Ph.D.'s, found a median age of 45. Similarly, while the Epps and Howze study showed very little difference in sex ratio between black sociologists and white sociologists (nearly 80 percent of both groups are males), Conyers's data showed that about 88 percent of black Ph.D.'s are males. The sex composition of black doctorates in sociology, therefore, is similar to the sex composition of all doctorates in sociology.[11] Age differences favor females, however. The data did not show any black female Ph.D.'s over 56 years of age.

Region of Birth   Most black sociologists, Ph.D. or not, were born in the South—nearly two-thirds. For the white comparison group in the Epps and Howze study, all but 15 percent were born in areas other than the South.

An examination of the size of place of birth for black doctorates in sociology showed that about 46 percent were born in urban localities with a population of more than 100,000 inhabitants. Only 12 percent were born in rural areas. Approximately one-fourth of black doctorates in sociology were born in cities of 2,500 to 25,000 inhabitants. When black doctorates in sociology were asked, "Before reaching 18 years of age, where was most of your life spent?" responses indicated most of them had spent most of these years in the same region and locality as had been indicated for place of birth. There was a tendency, however, for some black doctorates born in the South to have spent most of the first eighteen years of their lives in regions other than the South. This was true for about 15 percent of those who stated they were born in the South.

Education of Parents Data by Edwards,[12] Bond,[13] Conyers, and Epps and Howze, tend to suggest a tradition of literacy and a semblance of occupational stability for family of orientation of black professionals. While this suggests that, compared to all blacks, these social scientists come from privileged backgrounds, when black sociologists were compared with a white comparison group, the educational status of the parents of black sociologists was lower than that for the white group. About two-fifths of black parents of both sexes were high school graduates or had obtained some college education. The comparable proportion for whites was about two-thirds. Conyers's data on black doctorates in sociology showed mothers to have slightly higher educational attainment than fathers of black doctorates in sociology; 50 percent of the mothers to 40 percent of the fathers were high school graduates or above.

Occupationally, the fathers of black doctorates in sociology more frequently worked at professional jobs than at any other type of occupation—28 percent. This category was followed by laborers, 18 percent, and service workers, 16 percent. Mothers of black doctorates in sociology were more frequently reported as housewives —44 percent—than was the case for any other occupational category. This category was followed by household and services workers, 26 percent, and professional workers, 25 percent.

Marital Status   In regard to the marital status of black doctorates in sociology, about 80 percent are married and about 15 percent are single. When asked if they had ever been divorced, one-fourth said yes. The fact that one-fourth of the respondents have been divorced but only three or four have not yet remarried might suggest, as it is commonly claimed, that divorce is not a negation of the institution of marriage and that social pressures often exert influence to remarry.

When asked the number of children ever present in their families, the respondents reported an average of about 2. This is somewhat lower than the average reported for family of orientation of black doctorates in sociology and compares favorably with the national average.

Although no data were gathered on the professional status of the brothers and/or sisters of black doctorates in sociology, observation and studies would tend to suggest the possibility that Negro professionals "run" in families. [14] Data were gathered, however, on the number of brothers and sisters and the birth order for black doctorates. The average number of brothers and sisters per doctorate was 2.5, and 38 percent were firstborn or were the only child. [15]

Educational Characteristics

In this section we are interested in tracing the education of black sociologists from the elementary level of schooling to the attainment of the Ph.D., where applicable.

Elementary School   Data on black doctorates in sociology reveal that nearly 90 percent attended a public elementary school. Eighty-three percent attended elementary schools which were three-fourths to all black, with about three-fourths attending schools which had black students only. About 12 percent of black doctorates in sociology attended elementary schools which were predominantly white.

High School Level   Nearly three-fourths of black doctorates in sociology attended private high schools. This trend was reasonably pronounced for blacks until fairly recent times. Not only were there private boarding high schools, which blacks attended; but many of the predominantly black private colleges had high schools as part of their total curricula offering. We do not have comparable data for whites, therefore we cannot determine the extent to which this an atypical pattern. The high schools attended were more likely to be integrated than the elementary schools attended by black doctorates in sociology; nearly 19 percent attended high schools which were approximately all white, with an additional 5 percent attending high schools which were about three-fourths white. White sociologists, in contrast, were much more likely to live in regions outside the South and to have attended high school and college outside the South. About 95 percent of white sociologists attended all-white high schools.

College Level   Both the data of Conyers on black Ph.D.'s and the Epps and Howze data on black sociologists, Ph.D. and non-Ph.D., show that most black sociologists attended colleges located in the South, nearly 60 percent in both instances. Similarly, both sets of data show that slightly over 50 percent of black sociologists attended traditionally black institutions.

Private black institutions have produced more Ph.D's in sociology than any other type of undergraduate institution. About 39 percent of black Ph.D.'s attended private black institutions compared to 26 percent from predominantly black state institutions. Morehouse College alone has produced over a dozen. Predominantly white state institutions ranked third, with about 23 percent, and predominantly white private colleges ranked fourth, with about 10 percent of black undergraduates who subsequently obtained a Ph.D. in sociology. However, social science graduate students currently enrolled in degree programs tend to be graduates of predominantly white institutions (60 percent). While these data apply to all social sciences, there is no reason to believe that the pattern is different for sociology graduate students. This suggests a trend which reflects the shift of the black population nationwide and the removal of restrictions on admissions to white colleges and universities.

The major field of concentration for black doctorates in sociology has been sociology, with at least 60 percent having sociology as their major. Interesting in its own right is the fact that the mathematical, biological, and physical sciences were the next highest fields for majors in undergraduate colleges who subsequently obtained the Ph.D. in sociology. Equally interesting is the fact that these same fields of study were most frequently cited for minor fields of concentration at the undergraduate level for black doctorates in sociology; nearly 39 percent had minors in mathematics, biology, or physical sciences. These areas of minor concentration for black doctorates were followed by history, with about 13 percent.

The survey by Epps and Howze, which included nondoctorates, found that for both black sociologists and the comparison white sociologists, about 45 percent had sociology as an undergraduate major. The discrepancy between the two studies may reflect an earlier commitment to the field by black doctorates than for the other groups.

Master's Level Data from the two studies show striking similarities in their findings on the master's level. Both sets of data show that about 30 percent of the black sociologists in America received their master's degrees from institutions located in the South, followed by about a third from the North Central region, particularly the East North Central division. Very few master's degrees for blacks in sociology have come from institutions in the New England states or the mountain West, although the Epps and Howze data show about 10 percent of master's degrees in sociology coming from institutions in the West.

Black private institutions did not produce the largest number of master's degree holders who subsequently obtained the Ph.D. Such institutions produced about 26 percent, largely due to the very strong showing of Atlanta University, which has awarded over 200 master's degrees; over 20 of these recipients have subsequently obtained their Ph.D's in sociology. Fisk University has produced at least 16 persons who have later earned Ph.D. degrees. The leading type of school for blacks who obtained their master's, and subsequently the Ph.D., has been predominantly white state universities, which have produced about 47 percent. At both the undergraduate and master's levels, white sociologists were more likely than blacks to have attended major Ph.D.-granting institutions.

The major field of concentration for black sociologists at the master's level has been sociology, about 60 percent.

The Ph.D. Level   As far as we have been able to discover, a record of some kind has been gathered on practically all known black Americans who have ever earned the doctorate in sociology. We are now able to identify 160 such persons. It appears that the first doctorate in sociology earned by a black was conferred on the late Bishop R. R. Wright in 1911 by the University of Pennsylvania, and not on George Haynes from Columbia University in 1912. Contrary to popular belief, W. E. B. Du Bois did not earn a Ph.D. in sociology. Despite the contributions to sociology which Dr. Du Bois made during his illustrious career, his doctorate was in history and was awarded to him by Harvard in 1895. Incidentally, the powerful and productive Charles S. Johnson did not hold a Ph.D. in sociology, but a Ph.B. (Bachelor of Philosophy) from Chicago in 1918 and several honorary degrees—Virginia Union, Columbia, Harvard, Glasgow, Lincoln, and Central State.

Ph.D.-granting institutions in America have been unequal in their production of black Ph.D.'s in sociology. Less than one-half of the Ph.D.-granting institutions in sociology in America have awarded a doctorate to a black person. The University of Chicago, Ohio State University, Washington State University, Columbia University, and Indiana University have produced about 60 percent of the Ph.D.'s awarded a black person in sociology. The average number of Ph.D.'s ever awarded black persons by institutions awarding at least one doctorate in sociology to a black person is about four.

The University of Chicago leads all other institutions in the number of doctorates in sociology awarded to blacks. About 22 of the black Ph.D.'s now living have received their degrees from Chicago. With the exception of Ohio State University, which ranks second, with 16 living black doctorates in sociology, the University of Chicago has produced more than twice as many black doctorates in sociology as any other institution. When black doctorates, however, were taken as a percentage of *all* doctorates in sociology produced by a given university from 1955 to 1964, Washington State University led the pack with 28 percent. If the picture we are painting for the three highest producers of black doctorates in sociology is beginning to look too pretty, we would like to state that Chicago, Ohio State, and Washington State have produced only 5 or 6 black Ph.D.'s in sociology since 1965, and half of these came from the University of Chicago. We have no direct data on rates of Ph.D. production since 1967, however, and some institutional positions may have changed in recent years.

The overwhelming majority of black Ph.D.'s in sociology have received their degrees from prestigious and major Ph.D.-granting institutions in America, yet very few of these institutions have employed a black person within their departments of sociology on a regular basis. We say this at a time when over 70 percent of the black Ph.D.'s in sociology are employed in predominantly white settings, particularly white universities of one type or another.

The fact that most of the black Ph.D.'s in sociology were granted their doctorates from prestigious and major Ph.D.-granting universities in American correlates highly with region of the country in which the degree was obtained. Less than 8 percent of black doctorates received their doctorates from universities located in the South, and, with the exception of Tennessee, these universities (Maryland, Kentucky, and American and Catholic Universities of Washington, D.C.) are not truly in the Deep South.

Frank Clemente of the University of Kentucky has addressed himself to the question of racial differences in progress toward the doctorate in sociology by selecting a sample of 70 black holders of the Ph.D. and comparing them with a matched sample of 70 nonblack Ph.D.'s. He found that black sociologists receive the Ph.D. about 2.7 years later in life than nonblacks; the mean age at Ph.D. being 34.7 for blacks and 32 for nonblacks. Further, his data show that the years between the bachelor's degree and the Ph.D. are longer for blacks than nonblacks, a mean of 11.5 years for blacks and 8.8 for nonblacks. [16] These data ought to be viewed partly against a finding by Conyers which showed that about three-fourths of black graduate students who obtained the doctorate in sociology have taught for over four years before receiving their doctorates, as well as against many of the factors known to affect blacks and the attainment of higher educational objectives, such as: lower income levels; financial assistance in graduate schools; family considerations; language barriers; and obtaining various educational degrees at different rather than the same academic insitution.

As a group, black sociologists in the Epps and Howze sample are less likely than white sociologists in their survey to have obtained the Ph.D. degree (41 percent vs. 56 percent). One reason for this discrepancy has been the difficulty blacks have encountered in finding financial support for graduate study. The survey found that only 30 percent of black sociologists reported having received teaching assistantships (compared to 49 percent of whites). The same pattern was found for research assistantships, but the differential was not as great.

Career Patterns of Black Sociologists   Since 1945, several significant shifts in employment patterns of black sociologists have taken place. Before 1955, more than 60 percent of black sociologists were employed in the South. This proportion had dropped to 51 percent by 1960, and reached a low of 41 percent in 1968. In 1970, at the time of the survey of black social scientists, about 47 percent of black social scientists were employed in the South. This slight reversal may be attributed to a broadening of opportunities for blacks at traditionally white institutions in the South. It may also reflect the current emphasis on black consciousness and the appeal for blacks to return to their own institutions.

For most of the years covered by our research, whites were more likely to be employed by prestigious institutions, and they were likely to earn more money and have better working conditions than blacks with comparable training and experience. By 1970, however, the differences for holders of Ph.D. degrees were minimal. Blacks were equally likely to be employed by prestigious institutions, and they reported higher earnings. When we compared persons who had not earned the Ph.D., however, we found that blacks were much less likely than whtes with equivalent training to be employed by prestigious institutions; however, blacks were favored by earning differences. The favored income position of blacks is attributable to the relative scarcity of black sociologists at a time when their services are in great demand. If the supply increases sufficiently to meet demands, earnings will then reflect the changed market.

When black and white sociologists were compared on the basis of academic rank and tenure, the results indicated that about equal proportions of the two groups held the rank of full professor. However, when we compared sociologists at white institutions, blacks were underrepresented in the professorial rank. Blacks at black institutions were much more likely to be full professors. Therefore, it appears that while white institutions are hiring black sociologists, they are hiring them in the lower ranks. This suggests that there may be a problem when these junior professors become eligible for promotion to tenure.

As a group, black sociologists are more likely than whites to be tenured faculty members. Much of this difference is explained by the fact that a large proportion of blacks work at traditionally black schools where tenure policies are based almost exclusively on degrees earned and amount of teaching experience. Blacks working at traditionally white institutions do not differ substantially from their white colleagues in the attainment of tenure.

When we look at area of academic specialization, we find that black sociologists are underrepresented in methodology, social organization, and demography and population. They tend to be overrepresented in race relations, theory, and social problems. The pattern suggests that blacks concentrate in problem-oriented specialities rather than in areas that have little direct application to social problems. Blacks at white schools are especially concentrated in race relations and related areas. We believe this concentration reflects an interaction of personal interests and student demands.

One of the greatest problems faced by black sociologists is the fact that they tend to work at small institutions with limited resources. This is reflected in their teaching loads. More than half of the black sociologists working at black schools reported teaching loads of 12 hours or more per semester. Only about one-third of sociologists at traditionally white institutions carry such heavy loads. Associated with the heavy teaching load is the fact that black sociologists at black schools tend to devote most of their time to teaching and relatively little to research. Sociologists at traditionally white institutions are much more likely to have research commitments than are those at black colleges. When asked to list the most important problems they anticipated in future career development, the problem mentioned most frequently by both black and white respondents was "lack of opportunity for research." This problem is obviously most serious for blacks at black colleges. The need for additional education was also listed as an important problem by 17 percent of the black sociologists.

Survey data indicate that black sociologists participate in the activities of professional associations at about the same rate as their white colleagues, if we use attendance and presenting papers as criteria. Obviously, however, they play a lesser role in the governance of the national and regional associations. About the same proportions in both groups have held office in some professional organization when we include the black caucus and other special-interest group organizations.

Other Educationally Related Considerations

The achievement of the Ph.D. degree usually cannot be managed without financial aid, varied sources of personal and social influence, and an atmosphere conducive to achievement. Most achievements generally show a pronounced parental influence. [17] Too often, however, adequate differentiation of parental influence, or the relative importance of it to other variables, has not been made. Conyers found it was not parents who were the most important source of financial support or source of influence for black doctorates in sociology. Teaching and research assistantships and fellowships were the most important source of financial support and personal ambition; school teachers and mother were the most frequently cited sources of influence encouraging black doctorates in sociology to pursue higher degrees. It is realized that we are, in part, talking about a sequence of sources and influences as well as their interactional effects—unmeasured to a large extent by this study.

Problematic areas, such as perceived degree of discrimination within a department, the university, and the milieu of the locality in which the university is located can affect successful progress toward higher academic degrees by blacks. For example, black Ph.D.'s in sociology reported in the Conyers study that *some* to *a great amount* of discrimination was perceived by them in the following areas while they were pursuing their Ph.D. degree: (1) rooms or housing in town, 50 percent; (2) townspeople, 44 percent; (3) stores, recreation, shops, and the like, in town, 33 percent; (4) recommendation for jobs upon graduation, 27 percent; (5) assignment to college housing, 22 percent; (6) scholarships, fellowships, and financial aid, 16 percent; (7) inclusion by other students in informal activities, 14 percent; (8) college adminstration, 11 percent; (9) participation in graduate student affairs, 10 percent; (10) teachers in the sociology department, 9 percent; (11) grades in class, 9 percent; (12) students at the university, 8 percent. While it might be contended that areas cited above were more important a few years ago than now, it seems reasonable to assert that they probably had and do have more impact on blacks who "give up" than for those who survive.

A final note in this section is in order. In recent years a number of studies have been conducted on teacher morale and work satisfaction in black settings, particularly on the college level.[18] Thompson states:

All studies usually having to do with Negro colleges usually agree on at least one point; there is widespread feeling of dissatisfaction among the teachers which leads to "low morale."[19]

In an attempt to find out how black Ph.D.'s in sociology rate their work in predominantly black academic settings as compared with black Ph.D.'s in predominantly white institutions, Conyers asked both groups to rate their present employment in regard to 21 items. From a comparison of returns of 42 black Ph.D.'s at predominantly white institutions with 33 black Ph.D.'s in predominantly black institutions, it was found that blacks at predominantly white institutions rated from among 21 items 17 of them as *good* and *very good* to a higher extent than black Ph.D.'s at black institutions. The items rated higher by black sociologists at predominantly white institutions were:

1. *Quality of students:* 73 percent vs. 31 percent, a percentage difference of 42.
2. *Teaching load:* 87 percent vs. 53 percent, a percentage difference of 34.
3. *Cultural and educational environment for my children:* 76 percent vs. 43 percent, a percentage difference of 33.
4. *Research funds and opportunities:* 65 percent vs. 34 percent, a percentage difference of 31.
5. *Academic climate:* 84 percent vs. 55 percent, a percentage difference of 29.
6. *Salary:* 79 percent vs. 50 percent, a percentage difference of 29.
7. *Opportunity for specialization:* 74 percent vs. 50 percent, a percentage difference of 24.
8. *Secretarial assistance:* 59 percent vs. 35 percent, a percentage difference of 24.
9. *Fringe benefits:* 86 percent vs. 63 percent, a percentage difference of 23.
10. *Funds for departmental lectures:* 60 percent vs. 40 percent, a centage difference of 20.
11. *Office space:* 68 percent vs. 50 percent, a percentage difference of 18.
12. *Quality of the administration:* 73 percent vs. 57 percent, a percentage difference of 16.
13. *Research and student assistance:* 55 percent vs. 39 percent, a percentage difference of 16.
14. *Reputation of the department:* 72 percent vs. 57 percent, a percentage difference of 15.
15. *Departmental funds:* 42 percent vs. 31 percent, a percentage difference of 11.
16. *Supplies and materials:* 77 percent vs. 68 percent, a percentage difference of 9.
17. *Professional travel:* 60 percent vs. 58 percent, a percentage difference of 2.

The four items rated higher (as *good* or *very good*) by black Ph.D.'s in sociology at black schools than those at white schools were:

1. *Geographical area of the country*: 71 percent vs. 61 percent, a percentage difference of 10.
2. *Promotion and tenure*: 77 percent vs. 68 percent, a percentage difference of 9.
3. *Colleagues in department or division*: 83 percent vs. 80 percent, a percentage difference of 3.
4. *Civic and community participation*: 79 percent vs. 77 percent, a percentage difference of 2.

Some Political, Social, and Reputational Considerations

Political Affiliation   About two-thirds of black doctorates in sociology reported they lean toward the Democratic party; 14 percent indicated they are independents or have no particular political preference; 11 percent indicated socialist leanings and about 4 percent reported Republican leanings.

When asked whether they are presently members of a political party, 62 percent said yes. Also, nearly 18 percent of black Ph.D.'s in sociology have been elected or appointed to political office at one time or another. Twenty-two percent of the respondents said they have experienced changes in their political leanings since they were 25 years old.

Religious Affiliation   Two-thirds of black doctorates in sociology claim a religious affiliation, ranked as follows: (1) Episcopalian, 25 percent; (2) Methodist, 23 percent; (3) Presbyterian, 16 percent; (4) Baptist, 14 percent; (5) Congregationalist, 5 percent; and (6) Catholic, 5 percent. Only about 46 percent attends church as frequently as once a month, whereas about 47 percent attends church three or fewer times a year. About a third of black doctorates in sociology attends church once a year or not at all.

Along more purely social lines, it was reported that two-thirds of black doctorates in sociology have been affiliated with Greek-letter organizations, and many have been affiliated with masonic groups, the Elks, the Boulé, and other such groups. A significant proportion of black doctorates have held local, regional, and national offices within these organizations. Present active membership within these groups, however, is probably not applicable to more than a third of black doctorates in sociology.

Black sociologists have made noteworthy contributions to sociology; therefore, it was felt important to ask black doctorates in sociology which black sociologists, living or dead, have made the most noteworthy contributions to sociology. It was realized when this question was asked in 1967 that some persons who have made contributions to sociological knowledge had not earned their doctorates in sociology. For example, W. E. B. Du Bois, St. Clair Drake, and Allison Davis did not receive their doctorates in sociology. Further, it was realized that, among the study group, many would not know the race of all contributors to sociology. Furthermore, it was realized that the results obtained from this type of question can be modified by time. If the same question were asked today, perhaps other names than the ones reported below would appear. They are ranked on the basis of the number of times cited in the top five ranks.

Respondents believed that among black sociologists, living or dead, the following ten have made the most important contributions to sociology: (1) E. Franklin Frazier; (2) Charles S. Johnson; (3) W. E. B. Du Bois; (4) Oliver C. Cox; (5) Ira De A. Reid; (6) Hylan G. Lewis; (7) St. Clair Drake; (8) Mozell Hill; (9) Allison Davis; (10) Joseph Himes. That there is some concurrence in the profession in regard to some of these scholars is indicated by the American Sociological Association's establishment of a Du Bois-Johnson-Frazier Award Committee in 1971. The first award went to Oliver C. Cox. The Association of Social and Behavioral Scientists established a W. E. B. Du Bois Award three years ago and has awarded it to the following scholars: Oliver C. Cox (1970), Lewis W. Jones (1971), and Horace Mann Bond (1972).

Sociocultural, Ideological, and Policy Implications

Our research has indicated that substantial differences exist between black sociologists and others in the profession. We have also commented on the severe shortage of black persons trained in this area. We attribute this shortage to historical patterns of racial discrimination which resulted in differential recruitment, differential opportunities for advanced training, and differential opportunities for career development. All of the differences in opportunities have, until very recently, favored whites. The results of our research have documented racial inequities present in the careers of black sociologists, beginning with their earliest educational experiences and continuing through their current employment. Black sociologists encountered greater financial hardship, they found it more difficult to obtain higher education, their graduate training was extended for unusually long time periods, and they were often employed in a segregated academic market. Now, as a result of civil rights pressure, and in response to student demands, black sociologists are in great demand. What are the implications of this situation?

One obvious implication of our research is that sociology is dominated by whites. This includes professional associations, academic departments, and professional publications. It means also that the substantive content as well as the epistemology of the discipline are determined by whites. The central figures in the development of modern sociology were Europeans. There have been few competing influences. Therefore, the sociological perspective has tended to be a European perspective. What this has meant to black sociologists was stated clearly by James Moss in the following passage:

the sociology that I learned, and the concepts I internalized, were all cast within the framework of white perceptions and white interpretations. Indeed, while many will dispute this, the sociology I brought away with me from Columbia was the sociology of the white experience, with its Anglo-Saxon and Teutonic roots. It certainly did not nor does it now touch, except peripherally, upon the sociology of the black experience either in this country, or in Africa or the Caribbean. Nor do I think that the experience has been substantially different for most black scholars in America.[20]

Whether one agrees with Moss's contention that there is a "white stereotyping of subject matter in the social sciences,"[21] it is undoubtedly true that few black sociologists found black professors teaching in the sociology departments of the institutions where they obtained their doctoral degrees. Those black scholars who earned undergraduate or master's degrees at Howard, Fisk, Atlanta, Lincoln, and other black universities did have an opportunity to benefit from the scholarship and experiences of black sociologists such as Frazier, Johnson, Du Bois, and Cox. That none of the prominent black sociologists were offered professorships at major Ph.D.-granting institutions can only be attributed to the racial chauvinism that permeated the hiring policies of these institutions. It is undoubtedly true that the sociological perspective can be broadened considerably by the inclusion of more blacks (and other excluded groups) in policy-making positions in professional associations and in teaching, research, and administrative capacities in university departments. There is a need for professors who are sensitive to the complex forces of race in our society and who have the insight and imagination needed to provide a comprehensive interpretation and analysis of these phenomena. Black students have demanded that universities hire more blacks so that they too can have professors who share their experiences and with whom they can identify. There is also, however, a broader need. All students and professors can benefit from the wider perspectives on human experience which suggest the possibility of recasting and reformulating existing sociological conceptions of human behavior and human social systems.

Obviously there is a need for a rapid increase in the production of black sociologists. We have pointed out that even those institutions that have been most productive in the past are turning out very few black sociologists even today. How can this situation be remedied? Major efforts are needed by professional associations, government agencies, universities, and foundations in order to recruit more black Americans into sociology. Some suggestions about the kinds of steps these organizations may take are presented below.

First, sociology departments at black colleges should be strengthened. The black colleges still educate a substantial proportion of the total black college enrollment. Strengthening departments at these colleges would increase the pool of eligible students who might be recruited into graduate departments. Those black universities with graduate programs should also be provided with as much assistance as possible so that they can improve their offerings and increase their graduate student enrollments.

The second recommendation is that adequate funding be provided for black graduate students. In view of the relatively poor financial situation of many black students, the typical stipends such as assistantships, fellowships, and traineeships, may not be sufficient. Supplemental funding may be necessary to enable substantial numbers of black Americans to obtain graduate degrees in sociology.

A third consideration is that compensatory recruiting is necessary if blacks are to be represented in sociology in approximately the same proportion as they are found in the general population. It will not be enough for sociology departments to increase enrollments until blacks represent 12 percent of graduate students. They would have to enroll at least double that proportion to compensate for the relatively small proportion of blacks currently in the profession. Graduate departments should also allow for the fact that blacks are not only underrepresented in the profession, but they are especially underrepresented among those who have earned doctorates. Therefore, graduate departments should make special efforts to steer entering black graduate students into doctoral programs. A special effort should also be made to "reclaim" those who have dropped out of graduate programs for nonacademic reasons.

Our fourth recommendation is that graduate departments should institute programs designed to eliminate the problems encountered by black graduate students. Given the racial character of American society, black students can be expected to face personal problems as they attempt to cope with the predominantly white environment of the graduate school. Most graduate programs are difficult enough for white students; graduate deparments should, therefore, develop programs that will demonstrate that racial discrimination is not a problem. This implies that graduate departments should carefully examine their curricula and remove any cultural biases which currently exist.

Finally, professional associations and graduate departments should encourage black sociologists to specialize in areas in which few blacks currently specialize. There is an acute shortage of black demographers and statisticians. Blacks are also underrepresented in methodology and social organization. These shortages are especially important for those black institutions that are trying to develop strong sociology departments. We are also concerned about underrepresentation in methodology, demography, and social organization because scholars in these areas often influence policy decisions that affect blacks and other minorities. Black scholars can help to make sure that these specialties take into consideration perspectives other than those of middle-class whites. The American Sociological Association and the regional associations should establish programs to encourage the recruitment of black sociologists and to assist in their placement and career development. The Black Caucus in Sociology and individual black sociologists must also continue to engage vigorously in the struggle to improve the status of blacks in the profession of sociology.

Notes

1   For example, little or no differentiation by race occurs in the following studies: Leland J. Axelson, "Graduate Schools and the Productivity of Their Graduates," *American Journal of Sociology* 56 (September 1950): 171-75; Bernard Berelson, *Graduate Education in the United States* (New York, 1960); David G. Brown, *The Market for College Teachers* (Chapel Hill, 1961); Diana Crane, "Scientists at Major and Minor Universities: A Study of Productivity and Recognition," *American Sociological Review* 30 (October 1965): 699-714; Abbott L. Ferris, "Educational Interrelations Among Social Sciences," *American Sociological Review* 24 (February 1964): 103-14; Jerome G. Manis, "Some Academic Influences Upon Publication Productivity," *Social Forces* 29 (March 1951): 267-72; Stanley Schacter, "Birth Order, Eminence and Higher Education," *American Sociological Review* 38 (October 1963): 757-68; Elbridge Sibley, *The Education of Sociologists in the United States* (New York, 1963); Jules A. Wanderer, "Academic Origins of Contributions to the American Sociological Review," 1955-1965, *The American Sociologist* 1 (November 1966): 241-43.

2   Harry W. Greene, *Holders of Doctorates Among American Negroes* (Boston, 1946); G. Franklin Edwards, *The Negro Professional Class* (Glencoe, 1959); Horace Mann Bond, "The Negro Scholar and Professional in America," in *The American Negro Reference Book*, ed. John P. Davis (Englewood Cliffs, New Jersey, 1966), 548-88; and *A Study of Factors Involved in the Identification and Encouragement of Unusual Talent Among Underprivileged Populations* (Washington, D.C., Office of Education, U.S. Department of Health, Education, and Welfare, Project No. 5-0859 by Horace Mann Bond); Richard L. Simpson, "Professionalism and Work Satisfaction Among Southern White

and Negro Public School Teachers" (paper presented at the Southern Sociological Society, New Orleans, 1966); Kurt W. Back and Ida H. Simpson, "The Dilemma of the Negro Professional," *Journal of Social Issues* 20 (January 1964): 60-70; James A. Moss, "The Utilization of Negro Teachers in the Colleges of New York State" (Ph.D. dissertation, Columbia University, 1957); James A. Moss, "The Integration of Negro Teachers in Predominantly White Colleges," *Journal of Negro Education* 27 (Fall 1958): 451-62; James A. Moss, "The Utilization of Negro Teachers in New York State," *Phylon* 21 (March 1960): 63-70; Daniel C. Thompson, "The Teacher in the Negro Colleges: A Sociological Analysis" (Ph.D. dissertation, Columbia University, 1956); Daniel C. Thompson, "Career Patterns of Teachers in Negro Colleges," *Social Forces* 36 (March 1958): 270-76; and Joseph Himes, "The Teacher of Sociology in the Negro College," *Social Forces* 24 (March 1951): 302-5; James E. Conyers, "Negro Doctorates in Sociology," *Phylon* 29 (Fall 1958): 209-23. Edgar G. Epps and Glenn R. Howze, "The Status of Black Americans in the Field of Sociology" (paper presented at 66th Annual Meeting of the American Sociological Association, Denver, Colorado, 1971); Clyde Franklin and Alice Franklin, "The Marketable Position of Black Sociologists and the Black Brain Drain Controversy," unpublished, 1972; and Frank Clemente (two papers: "Racial Differences in Research Output" and "Racial Differences in Progress Toward the Doctorate," 1972).

3   Conyers wishes to acknowledge the financial support provided by a grant from the Atlanta University Center Research Committee. He also wishes to acknowledge assistance given him by William V. Frazier, Lois Benjamin, and Eddie Collins, former graduate students of Atlanta University. The assistance of Professor Martin Levin of Emory University and Patricia Murphy of the University of Massachusetts is also gratefully acknowledged.

Epps wishes to acknowledge the help provided by his collaborator at Tuskegee Institute, Glenn R. Howze, and the financial support provided by a grant from the Russell Sage Foundation. Norma D. Carson, Kasondra Maratty, Celia H. Jefferson, and Jo Howze, all of Tuskegee Institute, also provided invaluable assistance to us in the conduct of the *Survey of Black Social Scientists* (Report to the Russell Sage Foundation, 1971).

The Epps and Howze study is based on a sample of 1,030 black social scientists, of whom 222 are sociologists, and a comparison sample of 1,565 nonblack social scientists which included 187 sociologists. Data were obtained by mailed questionnaires in 1970. These respondents are the 57 percent of black social scientists and 56 percent of white social scientists contacted who returned usable questionnaires. Detailed information on sample selection may be obtained from the authors.

Conyers's study is based on 85 black sociologists who had earned the Ph.D. degree in sociology. The data were obtained by mailed questionnaires. The respondents constitute 70 percent of the 121 sociologists identified in 1967.

4   James W. Bryant, *A Survey of Black American Doctorates* (The Ford Foundation, 1970).

5   Fred E. Crossland, "Graduate Education and Black Americans"

(mimeographed and distributed by the Office of Special Projects, The Ford Foundation, 1968), p. 2.

6   Fred E. Crossland, *Minority Access to College,* a Ford Foundation report (New York: Schocken Books, 1971), pp. 15-16.

7   James E. Conyers, "Negro Doctorates in Sociology: A Social Portrait," *Phylon* 29 (Fall 1968): 209-23; and Laren Wispe et al., "The Negro Psychologists in America," *American Psychologist* 25:146.

8   "Interim Report of the Committee on the Status of Blacks in the Profession," (mimeographed and distributed by the American Political Science Association).

9   Letters to authors from Donald Deskins, May 1, 1970.

10   Bond, "The Negro Scholar and Professional," p. 566.

11   See Sylvia F. Farra, "The Status of Women in Professional Sociology," *American Sociological Review* 25 (April 1960): 270-76; and Sibley, *The Education of Sociologists,* p. 51. We did not attempt a separate analysis for female sociologists in this study because of the small samples involved.

12   Edwards, *The Negro Professional Class.*

13   Bond, "The Negro Scholar and Professional," p. 566.

14   Bond, "A Study of Factors Involved in the Identification and Encouragement of Unusual Academic Talent."

15   For a critical discussion of birth order and higher education, see Schacter, "Birth Order."

16   Clemente, "Racial Differences in Progress Toward the Doctorate."

17   See the previously cited works by G. Franklin Edwards and Horace Mann Bond.

18   See Daniel C. Thompson, "Problems of Faculty Morale" *Journal of Negro Education* 29 (Winter 1960): 37-46; Himes, "The Teacher of Sociology"; Simpson, "Professionalism," and Back and Simpson, "The Negro Professional."

19   Thompson, "Faculty Morale," p. 40.

20   James A. Moss, "In Defense of Black Studies," in *The Black Man in America: Integration and Separation,* ed. James A. Moss (New York: Dell Publishing Company, 1971), p. 122.

21   Ibid.

9

Nathan Hare

THE CONTRIBUTION OF BLACK
SOCIOLOGISTS TO BLACK
STUDIES

In his last published article, E. Franklin Frazier spoke of a "failure of the Negro intellectual" which he attributed to the Negro intellectual's seduction by "dreams," conscious and unconscious, of final assimilation.[1] While this appears to have applied particularly to sociologists of that day and to many of the present era, a new breed of black sociologist is now emerging on the American scene.

The new black sociologist has lost faith in what he regards as an oppressive society. He rejects, therefore, the value-free myth and similar sociological theories, and looks to a new sociology as an instrument for social change:

it is becoming rather clear that educational institutions are vital to a liberation movement, a fact of modern times in anti-colonial movements in the Third World ... there is a need to find new styles of scholarship, new forms of knowledge, new ways of knowing.[2]

The new black sociologist (almost eight out of ten are male) is increasingly less likely to have Southern origins, except that he is still more likely than not to have attended a predominantly black college. However, once his formal education is completed, he is highly more likely to teach at a predominantly white college. Despite his nationalistic leanings and his training in sociology, he is, like his older counterpart, uninclined to believe that black sociologists have made a significant contribution to black studies.

We pinpoint black studies because, just five years after Frazier's death and his criticism of Negro intellectuals, black intellectuals and students launched what was potentially the most significant social movement to appear in American scholarship—the movement to revamp the Negro college and to erect radicalized black education on white campuses (popularly known as "black studies").

We have chosen black studies as a focus for discerning the differences between old and new black sociologists and, in particular, the direction of the new black sociologist. Our data consist of analysis of writings on the subject of black studies and black scholarship by black sociologists—James Turner, Abd-al Hakimu Ibn Alkalimat (né Gerald McWorter), Maurice Jackson, Orlando Patterson, and Alphonso Pinckney—and questionnaire returns from 52 black sociologists holding the Ph.D. degree. The sample included 24 sociologists who were 45 years old and over, 18 who were 35 to 44, and 10 who were under 35. Differences by age were immediately apparent from an analysis of the questionnaires and confirmed, among other things, how young and old sociologists part company on the issue of assimilation.

Although the age trichotomy (less than 35, 35 to 44, and 45 and over) showed consistent patterns on most variables, this was not quite always the case, due in part, perhaps, to the fact that there were only ten individuals in the sample below the age of 35. When age was dichotomized, however, the age differences were always in the expected direction. Hence the age dichotomy was somewhat sharper than the trichotomy.

When asked to indicate open-ended criticisms of black studies, the group 45 years old and over gave assimilationist and conformist responses: "too ethnocentric"; "have not been related to the larger (predominant) culture and society"; "not integrated into the total academic program"; "amount to racial chauvinism"; "remain outside the central thrust of the academic program"; "too hastily developed"; "intermix polemics with logic"; "staffed by propagandists rather than scholars."

By contrast, the younger group, the less-than-45-year-olds, gave nationalistic rather than asimilationist criticisms as a rule, and called for greater power and self-determination for black studies and their personnel. For example: "most black studies programs are white controlled through the bureaucracy"; "most are not independent departments"; "blacks need more control over the programs"; "the programs are not concerned with developing a philosophy of blackness but rather merely describe forms of exploitation"; "material taught is not really relevant."

The young black sociologist, like blacks at large, is increasingly turning his back on assimilation as a goal. A sample of published statements by young black sociologists will attest to this fact. From a former University of Chicago faculty member:

> For increasing numbers of black people, assimilation is neither desirable nor likely at the present time; and all evidence tends to support this position.[3]

From a University of Chicago-trained Ph.D.:

> One of the patterns is for education to be simply a process of acclimation and adjustment to the white world. One goes to a white school to rub shoulders with them, "because, son, you got to make a livin' out in their world."[4]

From a Cornell University professor:

> any black studies program which purports to be educating black students for fuller participation in the American mainstream is counter-productive to black people's needs for development and self-control. Moreover, it is essential to our liberation that black youth are motivated to resist—not accept—the "mainstream" of the system which oppresses and destroys our people.[5]

A black University of California sociologist observes that black studies are not the study of race relations, and cautions against imitating the technique and findings of race relations specialists.[6] Similarly, a black Harvard University professor criticizes the "contributionism" of black social scientists and warns generally against mimicking the white scholar's values in our own research and scholarship.[7]

These black sociologists have lost faith, if not in sociology, in the existing society's values as passageways to the goals of black freedom. Accordingly, they reject that society and that science which, they feel, rejects them. In their view, the "very nature" of education in relation to the rest of society comes under serious scrutiny.[8]

There can be no freedom in the present system; it must undergo fundamental changes or be replaced entirely. The only way for it to be changed is to have a new constitutional convention and reconstruct the basic political documents serving as the basis of the social order. We must have a new constitution, a new flag, new symbols, new songs, a new economy, a new way of relating to the rest of the world, a new commitment for peace and justice everywhere. The new society must be hip in the hippest sense of that beautiful word. [9]

Among the most salient themes of conventional sociology which the new black sociologist rejects is the "value-free" approach to scientific analysis. The value placed on scientific analysis and methods must be joined by an equally important value placed on "empathy, involvement and commitment." [10]

Our search for understanding through social analysis is conditioned by how we resolve several long-standing controversies, not the least of which is the relationship between ideology and science. In the case of Africans captured in the West (particularly in the United States of America), this has all too often been resolved by black intellectuals acquiescing to a white social science. This has meant swallowing the most favorable white positions without piercing through to the implicit ideological assumptions really used to guide history with white interests. Many black social scientists seemingly have not really known the extent to which science is inevitably a handservant to ideology, a tool for people to shape, if not create, reality. [11]

In an article, "Toward a Sociology of Black Studies," a black University of California professor rejects the notion that scientists have no control over the application of knowledge. He therefore calls for "relevance" in black scholarship, and questions the "presumed directedness" of current sociology and scholarship. [12]

For many professional black educators any question of the relationship of ideology to what they teach makes them uneasy. They would most likely be inclined to consider the discussion of black studies, as we have presented in this paper, as a subjective approach to learning and a sort of sectarian encroachment that would demean the academic quality of their work. But, while it is true that facts must derive from objective discourse, we must not become confused by the facade that education is value-free and above the social system when in fact it is the axis for the developing and refining of ideas that are put into the development of the ideology of the society. Education for blacks must consider the need to break down "false consciousness." It must seek to reveal to black people—by facts; by emotionally powerful experiences and by argument—the machinations of opppression.[13]

Empirical research, another maintains, has resulted in the "falsification" of our understanding of social reality. "We have been looking at the trees and ignoring the essential nature of the forest."[14]

Alternatively, the science of sociology—indeed all scholarship, not least black studies—must become an instrument for social change and social action. Black studies programs that do not lead to action to alter basic power relations between whites and blacks are condemned as "insular" and "traditional." This is because "control over content and definition of the learning of our young is a pivotal facet of the liberation struggle."[15] All elements of the black freedom movement must "subvert and/or supplant the entrenched social system if it is to be a real source of radical change and not a false one."[16] The black intellectual, in particular, must discover "new styles of scholarhip, new forms of knowledge, new ways of knowing"[17] which not only serve to "demystify" the scholarly process but also to pull it out of the abstract and relate it to the daily lives of the students and their communities. Important, therefore, is a community component (almost unanimously recommended by our respondents) which consists of course-related activity and experiences in the community reminiscent of the old Park and Burgess approach.

Since scholarship is to become an instrument for social change and black liberation, the first step, as in any social movement, is to wed action to an appropriate ideology. Black educators are urged to "reinforce the development of consciousness and concern for the black community among students and contribute to the development and implementation of a new definition of the ends toward which black children are educated."[18]

Black education must make students consistently conscious of struggle and commitment. Too often the question of cultural values and political ideology is only superficially perceived. It is necessary at this time to define our long-range goals, and put into operation the work needed to fulfill these immediate objectives.[19]

In an article, "The Ideology of Black Social Science," one young sociologist maintains that the relationship between science and ideology is one of the most important controversies which we must resolve in order to gain true understanding through social analysis.[20] In this view, science and scholarship, not to mention social science, are not "value-free." Therefore, it is advocated, black sociologists must have a commitment to an ideology in opposition to the status quo.

A Survey of Black Sociologists: Belief Systems About Black Studies

This survey consists of 52 questionnaire returns from black sociologists with Ph.D. degrees. Although the majority of this group (64 percent) received their early training in a Negro college, most of them (69 percent) now work in a white college where there is a black studies program (73 percent). However, only 54 percent have ever taught black studies, mainly because they have not been asked to do so. Only 4 percent have ever refused to teach a black studies course.

Black sociologists are not particularly inclined to believe that the writings of black sociologists have had a significant impact on black studies (50 percent). Here there was a difference between those who had taught black studies and those who have not, with those who have taught black studies holding a higher regard for the writings of black sociologists in this field. In fact, this was the only item in the questionnaire on which those who had taught black studies and those who had not differed noticeably. Further, only 57.7 percent believe that black sociologists have taken any key role in developing and staffing black studies programs. Only 42.3 percent believe that the most important course in a black studies program is sociology.

Perhaps reflecting a deep understanding of the black studies movement, only 55.8 percent believe the popular notion that most Negro colleges have, since their inception, or since their faculties became predominantly black, been engaged in teaching black studies. This, however, is still a high percentage and again probably reflects the similarity between black sociologists' ideas on black studies and those of the populace at large.

Many individuals, equating black studies with the study of black people, believe that black professors in Southern schools have long taught black studies. Others, by contrast, hold that black studies grew out of the black consciousness movement of the late 1960s and properly consists of courses geared to the demands of that ideology; for example, to make education "relevant" to the black student and his community. Black studies emerge as a teaching device to help overcome generations of black exclusion from the educational process. Any course, in the view of such advocates, can be taught from a black point of view.

As many as 69.2 percent believe that the most important goal a black studies program can have is that of providing black students with significant knowledge and understanding of black and black-white relations in the United States. Thus, black studies would have the goal of solving the problems of racial conflict and black oppression. This is a significant departure from the purely "academic" function of scholarship and education.

However, 76.9 percent think it is better for black students graduating from college to receive degrees in the "traditional" subjects such as mathematics, engineering, biology, and sociology, than in black studies.

Almost half of the black sociologists (46.2 percent) believe that most black studies programs have not been able to attract competent black scholars. Only 51.9 percent believe that all black college students should be required to take at least one course in black studies. This may indicate a basic lack of support for the idea of black studies, as an identical figure also believe that whites should be required to take at least one course. However, only 7.7 percent believe that no college or university needs any specific course in black studies.

While 59.6 percent believe that interest in black studies programs on white campuses is waning, only 28.8 percent believe that interest on black campuses is waning. Like other responses above, this may reflect an accurate assessment of objective reality, as black studies as such came to Negro campuses as a delayed response to the initial thrust on white campuses.

Twenty-nine percent believe that black studies have had no significant effect upon curricular changes; and 59.6 percent believe that, in general, most black studies programs can provide a black college student with a better education than he could receive without such a program. This is only slightly more than half and indicates that black sociologists as a whole have not, to any significant degree, accepted the idea of black studies.

Young Black Sociologists Among the factors shown to have no consistent effect on the attitudes of black sociologists toward black studies were: region of childhood rearing, predominant color of college attended, nature of agency or college in which presently employed, and even whether respondents had ever taught black studies.

Age was found to have a consistent relationship. Here it is important to understand that age is not merely a demographic variable, or the consequence of aging alone; it also reflects generational changes in dominant ideas. Persons attending college or entering the field of sociology in an assimilationist era would be exposed to a different set of ideas than those developing in a more nationalistic era. It is possible, however, that other factors, not available in this study, could be found to have an equal or perhaps greater importance. For instance, political ideology would no doubt determine one's views toward black studies, regardless of age, although this is implied in our assimilationist-nationalistic dichotomy. This is not to say, however, that all blacks fell neatly into this division.

The factor of age has a dual effect in that it can represent generational differences or/and social trends. The only characteristic reflecting consistent differences among the respondents in this sample was that of age.

First, demographically speaking, the young sociologists have a higher proportion of females than the older group. They are less likely to have originated in the South and slightly less likely to have received their early education at a Negro college. They are highly less likely to be teaching now at a Negro college. Surprisingly, there is no difference in the percentages that have taught black studies when compared with the older sample. Yet none of the black sociologists 35 years old or less has ever refused to teach a black studies course.

When categorized by age (35 years old or less, 35 to 44 years old, and 45 years old and over) black sociologists exhibit consistent differences by age in their attitudes and beliefs about black studies. For instance, for the belief that Negro colleges have long taught black studies courses, the difference is striking, with older respondents more likely to be gripped by this fallacy (30.0, 50.0, and 67.7 percent, respectively, for the three age-groups).

Young black sociologists are highly more likely to see black studies as an instrument for solving racial problems, to believe that the most important goal any black studies program can have is that of providing black students with significant knowledge and understanding of blacks and black-white relations (90.0, 72.2, and 58.3 percent, respectively).

Fewer of the young sociologists believe that it is better for black students graduating from college to receive degrees in the traditional subjects such as mathematics, engineering, biology, and sociology, than in black studies (50.0, 66.7, and 75.0 percent, respectively). This indicates a greater devotion to black studies on the part of young black sociologists. However, the young sociologists are highly more likely to believe that most black studies programs have not been able to attract competent black scholars (70.0, 39.9, and 37.5 percent). But they are nevertheless somewhat more inclined to believe that all black college students should be required to take at least one course in black studies (60.0, 55.6, and 45.8 percent). This pattern does not hold for the requirement that all white students take at least one black studies course. None of the two younger groups (35 years old or less, and 35 to 44 years old) agreed that no college or university needs any specific course in black studies, while 16.7 percent of those 45 years old and over thought so. While the young sociologists showed no difference in the rating of the writings of black sociologists as contributors to black studies, there was a consistent difference in assessing the role of black sociologists as a key one (50.0, 44.4, and 33.3 percent, respectively).

Criticisms of Black Studies A typical criticism of black studies by black sociologists revolves around opposition to the emergence and the effects of student power. The programs are said to be too hastily conceived and implemented—"too hastily put together under fire from the students"—though no indication of the amount of time ideally required was offered by respondents. In any case, the students are criticized for demanding a new ideology on the one hand and weak ("Mickey Mouse") programs on the other that not only detract from the dignity of the programs, but also threaten the scholarly egos and identities, as one respondent put it, of the black sociologists.

This may reflect acceptance of the popular stereotypes about black studies—that the programs are not properly scholarly, in the traditional sense at least, and do not represent a genuine (established) academic discipline. Instead, such persons believe, black studies consist mainly of black militant rhetoric and "rapping." Black studies programs are staffed by propagandists whose scholarship is suspect and, partly due to a self-fulfilling prophecy, the programs are unable to attract a high-level black faculty. One respondent flatly stated that the programs are "staffed by incompetents."

Thus, not only are students criticized; black studies faculties also come under scrutiny. There is said to be little commitment on their part to engage in "basic intellectual effort and basic research on the subject matter of black studies beyond immediate political and financial contingencies." Teachers are thought to propagandize rather than seek critical knowledge, while students are not serious in their efforts to learn. These teachers and students are thought to be "confounding the problems of militancy and personal needs with intellectual discipline, intermixing polemics and logic." Hence black studies are thought to have a "nonacademic" (propagandistic) basis.

On the other hand, the young sociologists were highly more likely, when criticizing black studies, to chastize the college administrations. Much of the criticism of administrators revolved around a lack of a genuine support—inadequate financing, staffing and planning. Inadequate funding is seen as direct resistance as well as the absence of a serious administrative commitment to the programs. Perhaps more important, in their view, in that it was more often mentioned, is the struggle for power between administrations and black studies advocates. This results, they feel, in "gestures to keep the natives quiet," with the programs remaining "white-controlled"—keeping blacks appeased but outside the power structure and decision-making process of the campus. There is perceived reluctance to grant the programs departmental and independent status; there is a fear of black control. Black studies programs are too often designed and staffed by white faculty and are therefore suspect.

Whereas a few believe that the programs are not separatist or independent enough, many decry their separatism. This was particularly true among older respondents. "Really don't know much about black studies, but would tend to question the separatist aspects which envelop them." Or, "I have had experience with only one. The people involved in it were separatist and cultural nationalists. The program collapsed for that reason." Such assimilationists hold that the persons who need black studies most (white students) do not enroll significantly and that there is a need for training more white teachers for black studies work. They regret that black studies are not integrated enough into the general campus community and society at large. They further regret that black studies do not, in their view, prepare black students for an integrated role and, even in the study of blacks, fail substantially to discover and depict the contributions of blacks to American (white) society.

They are more rhetoric, fiction, mimicry than factual accounts of the significant life and cultures of Negroid peoples and their contributions past to present to human societies and nations.

Many bemoan the "too narrow" emphasis on the arts and humanities, calling for a stronger inclusion of social sciences but, more frequently, embracing the need for technical courses and the "hard" sciences. "There is not enough attention being given to the means by which the skills acquired by students in black studies are to be accommodated to the larger community."

Or, "I approve, but it must include the basic subjects such as English, mathematics, science."

Or, "The range of courses is not wide enough. They need more in such as economics, research methods, mathematics."

The Community as Laboratory One of the most frequent

notions set forth in response to the open-ended question about the ideal relationship between the black community and the black studies programs was the use of the black community as a practical laboratory for study and analysis.

In my view, the ideal relationship would be one that recognizes the primacy of the university as a seat of learning but which draws upon and incorporates experiences from real communities to facilitate that learning process for students and faculties. Experts of all levels of experience and training, academic or otherwise, could be utilized in seminars, research undertakings, and as resource persons for students involved in various practical projects. The community (sub-communities) with its permission could be the testing ground for theoretical assumptions and for the practical application of knowledge developed in response to local community needs.

Most crucial to black studies, in this view, aside from the ideology of social change, would be the community component of their methodology. This is designed to wed black communities, heretofore excluded, and the educational process, to transform the black community, making it more relevant to higher education at the same time as education is made relevant to the black community. Such education would bring both the college to the community and the community to the college. The community and its problems would constitute a laboratory, and there would be apprenticeship and fieldwork components to every course.

Even a course such as history might have the requirement that students put on panel discussions on black history in church basements or elsewhere for younger children. A class project could be the formation of a black history club, over the years organizing the black community thereby and raising black consciousness, at the same time helping to educate black youth through course-related tutorial programs. The black college student's mere presence in the community could provide an otherwise unavailable role model for young black children and, as the student tests out his theories learned in the classroom through these various apprenticeship activities (say, in black politics, black economics, black journalism, black theater), he would gain an intensive knowledge of and commitment to the community he was being taught to serve after graduation.

The black sociologists in general envision a "mutual" or "reciprocal" or "symbiotic" relationship between black studies and the black community. The black studies program would use people from the community as teachers and paraprofessionals while the community would recognize and utilize the competence and leadership of the black studies faculty toward community development and the elimination of social problems.

For instance:

Any program which addresses the needs of black people should keep in touch with the day-to-day concerns and activities of black people. A meaningful academic program should, among other things: (1) provide a service function to black communities; (2) solicit input from communities for program development; (3) encourage community to seek services of blacks on campus whenever possible; try to develop reciprocal relationships.

Or:

The university should be the research-investigative as well as mass-based education arm for the development of the black communities which in turn take action on the basis of education and research which in turn produces dynamic and progressive change.

Some black sociologists hold out a one-way impact—the black studies affecting the community on the one hand, or the community affecting the black studies program on the other.

In the relationship between community and black studies, I suppose there should be unified faculty-to-staff efforts toward in certain respects "representing" the black community ... in addition to a dedication (on the part of the faculty) to considerable research on blackness and on black-white relations.

On the other hand:

There should be research on and the solutions to problems confronting the black subcommunities. Such services should be made known to the communities and that they are available on request. They could also offer some assistance in organizing the communities during political campaigns, for relevant issues, etc.

In addition to programs oriented to black community development, including research focused on issues of concern to the black community, the black studies faculty would provide role models as teachers and consultants. Out of these efforts would emerge "communiversities" in which faculty would teach "free" courses to the black community. The black community in turn would play a major role in helping to develop curricula for the black studies program and share generally in its design.

Notes

1   E. Franklin Frazier, "The Failure of the Negro Intellectual," *Negro Digest* (February 1962).

2   Gerald McWorter, "The Nature and Needs of the Black University," *Negro Digest* (March 1968), p. 11.

3   Alphonso Pinckney, "The Assimilation of Afro-Americans," *The Black Scholar* (December 1969), p. 46.

4   Gerald McWorter, "Black University," p. 10.

5   James Turner, "Black Studies and a Black Philosophy of Education" (unpublished manuscript, 1970), p. 7.

6   Maurice Jackson, "Toward a Sociology of Black Studies," *Journal of Black Studies* (December 1970), p. 136.

7   Orlando Patterson, "Rethinking Black History," *Harvard Today* (December 1971).

8   Turner, "Black Studies," p. 1.

9   A. H. I. Alkalimat (Gerald McWorter), "The Ideology of Black Social Science," *The Black Scholar* (December 1969), p. 34.

10   McWorter, "Black University," p. 10.

11   Alkalimat, "Black Social Science," p. 28.

12   Jackson, "Toward a Sociology," p. 134.

13   Turner, "Black Studies," p. 10.

14   Alkalimat, "Black Social Science," p. 29.

15   Turner, "Black Studies," p. 8.

16   McWorter, "Black University," p. 6.

17   Ibid., p. 11.

18   Turner, "Black Studies," p. 4.

19   Ibid., p. 7.

20   Alkalimat, "Black Social Science," p. 28.

10

Jacquelyne Johnson Jackson

BLACK FEMALE SOCIOLOGISTS

Within both the general concerns of knowing and understanding professionals and efforts to increase the number of professionals who are members of minority groups, some gaps remain. One such gap involves black females. If one were to search for data about black female professionals, one would almost search in vain. If one were to search for black female professionals, one would almost search in vain. If one were to search for black female professionals in occupations generally rated as more prestigious than those of public school teaching, nursing, social work, and library science, again one would almost search in vain. Any number of variables may be useful in explaining this gap, but chief among them are persisting discrimination against black females precisely because they are both black and female; false assumptions about their professional superiority over black males; and scant interest in studying them due to their scarcity in the more prestigious occupations.

Most studies concerned with women professionals ignore blacks, and most studies concerned with black professionals ignore women. [1] More research should be focused upon professions and professionalism as related to black women. More efforts ought to be made to increase substantially the number of black women employed in professional occupations. Upgrading of educational, occupational, income, and employment levels of black females heading or likely to head families with dependent members is of paramount importance. [2] Such conclusions grew out of my examination of available literature on black women and from my comparisons of black women with black males and whites.

267

The general purpose of this study is to examine one small segment of black female professionals about whom almost nothing is known, namely, black female sociologists. Its specific purposes are those of reviewing briefly studies about black sociologists; comparing black sociologists by sex; providing impressionistic judgments on and a partial bibliography of black female sociologists; and emphasizing a need for more black female sociologists.

In addition to personal experiences and observations, the methodology employed included library research and a mailed questionnaire study involving 66 blacks (16.7 percent female) who hold doctorates in sociology. These were the respondents (representing a return rate of about 53 percent) to a questionnaire mailed to 125 potential subjects in spring 1972. They were eligible for inclusion by virtue of being black, having earned a doctoral degree in sociology in or since the year 1945, and by either being a natural citizen of the United States or having earned the doctoral degree and being currently employed within the United States. Those 125 individuals represented eligible sociologists whose current addresses were available. The total estimated number of potential subjects, including those for whom addresses were not available, was 150.

The questionnaire form—one page in length—requested limited background data (name, sex, age, marital status, and institution awarding and year of receipt of the doctoral degree)˙ and data about the dissertation, publications, current research gaps in available literature about blacks, and specification of the most important publication by any black sociologist. Library research was utilized to augment the data provided by respondents and, for nonrespondents and for potential subjects whose addresses were unknown, to obtain information about institution awarding and year of receipt of degree, dissertation title, and publications.

Important limitations in the data were imposed by temporal and monetary restrictions that prevented a highly systematic examination of each dissertation and publication of black female and male sociologists receiving a degree in or since 1945. The list of black sociologists was not exhaustive, and no claim can be made for completeness of bibliography for individuals not submitting a bibliography or submitting an incomplete one.[3]

Previous Studies of Black Sociologists

The most impressive conclusion I drew from my examination of previous studies of black sociologists available was the absence of any concern about females, as evidenced partially by the general failure to separate the data by sex.

Who is the black sociologist? Four pioneering published studies existed.[4] Two, by Conyers and by Hines, were presented initially at the 1967 annual meeting of the Association of Social and Behavioral Scientists (then the Association of Social Science Teachers) in Houston, Texas. The papers were presented in the sociology sessions I developed on "Contributions of Negro Sociologists to Sociology." The remaining two were written by Epps and Howze and by Franklin and Franklin.[5]

Hines's assessment of contributions by black scholars to pure and applied sociology was largely superficial, with an in-depth content analysis of their works and any bibliographic reference to black sociologists conspicuously absent. But his assessment was important in stressing the critical influence of racial status upon intellectual pursuits, symbolized here by a preoccupation with race relations (especially in community organization and education), where the dominant influence of Robert E. Park and the Chicago school was highly visible. In Hines's view, black sociologists had generally failed to contribute significantly to fields outside of race relations, such as theory, methodology, social organization, and social psychology.

Conyers based his largely demographic portrait upon data obtained from or about 121 black Americans identified as holders of a Ph.D. in sociology and still living in 1966. They approximated the population of living black doctorates in sociology. In addition to providing data about sex (*only 12 percent were female*), age (a median of about 45 years), marital status (80 percent married), institutions awarding the degrees (the three leaders, in descending order, were the University of Chicago, Ohio State University, and Washington State University), place of current employment (40 percent in black colleges and universities), and other relevant familial, educational, and organizational data, Conyers noted that his sample regarded E. Franklin Frazier as the black sociologist making the most important contributions to sociology. Conyers also raised anew several critical issues about the production of black sociologists, such as their significant underrepresentation among doctorates in sociology, but he failed to raise any questions about the significant underrepresentation of women, black women in particular, among doctorates in sociology in general.

Epps and Howze were primarily concerned with a comparative description of black and white social scientists with and without a doctorate. They, too, failed to separate their data by sex. The sparse data they collected in 1970 about approximately 96 black doctorates in sociology did, nevertheless, reveal interesting trends both continuous and discontinuous with the past. For example, approximately 91 percent of the degrees were received after 1950, with significant increases occurring in or since 1960; that is, about 32 percent of the degrees were conferred between 1951 and 1960, and approximately 58 percent since then. While about 64 percent of all the degrees were conferred by institutions regarded as major degree-granting institutions in sociology, their analysis revealed a recent trend of a decline in blacks receiving doctorates from the most prestigious institutions. By geographical location, 70 percent of all the degrees were earned from Northern institutions. The trend of increased attendance at Western institutions continued. A new trend (albeit slight) of attendance at Southern institutions also appeared. The earlier trend of a majority of black sociologists being employed outside black institutions, noted by Conyers, was also substantiated. In comparison with their white counterparts, black sociologists with and without the doctorate were underrepresented in the specialized areas of methodology, social organization, demography, and population, and overrepresented in race relations, theory, and social problems. Compared with all black social scientists, black sociologists reported greater publication frequencies and, in this respect, failed to differ significantly from their white peers. Approximately 60 percent of the sampled black sociologists had published at least one book and about 79 percent had published at least one article. Epps and Howze did not provide any data about the content, quality, and location of these publications.

Franklin and Franklin were specifically concerned, in 1971, with the marketability of black sociologists and the impact of this factor upon departments of sociology in black institutions. After investigating the employment sites of 144 black sociologists holding the doctorate, and finding 40 percent of them in black institutions, they concluded that blacks employed in predominantly white academic settings were significantly overrepresented in the least prestigiously ranked institutions and significantly underrepresented in the most prestigiously ranked ones. That is, blacks have not received preferable hiring in comparison with nonblacks in the most prestigious institutions. Black colleges and universities have not been competing with those institutions for black sociologists. Instead, they have been competing with the least prestigious of the predominantly white institutions. Franklin and Franklin failed to analyze their data by sex and by prestige status of individual black sociologists. The provided no comparison of employment statuses of black female and male sociologists. Such information would have been extremely useful in evaluating the marketability of black sociologists in predominantly black and predominantly white departments of varying prestige.

These four studies actually provide us with extremely limited knowledge of the processes and patterns of becoming and being black sociologists, and with almost no data about those processes among black females. But, in the present context, they are extemely significant in emphasizing not only the dearth of data about black females but also in bringing into sharp focus the relative historical unimportance of black females as sociologists. In part, this unimportance can be attributed directly to the numerical dearth of black female sociologists.

An examination of the limited data available about women sociologists was also fruitless in revealing any cogent information or concerns about blacks.[6] Such studies need not be reviewed here for at least three reasons. One is the specific focus of this work upon black sociologists. The remaining two, as explained in greater detail elsewhere,[7] are that cross-racial comparisons often mask pertinent findings about blacks themselves and that comparisons about gaps in educational, occupational, income, and employment statuses of professional black women are most appropriate when the comparison group contains those occupying the highest overall status in these areas—and in these cases those occupying that status happen to be white men.

Sex Comparisons of Black Sociologists

Sex comparisons of black sociologists can be useful in enlarging our knowledge about black female sociologists and in providing additional information about the effects of sex upon professionalism when race is held constant. Two overlapping data sources were available for these comparisons: library research and the questionnaire data. Following comparisons by sex of academic training of black sociologists known to have received the Ph.D. in sociology in 1945 or after is a comparison of data obtained from the sample.

Analysis of available information about institutions awarding and years of receipt of Ph.D. degrees in sociology for 145 black sociologists identified as receiving such degrees between the years 1945 and 1972 revealed that only 21 (14.5 percent) of that total were females. Table 1, containing a numerical and percentage distribution of years of receipt of doctorate by sex revealed both significant underrepresentation of females (as compared with their proportionate representation in the black population) and significant differences by sex in time of receipt of degrees. About 62 percent of the females and 48 percent of the males received degrees after the year 1960. That difference was significant at the .05 level of confidence ($x^2 = 4.1826$, df = 1). The modal time period for females was between 1965 and 1968; for males, 1961 and 1964.

The female modal time period coincided with the time period in which the percentage of female-earned degrees, as compared to total degrees, was also the highest. As shown also in table 1, 26.9 percent of all degrees earned between 1965 and 1968 were earned by females. The low years occurred between 1957 and 1960.

When institutions were ranked by the number of degrees awarded to blacks irrespective of sex, the University of Chicago led, followed by Ohio State University, a finding consistent with Conyers's report of the two institutions most likely to have awarded

TABLE 1.
Numerical and Percentage Distribution of Years of Receipt of Ph.D. Degrees in Sociology by Blacks, by Sex, 1945-72

Year	Female		Male		Both Sexes		Female %
	No.	% of total female degrees, 1945-72	No.	% of total male degrees, 1945-72	No.	% of total degrees, 1945-72	of total degrees, each time period
1945-48	1	4.8	9	7.3	10	6.9	10.0
1949-52	2	9.5	17	13.7	19	13.1	10.5
1953-56	3	14.3	19	15.3	22	15.2	13.6
1957-60	2	9.5	20	16.1	22	15.2	9.1
1961-64	4	19.0	23	18.5	27	18.6	14.8
1965-68	7	33.3	19	15.3	26	17.9	26.9
1969-72	2	9.5	17	13.7	19	13.1	10.5
Total	21	99.9*	124	99.9*	145	100.0	14.5

*Rounding errors.

doctorates to black sociologists. Tied in third place for these 145 black sociologists were Columbia University and Washington State University.

When females only were considered, the picture changed. Radcliffe College, the University of Chicago, and Washington University had awarded two degrees each to females, and the remaining degrees (one each) had been conferred by Brandeis, Bryn Mawr, Case-Western, Cornell, Northwestern, Ohio State, State University of Iowa, the Universities of Georgia, Illinois, Nebraska, Pennsylvania, Southern California, Texas, Wisconsin, and Washington State. The spread of institutions attended by females ($\bar{X} = 0.9$) was much greater than that characteristic of males ($\bar{X} = 0.3$). In addition, a much larger proportion of males than females graduated from institutions regarded as having the most prestigious departments of sociology.

The above comparison by sex highlighted the significant underrepresentation of females among black sociologists, their later (average) entry into the field, the wider range of institutions awarding them degrees, and the less prestigious status of those institutions.

The limited background data obtained from 66 subjects in the questionnaire study indicated that, in addition to the majority being male, females were somewhat (but not significantly) younger than males in current ages and their ages at the time of receipt of their degrees. For the 9 (of 11) females and 50 (of 55) males reporting age, their median current ages were 35.0 and 42.0 years, respectively. The mean female age of 38.2 years (s. d. = 9.3 years) was 6.9 years less than the mean male age of 45.1 years (s. d. = 10.3 years). The median ages at receipt of degree were 28.0 and 32.5 years, respectively, for females and males, with the female mean of 29.7 years (s. d. = 6.3 years) being 4.8 years less than the male mean of 34.5 years (s. d. = 5.2 years). Males were more homogeneous by age at receipt of degree than were females, but greater variability characterized their current ages than was true for females.

Sex differentiation by marital status was readily apparent. For the ten females reporting marital status, 30 percent had never married, 30 percent were currently married, and 40 percent were separated, widowed, or divorced. Comparable data for the 51 males providing similar information were 5.9 percent either had never married or were separated, widowed, or divorced, and 88.2 percent were married. Thus, black sociologists were significantly more likely to have been married if they were male than female ($x^2 = 18.5478$, df = 2, p < .001). The percentage of 78.7 of all subjects married approximated the 80.0 percent reported as married by Conyers. It may also be noted, in passing, that remarriage was much more frequent among males.

Similarities and differences by sex were apparent by type of current employers. About 18 percent of both females and males were employed in predominantly black institutions. The majority of those males were in administrative capacities, such as departmental chairmen, deans, or directors of major programs. *None of the females were employed in administrative capacities,* which also suggests their lower median incomes as compared with their male counterparts. The remaining 82 percent of females were all located in predominantly white universities; the remaining males, with the exception of one retired male, were located either in predominantly white academic or nonacademic settings. None of the sampled females and few of the males were employed in the Deep South.

Unfortunately, no data were obtained about sources of support for graduate training or about the subjects' previous research and its chronology, funding patterns, costs, and utilization. From the sample as a whole, however, a much larger proportion of females than males were currently engaged in research. In fact, 100.0 percent of the females and 73.1 percent of the males reported current research. This sex difference disappeared when comparisons were restricted to those employed in nonadministrative positions in colleges and universities. Data available from 9 females and 52 males indicated that 66.7 percent of the former and 61.5 percent of the latter had published at least a portion of their dissertation content. This similarity by sex could be due to any number of factors, including the possibility that sex is not an important variable affecting publication. But the slightly higher rate of publication of dissertation content by females may also have been induced par-

tially by the more recent receipt of their degrees and by a con-
comitant (although currently subsiding) demand for publications
by blacks on blacks.

About 30 percent of the females (N=10) and 65 percent of the
males (N=52) indicated that they had served as principal investigator of at least one research project since obtaining the doctorate.
An additional 10 percent of the females had acted as coinvesti-
gators. Overall, females were far less likely to have collaborated on
research (and on publications as well).

The reported current research of females could not be distinguished from that of males by its emphasis upon blacks. That
generalization is equally apt for dissertations produced by both
sexes. Such an emphasis is readily understandable and is legitimate.
In addition to the fact that black sociologists are obviously themselves *black,* a significant proportion of their professors at major
institutions were themselves involved in race relations research and
teaching or involved in other research where they desired data about
blacks. A number of contemporary black sociologists were likely to
have been influenced in selecting areas of specialization by those
professors most receptive to them. Further, a number of contemporary black sociologists were trained under or came under the
direct or indirect influence of W. E. B. Du Bois, Charles S.
Johnson, or E. Franklin Frazier, all of whom were, *inter alia,* race
relations specialists. And, as Hines suggested, black sociologists
have most often utilized their immediate environments as data-
collecting locales.

Hence, it is not unusual that black sociologists—including black
females—have been and are interested in blacks, or that much of
their work has concentrated upon some aspect of black oppression in
the United States. A majority of the dissertations by black sociologists were undertaken independently of any collaboration on research projects involving their major professors. Such opportunities
have been far fewer for black than for white graduate students in
sociology. Thus, it is not unusual that black sociologists seeking
research subjects selected blacks. In this respect, many blacks have
been most cooperative. During at least the years preceding, during,
and shortly following my own sojourn as a graduate student, a

number of blacks were quite willing to participate as subjects if that participation aided any black in acquiring further education.

Recent opposition by some blacks to social science research on blacks has been directed primarily towards white social scientists, and especially towards those whites generously funded by public or private funds to undertake research about blacks. Confronted with increasing difficulties in obtaining data from black subjects (due to such causes as the purported fears of white investigators in entering black neighborhoods) and increasing sophistication among blacks themselves about research (such as beliefs that research should be relevant and lead to progressive social change), white principal investigators have increasingly and strategically utilized black interviewers to obtain data from black subjects. While such blacks have generally not been senior members of investigative teams and thus have had no authority in analyzing and interpreting data collected, it should also be noted that, in a few instances, contemporary black sociologists have had some access to data collected as a basis for their dissertations, as in the cases of Johnson and Pinckney.[8] Perhaps the best example of this occurrence among black female sociologists is the case of Ladner.[9]

The current research of black females differed only in degree from that of males. Females were more likely to focus upon specific problems involving or believed to involve black women, black youth, black aged, and black poor, and less likely to focus upon methodological issues (except as those issues related to inappropriate designs for investigating blacks). The males exhibited far greater interest in studies related to criminal behavior, manpower, rural settings, and, interestingly, student unrest. Few of both sexes were involved in investigating or evaluating educational programs, such as Black Studies or Project Head Start. Almost none were engaged in research utilizing subjects of other minority groups within the United States. One exception was a male investigator's project on "Interethnic relationships in New England, with special attention to Puerto Ricans in Boston." In those projects where whites were included as research subjects (and they were very few indeed), the predominant focus was upon their negative impact upon blacks.

Much current research undertaken by the sample could aid in

reducing significant gaps the sample identified as characteristic of available literature on blacks. No sex differences were apparent in these specifications. At least 80 percent of the sample characterized existing literature on blacks as highly inadequate in theoretical conceptions, methodological approaches, and data utilization. Most pinpointed such gaps as those of "utter misuse of quantification methods by whites in the study of blacks," "paucity of research and analysis by blacks," "lack of rigorous empirical indicators of values and lifestyles of blacks independent of socioeconomic variables," "research on middle-class blacks," "insufficient sampling of blacks to justify generalizations reached through supposedly valid empirical research," and "comprehensive studies of black family life."

Although any number of examples could be given to illustrate the varying kinds of concerns the sample expressed about available literature on blacks, two may suffice. The first illustration concerns "bad" literature about blacks. In investigating religious attitudes of a *nonrandom* sample of aged black and white subjects, subdivided occupationally on the basis of major lifetime employment as nonmanual or manual workers, Heyman and Jeffers reported that manual blacks were significantly more religious than manual whites.[10] Jackson's reanalysis of that data showed the inappropriate methodological procedure of merely dividing subjects by occupational categories of nonmanual and manual workers. The vast majority of white manual subjects had been employed in semiskilled and skilled positions. The vast majority of black manual subjects had been engaged in domestic or unskilled labor. When Heyman and Jeffers's subjects were compared by race within specific occupational categories of semiskilled and skilled workers and domestics and unskilled workers, no significant differences by race characterized their religious attitudes. Blacks were no more religious than whites in their sample. These investigators were differentially influenced by the "known fact" that in the South blacks are more religious than whites.[11]

The second illustration expresses the sample's concerns about the need for competent black critics of literature affecting blacks. In this respect, Taylor's definition of *quantitative racism* is useful ("intentional *or* unintentional misuse of statistical and quantitative methods in the behavioral sciences to show, either directly or in-directly, explicitly or implicitly, some kind or type of ethnic superi-ority, usually with respect to black-white differences").[12] In his cogent analysis of such common errors as "reification, incorrect calculations of 'heritability,' invalid syllogisms, equating SES with environment, misreading of tables and figures, problems of culture-bias, unnecessary statistical manipulations, incorrect causal infer-ences, inconsistent interpretations of regression toward the mean, and other errors,"[13] Taylor did not reject the scientific method. He rejected its misuses. He urged more sophisticated criticism by black social scientists of research related to blacks by those he defined as racist social scientists, such as Jensen. Black social scientists should go beyond merely indicating emotionally that "Jensen is wrong" by specifying precisely why Jensen is wrong. His cautions remind us that illegitimacy data never specify the race of the father, just as homicide data generally fail to specify clearly the race of the mur-derer.

Perhaps due to certain differences in their publication patterns, as discussed in greater detail below, black female sociologists were more reluctant in singling out what they regarded as their most important work than were black male sociologists in this sample. When asked to single out the most important work by any black sociologist, the agreement was far greater among females that the single, most important work was E. Franklin Frazier's *The Negro Family in the United States* (Chicago: University of Chicago Press, 1939). Interestingly enough, only one female singled out any work of W. E. B. Du Bois as the most important work, but about ten males specified Du Bois.

Taking the sample as a whole, and based upon responses from 60 of 66 subjects, the modal response (30.0 percent) for the most important work by any black sociologist was Frazier's *The Negro Family in the United States*, followed by Cox's *Caste, Class and Race* (23.3 percent), Frazier's *Black Bourgeoisie* (11.7 percent), Du Bois's *The Philadelphia Negro* (8.3 percent), and Drake and Cayton's *Black Metropolis* (6.7 percent). The remaining 20.0 per-cent singled out Du Bois's *The Souls of Black Folks* and *Black Reconstruction* (3.3 percent each), and Frazier's *Race and Culture*

Contacts (1.7 percent), Du Bois's *The Study of Negro Problems* (1.7 percent), *Suppression of the Slave Trade* (1.7 percent), and, in general, his early urban work (1.7 percent), the collective work of Charles S. Johnson (1.7 percent), Taylor's *Balance of Small Groups* (1.7 percent), McDaniel's "Structural Conduciveness and the Occurrence of Race Riots in America" (1.7 percent), and the writings of Nathan Hare (1.7 percent).[14]

When all works produced by the same author were grouped collectively, 43.3 percent of 60 respondents regarded Frazier as the most important black sociologist; 23.3 percent gave that honor to Cox, and 20.0 percent gave it to Du Bois. Noticeably absent, of course, was any work by a black female sociologist. Excepting Taylor's work, all publications cited were primarily concerned with the status of blacks.

This sample's specification of the most important sociological work by a black sociologist was not directly comparable to Conyers's specification of black sociologists making the most important contributions to sociology. His rank order, based upon the number of times each individual was cited as being among the "top five," placed Frazier in first position, followed by Johnson, Du Bois, and Cox. That ordering is at variance with this sample's specification of Frazier, Cox, Du Bois, and Drake and Cayton. The significantly lower ranking of Johnson in this sample may be due to important differences between it and Conyers's sample. In the latter, more subjects were much more likely to have studied or worked under or known about Johnson. The recent revival of interest in Du Bois's works has not yet extended to Johnson, perhaps because Johnson has never been regarded as an ideological hero by younger black scholars and militants and, less often perhaps, because those younger scholars and militants have never been exposed to his work. The significantly earlier death of Johnson than of Du Bois may also be a factor. Whatever the case may be, Frazier continues to be regarded—perhaps by black and white sociologists alike—as the most important black sociologist past or present.

This comparison of black female and male sociologists in the sample can be summarized by emphasizing the significant differences in marital statuses and employment positions and locations.

Females were far less likely to have been married, with a spouse, and far less likely to have been employed in administrative capacities within academic institutions or to have been employed at all in nonacademic settings. While not significantly different, they were younger than their male counterparts and received their degrees at an earlier average age than the latter. Their current research projects were far more likely to have been focused upon problematic considerations affecting blacks, but they were in essential agreement with the males about significant research gaps characterizing literature about blacks. Although subjects of both sexes most often singled out Frazier as the author of the most important publication by a black sociologist, the females were even more likely to have singled out Frazier and less likely to have specified such individuals as Du Bois.

Dissertations and Publications by Black Female Sociologists

As previously indicated, the primary purpose of this section is the provision of a partial bibliography and the sharing of certain impressionistic judgments. The bibliography is incomplete because it does not include works published after this study was completed and because of my failure in uncovering publications in my library research for those females who did not provide their own bibliographies due to such reasons as changes in their surnames unknown to me, failures to respond to the questionnaire, or my failure to send questionnaires because of unknown addresses.

Dissertation titles by author, institution, and year are listed (under "Dissertations") for each of the 21 black females identified as having received a Ph.D. degree in sociology in 1945 or since. While varying in problems selected for investigation and in methodological approaches, most of these dissertations were concerned specifically with blacks. The vast majority were concerned with social organization (including social stratification) or with social psychology (including social movements). Some were largely descriptive, while others were more heavily oriented toward theory, including those designed to test existing theories; all were generally pioneering in that they either explored fields in which relatively little research had been done or they applied research to blacks. Almost none involved any longitudinal research, but almost all employed quantitative methods of analysis. Primarily issue-oriented, the topics generally reflected issues of great concern either within sociology or within the larger American society at the time the authors undertook and completed their dissertations. Finally, almost all were concerned with attitudes and behaviors in urban environments only, and only one was set outside the United States.

A number of topics were obviously missing from these investigations, but several in particular may be noted. None focused upon current problems of black women as related to education, income, and employment (including professionalization), and none focused upon black sociologists, including women.

A publication count was based upon bibliographies provided by the sample information obtained from 14 black sociologists not in the sample, and the library research on publications by all of the 145 black sociologists identified as being eligible for inclusion as contemporary black sociologists. As of May 1972, 83 works were located for the 21 black female sociologists and 512 works for the 124 black male sociologists.

The mean number of articles by females appearing in journals (2.0) was lower than the mean of 3.4 for males. However, the female mean of 1.9 for "all other works" (books, monographs, chapters in books, magazine articles, and articles in in-house but nonprofessional journals) was higher than the male mean of 0.9. The overall mean of 4.3 works per male sociologist was slightly higher than that of 4.0 for females.

Epps and Howze, who found no significant differences in the number of publications produced by black and white sociologists in their sample, indicated that about two-fifths of each group had no publications. About 29 percent of the blacks and 24 percent of the whites had from one to three publications, and the remaining in both groups had four or more publications. Sociologists in their sample were not restricted to doctorates, and publication data were not reported by sex. Their data and the data cited above in this study, however, are similar in terms of skewness. That is, a minority of sociologists have relatively high publishing rates, while a majority rarely publish.

While no significant differences appeared to characterize gross publication rates by sex in this study, there were differences in publication sources. Table 2 provides information about major publication sources by sex for 43 articles written by black female and 396 articles written by black male sociologists. The most frequent source for females was *Phylon*, followed by the *Journal of Social and Behavioral Sciences*, with *The Black Scholar* and *The Gerontologist* in third position. The first three journals are black journals, although each publishes works by nonblacks. The journals in which males were most likely to have published, also in descending order, were *The Journal of Negro Education*, *Phylon*, and the *Journal of Social and Behavioral Sciences*. These journals were established by blacks and have always operated from black institutions. Thus it appears that the publication sources most likely to be available to black female and male sociologists are those which are "black-controlled."

TABLE 2.
Publication Sites of Articles Located for Black Female and Male Sociologists

Publication site	% Female	% Male
Percent	100.0	100.0
Phylon	11.6	7.6
*Journal of Social and Behavioral Sciences**	9.3	6.8
The Black Scholar	7.0	1.2
The Gerontologist	7.0	0.2
Aging and Human Development	4.7	0.0
The Family Coordinator	4.7	0.0
The Journal of Negro Education	2.3	8.8
American Sociological Review	2.3	5.3
Social Forces	0.0	5.3
Journal of Human Relations	2.3	5.1
American Journal of Sociology	0.0	2.8
Sociology and Social Research	2.3	2.5
All other	46.5	54.4

Note: For sociologists, N = 21 (females) and 124 (males); for articles, N = 43 (by females) and 396 (by males).
*Formerly *Journal of the Association of Social Science Teachers*, whose current editor (1973-76) is Dr. Johnnie Daniel, a black male sociologist.

As shown in table 2, the major journals in sociology contain almost nothing by black female sociologists. In fact, only 4.6 percent of female articles appeared in the *American Sociological Review* and *Sociology and Social Research*; none were in *Social Forces* and the *American Journal of Sociology*. Black male sociologists were significantly more likely to have been published in those major journals in sociology than were females. Almost 16 percent of their articles appeared in the just-mentioned journals. The section on "Publications" in the bibliography contains a listing of all publications located for black female sociologists. It may be examined for additional information about their publication sources.

Although I could not examine all publications by black female and male sociologists, I did read carefully a number of them. I was impressed especially with their concentration upon social issues or problems of particular relevance to blacks, upon their explicit recognition that values of investigators affect research about blacks and black-white relationships (even when the scientists are white!), and their great concern about appropriate utilization of their findings. Most of their research may be regarded as "small-scale," due perhaps to great difficulties encountered by most contemporary black sociologists in obtaining large research grants. Yet the quality of their research is generally good. Their research definitely warrants consideration from those most interested in striving toward better knowledge and understanding of blacks.

Further Development of Black Female Sociologists

It may be relevant to note here that very few black females ever receive higher education. In 1971, only 2.9 percent of black females 25 years of age and older had completed four years of college and only an additional 1.4 percent had completed five or more years, as compared with 3.0 and 1.7 percent, respectively, for their black male counterparts.

Unfortunately, no data by sex showing the number of blacks receiving undergraduate degrees in sociology were available, but some indication of the greater proportion of females receiving such degrees from predominantly black institutions was available. For example, in 1968-69, 72.6 percent of the recipients of bachelor's degrees in sociology were female, and a majority of those receiving a master's degree in sociology in the black institutions were also female. It appears that, in the past at least, the majority of black recipients of bachelor's degrees in sociology were female, but that only a very small proportion of those receiving doctoral degrees were females.

Racial and sexual discrimination adversely affecting higher educational attainment among black women must be abated. We clearly need to know more about processes affecting the development of black female sociologists. Factors contributing toward greater numerical increases in black female sociologists include greater access to scholarships and fellowships for graduate education (which, when necessary, should include adequate provisions for housekeeping and child-care services); greater identification of potentially good female students in their undergraduate years and in their high school years and encouragement from faculty motivating them to become professional sociologists; greater visibility of existing black female sociologists who may serve as appropriate models; more selective recruitment of sociology majors in undergraduate departments of sociology, including those in black institutions; and greater training of these students as budding sociologists, making certain that they are initially aware of the most appropriate routes to follow in becoming a sociologist and that they know clearly the distinctions between sociology and social welfare or social work.

Summary

After noting the dearth of data available about black female sociologists, this study focused upon comparisons between black female and male sociologists, utilizing limited data obtained from a questionnaire study of 66 black sociologists and from library research. Among comparisons noted were those of the wider range and generally less prestigious status of universities awarding Ph.D. degrees to females, somewhat younger ages of females currently and at time of receipt of degree; significant differences in marital status since females were far more likely to have been without spouses; and the much greater constriction of females as measured by their employment locations and positions since they were far less likely to have been employed in administrative capacities within academic institutions or to have been employed at all in nonacademic settings. The sexes were generally indistinguishable by such variables as current research and specification of research gaps characterizing available literature on blacks. However, females were more likely to have been engaged in research focusing specifically upon problematic considerations affecting blacks. Although subjects of both sexes most often singled out E. Franklin Frazier's *The Negro Family in the United States* as the single most important publication by a black sociologist, females were much more likely to have singled him out. In their own research, most of the sampled black sociologists could be said to have followed Frazier's lead in their concerns about meaningful research on blacks by blacks.

The bibliography is of especial significance in providing dissertational and publication data for most of the black females identified as sociologists who completed their work in or since the year 1945, and, in addition, the text provided some limited comparison of publication sources for black female and male sociologists. While both groups differed, in that males appeared to have had somewhat greater access to publication in major journals in sociology, they were alike in their modal dependence upon black journals, particularly upon *Phylon, Journal of Social and Behavioral Sciences, The Journal of Negro Education,* and *The Black Scholar*.

In voicing concerns about further development of black female sociologists, several broad suggestions for increasing the supply were proffered. Greater development and utilization of black female sociologists could well be a major factor in improving significantly our knowledge and understanding of blacks and of black-white relationships in the United States.

Notes

1   See, for example, Jessie Bernard, *Academic Women* (University Park, Pennsylvania: The Pennsylvania State University, 1964); or G. Franklin Edwards, "Occupational Mobility of Negro Professional Workers," in Ernest W. Burgess and Donald J. Bogue, eds., *Contributions to Urban Sociology* (Chicago: The University of Chicago Press, 1964), pp. 443-58.

2   For an extensive discussion of comparative educational, occupational, income, and employment levels by race and by sex, see Jacquelyne J. Jackson, "Black Women in a Racist Society," in Charles V. Willie, Bernard Kramer, and Bertram Brown, eds., *Racism and Mental Health* (Pittsburgh: University of Pittsburgh Press, 1973).

3   Since completing this study, I have located four additional black sociologists. One was Delores P. Aldridge, from Purdue University, 1971; one was from Ohio State University in 1972; one, either in 1971 or 1972, from Washington University; and one from Mississippi State University, 1971.

4   For an additional publication, based upon a combination of their previous findings, see James Conyers and Edgar Epps, Chapter 8 above.

5   James E. Conyers, "Negro Doctorates in Sociology in America: A Social Portrait," *Phylon* 29 (1968): 209-33; Ralph H. Hines, "The Negro Scholar's Contribution to Pure and Applied Sociology," *Journal of Social and Behavioral Sciences* 8 (1967): 30-35; Edgar G. Epps and Glenn H. Howze, *Survey of Black Social Scientists* (Tuskegee Institute, Alabama: Carver Research Foundation of Tuskegee Institute, 1971); and Clyde W. Franklin, Jr., and Alice P. Franklin, "The Status of Black Sociologists in the United States and the Black Brain Drain Controversy," *The Journal of Afro-American Issues* 1 (1972): 61-67.

6   While the very scarcity of black female sociologists may have accounted for failure to analyze them, it is significant to note that no concerns were expressed about the need for developing black females as sociologists in these works.

7   See Jackson, "Black Women," and idem, "Social Gerontology and the Negro: A Review," *The Gerontologist* 7 (1967): 168-78.

8   See Robert B. Johnson, "The Nature of the Minority Community— Internal Structure, Reactions, Leadership, and Action" (Ph.D. diss., Cornell University, 1955), and Alphonso Pinckney, "The Anatomy of Prejudice—Majority Attitudes Toward Minorities in Selected American Cities" (Ph.D. diss., Cornell University, 1961), which evolved out of the research directed by Robin M. Williams, whose larger study was eventually published as *Strangers Next Door: Ethnic Relations in American Communities* (Englewood Cliffs, New Jersey: Prentice-Hall, 1964).

9   See Joyce A. Ladner, "On Becoming a Woman in the Ghetto: Modes of Adaptation" (Ph.D. diss., Washington University, 1968), which grew out of a research project directed by Lee Rainwater on Pruitt-Igoe.

10   Dorothy Heyman and Frances Jeffers, "Study of the Relative Influence of Race and Socio-economic Status Upon the Activities and Attitudes of a Southern Aged Population," *Journal of Gerontology* 19 (1964): 225-29.

11   Jackson, "Social Gerontology."

12   Howard F. Taylor, "Quantative Racism: A Partial Documentation," *The Journal of Afro-American Issues* 1 (1972), p. 1.

13   Ibid.

14   Oliver C. Cox, *Caste and Race* (Garden City, N.Y.: Doubleday, 1948). E. Franklin Frazier, *Black Bourgeoisie: the Rise of a New Middle Class in the United States* (New York, 1957). W. E. B. Du Bois, *The Philadelphia Negro: A*

Social Study (New York: Schocken, 1967; originally published in 1899). St. Clair Drake and Horace Cayton, *Black Metropolis* (New York: Harcourt, Brace, 1945). W. E. B. Du Bois, *The Souls of Black Folk: Essays and Sketches* (Chicago: McClurg, 1903) and *Black Reconstruction* (New York: Harcourt, Brace, 1935). E. Franklin Frazier, *Race and Culture Contacts in the Modern World* (New York: Knopf, 1957). W. E. B. Du Bois, *The Negro American Family* (New York: Negro Universities Press, 1969), and *The Suppression of the African Slave Trade to the United States of America, 1638-1870* (New York: Longmans, Green, 1896). Howard F. Taylor, *Balance in Small Groups* (New York: Van Nostrand Reinhold, 1970). Clyde O. McDaniel, Jr., "Structural Strain, Structural Conduciveness, and the Occurrences of Race Riots in America," *Psychology: A Journal of Human Behavior* 8 (1971).

Bibliography

Dissertations

Aldridge, Delores P. "Alienation of Self-esteem of College Students as Related to Socio-economic Background, Race and College Experiences." Purdue University, 1971.

Bagley, Cora E. "Consensus and Organizational Effectiveness." University of Wisconsin, 1968.

Beatty-Brown, Florence R. "The Negro as Portrayed by the St. Louis Post-Dispatch from 1920-1950." University of Illinois, 1951.

Carter, Barbara. "On the Grounds: Informal Culture in a Girls' Reform School." Brandeis University, 1972.

Carter, Wilmoth. "The Negro Main Street of a Contemporary Urban Community." University of Chicago, 1959.

Clarke, Jacquelyne J. "A Comparison of the Goals and Techniques of Three Negro Civil-Rights Organizations in Alabama in 1959." The Ohio State University, 1960.

Cox, Henrietta S. "Social Classes as Subcultures—Variations in Value-Orientations in Selected Areas of Mother-Child Behavior." Washington University, 1964.

Curwood, Sarah T. "Role Expectation as a Factor in the Relationship between Mother and Teacher." Radcliffe College, 1956.

Diggs, Mary H. "A Comparative Study of Delinquent Behavior Manifestations in One Hundred Delinquent and One Hundred Non-Delinquent Negro Boys." Bryn Mawr College, 1945.

Forrest, Audrey W. "Social Perspectives—A Comparative Analysis." University of Nebraska, 1964.

Gordon, Joan L. "Some Socio-economic Aspects of Selected Negro Families in

Savannah, Georgia, With Special Reference to the Effects of Occupational Stratification on Childrearing." University of Pennsylvania, 1955.

Hamilton, Ruth S. "Patterns of Participation Among Selected Voluntary Associations in Accra, Ghana." Northwestern University, 1966.

Hardin, Anna F. "Social Factors in Student Counseling Needs: A Comparative Study of Student Counseling Clients and Non-Clients Among College Freshmen." Washington State University, 1956.

Hill, Adelaide C. "The Negro Upper Class in Boston—Its Development and Present Social Structure." Radcliffe College, 1952.

Johnson, Clara L. "Racial Attitudes of Negroes as a Function of Objective Power Relations, Feelings of Powerlessness, and Social Class." University of Georgia, 1970.

Joseph, Gloria. "A Study of Group Conflicts and Leadership in a Riot-Victimized Northern City." Cornell University, 1967.

Ladner, Joyce A. "On Becoming a Woman in the Ghetto: Modes of Adaptation." Washington University, 1968.

Perry, Wilhelmina E. "The Urban Negro With Special Reference to the Universalism-Particularism Pattern Variable." University of Texas at Austin, 1967.

Queeley, Mary A. "Innovation in an Urban Slum School." University of Chicago, 1965.

Rose, LaFrances R. "A Test of Three of Harry Stack Sullivan's Developmental Theory of Personality: Juvenile Era, Preadolescence, and Early Adolescence Stages." State University of Iowa, 1964.

Wilkinson, Doris Y. "Expectation Congruence: Implications for the Analysis of Intergenerational Continuity." Case-Western Reserve University, 1968.

Williams, Dorothy S. "Ecology of Negro Communities in Los Angeles County, 1940-1959." University of Southern California, 1961.

Publications *

Carter, Wilmoth. "Negro Main Street as a Symbol of Discrimination." *Phylon* 21 (1960): 234-42.

———. *The Negro of the New South.* New York: Exposition Press, 1967.

———. *The Urban Negro in the South.* New York: Vantage, 1962.

Clarke, Jacquelyne J. "On the Sociological Nature of Man," in *The Nature of Man,* edited by Leonard H. Spearman. Baton Rouge, Louisiana: Southern University, 1961.

* Of those individuals listed in the "Dissertations" section, publications data were obtained from the persons themselves for Bagley (now Marrett), B. Carter, W. Carter, Clarke (now Jackson), Cox, Curwood, Diggs, Hamilton, Johnson, Ladner, Queeley, Rose, and Wilkinson.

————. "Standard Operational Procedures in Tragic Situations." *Phylon* 22 (1961): 318-28.

————. *These Rights They Seek.* Washington, D.C.: Public Affairs Press, 1962.

Curwood, Sarah T. *Head Start in Action. A Survey and Evaluation of a Head Start Program in the Commonwealth of Massachusetts.* Massachusetts Committee on Children and Youth, Monograph I, October, 1966.

————. "Mothers and Ghetto Schools." *Integrated Education* 3 (1965): 35-43.

————. "A Report on Lippitt Hill." Providence, Rhode Island: Providence School Department, September, 1963.

Diggs, Mary H. "Some Problems and Needs of Negro Children as Revealed by Comparative Delinquency and Crime Statistics." *Journal of Negro Education* 19 (1950): 290-97.

Hamilton, Ruth S. "The Savannah Story: Education and Desegregation." In *Our Children's Children,* edited by Raymond W. Mack, pp. 109-40. New York: Random House, 1968.

————. *Urbanization in West Africa.* Evanston, Illinois: Northwestern University Press, 1965.

Hill, Adelaide C. "Negro Fertility and Family Size Preferences: Implications for Programming of Health and Social Services." In *The Negro American,* edited by Talcott Parsons and Kenneth B. Clark, pp. 205-24, Cambridge, Massachusetts: Houghton Mifflin, 1966.

*Jackson, Jacquelyne J. "Aged Blacks: A Potpourri Towards the Reduction of Racial Inequities." *Phylon* 32 (1971): 260-80.

————. "Aged Negroes: Their Cultural Departures from Statistical Stereotypes and Selected Rural-Urban Differences." *The Gerontologist* 10 (1970): 140-45. Reprinted in *Research Planning and Action for the Elderly,* edited by Donald P. Kent, Robert Kastenbaum, and Sylvia Sherwood, pp. 501-13.

————. "The Association of Social and Behavioral Scientists." *Race* 13 (1971-72): 93-94.

————. "The Blacklands of Gerontology." *Aging and Human Development* 2 (1971): 156-71.

————. "Black Professional Organizations: A Case Study." *The Journal of Afro-American Issues* 1 (1972): 75-91.

————. "A Black Sociologist Crystallizes Social and Psychological Needs to the Characteristics and Special Problems of Ghetto Youth." In *Multimedia Materials for Afro-American Studies,* edited by Harry A. Johnson. New York: R. R. Bowker Company, 1970.

————. "Black Women in a Racist Society." In *Racism and Mental Health,*

---

* See also entries for Clarke, Jacquelyne J.

edited by Charles V. Willie, Bernard Kramer, and Bertram Brown. Pittsburgh: University of Pittsburgh Press, 1973.

———. "But Where Are the Men?" *The Black Scholar* 3 (1971): 30-41.

———. "Comparative Lifestyles and Family and Friend Relationships Among Older Black Women." *The Family Coordinator* 21 (1972): 477-85.

———. "Compensatory Care for the Black Aged." *Occasional Papers in Gerontology*. No. 10. Institute of Gerontology, The University of Michigan-Wayne State University, pp. 15-23.

———. "An Exploration of Attitudes Toward Faculty Desegregation at Negro Colleges." *Phylon* 28 (1967): 338-52.

———. "Face to Face, Mind to Mind, It 'Sho Nuff Ain't No Zombie Jamboree." *Journal of National Medical Association* 64 (1972): 145-50.

———. "Family Organization and Ideology." in *Comparative Studies of Blacks and Whites in the United States, 1966-1970*, edited by Ralph M. Dreger and Kent S. Miller. New York: Academic Press, 1972.

———. "Kinship Relations Among Negro Americans." *Journal of Social and Behavioral Sciences* 16 (1970): 5-17.

———. "Marital Life Among Aged Blacks." *The Family Coordinator* 21 (1972): 21-27.

———. "Negro Aged and Social Gerontology, A Critical Evaluation." *Journal of Social and Behavioral Sciences* 13 (1968): 42-47.

———. "Negro Aged in North Carolina." *North Carolina Journal of Mental Health* 4 (1970): 43-52.

———. "Negro Aged Parents and Adult Children: Their Affective Relationships." *Varia* (Spring Issue, 1969): 1-14.

———. "Negro Aged: Toward Needed Research in Social Gerontology." *The Gerontologist* 11 (1971): 52-57.

———. "Our Association, 'Where It's At, Baby!'" *Journal of Social and Behavioral Sciences* 16 (1970): 53-60.

———. "Research, Training, Service, and Action Concerns About Black Aging and Aged Persons: An Overview." In *Proceedings of the Research Conference on Minority Group Aged in the South*, edited by Jacquelyne J. Jackson, pp. 41-47. Durham, North Carolina: Duke University, 1972.

———. "Sex and Social Class Variations in Black Adult Parent-Adult Child Relationships. *Aging and Human Development* 2 (1971): 96-107.

———. "Social Gerontology and the Negro: A Review." *The Gerontologist* 7 (1967): 168-78. Reprinted in *Sociological Symposium*, No. 2 (Spring 1969): 101-21.

———. "Social Implications of Housing Relocation Among Low-Income Southern, Urban Blacks." *The Gerontologist* 12 (1972): 32-37.

———. "Two Black Boycotts: A Contrast of Success and Failure." *Afro-American Studies, An Interdisciplinary Journal* 2 (1971): 87-94.

———. "Where Are the Black Men?" *Ebony* 27 (1972): 99-102, 104, 106.

Jackson, Jacquelyne J. and Ball, Mercerdee E. "A Comparison of Rural and Urban Georgia Aged Negroes." *Journal of the Association of Social Science Teachers* 12 (1966): 30-37.

Jackson, Jacquelyne J., and Davis, Abraham, Jr. "Characteristic Patterns of Aged, Rural Negroes in Macon County." In *A Survey of Selected Socioeconomic Characteristics of Macon County, Alabama, 1965,* edited by Beulah C. Johnson, pp. 122-57. Tuskegee, Alabama: Macon County Community Action Program Office, 1966.

Jackson, Jacquelyne J. and Jackson, Viola E. "Needed: Personalized Modes of Learning." *Educational Leadership* 30 (1972): 20-22.

Jackson, Jacquelyne J., editor. *Proceedings of the Research Conference on Minority Group Aged in the South.* Durham, North Carolina: Duke Unversity, 1972.

Ladner, Joyce A. "Birmingham Funeral." *New American* 3 (1963): 2.

———. *Black Repression: An Analysis of Institutional Racism in the Seventies.* Third World Press, forthcoming.

———. "Intervention Strategy and Unemployment." St. Louis: Social Science Institute, Washington University, 1964.

———. "Planned Parenthood and Intervention Research." St. Louis: Social Science Institute, Washington University, 1964.

———. "Racism and Comprehensive Planning." *Journal of the American Institute of Planners.* 35 (1969): 68-74.

———. "Tanzanian Women and Nation Building." *The Black Scholar* 3 (1971): 22-29

———. *Tomorrow's Tomorrow: The Black Woman.* Garden City, New York: Doubleday Publishing Company, 1971.

———. "What 'Black Power' Means to Negroes in Mississippi." *Trans-action* 5 (1967): 7-15. Reprinted in *Blacks in the United States,* edited by Norval D. Glenn and Charles M. Bonjean, pp. 444-57. San Francisco: Chandler Publishing Co., 1969.

———. "White America's Response to Black Militancy." In *Black Americans,* edited by John F. Szwed, pp. 205-18. New York: Basic Books, 1970.

———. "Women in Poverty: Its Roots and Effects." In *What Is Happening to American Women,* edited by Anne Scott. Atlanta: Southern Publishers Press, 1970.

Ladner, Joyce A., and Hammond, Boone E. "Socialization into Sexual Behavior." In *The Individual, Society, and Sex: Background Readings for Sex*

Educators, edited by Carlfred Broderick and Jessie Bernard, pp. 41–52. Baltimore: Johns Hopkins University Press, 1969.

Ladner, Joyce A., and Stafford, Walter W. "Black Repression in the Cities." *The Black Scholar* 1 (1970): 38-52.

(Poussaint, Alvin F.) and Ladner, Joyce A. "Black Power: A Failure for Racial Integration Within the Civil Rights Movement." *Archives of General Psychiatry* 18 (1968): 385-91. Reprinted as "Helping Hands Were Out of Touch" in *National Observer,* 12 August 1968.

Ladner, Joyce A., editor. *The Death of White Sociology.* New York: Random House, 1973.

Marrett, Cora B. "The Brown Power Revolt: A True Social Movement?" *Journal of Human Relations* 19 (1971): 356-66.

———. "On the Specification of Interorganizational Dimensions." *Sociology and Social Research* 56 (1971): 83-99.

Marrett, Cora B; Hage, Jerald; and Aiken, Michael "Organization Structure and Communications." *American Sociological Review* 36 (1971): 860-71.

Queeley, Mary A. "Nongrading in An Urban Slum School." In *Innovation in Mass Education,* edited by David Street, pp. 52-90. New York: John Wiley and Sons, 1969.

Rose, LaFrances R. *Interpersonal Relations Among School Children in an Iowa City.* A Research Report of the Iowa Urban Community Research Center, 1965.

Wilkinson, Doris Y. "Alienation and Presidential Choices." *Independent Journal of Social Research* 11 (1970).

———. "Coming of Age in a Racist Society." *Youth and Society* 3 (1971): 100-118.

———. "Dating Status of American College Women As a Predictor of Interactional Decline with Parents." *International Journal of Comparative Sociology* 11 (1970): 300-306.

———. "Political Assassins and Status Incongruence: A Sociological Interpretation." *British Journal of Sociology* 21 (1970): 400-412.

———. "The Poverty of American Sociologism." *International Behavioral Scientist* 1 (1969): 74-84.

———. "Sociological Imperialism: A Brief Comment on the Field." *Sociological Quarterly* 9 (1968): 397-400.

———. "Sociological Orientation to Artistic Creations." *Independent Journal of Social Research* 10 (1969): 40-47.

———. "The Status Characteristics and Primary Group Relationships of American Political Assassins." *Political Scientist* 6 (1969): 37-47.

———. "Status Differences and the Black Hate Stare: A Conversation of Gestures." *Phylon* 30 (1969): 191-96.

———. "Tactics of Protest as Media: The Case of the Black Revolution." *Sociological Focus* 3 (1970): 13-21.

———. "Through the Looking Glass Self Darkly: A Glossary for the Profession." *Sociological Focus* (1972): 67-78.

———. *Workbook for Introductory Sociology.* Minneapolis: Burgess Publishing Company, 1968.

Wilkinson, Doris Y., editor. *Black Revolt: Strategies of Protest.* Berkeley, California: McCutchan Publishing Company, 1969.

Other References

Bernard, Jessie. *Academic Women.* University Park, Pennsylvania: The Pennsylvania State University, 1964.

Conyers, James E. "Negro Doctorates in Sociology in America: A Social Portrait." *Phylon* 29 (1968): 209-33.

Conyers, James E., and Epps, Edgar G. "A Profile of Black Sociologists," in Blackwell and Janowitz, eds., *Black Sociologists.* Chicago: University of Chicago Press, 1974.

Cox, Oliver C. *Caste, Class and Race.* Garden City, N.Y.: Doubleday, 1948.

Drake, St. Clair, and Cayton, Horace. *Black Metropolis.* New York: Harcourt, Brace, 1945.

Du Bois, W. E. B. *Black Reconstruction.* New York: Harcourt, Brace, 1935.

———. *The Negro American Family, 1908.* New York: Negro Universities Press, 1969. Originally published by the Atlanta University Press, as a social study made by the 1909 and 1910 classes of Atlanta University, together with the Proceedings of the 1908 Conference for the Study of the Negro Problems.

———. *The Philadelphia Negro: A Social Study.* New York: Schocken, 1967. Originally published in 1899.

———. *The Souls of Black Folk: Essays and Sketches.* Chicago: McClurg, 1903.

———. *Suppression of the African Slave Trade to the United States of America, 1638-1870.* New York: Longmans, Green, 1896.

Edwards, G. Franklin. "Occupational Mobility of Negro Professional Workers." In *Contributions to Urban Sociology,* edited by Ernest W. Burgess and Donald J. Bogue, pp. 443-58. Chicago: The University of Chicago Press, 1964.

Epps, Edgar G., and Howze, Glenn H. *Survey of Black Social Scientists.* Tuskegee Institute, Alabama: Carver Research Foundation of Tuskegee Institute, 1971.

Franklin, Clyde W., Jr., and Franklin, Alice P. "The Status of Black Sociologists in the United States and the Black Brain Drain Controversy." *The Journal of Afro-American Issues* 1 (1972): 61-67.

Frazier, E. Franklin. *Black Bourgeoisie: The Rise of a New Middle Class in the United States.* New York, 1957.

————. *The Negro Family in the United States.* Chicago: University of Chicago Press, 1939.

————. *Race and Culture Contacts in the Modern World.* New York: Knopf, 1957.

Heyman, Dorothy, and Jeffers, Frances. "Study of the Relative Influence of Race and Socio-economic Status Upon the Activities and Attitudes of a Southern Aged Population." *Journal of Gerontology* 19 (1964): 225-29.

Hines, Ralph H. "The Negro Scholar's Contribution to Pure and Applied Sociology." *Journal of Social and Behavioral Sciences* 8 (1967): 30-35.

Johnson, Robert B. "The Nature of the Minority Community—Internal Structure, Reactions, Leadership, and Action." Ph.D. dissertation, Cornell University, 1955.

McDaniel, Clyde O., Jr. "Structural Strain, Structural Conduciveness, and the Occurrence of Race Riots in America." *Psychology: A Journal of Human Behavior* 8 (1971).

Pinckney, Alphonso. "The Anatomy of Prejudice—Majority Attitudes Toward Minorities in Selected American Cities." Ph.D. dissertation, Cornell University, 1961.

Taylor, Howard F. *Balance in Small Groups.* New York: Van Nostrand Reinhold, 1970. Translated into Japanese by Reimei Shobo, Inc. of Tokyo, Japan.

Williams, Robin M., Jr., et al. *Strangers Next Door: Ethnic Relations in American Communities.* Englewood Cliffs, New Jersey: Prentice-Hall, 1964.

IV. Theoretical Issues

11

Walter L. Wallace

SOME ELEMENTS OF

SOCIOLOGICAL THEORY IN

STUDIES OF BLACK AMERICANS

This paper attempts to analyze a few hypotheses put forward in the scholarly literature about Black people, and about Black-White* relations, in the United States. My attention will be limited to certain aspects of the substantive content of these hypotheses, as distinct from their empirical truth or falsity; distinct from the motivations of their authors; and distinct from their logical and practical testability. Thus, the only aim of this paper is to advance our understanding of the meaning—and in a few cases, the practical implications—of some leading ideas that have been expressed about Black Americans. I explicitly and deliberately leave to other times, other places, and partly to other persons, the determination of why and how these ideas are expressed, and how verifiably true they may be.

My analysis will be couched in sociological terms—more precisely, in terms of part of a system of conceptual elements that I have found useful in understanding sociological theory and sociological work in general. Of course, not all studies of Black Americans

---

* By capitalizing "Black" and "White," I intend to abstract only the contemporary, American, social-identity designations of those terms and to give as much honor to them as to other capitalized social-identity designations such as Anglo-Saxon, Jew, Puerto Rican, Chicano, Mexican-American, American Indian, Italian-American. In addition, I hope the capitalization will help separate the terms' metaphorical social-identity references from their metaphysical connotations of evil and goodness, mystery and clarity, dullness and enlightenment, as well as from their strictly psychophysical denotations of totally absorbent and totally reflective visual colors. For both of these purposes, of course, "Afro-American" is superior to "Black American" except that the idea of "Black-White relations" cannot be so neatly expressed with it.

are explicitly sociological or theoretical. Some belong more directly to history, psychology, or political science in their orientations, and some in each discipline claim to be only descriptions, devoid of theory. But implicit sociological propostions can be discerned in almost any study dealing with Black Americans, largely because the term "Black Americans" itself unavoidably implies social relations, both among members of that category and between them and members of other categories. Thus, the term "Black Americans" readily calls up "the Black community" on the one hand, and the "White community" and "Black-White relations" on the other, as correlative terms of sociological import. It is this sociological import—whether implicit or explicit—and more particularly some of the theoretic concepts and propositions contained in it, that I wish to analyze here.

The instrument used in this analysis is part of a system first developed for the purpose of systematically differentiating and integrating the principal substantive orientations in modern sociological theories (Wallace 1969:1-59). The fact that this system originated in such an effort should not be overlooked because it helps to explain the limitations of this paper that were mentioned earlier. Thus, suppose I am asked *why* I shall not try to say anything new about the truth-value of this or that statement about Black Americans, and *why* I shall not approach any such statement either "on its own terms" or in terms of psychological theory, or political science theory, or historiographic theory (or morality, for that matter). The answer is because I start out in this effort from a systematic analysis of sociological theory, not from a study of empirical data, not from my unsystematic personal convictions about the facts, and not from my scanty knowledge of other, nonsociological, frames of reference.

Certain disadvantages and advantages flow immediately from this point of departure. On the one hand, the application of ideas derived from the analysis of sociological theory to studies of Black Americans risks becoming not an "application," but an "imposition" that misrepresents these studies and distorts our view of them to fit some narrow, discipline-bound perspective. On the other hand, we desperately need a common interpretative framework for the rapidly expanding literatures and vocabularies of Black studies as well as sociology; otherwise, we must soon abandon hope of comprehending either of them. Therefore, I propose to risk the disadvantage In the whirl of words and phrases whose popularity so quickly rises and falls (Who now writes about "colored people" or "jim crow"?) we must somehow devise a system for getting to the heart of hypotheses, old and new, about Black Americans. Such a system should enable us to understand and compare hypotheses in relatively unambiguous and agreed-upon ways. Ideally, we ought to be able to reduce every such hypothesis—however complex or simple, however familiar or original—to its underlying "skeleton," that is, to some relatively unambiguous and readily understandable combination of elemental concepts. Indeed, I believe that until theoretically oriented sociologists who are interested in studying the Black community and relations between the Black and White communities can speak in terms of such theoretic elements underlying the full range of rhetoric and research in this field, we shall contribute only the most superficial insights (or only duller polemics) to the struggle for Black freedom and to the development of scientific sociology.

I have said that only *part* of an analytical system will be employed here. More specifically, this essay concentrates on two complementary sets of theoretic elements in sociology: attention is called first to the distinction between social organization and culture as *types* of social phenomena, and then to the distinctions between interpersonal, institutional, community, societal, and intersocietal *levels* of social phenomena. By applying these well-established and general sociological concepts, I hope to produce an analysis of a few hypotheses about Black Americans that will transcend the passing vagaries of personal style and collective fashion as well as the more persistent distinctions of academic discipline.

Note that my analysis is of single hypotheses, not of interrelated sets of hypotheses or theories, and emphatically not of their authors' larger bodies of work. It is important to bear this in mind, because any given theory always encompasses several hypotheses of differing content, and the work of any given author always embraces a variety of hypotheses if not, indeed, a variety of theories. As a consequence, when the same work or author is cited below in different analytic contexts, that does not necessarily indicate internal contradiction or indecisiveness, but simply substantive variety. Of course, analyses of theories and of authors' bodies of work (analyses that might conceivably uncover such internal contradictions or indecisiveness) can be built up from analyses of single hypotheses, but that is not the aim of this paper. My aim here is a far more modest and elementary, though fundamental, step in that direction.

It should also be understood that this analysis will not even approximate completeness—either in the elements of sociological theory that are examined or in the hypotheses concerning Black Americans to which these elements are applied. In fact, completeness could not possibly be achieved in the brief compass of this essay, and the theoretical elements and the Black studies hypotheses that form the subject matter of this paper have been selected largely with this editorial consideration in mind. But despite this incompleteness, the theoretic elements discussed here are related to each other in what I believe are complementary ways that enable them to stand as an independent subset of the larger schema.

One thing more, by way of introduction: It may be thought that the analytical tools to be employed here are only useful retrospectively, in examining studies that have already been done. But it may well be that these tools can also have a prospective use in providing elements from which new studies of Black Americans, and new theoretical propositions in such studies, may be constructed.

Types of Social Phenomena

Perhaps the single most important conceptual distinction in all sociological theory (even though this distinction is sometimes only implicit) is between two broad types of social phenomena. One of these types is conventionally called "social organization" while the other is called "culture." Briefly, by "social organization" we refer to patterns or regularities in who-does-what-to-whom: who talks or listens to whom, who feeds or starves whom, who hits or caresses whom, who helps or hinders whom, who approaches or avoids whom, and the like. The essential thing is that social organization necessarily involves externalized, *physical* action regularly occurring between people. By "culture," however, we refer to patterns or regularities in who-thinks-or-feels-with-whom, and thereby we implicate the subjective dispositions—the symbols, beliefs, perceptions, loyalties, memories, expectations, opinions, values, hopes, fears, loves, hates, and the like—that people hold in common, or in complementarity, or in conflict. Therefore, in contrast with "social organization," "culture" always involves internalized, *psychical* behavior regularly shared between people.

Thus, social organization and culture are concepts referring to two distinct ways in which one individual or group may be behaviorally related to another (that is, two ways in which social phenomena may be defined)—related in terms of regularities or patterning in their joint physical behavior (roughly speaking, their "bodies'" behavior), and in terms of regularities or patterning in their joint physical behavior (roughly speaking, their "minds'" and "hearts'" behavior).

Several important problems in studies of Black Americans revolve around the theoretic distinction between social organization and culture. Consider, for example, two very well-supported empirical generalizations. The first is that both social organization and culture are universal among human beings. Wherever and whenever human beings have been found, they have been observed to act upon one another and jointly construct shared meanings, no matter how fleetingly. The only exceptions may be the extemely few (and disputed) cases of "feral" men and extreme isolation. But even granting these dubious exceptions, it seems safe to say that very nearly all human beings participate in some social life—that is, in some organization and in some culture. The generalization seems so safe, indeed, that it is altogether taken for granted and raised to the level of a general "principle" in sociology.

A second, widely accepted empirical generalization—another "principle" of sociology—is that although social organization and culture are logically independent with respect to their contents, they are connected in actual fact (that is, empirically covarying and therefore causally related, directly or indirectly). It is at this point, in mediating or transmitting the causal impact of culture on social organization and of social organization on culture, that communication (including language) finds its pivotal role in sociological theory. Contrasting hypotheses about the direction of influence between social organization and culture may be found in Weber's (1930) contention that the "spirit" (culture) of capitalism helped to explain (cause) the rise of its exchange relationships (social organization), and Engels's hypothesis that "the final causes of all social changes ... are to be sought not in men's brains [culture] ... but in changes in the modes of production and exchange [social organization]" (1968:417). The main point for present purposes, however, is that both men agreed on the hypothesis that *some* empirical causal dependence exists between social organization and culture. Closer to home, the logical independence of these two types of social phenomena underlies Du Bois's statement that "not every builder of racial cooperation and solidarity [social organization] is a Jim Crow advocate, a hater [culture] of white folk. Not every Negro who fights prejudice and segregation [social organization] is ashamed [culture] of his race" (1919:268). But an empirical hypothesis of mutual causal dependence or interaction between social organization and culture would lead us to expect statistical tendencies in the directions that Du Bois denied, as well as in the directions that he emphasized. Similarly, one might logically add that not all White persons who objectively discriminate (social organization) against Blacks do so because they are subjectively race prejudiced (culture), nor do all White persons who are race prejudiced (culture) objectively discriminate (social organization) against Blacks, but empirical tendencies seem likely to operate in both of these directions.

One recent study pertaining to Black Americans was addressed to "the question of whether slavery caused prejudice or prejudice caused slavery" (Jordan 1962:106-7). This is a particular formulation of the more general question of whether social organization causes culture or culture causes social organization. Jordan's conclusion, reminiscent of Engels's later letters on a similar interaction between "economic base" and "social superstructure," is that "both [slavery and prejudice] may have been equally cause and effect, constantly reacting upon each other, dynamically joining hands to hustle the Negro down the road to complete degradation" (1962:112).

Frazier, in most of his published statements, tended to identify social organization as causal influence on culture, rather than the reverse. For example, he argued that the cultural "traditions" of the new Black middle class—the culture that he so bitterly scorned —were consequences of social organizational changes, particularly increased occupational mobility and differentiation among Northern, urban Blacks. These were changes brought about by other social organizational changes: two world wars, economic expansion, the migration of Black people to Northern cities, and so on (1955:256-66). However, although Frazier hypothesized the social organization-to-culture causal sequence in *most* of his statements, in at least one publication he seems to have adopted the reverse sequence. After becoming deeply impressed with the post-World War II emergence of Black African nations, Frazier urged Black intellectuals to construct "a new self-image or new conception" of Black Americans, presumably so that this new cultural self-conception might influence the status of Black people in the American social organization, and so allow us to "leave a worthwhile memorial—in science, in art, in literature, in music—of our having been here" (1962:279).

In contrast with Frazier's hypothesis of the causal primacy of social organization over culture, Myrdal argued chiefly for the reverse. The very title of *An American Dilemma* suggests the view that the main determinant of race relations is cultural (Myrdal's term is "moral") and not social organizational. More specifically, for Myrdal, the American "dilemma" represents the unresolved clash of two cultural "creeds"—one is cosmopolitan, in the sense that it applies to individuals in their roles as participants in the nationwide social organization, and the other is local, in the sense that it applies to individuals in their roles as participants in neighborhood, community, or regional social organizations of smaller scope and narrower interests (1944:lxxii-lxxiii). But again, this is Myrdal's *chief* hypothesis. There is also in his work the subsidiary claim that various social organizational phenomena, such as labor unions, cities, schools, and the like can exert causal primacy over the cultural dilemma, so that local creeds will eventually be brought into line with the cosmopolitan one (1944:80).

But whether the answer favors one, or the other, or neither side of the equation, to ask "What causes what? Which comes first: social organization or culture?" is to confront a crucial problem. And the problem is crucial, not only for theory in sociology, but for strategy in social action. In the latter realm, the insurgent side asks, "How much of available resources should be allocated to fomenting strikes, boycotts, picket lines, sabotage, assassination, guerrilla warfare and other acts directed primarily to disrupting the established system's social organization, and how much to producing revolutionary speeches, slogans, songs, pamphlets, posters, poems, plays, and other propaganda directed primarily to disrupting the established social system's culture?" And for its part, the defending establishment asks "How much of available resources should be allocated to guaranteeing business as usual on the social organization side, and how much to guaranteeing beliefs as usual on the culture side?"

In this connection, apparently Cruse favors the hypothesis that culture is more influential over social organization than the reverse (unless, of course, the social organization is in the cultural sphere). Cruse rejects Karl Marx as theoretician for Black Americans in favor of C. Wright Mills; rejects the mode of production as societal determinant in favor of what might be called the mode of ideation and communication; rejects the proletariat as revolutionary force in favor of the intelligentsia. "Whoever controls the cultural apparatus ...," Cruse asserts, "also controls the destiny of the United States and everything in it" (1967:474). With this theoretical position, it follows that Cruse prefers the strategy of selecting culture, rather than social organization, as the primary target of insurgent social action. He therefore argues that "the first step toward economic autonomy must be [to] wrest ownership of all cultural institutions (theaters, halls, club sites, and movie houses) out of the hands of private, outside concerns, for the key idea is cultural institutions ... owned and administered by the people of [the Black community]" (1967:87). In a sense, having stood Marxist social theory on its head, Cruse then proceeds, consistently, to stand Communist action strategy on its head.

Turning from these practical implications of the social organization-versus-culture distinction, let us examine briefly some of its theoretical implications and their bearing on studies of Black Americans. Obviously, the principles of the human universality of both kinds of social phenomena, and of causal linkages between them, mean that we should be surprised to find that human beings who have a distinctive social organization do not also have a distinctive culture, and vice-versa.

It is therefore an altogether startling fact that some sociologists who explicitly recognize the existence of distinctively Black American social organization (for example, the Black urban community, the Black church, Black fraternal organizations) nevertheless deny the existence of any distinctively Black culture. Glazer and Moynihan maintain that "the Negro is only an American, and nothing else. He has no values and culture to guard and protect" (1963:53). And Frazier argued that "unlike other racial or cultural minorities the Negro is not distinguished by culture from the dominant group. Having completely lost his ancestral culture, he speaks the same language, practises the same religion and accepts the same values and political ideals as the dominant group" (1957:680).

Now consider another startling fact: the supposed absence of a distinctive culture among a people having an admittedly distinct social organization is employed, by the same scholars, as a reason for eliminating (through "assimilation") this nonexistent culture. As a result, it becomes clear that those who claim that Blacks have no distinctive culture really mean that Blacks have no "healthy" distinctive culture.

Thus, Myrdal claimed that "American Negro culture . . . is a distorted development, or an unhealthy condition of American culture" (1944:928), and Frazier saw "the segregated Negro community [as] essentially a pathological phenomenon in American life" (1947: 291). But when one asks about the criterion of "health" or "normality" underlying these judgments, no abstract philosophical ideal is offered, against which any and all real cultures would certainly be found "pathological" to some degree, and no cultural relativism within which every surviving real culture would appear "healthy" to some degree—instead, the actually existing American White culture is set up as the standard. Myrdal baldly argued that "the notion popularized by anthropologists that *all* cultures may be good under the different conditions to which they are adaptations ... does not gainsay our assumption that *here, in America,* American [White] culture is 'highest' in the pragmatic sense that adherence to it is practical for any individual or group which is not strong enough to change it" (1944:929). So Moynihan, twenty-one years later, could continue this ethnocentric and opportunistic line of argument by claiming that "it is a clear disadvantage for a minority group to be operating on one principle, while the great majority of the population, and the one with the most advantages to begin with, is operating on another" (1965: 75).

Intimately related to these issues of whether any distinctively Black American culture exists at all, and if so, whether and by what criterion it is "healthy" or "pathological," is the question of the autonomy of that culture—that is, the extent to which its development is attributable to endogenous or exogenous influences. Myrdal believed that "the Negro's entire life [and culture] ... are, in the main, to be considered as secondary reactions to more primary pressures from the side of the dominant white majority" (1944: lxxv), and viewed the "glorification of things African, especially in music and art [*and*] the back-to-Africa movement after the First World War, [as] a reaction to discrimination from white people, on the one hand, and a result of encouragement from white people, on the other hand. Thus, even the positive movement away from American culture has its source in that culture" (1944:928). Similarly, Meier and Rudwick (1970) argue that the changing currents of integrationist and separatist ideology flowing within Black American culture have been responses to external changes in the level of rejection of Blacks by the White community, rather than responses to changes within Black communities themselves. Billingsley too, in his study of Black families, claims that "Both the [Black] family and the [Black] community are creatures of the wider [White] society, which provides or withholds the resources for its creation, survival, and development" (1968:150). In the same general vein, Frazier argued that "the sociological explanation of the system of racial separation and the disfranchisement of the Negro is to be found in the unresolved class conflict and the resulting political struggles among the whites in the South" (1953:5-6), and he referred to "the confinement of the Negro to unskilled occupations and domestic service as an aspect of the political struggle in the South, not between the whites and Negroes but between the white propertied classes and white working classes" (1955:109). Thus, Blacks were seen by Frazier, at that time, as pawns in a struggle among whites— a view in some contrast with his own bitter observation only five years later that, in the nation's commemoration of the Civil War, that war "is supposed to have been the result of a misunderstanding of two brothers, white brothers, of course, and the Emancipation of the Negro is forgotten" (1962:279). Of course, Frazier's earlier statement contrasts even more sharply with Du Bois's hypothesis that "The American Negro not only was the cause of the Civil War but a prime factor in enabling the North to win it" (1943:79)—no mere pawn, but the principal actor, in Du Bois's view.

And, of course, the hypothesis that the Black community lacks autonomous development may well underlie the coupling of widespread inattention to Black social life in its own right with careful attention to "race relations" and to the attitudes of Whites toward Blacks. Myrdal's *An American Dilemma* is an example of this, insofar as only two chapters (chapters 43 and 44) out of a total of forty-five are devoted specifically to Black social organization and culture.

In summary, then, we have three major questions in studies of Black Americans that center around the fundamental theoretical distinction between culture and social organization: (1) Given that distinctively Black American social organization obviously exists, does an equally distinctive Black American culture exist? (2) Given that distinctively Black American social organization and culture exist, in what respect and to what extent are they healthy or pathological, by what standard? and (3) in what ways, and to what degree, are developments in Black American social organization and culture autonomous from, or dependent on, developments in White American social organization and culture?

Regarding the first question, several theorists have argued or acknowledged that despite tendencies toward correspondence or "matching" between social organization and culture, significant discrepancies between them can emerge and persist. For example, Marx called one variety of this discrepancy "false" consciousness and another variety "Communist Party" consciousness. In the first, Marx claimed that certain cultural elements can lag behind social organization; in the second, he claimed that similar elements can lead social organization. Further, Anthony Wallace's (1956) concept of "revitalization" refers to a change primarily in culture (in the "mazeway"), while Lenin's (1932) concept of "revolution" refers to a change primarily in social organization (in the "state") —but both changes are claimed to accomplish the same thing: drastic reduction of an acknowledged gap between social organization and ideology.

Therefore, one way of conceptualizing the current resurgence of Black separatist ideology is not as a deviation from prior integrationist ideology, but as a convergence of Black culture toward Black social organization. In other words, by lending support to a resurgence of separatist ideology and Black consciousness in general, the persistently distinctive social organization of the Black community may be drawing an aspect of its associated culture—namely, its ideology—back into greater consonance with its own distinctiveness. Indeed, the history of Black ideology in the United States seems to reveal periodic ideological divergences from and convergences toward Black social organization.

Regarding the second question, the contention that Black American social life is pathological is, at least from the viewpoints of cultural relativism and functionalism, untenable on its face. One has only to point to the facts that Black Americans have survived, that we have contributed in important ways to mankind's survival, and that we have done both in a hostile environment during nearly fourteen generations as slaves followed by four generations, so far, as domestic colonials and members of the out-caste. It will be indeed a bizarre definition of "pathology" that condemns as wholly pathological a social life productive of these outcomes in the face of these obstacles.

Finally, regarding the third question, it seems a safe general hypothesis that whatever exists, exists by virtue of some balance between forces internal and forces external to it, but that, in any given case, the balance will vary over time. Thus, the periodic rise of integrationist ideology in the Black community, while other aspects of culture and most aspects of social organization remain separate, may be responsive more to influences impinging from outside—that is, from the White community—than to those emanating from within the Black community. The rise of separatist ideology, however, may be just the reverse: it may be more responsive to internal influences in the Black community than to external influences. The periodic divergences and convergences between Black ideology and Black social organization, to which I referred above, may therefore be a response to the repeated ebb and flow of exogenous and endogenous influences throughout the history of the Black community in the United States.

In the discussion so far, I have tried to point out some implications of the conceptual distinction between social organization and culture. That discussion may be thought of as having focused on a "horizontal" dimension, wherein two equally important types of social phenomena were identified and interrelated. By contrast, the next discussion focuses on a "vertical" dimension, signalized by its reference to "levels" rather than "types" of social phenomena. Thus, I propose to shift the focus from a nominal ordering to an ordinal ordering of social phenomena. It is important to emphasize that, together, these two orderings yield a self-contained two-dimensional space: the social organization-culture dimension intersects the levels dimension, such that social phenomena are postulated as having level-specific types of social organization and level-specific types of culture. For example, a two-person group (two friends, two enemies, two lovers) will have its own social organization and its own culture, different in kind from the social organization and culture of, say, a factory, a city, or a society.

Levels of Social Phenomena

Five levels of social phenomena may be distinguished in theoretical writings in sociology: the interpersonal or small-group level; the intergroup or institutional level; the interinstitutional or community level; the intercommunity or societal level; and the intersocietal level. In order to indicate, in a general way, what this "levels" distinction means for theory in sociology, and therefore for studies employing such theory, consider two extremes: some sociological theories may be termed "atomistic" because they claim that in order to understand the largest, most inclusive, social phenomena (say, societies and intersocietal systems) one must first understand the smallest, most exclusive, social phenomena (say, two-person groups), since the largest are only more or less elaborate combinations of the smallest. These theories see all social phenomena as built *up* from, and thus explained by, interpersonal relations. Wagner (1963) has suggested that "interpretative-interactional theories" are of this type; and Parsons (1960) has suggested that his own "social action" theory—including, especially, the pattern variables—is located here.

At the other extreme, we have "structure-functionalism," according to Wagner (1963), and Parsons's AGIL functional imperatives (1960). These theories may be termed "wholistic," because they claim the reverse of atomistic theories, namely, that the smallest social phenomena can only be understood in light of the larger wholes of which they are parts. In this view, all social phenomena are built *down* from, and thus explained by, the most inclusive societal and intersocietal frameworks.

Between these extremes are varieties whose sense I have tried to capture by posing three intermediate levels of social phenomena from which primary causal influence may be said to proceed either upward toward more inclusive social phenomena, or downward toward less inclusive social phenomena, or both. Thus, theories that claim explanatory primacy for voluntary associations (including social movements), or for bureaucratic organizations, or for the family, or for the community, or for the society, would be specified as types variously intermediate between those claiming primacy for interpersonal interactions, at one extreme, and others claiming primacy for international affairs, at the other.

Since it is clear that individual human beings participate in social phenomena at all levels, and that a given individual may participate at all levels and may do so even simultaneously, it follows that differences between levels cannot rest on differences between participants. They must rest, instead, on differences in the manner in which participants in social phenomena at each level are "arranged"—that is, differences in the number of participants that are involved and in certain of their relationships to each other.

Now it is a further generalization or "principle" of sociology (analogous to a similar one in physical chemistry) that such different arrangements, sometimes of the same participants, have different consequences. These consequences, especially when they are compared from a "lower" to a "higher" level of social phenomena, have been called "emergent" qualities since they appear to grow out of the arrangements rather than to be inherent in the components (Blau 1960:3-4). One such emergent consequence—frequently hypothesized and almost as frequently observed—is that the same human being will behave differently when participating in, and therefore under the influence of, social phenomena at different levels.

Myrdal exemplifies this latter hypothesis in claiming that "when the man in the street acts through his orderly collective bodies, he acts more as an American, as a Christian, and as a humanitarian than if he were acting independently" (1944:80). Indeed, the theoretic distinctions among levels of social phenomena that I suggest here play a key role in the entire analysis set forth in *An American Dilemma*. I have already indicated that this work (despite its avowed assumption of "a general interdependence between all the factors in the Negro problem" [1944:75]) seems clearly to assign primary causal influence to culture over social organization. But cutting across this assessment, Myrdal claims that the personal level is the primary locus from which the influence of culture operates. Myrdal says, " 'The American Dilemma', . . . is the ever-ranging conflict between, on the one hand, the valuations preserved on the general plane which we shall call 'The American Creed,' where the American thinks, talks, and acts under the influence of high national and Christian precepts, and, on the other hand, the valuations on specific planes of individual and group living . . . " (1944:lxxi). Note that Myrdal refers explicitly to this dilemma as occurring at the "personal" level, and thus *within* individuals: "the essence of the moral situation is ... that the conflicting valuations are held by the same person" (1944:lxxi). However, from a sociological point of view this necessarily implies a primary focus at the interpersonal level, insofar as Myrdal repeatedly intimates that the dilemma is generated and transmitted (that is, taught and learned) *between* individual Americans rather than in some way given *within* each individual American.

Myrdal's implicit primary focus at the interpersonal level is reinforced when he explicitly denies causal primacy to the institutional level of social phenomena: "Though our study includes economic, social, and political race relations, at bottom our problem is the moral dilemma of the American" (1944:lxxi). This causal specification is not advanced unequivocally, to be sure, since Myrdal also argues that "through huge institutional structures, a constant pressure is brought to bear on race prejudice, counteracting the natural tendency for it to spread and become more intense" (1944:80). Curiously enough, however, near the end of his treatise Myrdal apparently retracted this latter stress on the institutional level as exerting beneficent causal primacy in "the type of society we call democracy" (1944:80). Instead, when answering the interpersonal-level question of "why ... potentially and intentionally good people so often make life a hell for themselves and each other when they live together," he blames the same institutions that earlier he had acclaimed: "the fault is ... that our structures of organizations are too imperfect, each by itself, and badly integrated into a social whole" (1944:1023).

But despite these attributions of causal primacy to the institutional level, Myrdal's preferred hypotheses seem to favor its location at the personal and therefore the interpersonal level. In contrast with this position, Moynihan, and Billingsley (as Billingsley points out [1968:33]), share the hypothesis that the pivot of social organization and culture at all levels is the family—a social phenomenon at the institutional, rather than interpersonal, level. Moynihan asserts that "the family is the basic social unit of American life" (1965:51); Billingsley goes further in claiming that "the family is the most basic institution of any people, the center and source of its civilization" (1968:Foreword). But again, both Billingsley and

Moynihan have other hypotheses; these are reflected in their calls for action at the societal level (through the federal government) with respect to the family at the institutional level, and Billingsley even says, in a more wholistic mood than that quoted above, that "the greater force for defining, enhancing, or obstructing comes from the wider society to the family and not the other way around" (1968:150).

Carmichael and Hamilton offer an example of the view that assigns causal primacy neither to the interpersonal, nor the institutional, but to the interinstitutional or community level. They say, "The concept of Black Power rests on a fundamental premise: Before a group can enter the open society, it must first close ranks. ... Traditionally, each new ethnic group in this society has found the route to social and political viability through the organization of its own institutions with which to represent its needs within the larger society" (1967:46); "the power must be that of a community, and emanate from there" (1967:46). In writing of school integration, they argue that "the goal is not to take black children out of the black community and expose them to white middle-class values; the goal is to build and strengthen the black community" (1967:55). Genovese's argument in this same mood should also be mentioned: "The assertion of Black hegemony in specific cities and districts—nationalism if you will—offers the only politically realistic hope of transcending the slave heritage" (1966:47). In a similar statement, Cruse argues that "the large cities, especially in the North, are where the decisive struggles of the Negro movement will be waged. It will be a difficult struggle, but the Negro movement must win political and economic power within these urban communities" (1967:448).

Now it should be clear that, in the above quotations, "nationalism" does not necessarily mean more than "community control," where the communities are an increasing number of inner cities scattered across the country. This suggests that a new, Black, and distinctively latter-half-of-the-twentieth-century definition of nationalism may be developing. In this definition, geographical contiguity of territory may be of little importance—or at least of far less importance than in the nationalisms of earlier days. In certain expressions termed "Black nationalist," therefore, one may discern an image of a Black American nation consisting of a large number of geographically dispersed parts existing entirely with the present-day United States, maintaining, it is hoped, peaceful relations with the United States along thousands of miles of discontinuous border, and linked together by some single Black governmental power and common cultural elements.

Thus, while Turner deplores the "geographical dispersion [of Black Americans] which has been a liability in the sense that it has depressed a sense of territoriality and thus common nationalist-orientation among black people" (1970:13), he calls for a mixed strategy whereby Blacks would capture "control over all institutions within the area [that Black people in the several, geographically dispersed metropolises] occupy," and also "support ... black nation-building in [the more solidary] areas of the South where blacks are in great numbers" (1970:12-13).

Perhaps the clearest and least ambivalent examples of the societal-level hypothesis are to be found in the works of Marxist students, who assign causal primacy in the internal and external social relations of Black Americans to capitalism as an all-pervading societal (and intersocietal) system. Cox, for example, attributes all racial antagonism to capitalism:

> Our hypothesis is that racial exploitation and prejudice developed among Europeans with the rise of capitalism and nationalism and that because of the world-wide ramifications of capitalism, all racial antagonisms can be traced to the policies and attitudes of the lead capitalist people, the white people of Europe and North America (1948:322).

Haywood reflects the same societal-level orientation, although his view is not only Marxist but Stalinist as well. Arguing that the Black Belt of plantation counties in the Deep South constitutes an "internal colony," he declared that "The Negro question has now definitely become the problem of an oppressed nation striving for national freedom against the main enemy, imperialism" (1948:143). Haywood therefore called for the founding of a Black nation in the Black Belt, based upon a single integral territory, and incorporating the Whites in that area as a national minority in the same way, presumably, that Blacks remaining in the United States would become a national minority, rather than solely a racial minority.

A non-Marxist societal-level hypothesis is that of Warner, whose location of primary causal influence over race relations at the societal level is reflected in his combination of "color caste [as] an example of status in which the position of the individual is fixed" with "social class, where movement and freedom of the individual are stressed" (1962:88-89).

Finally, of course, the nationalist advocacy of an African national homeland should be mentioned. In 1922, petitioning the League of Nations on behalf of "four hundred million Negroes of the world," Garvey's Universal Negro Improvement Association said, "We believe that as a people we should have a Government of our own, in our homeland—Africa," and again in 1928: "The entire regions of West Africa could be brought together as one United Commonwealth of Black Nations and placed under the government of black men, as the solution of the Negro problem, both in Africa and the Western World" (quoted in Essien-Udom 1962:252).

It should be noted that this call for an African homeland, reflecting a societal-level hypothesis, reflects also an intersocietal-level one insofar as the petitions were presented to the League of Nations and insofar as the proposed nation would have been homeland to Blacks of all nations. In both senses, then, the United Commonwealth of Black Nations would have been predicated on an intersocietal-level as well as a societal-level hypothesis.

Now, going beyond sociological hypotheses regarding the way things *are*, but with the aid of such hypotheses, we may usefully recast one principal ideological theme regarding the way things *should* be. "Integration or separation" are the terms in which it is usually framed, but it is better formulated as a more complex question: At what levels should separation take place and at what levels should integration take place?

Let me try to specify what this question means. Consider the possibility of separate Black and White institutions (say, separate churches, fraternal and social organizations, political parties, families) within integrated Black-White communities. This would mean separatism at the institutional level and perhaps also below, but integration of Black and White institutions at the community level. Similarly, the possibility of separate Black communities would mean separation at that level and perhaps also below, but integration of such communities at the societal level. In the same way, one can conceive of separation at *all* levels, including the intersocietal one, such that the human population of the earth would be divided into two or more genuinely isolated systems. On the other hand, integration at all levels down to and including the interpersonal one may also be imagined. Moreover, each variation may cast separation or integration, at each level, in the role of temporary means or permanent end. Thus Jencks seems to see community-level separation more as means than end: *"enroute to integration,* the Negro community needs to develop a greater independence—a chance to run its own affairs ..." (quoted in Carmichael and Hamilton 1967: 45). Carmichael and Hamilton convey a similar implication: *"Before a group can enter the open society,* it must first close ranks" (emphases added) (1967:44).

Du Bois, in an early discussion of integration and segregation at the interpersonal and institutional levels, appears to have been ambivalent:

> You cannot build up a logical scheme of a self-sufficing, separate Negro America inside America or a Negro world with no close relations to the white world. If there are relations between races they must be based on the knowledge and sympathy that come alone from the long and intimate human contact of individuals.
>
> On the other hand, if the Negro is to develop his own power and gifts; if he is not only to fight prejudices and oppression successfully but also to unite for ideals higher than the world has realized in art and industry and social life, then he must unite and work with Negroes and build a new and great Negro ethos (1919:267-68).

During his long lifetime, however, Du Bois increasingly came to resolve this ambivalence in favor of separation at the institutional level, and not only for "negative reasons" involving defenses against rejection of Blacks by Whites (which would tend to define separation as a temporary means), but for "positive reasons" involving the special potential of Black people (which seems to cast separation in the role of more permanent end). Indeed, Du Bois (1970) seems to have evolved, under the impact of repeated disappointments with White America, from an early advocacy of integration at the interpersonal level (around 1920) to advocacy of separation at the institutional and community levels (around 1935), and finally, toward the end of his life (around 1960), to the advocacy of separation at the societal level.

Frazier moved too, apparently under the impact of the emergence of Black African nations after World War II, from strong adherence to integration at all levels to a tentative advocacy of separation at the societal level. He shifted from claiming that "the segregated Negro community . . . is essentially a pathological phenomenon in American life" and "[integration] will cause Negroes generally to acquire a saner conception of themselves and of their role in American society," in 1947 (1947:291), to urging the Negro intellectual to "dig down into the experience of the Negro and bring about a transvaluation of that experience so that the Negro could have a new self-image or new conception of himself," to acknowledging that "I can not envision any assimilation in the foreseeable future," and to warning that "integration [for the Negro intellectual] should not mean annihilation—self-effacement, the escaping from his identification," in 1962 (1962:279).

Conclusion

I have tried briefly to set forth and illustrate two related analytic schemes for revealing similarities and differences among a variety of ideas contained in studies of Black Americans. These schemes have included distinctions between two kinds of social phenomena and between five levels of social phenomena. To repeat a claim made at the outset of this paper, I propose that these schemes may find use, not only in understanding studies that have already been completed, but in forming the primitive elements of new studies and new theories still to be constructed.

Now, in closing this paper, let me draw attention to the obvious: the relationship between scientific theory and empirical observations is reciprocal; observations depend on theory, since we tend to see what we look for, and theory depends on observation, since we tend to interpret what we see. If we change our theory—for whatever reason, including deliberate ideological ones—we are apt to look for, and see, different things. If we see a new thing—again, for whatever reason, including unintended, accidental ones—we are apt to develop a new theory. Insofar as the literature on Black Americans and on Black-White relations in the United States reports or predicts observations, general sociological theory necessarily plays a part in it. This has been the principal theme of my paper. But that literature has its specialness—its wholly unique realm of observation and hypothesis—and therefore it has played a part in the development of theory and will play a still more crucial part there. This latter relationship has been a principal theme of other papers at the national conference on black sociologists.

It is perhaps just such reciprocity between general sociological theory and studies of Black Americans that can be most fruitful for Black freedom, for understanding the nature of Black social organization and culture at all levels, and for scientific sociology.

References

Billingsley, Andrew. *Black Families in White America*. Englewood Cliffs, N. J.: Prentice-Hall, 1968.

Blau, Peter. *Exchange and Power in Social Life*. New York: Wiley, 1960.

Carmichael, Stokely, and Hamilton, C. *Black Power*, New York: Random House, 1967.

Cox, Oliver, C. *Caste, Class, and Race: A Study in Social Dynamics*. New York: Doubleday, 1948.

Cruse, Harold. *The Crisis of the Negro Intellectual*. New York: Morrow, 1967.

Du Bois, W. E. B. *W. E. B. Du Bois: A Reader*. Edited by Meyer Weinberg. New York: Harper Torchbooks, 1970.

———. "Reconstruction, Seventy-Five Years After." *Phylon* 4 (1943). In *W. E. B. Du Bois: A Reader*. Page numbers refer to the latter.

———. "Jim Crow." *The Crisis* (January 1919). In *W. E. B. Du Bois: A Reader*. Page numbers refer to the latter.

Engels, Frederick. *Socialism: Utopian and Scientific*, in *Karl Marx and Frederick Engels, Selected Works*. New York: International Publishers, 1968.

Essien-Udom, E. V. *Black Nationalism*. Chicago: University of Chicago Press, 1962.

Frazier, E. Franklin. "The New Negro Middle Class." First published in 1955. In *E. Franklin Frazier on Race Relations*, edited by G. Franklin Edwards.

Chicago: University of Chicago Press, 1968. Page numbers refer to the latter.

———. "The Failure of the Negro Intellectual." First published in 1962. In *E. Franklin Frazier on Race Relations*. Page numbers refer to the latter.

———. "Theoretical Structure of Sociology and Sociological Research." First published in 1953. In *E. Franklin Frazier on Race Relations*. Page numbers refer to the latter.

Genovese, Eugene D. "The Roots of Black Nationalism." First published in 1966. In *Americans From Africa*. Vol. 2, *Old Memories, New Moods*, edited by Peter I. Rose. New York: Atherton, 1970. Page numbers refer to the latter.

Glazer, Nathan, and Moynihan, Daniel Patrick. *Beyond the Melting Pot*. Cambridge, Mass.: M.I.T. Press, 1963.

Haywood, Harry. *Negro Liberation*. International Publishers, 1948.

Jordan, Winthrop D. "Modern Tensions and the Origins of American Slavery." *Journal of Southern History* 28 (February 1962): 18–30. In *Americans From Africa*. Vol. 1, *Slavery and Its Aftermath*, edited by Peter I. Rose. New York: Atherton, 1970. Page numbers refer to the latter.

Lenin, V. I., *State and Revolution*. New York: International, 1932.

Meier, August, and Rudwick, Elliott. *From Plantation to Ghetto*. Revised edition. New York: Hill and Wang, 1970.

Moynihan, Daniel Patrick. *The Negro Family: The Case for National Action*. First published in 1965. In *The Moynihan Report and the Politics of Controversy*. Cambridge, Mass.: M.I.T. Press, 1967. Page numbers refer to the latter.

Myrdal, Gunnar. *An American Dilemma*. New York: Harper and Row, 1962.

Parsons, Talcott. "Pattern Variables Revisited: A Response to Robert Dubin." *American Sociological Review* (August 1962), pp. 467–83.

Turner, James. "Blacks in the Cities: Land and Self-Determination." *Black Scholar* 1 (April 1970): 9-13.

Wagner, Helmut. "Types of Sociological Theory." *American Sociological Review* 28 (October 1963): 735-42.

Wallace, Anthony F. C. "Revitalization Movements." *American Anthropologist* 58 (1956): 264-81.

Warner, W. Lloyd. *American Life: Dream and Reality*. Chicago: University of Chicago Press, 1962.

Wallace, Walter L. *Sociological Theory*. Chicago: Aldine-Atherton, 1969.

Weber, Max. *The Protestant Ethic and the Spirit of Capitalism*. Translated by Talcott Parsons. London: George Allen and Unwin, Ltd., 1930.

12

William J. Wilson

THE NEW BLACK SOCIOLOGY:
REFLECTIONS ON THE
"INSIDERS" AND "OUTSIDERS"
CONTROVERSY

Robert K. Merton has remarked that "when a once largely powerless collectivity acquires a socially validated sense of growing power, its members experience an intensified need for self-affirmation. Under such conditions, collective self-glorification, found in some measure among all groups, becomes a predictable and intensified counterresponse to long standing belittlement from without" (1972, pp. 18-19).[1] The black liberation movement in the United States, especially since the ascendancy of the Black Power philosophy in the late sixties, has been marked by an avowed effort not only to reject the ideology of racism, but also to overcome the effects of racist oppression via cultural revitalization (that is, through strong emphasis on black cultural heritage and black identity). So widespread is the cultural revitalization movement that all segments of the black community in the United States have felt its influence (Wilson 1973, p. 201). It is no coincidence, therefore, that the quest for self-affirmation among black intellectuals, as reflected in the attempt to develop "black perspectives" to guide research and writing on the black experience, corresponds with the era of cultural revitalization and black glorification. Whether one focuses on the writings and research of black social scientists, black historians, or black humanists, the "black perspective" is informed by a belief that the black scholar "must de-colonize his mind so that he may effectively guide other intellectuals and students in their search for liberation" (Hare 1969, p. 58). The present essay critically ex-

322

amines black sociologists' arguments and claims for a "black perspective" in the study of race.

The Insiders Doctrine in Sociology

In his perceptive essay, Robert K. Merton (1972) has captured the rationales used by some black sociologists to explain the need or to justify the claim for a sociology of the black experience based exclusively or largely on the writings of blacks. Essentially, the rationale is conveyed in the Insiders doctrine—the view that individuals of a particular race or ethnic group have a greater intellectual understanding of the experiences of that group. In some instances, it is claimed that there is a fundamental causal connection between the skin color of a sociologist and his ability to conduct adequate and meaningful inquiry into the black experience. Black supporters of this view argue, therefore, that because white sociologists have neither directly engaged in the black experience nor been socialized in the life of black people they do not possess the unique values and perspectives necessary to orient oneself to the problem or to fully comprehend the subtleties of black life styles, the nuances of black behavior, and the meanings of black conduct. Thus, according to Joyce Ladner, the inability of white social scientists

to understand the nature and effect of neo-colonialism in the same manner as Black people is rooted in the inherent bias of the social sciences. The basic concepts and tools of white Western society are permeated by this partiality to the conceptual framework of the oppressor. It is simply enough to say that the difference between the two groups—the oppressor and the oppressed—prevents the former from adequately comprehending the essence of Black life and culture because of a fundamental difference in perceptions, based upon separate histories, life styles and purposes for being. Simply put, the slave and his master do not view and respond to the world in the same way (1971, p. xvii).

Likewise, Andrew Billingsley, irritated by the white social science "distortions" of "black realities," declares that "it is clearly the task of young Black social scientists, who can combine their own experience with their technical competence, to clarify for us the nature of these realities" (1972, p. xvii).

Although Billingsley's statement may be taken by some to support the more stringent claim of a causal connection between skin color and quality of research on the black experience, it may also be used to buttress the less extreme version that because of their dissimilar backgrounds and experiences white and black sociologists will approach the subject matter of race with different foci of interests.[2] Abd-l Hakimu Ibn Alkalimat (Gerald McWorter, 1969) maintains, for example, that race relations studies during the past fifty years have essentially "served a white ideology, while black ideologies have lacked the support of a systematic analysis" (1969, pp. 28-29); that white social science stresses emphasis on concepts easily operationalized or quantified whereas black social science gives primacy to concepts having a sociopolitical content (for example, white social scientists rely heavily on concepts such as "prejudice" and "discrimination" both of which are readily operation. Black social scientists, on the other hand, rely heavily on the concept "racism" which is more suitable to capture the essential features of race exploitation); and that the "conceptual framework presented as white social science reflects an *equilibrium model* of society based on evolutionary change" whereas "the concepts of a black social science reflect a *conflict model* of society bound together by coercion and changed by revolution" (1969, p. 35).

Ibn Alkalimat's views are consistent with those of other black sociologists critical of the research of white scholars on the grounds that it does not contribute to black liberation. Rather than focusing on white racism as a system of exploitation, they maintain, white sociologists have devoted an inordinate amount of time and space to studying and classifying black attitudes and behavior patterns; research which, far from aiding the black struggle, may be used by the government and other agents of oppression to control the black population.[3]

In the final analysis, the combined arguments that (1) whites are basically incapable of grasping black realities and (2) that because of the very nature of their experiences blacks and whites will approach the subject of race with different foci of interests have prompted some black sociologists to demand that white sociologists be excluded from researching and studying the Afro-American experience.

However, despite the emphasis given to the "black perspective," a coherent and integrated body of thought among proponents of the insiders doctrine that could clearly establish the direction and set the tone for a new black sociology does not exist. Nonetheless, it is possible not only to react to programmatic statements about black sociology but also to comment on works assumed to be representative of Insider themes and which provide justifications of their claims. My discussion then will assess these matters in terms of (1) the logic of scientific inquiry; (2) black approaches to analyzing racial experience; and (3) the possible consequences of the insider doctrine.

Insiderism and the Logic of Scientific Inquiry

If it is correct to assert that the discovery and verification of knowledge pertaining to racial group experiences is not logically distinct from the development of knowledge in other areas of study, then the claim that white sociologists, regardless of their competence, are excluded in principle from adequately comprehending the black experience raises a number of issues pertinent to the logic of scientific inquiry. To be more specific, *any* comprehensive investigation of human groups is obviously aided by valid information into the intentions, dispositions, beliefs, and other subjective experiences of groups. However, there are some levels of inquiry that yield definitive propositions of racial group interaction that do not require firsthand knowledge of group experiences. Herbert Blumer's (1965) statement on industrialization and race relations, for instance, was not postulated on the basis of "privileged" knowledge of say, the black experience, but rather on a careful analysis of historical and comparative data. Blumer noted that the racial tension and conflict usually attributed to societies undergoing industrialization are not likely to occur in regions with an established racial order but rather in societies where "industrialization may bring together racial groups which previously have not had relations with each other or only tenuously defined positions with regard to each other" and where "a firmly established racial order is definitely undergoing disintegration" (1965, p. 237).[4] Likewise, Robin Williams's proposition that "intergroup hostility and conflict are the more likely the greater the general level of tension in the society as a result of economic depression, prior cultural conflict, or various levels of social disorganization" (1947, p. 57) does not presume that Williams actually had experienced racial conflict himself, nor is the proposition invalid because Williams is not a member of a racial minority group.

Nonetheless, the foregoing examples do not involve statements that attempt to recapture the subjective aspects of the black experience in any comprehensive way, but rather are theoretical statements that explain a limited level of dominant and minority group interaction. Black supporters of the Insiders doctrine, therefore are likely to dismiss these examples by arguing that they do not represent the "unique" black experience and that it is here where white sociologists are deficient.

But there is no factual evidence to suggest that a sociologist has to be black to adequately describe and explain the experiences of blacks, in the same way that there is no evidence that a criminologist must be a criminal to understand criminal behavior; that a psychologist must be emotionally unstable if he is to competently study abnormal behavior; or that a historian be a Southern aristocrat to fully comprehend the behavior of the Southern landowning aristocracy.[5] Moreover, although the contrary is sometimes assumed, the black experience is not uniform. Despite the fact that all blacks may have been victimized by racist behavior, at one time or another, black experiences nevertheless vary by social class, region of the country, and age. Indeed some middle-class black sociologists may have experiences closer to those of middle-class whites than to those of lower-class blacks and thus they may have no more direct insight into the plight of ghetto blacks than do middle-class white sociologists. However, even if we accept the argument that, regardless of their station in life, blacks have a common experience which is altogether different from the experiences of whites, we must still confront the fundamental question of what really counts as an adequate understanding of this experience.

Some works by white sociologists, such as the Moynihan Report

(1965), have been soundly and convincingly criticized by black sociologists (cf. Billingsley 1968; Willie 1968; and Staples 1970) on the grounds that they distort the realities of black life. (It is interesting to note, however, that shortly after the publication of the Moynihan Report black social scientist C. Eric Lincoln [1965] wrote a paper on the black family that was vulnerable to the same criticisms leveled against Moynihan.) Other works by white social scientists on the black experience such as those by Elliot Liebow (1966) and Ulf Hannerz (1969) have been used and little criticized by black sociologists. Nevertheless, even if we invoke an Insider claim that participant observation studies of the black ghetto by black social scientists would have developed conclusions radically different from those presented by Liebow and Hannerz, the need for direct verification of any of the formulations or conclusions reached would not be negated. An adequate understanding of any subject matter within the purview of science is not simply a matter of having lived that experience but rather a demonstration that the items described and the propositions relating the items are, in fact, valid, and involve as a necessary condition for their being accepted the *possibility* of being verified through controlled observation by any person capable of doing so.

Accordingly, because the observations and formulations relating several aspects of the black experience are made by black sociologists, this does not, by itself, establish *knowledge*; neither does it mean that the observations are ipso-facto true, nor does it eliminate the need for scientific verification. To put the matter differently, the facts that a sociologist is black and that his background closely parallels those of a majority of blacks may, in many instances , be heuristically important in his attempts to *originate* admissible hypotheses to explain the experiences of blacks. But, to reiterate, his unique history is no substitute for objective evidence, measured in conformity with the logical principles of controlled inquiry, to verify his statements concerning the black experience.

To state that the experiences of a black sociologist may be heuristically important in the *development* of suitable hypotheses is to suggest, of course, that he may bring to his investigation certain values and orientations different from those of the white sociologists and that these may influence his selection of research topics and the manner in which he collects and interprets his data. The values and orientations of scientists are thus important in affecting the advancement of knowledge, but they do not substitute for the process of having their evidence and arguments meet the standards of validity imposed by the scientific community (Wilson 1973; Rudner 1968). However, black Insiders may take strong exception to this position by arguing that the ultimate aim of black social science should not be to achieve scientific adequacy but to conduct research and produce writings that aid in black liberation. To some extent, this orientation is implied by Ibn Alkalimat's statement that white social science uses concepts that are easily operationalized and quantified whereas black social science relies on concepts that have a sociopolitical content. However, there is nothing in the position I have developed thus far which would rule out the possibility of using concepts with a sociopolitical content (such as "racism" or "internal colonialism") in a framework designed to explain the black experience. Nor must the concepts be operationally defined in the strict manner in which a good deal of the empirical research narrowly defines "prejudice" and "discrimination." Certainly, in any scientific discipline it is necessary that the concepts have some basis in reality, but there is no logical reason why the empirical definitions of these concepts cannot be indirect (given significance on the basis of relations with other empirically defined concepts in a theoretical framework) or broad (based on comparative, historical, or structural data). It is a mistaken assumption that all theoretical concepts have to be immediately observable via a set of experimental operations (cf. Wilson and Dumont 1968). Nor is there anything in the comments I have made above which prevents black sociologists from using their research to advance the cause of black liberation. In the process of discovering or developing ideas, the data collected, hypotheses formulated, or theories developed could be designed to achieve any objective. All I am emphasizing is that the conclusions, propositions, and theories must be capable of confirmation and refutation if they are to be admissible as scientific knowledge. In short, whereas an individual scientist's unique experiences and orientations cannot be substituted for knowledge in the context of validation, they may play an important role in inventing and postulating hypotheses in the context of discovery.

Black Approaches to Race Relations—The New Black Sociology

The association between skin color and quality of study and research on the black experience, as our previous comments suggest, is neither logically nor empirically established and represents at best an unconfirmed hypothesis which must await developments in sociological research and theory. On the other hand, the less stringent view that black and white sociologists approach the subject of race with different foci of interests can be subjected to immediate empirical test. Although there are presently no systematic studies which authoritatively deny or affirm this assertion, work by black sociologists during the present period of black cultural revitalization suggests that it may have some basis in fact. However, the extent to which these new approaches represent a departure from the work done by white sociologists and the extent to which they can be readily traceable to the life experiences of black sociologists remains obscure. A thorough treatment of these questions with respect to the major aspects of race relations is outside the scope of this paper. However, I would like to consider them briefly in relation to the work of contemporary black sociologists on the black family—work which is said to embody the new black sociology and which is most frequently used to justify the Insiders doctrine.

The basic model used to organize data and guide interpretations is a central consideration in assessing the general orientation of the study of the black family. I have already mentioned Ibn Alkalimat's claim that white social science employs "an equilibrium model of society based on evolutionary change" whereas black social science uses "a conflict model of society bound together by coercion and changed by revolution" (1969, p. 35). Ibn Alkalimat's observations are quite consistent with Horten's (1966) comments on order and conflict theories.

As a generalization, groups or individuals committed to the maintenance of the status quo employ order models of society and equate deviation with non-conformity to institutionalized norms. Dissident groups,
striving to institutionalize new claims, favor a conflict analysis of society and an alienation theory of their discontent.... Society is a
natural system for the order analyst; for the conflict theorist it is a
continually contested political struggle between groups with opposing
goals and world views (1966, pp. 703-5).

However, an examination of those works on the black family
purported to reflect the black perspective and to represent the new
black sociology, reveal that far from incorporating a conflict approach the writings actually embody an order-equilibrium model
in which primacy is given to concepts such as "adaptation,"
"adjustment," and "normative consensus." It is necessary to point
out that this approach is a reaction to studies of the black family
that have stressed family disorganization, pathology, and value
disintegration, while ignoring black family strengths. Thus in the
words of black sociologist Robert Staples, "a relevant sociology of
the Black family will seek to discover the strengths in the Black
community that have allowed any form of Black family life to exist
under so many years of hardship" (1971, p. 4). The study widely
regarded as the prototype of this new black sociology is Andrew
Billingsley's *Black Families in White America*. However, Billingsley's book, which is a well-documented and carefully written piece of
scholarship, relies very heavily on the equilibrium-systems theory
model developed by Talcott Parsons. Billingsley states:

Drawing on the theoretical works of Talcott Parsons, Milton Gordon,
and others, we have urged that the Negro family be viewed as a social
system, imbedded within a network of both smaller and larger subsystems located within the Negro community and in the wider society.... It is, in our view, an absorbing, adaptive and amazingly
resilient mechanism for the socialization of its children and the civilization of its society (1968, pp. 32-33).

These comments hardly reflect a model in which the units are
"bound together by coercion and changed by revolution." But they
are central, nonetheless, to a book which has had significant influence on the way many black scholars, even those who support the

Insiders doctrine, approach the study of the black family (cf. Hill 1972; Ladner 1971; and Staples 1970), and this influence persists despite the fact that the theoretical orientation is based on "mainstream sociology" (that is, Talcott Parsons's system theory [1951 and 1955] and Milton Gordon's [1964] theory of assimilation). Nowhere is this influence more clearly demonstrated than in Robert Hill's recent, and widely publicized, book, *The Strengths of Black Families* (1972). In establishing the theoretical framework for his book, Hill states:

The classic analysis of the family as a social system by Parsons yield several helpful dimensions of family strengths. One of these dimensions, the ability to provide the necessary functions (both expressive and instrumental) to members and non-members, is basic to a viable family unit. We, therefore, operationally define as family strengths those traits which facilitate the ability of the family to meet the needs of its members and demands made upon it by systems outside the family unit (1972, p. 3).

The stress on black family strengths and the contribution of black family functions to the larger society shifts the analysis away from concepts such as "alienation," "value dissensus," and "nonconformity," which are usually associated with the power-conflict model, to order-consensus concepts. Thus in reviewing the literature on work norms among black and white Americans Hill is critical of the conflict-alienation interpretation of Jan Dizard (1968), who questions whether blacks and whites share the same values about the American occupational system and posits the view that blacks "having been kept out of the mainstream for so long ... may ... have rejected this mainstream and created 'streams' of their own" (1968:408); and, therefore, that these alienated males will fail to support work programs based on the values of middle-class white society. Hill stresses instead the fact that the research strongly upholds the view that whites and blacks are highly similar "in job aspirations and satisfaction, feelings of personal security in employment, as well as certain other work-related attitudes" (1972, p. 10).

This analysis leads me to conclude, therefore, that there may be little basis for maintaining that the black perspective in sociology is free of ambiguity. It seems ironic that the equilibrium-systems model that Ibn Alkalimat identifies with white social science is also central to the writings of black sociologists on the black family, writings that black supporters of the Insider doctrine proudly proclaim as representing the emerging black sociology.[7] It is true that consensus and conflict models vary widely and their use in particular explanatory frameworks does not necessarily reflect any basic ideological commitment. Most certainly if the aim of an investigator is to show the manner in which a particular racial or ethnic group is able to adapt or adjust to ongoing arrangements or to contribute to the functioning of the entire society, a systems-equilibrium model may be appropriate for explaining observed behavior. Likewise, human situations involve not only degrees of consensus and degrees of conflict, but also overlapping dialectical relationships between conflict and consensus. The problem here, as with the sole use of a purely conflict model, has to do with *selective* attention to certain situations and problems while ignoring others.[8] And this is as true for black sociologists who use the systems framework to account for strengths in the black family as it is for white sociologists who use the framework to explain order and equilibrium in a society.

If there is a difference between the way contemporary white sociologists and black sociologists study the family it has to do with the latter's focus on family strengths as opposed to weaknesses. However, even this approach is not the sole preoccupation of blacks. One of the earliest and most persuasive rebuttals to the Moynihan thesis concerning black family weaknesses was made by white sociologist Elizabeth Herzog (1966), who complained about the lack of attention given to black family strengths. Several other white sociologists (Bernard 1966; Reissman 1966; Hannerz 1969; Liebow 1967; and Coles 1964) have placed strong emphasis on black family strengths. Furthermore, the very scholars that Joyce Ladner (1971), one of the leading supporters of the Insider doctrine, criticized for "tacitly comparing the Black family to that of the white middle class, and thereby emphasizing its weaknesses, instead of trying to understand the nature of its strengths" were older generation black sociologists (cf. Frazier 1939; Drake and Cayton 1962; Johnson 1941; and Lewis 1955).

Thus, it is far from certain that any clear association can be established between black and white sociologists and their approach to race, when writings on the subject are considered over an extended period of time. And although it may be safe to hypothesize a connection between one's race and one's approach to race-related matters today, no sharp lines can be drawn between the writing of black and white scholars, and there is no guarantee that what is taken to represent the black perspective today will not be rejected by a new group of Insiders tomorrow.

Pitfalls of the Insiders Doctrine

Professor Wilson Record's article in this volume ("Response of Sociologists to Black Studies") raises some serious questions about the possible ramifications and consequences of the Insiders and Outsiders doctrine. Whereas I have concentrated on the doctrine as it has been developed by some black sociologists, Record has examined the doctrine's impact in the classroom. Full adherence to the doctrine requires that any courses dealing with the black experience be taught solely by blacks. This doctrine and the strong support it receives from many black students and black studies programs have, according to Record, precipitated a crisis for many white sociologists who teach race relations, causing some of them to abandon the field altogether.

The major pressure on white professors of race relations is in the classroom. Here black students, caught up in the current movement of race glorification in the aftermath of black protest and influenced by the Insiders doctrine as articulated by militant black scholars, approach the subject of race with heightened sensibilities, leading them to mistrust white professors and to often misinterpret their teachings about race. If Record's data accurately reflect the way white professors are responding to pressures both from students and black teachers, then those of us committed to the academic development of race relations should take pause. Let me elaborate.

Black Insiders would, of course, be happy to see black scholars gain a monopoly on the teaching, research, and writing about blacks, arguing that the white exodus would preserve the "integrity" of black studies. No doubt some black sociologists believe this, despite questions that can be raised about the validity of the doctrine, and therefore strongly support a black monopoly in the field of race relation. For others, however, support for the Insider doctrine is motivated by a desire to enhance their own professional status by removing white competition. To the degree that this sentiment is widespread, it increases the possibility that poorly trained hustlers and charlatans will enter the field of race relations to fill the vacancies created by the white exodus. It is no doubt true that some of the white "defectors" are themselves poorly trained and therefore are unable to offer the intellectual challenge that race relations affords, but the exodus may also remove a significant number of highly trained, imaginative, and productive white scholars. This is certainly not to say that there are not many capable and productive black sociologists in race relations, but it is to say that there are not nearly enough with the training and competence to fill a vacuum created by a large white exodus. This point is more clearly seen when we are reminded that less than 2 percent of the sociologists who listed race and ethnic relations as a field of interest in the 1970 *Directory of Members of the American Sociological Association* are black.[9] The field of race relations, therefore, may be in danger of losing a great deal of its intellectual thrust, and both teaching and writing in the field could suffer if pressures on competent white scholars force them to switch to less controversial fields of study.

This argument does not imply that black sociologists should not be critical of the writings and research of white scholars, or of other blacks for that matter, but it is to urge that the field of race relations be free to develop like any other substantive area in sociology, with the discovery and codification of knowledge, with the search for truth, and with the absence of arbitrary barriers imposed by Insiders and Outsiders doctrines. The real challenge of contemporary black sociologists is to continue the tradition of critical thinking and scholarship provided by the older generation of black sociologists. The classical works of E. Franklin Frazier, Charles S. Johnson, W. E. B. Du Bois, Oliver Cromwell Cox, St. Clair Drake, and Horace Cayton played a significant role in shaping the field of race relations. None of these scholars were detached observers, but their work reflected a commitment to autonomous standards of scholarship even though their orientations were undoubtedly influenced by their experiences as black Americans.[10]

Notes

1   Merton's argument is not an after-the-fact formulation. The above quotation is an observation of a quarter century ago. See Merton (1948:204).

2   The basic argument here, states Merton, is that "the Insiders, sharing the deepest concerns of the group or at least being thoroughly aware of them, will so direct their inquiries as to have them relevant to those concerns. So, too, the Outsiders will inquire into problems relevant to the distinctive values and interest which they share with members of *their* group" (1972, p. 16).

3   This is a view widely expressed among younger black sociologists at the recent Black Caucus Meetings held during the annual meetings of the American Sociological Association, and is reflected in some of the resolutions passed by the caucus.

4   As I have attempted to show elsewhere (Wilson 1973) there is a good deal of empirical support for these propositions.

5   For many of the arguments developed in the latter part of this section, I am indebted to Ernest Nagel (1961), especially Chapter 13.

6   For one criticism of Hannerz's conclusions see Hill (1972, p. 12).

7   The ambiguity of the "black perspective" is illustrated in Andrew Billingsley's Foreword to Hill's *The Strength of Black Families*. Billingsley, who had earlier used a Parsonian model to interpret the black family, writes: "A few years ago, Talcott Parsons became the high priest of social science by his development of the equilibrium model of social analysis. Parsons is still perhaps the most respected American social scientist, in large part because most other social scientists share his values and his commitment to the status quo. Social change is only a slogan in social science. Elsewhere we have called for the overthrow of the current ruling elite in social science which is largely comprised of white males over forty. It is heartening to see that a number of fresh perspectives of social science are emerging. Dr. Hill's work is a striking example of this new perspective." Yet, as I have attempted to show, the very framework used by Hill to analyze black family experiences was developed by Talcott Parsons.

8   For a detailed discussion of this point, see Schermerhorn (1970:50-59).

9   The problems presented by such a small number of black sociologists writing in the area of race relations, or any other subject area, was revealed when the editor of *Sociological Inquiry* proposed a special black issue of that journal in 1969. (This decision was made in response to Black Caucus complaints about the small number of articles by blacks in sociology journals.) A black consulting editor of *Sociological Inquiry* attempted to organize the issue by inviting black sociologists to submit papers. After a year of trying to obtain publishable manuscripts, the consulting editor dropped the project, stating that she "was unfortunately unable to get enough papers."

10   For a similar discussion of this point in relation to black scholars in general, see Merton (1972, pp. 42-43).

Bibliography

Bernard, Jessie.
    1966   *Marriage and Family Among Negroes*. Englewood Cliffs, N.J.: Prentice-Hall.
Billingsley, Andrew.
    1968   *Black Families in White America*. Englewood Cliffs, N.J.: Prentice-Hall.
    1972   Foreword to Robert B. Hill, *The Strength of Black Families*. New York: Emerson Hall, pp. xi-xvii.
Blumer, Herbert.
    1965   "Industrialisation and Race Relations," *Industrialisation and Race Relations: A Symposium*, ed. Guy Hunter, London: Oxford University Press.
Coles, Robert.
    1964   *Children of Crisis*. New York: Little Brown.
Dizard, Jan E.
    1968   "Why Should Negroes Work?" in *Negroes and Jobs: A Book of Readings*, ed. Louis A. Ferman, Joyce L. Kornbluh, and J. A. Miller. Ann Arbor: The University of Michigan Press.
Drake, St. Clair, and Horace R. Cayton.
    1945   *Black Metropolis*. New York: Harcourt, Brace and Company.
Frazier, E. Franklin.
    1939   *The Negro Family in the United States*. Chicago: University of Chicago Press.
Gordon, Milton M.
    1964   *Assimilation in American Life*. New York: Oxford University Press.
Hannerz, Ulf.
    1969   *Soulside: Inquiries into Ghetto Culture and Community*. New York: Emerson Hall.
Hare, Nathan.
    1969   "The Challenge of a Black Scholar," *The Black Scholar* 1 (December): 58-63.

Hill, Robert B.
  1972   *The Strength of Black Families.* New York: Emerson Hall.
Horton, John.
  1966   "Order and Conflict Theories of Social Problems as Competing
          Ideologies," *American Journal of Sociology* 71 (May): 701-13.
Ibn Alkalimat, Abd-l Hakimu (Gerald McWorter).
  1969   "The Ideology of Black Social Science," *The Black Scholar* 1
          (December): 28-35.
Johnson, Charles S.
  1941   *Growing Up in the Black Belt.* Washington, D.C.: American
          Council on Education.
Ladner, Joyce A.
  1971   *Tomorrow's Tomorrow: The Black Woman.* Garden City, N.Y.:
          Doubleday.
Lewis, Hylan.
  1955   *Backways of Kent.* Chapel Hill: University of North Carolina
          Press.
Liebow, Elliot.
  1967   *Tally's Corner: A Study of Negro Streetcorner Men.* Boston:
          Little, Brown.
Lincoln, C. Eric.
  1965   "The Absent Father Haunts the Negro Family," *The New York
          Times Magazine* (November 28).
Merton, Robert K.
  1948   "The Self-Fulfilling Prophecy," *Antioch Review* (Summer),
          pp. 193-210.
  1972   "Insiders and Outsiders: A Chapter in the Sociology of Knowl-
          edge," *American Journal of Sociology* 78 (July): 9-47.
Moynihan, Daniel P.
  1965   *The Negro Family: The Call for National Action.* Washington
          D.C.: U.S. Department of Labor.
Nagel, Ernest.
  1961   *The Structure of Science: Problems in the Logic of Scientific
          Explanation.* New York: Harcourt, Brace & World.
Parsons, Talcott.
  1951   *The Social System.* New York: The Free Press.
Parsons, Talcott, and Robert F. Bales.
  1955   *Family Socialization and Interaction Process.* New York: The
          Free Press.

Reissman, Frank.
    1966   "In Defense of the Negro Family," *Dissent* (March-April): 141-55.
Rudner, Richard S.
    1966   *Philosophy of Science.* Englewood Cliffs, N.J.: Prentice-Hall.
Schermerhorn, Richard.
    1970   *Comparative Ethnic Relations: A Framework for Theory and Research.* New York: Random House.
Staples, Robert.
    1970   "The Myth of the Black Matriarchy," *The Black Scholar* (February): 9-16.
    1971   *The Black Family: Essays and Studies.* Belmont, California: The Wadsworth Publishing Company.
Williams, Robin M., Jr.
    1947   "The Reduction of Intergroup Tension," *Social Sciences Research Council Bulletin,* no. 57.
Willie, Charles V.
    1970   *The Family Life of Black People.* Columbus, Ohio: Charles E. Merrill.
Wilson, William J.
    1973   *Power, Racism, and Privilege: Race Relations in Theoretical and Sociohistorical Perspectives.* New York: The Macmillan Co.
Wilson, William J., and Richard G. Dumont.
    1968   "Rules of Correspondence and Sociological Concepts," *Sociology and Social Research* 52 (January): 217-27.

V. Institutional Adaptations

13

James E. Blackwell

ROLE BEHAVIOR IN A CORPORATE

STRUCTURE: BLACK

SOCIOLOGISTS IN THE ASA

I

The major purpose of this discussion is to analyze differential role behavior of black sociologists within the American Sociological Association as responses to latent or manifest discriminatory practices within the organization. It is argued that, in spite of external and internal perceptions of the association as a "traditionally liberal" organization, its elitist practices have until recently given it a highly conservative character. The major focus here is on the experiences of black members in the association; however, failure to point out that other groups have encountered similar deprivations would obviously be a gross distortion of reality.

The American Sociological Association was founded in 1905, and blacks have either attended its meetings or been members almost since the founding period. They have always been in a minority situation both within the larger society and in the ASA. The experiences parallel. This situation may be characterized by categorical treatment or structural discrimination in general, denial of access to the major values of the association (controlled participation), social isolation, slights, self-consciousness among black members, role ambiguities, and uncertainties among many members, black and white, concerning the appropriateness of their responses to each other. Axiomatically, many of these situations are a consequence of historical forces operative at various stages in the association's development. Others may in part be traced to structural changes or shifts in the nature of the association itself.

In terms of numerical strength, control over the decision-making

341

process, access to status-conferring systems, or along almost any discernible measure evoked, a pattern of dominance-subordination has characterized the internal structure and external relations among the membership of the ASA. The dominant group, almost always white male, consistently maintained and exercised power to define eligibility and acceptability for roles either assigned or achieved by the members. Necessarily, and within the framework of the most prevalent ideology of expected or socially sanctioned minority group behavior, blacks who became members were expected to achieve along a prescribed system of normative behavior defined by this dominant group in order to become integrated into the dominant system. It was somewhat assumed somewhere along the way that universalistic criteria for gaining access to "scarce values" were at once known, shared, and pervasive in the dominant system. Although there is considerable dispute as to what constitutes the "universalistic criteria," we may assume, for the sake of argument, that these included scholarly standing in the field of sociology (professional visibility) as measured by the quantity of publications, that is, the number of articles published in prestigious or "refereed" journals as opposed to articles published in popular magazines or newspapers. It is claimed that these criteria extended to participation in the annual program of the association, and, to a lesser degree, participation in the activities of regional societies. All such criteria supposedly attest to the national reputation of an individual among his peers which theoretically enhances the opportunity for peers to confer higher recognition on him by electing him to a leadership position with the American Sociological Association. These are undoubtedly ideal expectations, since actual behavior often contradicts such principles.

Our major hypothesis is that black members of the ASA have historically sought inclusion in the affairs of the association, but that the utilization of so-called "universalistic criteria" has served to limit, if not exclude, blacks from access to the "shared values" [1] available to the majority of white members of the ASA. Essentially, consistent with orthodox perspectives of sociologists concerning the eventual modes of incorporation of "alien groups" in the larger social structure, assimilation has been the primary goal of black sociologists. Inasmuch as this goal was consistently blocked, it is argued, black sociologists came to accept one of three alternative methods of dealing with the basic problem. Either they would engage in an organized protest to effectuate inclusion; separate to form a parallel organization of black professional sociologists; or, finally, accept the status quo of peripheral membership. It is further argued that although the major effort was toward incorporation, polarization or disunity existed among black sociologists of a sort not uncharacteristic of that which prevailed in the latter stages of the civil rights movement of the sixties. The result of the struggle with the ASA was, among other things, a convergence of black demands with existing professional standards.

The response pattern made by black sociologists, therefore, to perceived patterns of discrimination or exclusion not only tend to vary at any given time but, it is observed, reflect patterns that seemed prevalent in the larger community in its relation to the larger white society's structural and psychological discriminatory practices against it. Although numerous attempts have been made to systematize these patterns into handy classificatory schema, they may be reduced for our purposes to acceptance, withdrawal or avoidance, assimilation, contention, and revitalization.[2]

II

The membership of black sociologists in the American Sociological Association has never approximated the proportion of blacks in the larger population. Neither is it likely to attain this percentage at any time in the discernible future, for reasons that we shall identify later in this discourse. However, the membership is disproportionately lower than it would have been if, admittedly in hindsight, the leadership structure had taken appropriate steps to encourage blacks to become members and to participate in the affairs of the society in its early history.[3] It would, in my view, be stretching scholarly imagination to conclude that all of our early founders were racially prejudiced. In some instances, in the absence of scholarly scientific proof to the contrary, a more correct assumption may be that the behavior of some of the founding fathers of sociology in the United States represented a disjunction between positive racial attitudes at the personal level and negative behavioral patterns at a societal level. Logic makes it difficult to accept the notion articulated by some that black scholars such as W. E. B. Du Bois were rejected by the ASA because they were "radicals qua radicals" and not because they were black. There may be a measure of truth in that assertion; however, little imagination is required to ascertain that the presence of both conditions, "black" and "radical," did not and does not promote a high degree of acceptability among sociologists at any moment in history.

During the early period, when the ASA was itself a loosely organized body, no significant steps were taken by the organization either to increase the number of blacks among its total membership or to incorporate its few black members into its structure or to enable them to play leadership roles. However, there is evidence that the most persistent objective of black sociologists regarding the association is and remains assimilation into the mainstream of the organization. This goal has endured even when efforts directed toward inclusion were thwarted, as was denial of opportunity to meet universalistic criteria for acceptance. Blacks were confronted with social oppression, structural isolation and psychological uncertainties, as they attempted to attend the annual meetings of the society and associated activities. In 1934, while the ASA was holding its annual meeting in Atlantic City, Charles S. Johnson, who had already distinguished himself as a scholar/teacher and who would attend annual meetings of the association for more than thirty years prior to his death, was subjected to categorical treatment (discrimination) by the hotel management. He was ordered to use the rear elevator when entering the hotel. He refused and, consistent with the external image of learned organizations in general, the American Sociological Association established a new policy on convention sites. The policy mandated that the organization would not hold its annual meetings at any locale which discriminated against any of its members.

The implementation of such a policy was particularly noteworthy since it came at a most antiliberal time in the United States. Inter alia, the KKK was in its heyday. Blacks were required to be better than the average whites in order to be accepted in graduate schools of sociology or to hope for some paternalistic professor to confer upon them the classification of "high probability" toward the achievement of the doctorate. In short, because of admissions policies, including quotas, eligibility would be conferred on an exceptionally few black persons as sociologists. Eligibility for full participation in the affairs of the association would be conferred on even fewer.

The policy enunciated in 1934, regarding meetings, meant that the ASA, for more than three decades, would not hold any subsequent meetings in the South, where racism was more blatant. The policy neither dealt with nor anticipated the subtle forms of racism which black members would encounter in the Northeast and West, nor did it predict the residual consequence that a sizeable number of practicing sociologists, black and white, would be effectively eliminated from attendance at national meetings and from informal interaction with professional colleagues because of the economic hardships incurred in attending meetings at long distances. Most black teachers of sociology or practicing sociologists in general were located in the South, working at predominantly black and often impoverished institutions. In most instances, budgetary constraints and limited encouragement for intellectual pursuits deterred blacks from participation. Those who managed to attend felt the strains of social isolation and self-consciousness so strongly that they soon withdrew into informal friendship cliques. Due to an involuntary, ascribed lowered status, many blacks voluntarily segregated themselves at national meetings for a social life free from the "put on" or perceived false friendship. One quite predictable outcome was the development of parallel structures, since blacks were not invited to read papers, participate in panels, or hold office. One structure whose origin can be traced to such factors is the Association for Social and Behavior Sciences. Thus, when the white sociologists were dining at the hotel restaurant or holding reunions in facilities which were open to them, black sociologists held their sessions in black establishments in the black community. One must remember that the advent of access to public accommodations is a phenomenon of the 1960s and not of earlier periods in this century. Withdrawal and avoidance patterns, such as the formation of parallel structures, represented protest forms prevalent at the time. In a real sense, they came to be accepted as institutionalized characteristics of minority (black)—dominant (white) existence. [4]

For several years the ASA did not seem prepared, by encouraging full assimilation of black members, to move beyond the policy enunciated in 1934. There was no evidence that its members argued for radical alterations in its internal structure which would assure equal access to the means for achievement and recognition in the field. Among black sociologists a negative belief system emerged regarding the possibility of high status achievement or recognition as a sociologist rather than as a "black sociologist." Contrarily, it was generally believed that articles submitted for publication in the established journals associated with professional sociology such as the *American Sociological Review* and the *American Journal of Sociology* were not likely to be accepted. Some believed that articles submitted by black sociologists employed in black colleges and universities, where 99 percent of them worked, were not even likely to be read, since by definition they were of inferior quality. Tentative data collected by Jacquelyne J. Jackson leads her to conclude, perhaps somewhat hastily, that blacks who received their doctorates from the University of Chicago seemed to have been successful in the publication of at least one article in the *American Journal of Sociology*, but nothing more. [5] This finding appears to be closely correlated with the factor of sponsorship; that is, where blacks had white sponsors (academic paternalism) who possessed access to the publication process, the blacks' chances of publishing in the mainstream journal were increased, though not significantly, since few have ever published in ASA refereed (professionally approved) journals. One consequence of this practice was the establishment of journals catering largely to research done by black social and behavioral scientists though characteristically open and available for articles submitted by anyone regardless of race, color, or creed. The term "characteristically" is used here to connote a continuous pattern of behavior as evidenced in the openness of black institutions to nonblacks, especially whites, at the same time that institutional closure cum exclusion prevails within the dominant structure.

Since institutional dualism exists in the larger society, in terms of black-white relations and the formation of parallel structures, the same phenomenon developed in academic and professional institutions. The "two-ness" described by Du Bois in *The Souls of Black Folk* also characterized, then and now, black sociologists as members of the American Sociological Association. For most, the primary identity is as a sociologist-scholar and secondarily as a member of a racial or ethnic category. However, many believe that others order their perceptions of black sociologists first in terms of a racial category rather than as a professionally competent sociologist. In short, these people see "race" first, which influences subsequent modes of interaction. An extension of this premise is that the competence of blacks is neither likely to be recognized nor rewarded by significant segments of the sociological fraternity. Or, if rewards are to be conferred, a higher degree of selectivity (dual standards, as it were) will be exacted in their case than would otherwise be the norm.

The dualism engenders status ambiguities, role conflicts, isolation, and contention. It is a function of limited access to those values held by the dominant group. Historically, blacks who worked at small, predominantly black colleges have not enjoyed access to research funds. For that matter, today in the 1970s, in comparison to white social scientists in general, blacks do not have equal access to research funds even when the major focus of the research is on blacks as subjects. This situation may in part be attributed to unsubstantiated notions of the inability of blacks to carry out sophisticated research projects, as well as to limited knowledge of blacks concerning available avenues to funding sources, a restricted sphere of influence in awarding research grants, a very narrow range of contacts with people who simply know where the funds are located and how to attain them, and discrimination in the awarding of funds to white and black scholars.

Not only did blacks develop their own associations but they tended to follow the path of their white counterparts in the programmatic activities of these associations. Thus, black associations provided opportunities for the reading of papers based upon scholarly research, participation on panels or taking the leadership in seminars or in the development of national and regional problems. Many blacks achieved high professional visibility in an all-black professional world. In this context, self-consciousness, identity-confusion, role-management, and tokenism were not serious problems; at least they were not insurmountable.

Until 1969, the participation of black sociologists in the affairs of the American Sociological Association is best described as "abject tokenism." This is true irrespective of the measure employed to determine participation. The fact is hardly contestable, regardless of shallow assertions that sociology is a liberating discipline, especially in the field of interracial behavior, or despite the fact that many individual white sociologists have striven arduously as individuals to create a better world both in the profession and in society at large.

In the sixty-seven years since its founding in 1905, the ASA has had only one black sociologist elevated by his peers to its highest elective position. The late E. Franklin Frazier, elected in 1947, served as president in 1948. Only four blacks were ever nominated for the vice-presidency: Charles S. Johnson, Ira De Augustine Reid, Preston Valien, and Joseph Himes. Johnson and Reid succeeded in becoming elected and did serve as vice-presidents of the association. Between 1946 and 1969, the most enlightened period in the civil rights movement of this century, only four black sociologists were elected to serve on the council, which is of course the singularly most important decision-making body of the organization! It is a gross injustice to charge, as some have implied, that blacks who attempt to gain access to the committee structure of the association or to its decision-making units are nothing more than "house niggers." The very use of this type of epithet to characterize those who seek inclusion raises questions about the prejudices and motivations of the users. Could it be that the users of such derogatory terms would in fact prefer to maintain the status quo of an all-white body, limiting if not preventing participation of blacks in the profession in any form while masking their real motives under the call for "universalistic criteria"? Could it be that such persons are in fact apologists for white privilege and black exclusion? Could their charges of "reverse racism" underscore deeply rooted racial prejudices of their own?

A closer examination of the membership structure of the American Sociological Association during the four-year period prior to and including the year of the first overt manifestation of dissatisfaction of blacks with the operation of the association, at the 1968 Boston meetings, is instructive.

Participation of Black Sociologists in ASA, 1965-68

Year	Number on Elective and Appointed Committees*	Total Membership of Committees	Number Chairing Sessions
1965	1	203	0
1966	2	203	0
1967	3	194	0
1968	2	203	0

*This includes membership on the council of the association. In each of the periods, approximately thirty-three standing, constitutional, and ad hoc committees were in existence. (See *The American Sociologist* for 1965, 1966, 1967, and 1968.)

It is clear from the above data that white sociologists monopolized advantages that accrued from membership in the association, especially in terms of the participation structure and professional visibility. Black sociologists soon concluded that membership without a voice or membership without power is indeed empty. The use of such terminology suggests a political stance; however, in my view, political perspectives are not a creation of the black sociologist's efforts toward inclusion. Neither are they a consequence of the Sociology Liberation Movement nor of the Women's Caucus. The Black Caucus demands would have come into existence in any case. I submit that politicization has characterized the association since it shifted from a small, informal society in 1939,[6] with approximately 1,000 members, to a more formal organization in the 1960s, when its membership had reached 9,000. Informal politicking had characterized many elections of the association prior to 1968 and has continued thereafter. Witness the number of letters circulated in behalf of a particular candidate for an elective office each year.

The assumed political behavior of black sociologists at the 1968 annual meetings in Boston must be viewed in terms of the historical factors of denial under which most black sociologists functioned. The stance taken in Boston could have been predicted by astute observers of human nature, and it was long overdue. For several years, it is estimated that black membership in the association was approximately 2 to 3 percent of the total. There would have been little concern over the issue of black participation and conferring of eligibility or access to highly desired values had black sociologists enjoyed relatively high visibility which approached parity. For several years the same two black sociologists were given the opportunity to demonstrate ability to help govern, in a limited manner, the affairs of the association. For example, the most persistent of these two has been Hylan Lewis, who served for several years as a member of the Ad Hoc Committee on UNESCO and represented the association in Washington, D.C., in 1966, on the Natural Sciences Commission of the U.S. National Commission for UNESCO.

Black sociologists, of course, were cognizant of the utilization of so-called universalistic criteria as determinants for eligibility in the corporate leadership structure but remained uncertain as to what constituted them. What were the actual determinants employed: Scholarly reputation? High professional visibility? Friendship cliques? Control over the spheres of dominance? Excellent sponsorship? Whatever they were, it was evident in 1968 that only one black sociologist appeared on the program of the annual meeting. Blacks were not members of the council of the association. Blacks were all but absent from the committee structure of the association. Only one black sociologist had been consistently involved in the visiting scientist program, Professor Butler Jones. Research funds were as a rule not available to blacks even when the primary focus was on blacks, and their articles were not likely to be published in mainstream journals. In this context, black sociologists asked: What does it mean to be a black sociologist in a predominantly white community of scholars? Is there not a blatant inconsistency between the external image of a liberal organization and the reality of deleterious conservatism within its internal structure? What are the alternative courses of action facing black members of the association? These questions were posed at a time when radical social and political changes were occurring within the black community in

America. They were undergirded by ideological issues which rendered a quiet quest for assimilation (or its acceptance as the desired goal) untenable as a primary solution to problems of accommodation between the races. They were raised at a time when the pacifist character of the civil rights movement was giving way to the new forms of militancy and confrontation in the black liberation movement. It was naïve to assume that black sociologists, whose lives always reflected a "strange dualism," could stand aloof from the conditions in which they found themselves as paying members of the American Sociological Association. They had unsuccessfully attempted professional acculturation, a process which in itself carries the seeds of intergroup conflict. Could structural assimilation then be achieved without formal protest? Could their rights and opportunities as members be expanded under the then existing situation of unexpressed concern? The response manifested itself in a heightened self-consciousness, self-awareness, and a group identity which combined to form a nascent "caucus" as the instrument for further expressive behavior.

The Caucus of Black Sociologists, a loosely structured ad hoc body under the leadership of Professor Tillman Cothran of Atlanta University, was formed in 1968 as a reaction to past denials and in order to advance the objective of professional inclusion. This is the major thrust of the resolutions presented by the caucus at the Boston meetings:

Whereas historically Black Americans have been excluded from the mainstream of institutional and professional life in the United States;
Whereas the large number of Black sociologists in America have not participated fully in the activities of the American Sociological Association;
Whereas Black sociologists have only token representation in the formal and informal structure of the Association;
Whereas the growth of sociology in the United States has been related to minority and ethnic group problems and is today increasingly focused on the dominant domestic issue—the struggle for justice and equality for Black Americans;
Whereas the experiences and professional competence of Black sociologists are indispensable for sound interpretation of research and theory related to the Black Community;

Whereas a pattern has developed in the Association which allows unfair advantage to certain renowned members of the Association to hold multiple chairmanships and representation on panels,

BE IT THEREFORE RESOLVED:

1. That the Council of the Association should always have representation from the Black membership;
2. That a greater effort should be made to assign Black sociologists to membership and chairmanships on standing and ad hoc committees;
3. That the Black sociologists should serve more frequently as chairmen of sections in programs of Association meetings;
4. That Black sociologists should always be represented as presentors of papers and as discussants on programs which have major relevance to the Black community;
5. That criteria of acceptance of papers for the American Sociological Association journals should be clearly enunciated and publicized so that all members, especially Black members, will have equal opportunity for the acceptance of their papers, and
6. That Black sociologists be secured as readers and referees of papers for publication in the American Sociological Association's journals.[7]

This six-part resolution was passed by a majority vote of the members at the August 28 business meeting and approved by the council on the same date, as expressed in the following Council Resolution:

Whereas, historically black Americans have been excluded from the mainstream of institutional and professional life in the United States, be it resolved, That the American Sociological Association shall make every effort to ensure that black sociologists are brought into fullest participation in all aspects of the governance and other activities of the Association.[8]

The demands presented by the Caucus of Black Sociologists were consistent with assimilationist ideology. Black sociologists desired inclusion and recognition along the same dimensions applied to white counterparts, and nothing more. They called for a critical assessment of the opportunity structure within the association regarding realization of full participation. In terms of history, these were indeed radical changes that were being sought, for no blacks served as section chairmen and comparatively few had ever served as session organizers at annual meetings. In another sense, these were relatively innocuous requests, except that, as is always the case with holders of power, a few sociologists would of necessity either relinquish or fail to attain some of their privilege of participating in "governance and other activities of the Association," were these goals to be realized. Harmless though these goals may have been to the majority who voted for the resolutions, a few nonblack sociologists would inevitably raise the cry of "special privilege to blacks" and "reverse racism" in subsequent letters to *The American Sociologist*. An identical phenomenon occurred in 1971 following positive action among the regular members and by the council on resolutions presented by the Caucus of Black Sociologists at the 1970 meetings in Washington, D.C.

Following the approval of the 1968 council resolution, the Committee on Committees, an all-white body, requested the Caucus of Black Sociologists to submit a list of black sociologists who could be recommended to the council for appointments on standing and ad hoc committees. Seven blacks were appointed to various committees of the association for 1969. Professor Tillman Cothran was nominated but not elected to the Committee on Publications. Professor Joseph Himes ran unsuccessfully for membership on the council. Professors Hylan Lewis and G. Franklin Edwards were nominated for membership on the Committee on Committees; the latter won a seat for 1969. A significantly larger number of blacks were scheduled to participate in the 1969 program in San Francisco. The association had also assigned space for meetings or other special activities to the ad hoc caucus, the women's group and the radical-sociological liberationists.

Although some were positive steps toward meeting the goals articulated by the Caucus of Black Sociologists, the actions taken by the council remained tepid forays into academic tokenism in the view of the disaffiliated and more activist group which was prominent in the caucus movement at San Francisco. Though short-lived, a struggle developed between those whose goal, on the one hand, remained "assimilation into the mainstream" and those who, on the other hand, advocated separation with reparations from the almost exclusively white American Sociological Association. A precedent had already been established for this course of action with the establishment of the Association of Black Psychologists. Why not display solidarity and self-identity by withdrawal and avoidance?

Would this action not draw dramatic attention to the racist nature of the association? This stance was also consistent with a growing movement at the time among young graduate students and older sympathizers. The rationalization or justification was basically that the most profound consequence of the drive toward assimilation and incorporation was abject tokenism. Otherwise, assimilation was a dismal failure. The return to parallel structures would provide blacks with a better opportunity to decide their own fate and expand the scope of professional participation through research concerning the black community. It could also serve a protective or ego-safeguard function by shielding blacks from the negative aspects of subordinate roles. This process alienated a number of "establishment-oriented" black sociologists. Potentially, it could be both disruptive and divisive. The unity evidenced at Boston was threatened but salvaged by an understanding of the costs of such divisions. The resolutions presented in 1969 in behalf of the still ad hoc Caucus of Black Sociologists, then under the temporary leadership of Professor Ernest Works, again proves instructive:

1. Statement of the Black Caucus:
The Black Caucus has considered at great length the relation of black sociologists to the American Sociological Association. On the basis of our discussions we have concluded that the procedures employed by the ASA effectively exclude black sociologists from meaningful participation in the activities of the Association. We define this situation as intolerable and feel that remedial action should be taken forthwith. We, therefore, demand that the following be complied with by the ASA:

1. That the Executive Council of the ASA call a special meeting and communicate to the Black Caucus what specific steps have been taken to implement the demands of the Black Caucus at the 1968 meetings.
2. That Black members of the ASA be appointed to all of the decision-making bodies whose actions influence the decisions of the ASA.
3. That multiple participation in sessions of the ASA be stopped and that participation be distributed more evenly among (the members) of the Association.
4. That the ASA undertake a program designed to provide scholarships and other forms of financial assistance for black students interested in sociology.

5. That the ASA arrange for special sessions for Black sociologists at the 1970 meetings.

The Black Caucus has also discussed the relationship of the ASA to social issues and found the relationship lacking. We feel that silence and inaction on social issues is tantamount to support of the conditions which underlie the issue. We therefore go on record as categorically opposed to:

1. The War in Vietnam
2. Counter-insurgency research
3. Political oppression of the Black Panther Party
4. Political oppression of black brothers and sisters who are trying to make our educational institutions more relevant to the black experience.
5. The shabby treatment of brother Nathan Hare at San Francisco State College.
6. The use of welfare to make the black population a dependent population.
7. Black capitalism which, in our view, is a sham.
8. The scheduled execution of brother Ahmed Evans in the State of Ohio for September 23, 1969. [9]

Inasmuch as the second half of the statement represented only the sense of the Black Caucus and required no formal action by the association, the participants voted its approval of the five positions in the first half of the statement at its business meeting on September 3, 1969. The 1970 council, meeting on September 5, 1969, approved the following motions in response to those presented by the Black Caucus:

Motion: That the Council has received the resolution of the Black Caucus, and Council reaffirms its continuing concern for the active participation of all minority groups in Association affairs. The *spokesman* for the Black Caucus is to be informed of the steps that have been taken by the Association to increase black participation in the program of the Annual Meeting, noting that these rules are under review by a new committee with the hope of widening participation. Seconded and approved.

Motion: That the Association provide up to $500.00 to a designated black sociologist to make an informal survey of various funding agencies as to the steps they are taking to support black sociologists by means of fellowships, research grants, etc. Seconded and approved. [10]

The council also pointed out that a session was being organized in race and ethnic relations and that "an invitation is to be extended to another member of the Black Caucus to organize a session on black sociology for the 1970 Annual Meetings." [11]

The motion passed by the council seemed to have been designed to placate for the moment rather than to take forthright steps that would assure a widened participation of blacks in the activities of the association. However, on January 21, 1970, Professor E. M. Volkart, then the ASA executive officer, addressed a letter to Professor Ernest Works, the ad hoc chairman of the Black Caucus. This letter reviewed in brief the various roles played by black sociologists in the association as well as the steps taken by the council to meet the caucus demands. [12]

As a result of action taken by the Ad Hoc Caucus of Black Sociologists in the 1968 and 1969, black members became more visible in the affairs of the association. Professor Tillman Cothran was *appointed* to the Committee on Publications in 1969. [13] One black member, Professor Joseph Himes, was nominated but lost in his bid for membership on the council. Two members of the association, Professors Lewis and Edwards, contested seats on the Committee on Committees but only G. Franklin Edwards was successful. Professor Troy Duster was at the same time serving as a member of the editorial board of the TAS.

The national slate for the 1970 elections included one black member for vice president-elect—Professor Joseph Himes; two for the council—Professors Cothran and Lewis; three for the Committees—Professors Charles V. Willie, Charles U. Smith and James A. Moss; and one for the Committee on Nominations—Professor Troy Duster. Of the seven black sociologists nominated on the 1970 slate, only one, Professor Charles V. Willie, was elected.

The 1970 Council appointed black sociologists to the following committees:

Constitutional Committees

Tillman Cothran	1971 Program Committee
Butler Jones	Committee on Regional Affairs
Charles Smith	Committee on Training and Professional Ethics
G. Franklin Edwards	Committee on Training and Professional Ethics

Standing Committees

William J. Wilson	Awards Selection Committee
Hylan Lewis	Committee on Research and Teaching
Tillman Cothran	Committee on Public Information
William J. Wilson	Committee on Professional Ethics
Joseph S. Himes and Albert J. McQueen	Committee on Teaching Undergraduate Sociology
Hylan Lewis	Committee on UNESCO
J. Herman Blake	Committee on Public Policy

Ad Hoc Committees

Joyce Ladner	Committee on Rights and Privileges of Membership
Ruth S. Hamilton	Teacher-Sociologists

Boards

Charles V. Willie	Board of Directors of SSRC

Frustration and anxiety increased within the community of black sociologists after observing the outcome of the 1970 election and the "progress" made toward broader participation. Clearly, the accomplishments were unsatisfactory. These setbacks necessitated appeals for new steps or different tactics not only to realize the goal of broader participation but for persuading the ASA to deal more forthrightly with issues of scholarship, research funds, and other matters affecting blacks in the profession.

To those who observed the meetings of the caucus in San Francisco and who were present at the first caucus business meeting in Washington, D.C., in 1970, it soon became evident that a formal organizational structure was imperative if the goals were to be reached. The leadership had to be clearly defined, goals rearticulated, and strategies precisely honed. An administrative structure based upon concepts of organizational and role management, role property use and role property, was also needed. Professor James E. Blackwell, chairman of the Department of Sociology and Anthropology at the University of Massachusetts at Boston, was requested to serve as chairman of a committee whose major purpose was to devise plans for the development of a formal structure and to formulate resolutions commensurate with new goals. Professor Blackwell was also requested to serve as the interim national chairman of the new organization, the Caucus of Black Sociologists, until a national election could be conducted in November, 1970. He subsequently served for two years.

The resolutions presented in Washington, D.C., reflected this new thrust as well as the decision to make the system work for black sociologists. The alternative was unequivocal separation from the American Sociological Association. A decision had been made. Remaining within the ASA was conditional upon positive and immediate responses. The resolutions called attention to the fact that it was the failure of the association to make adequate responses to the previously articulated demands of the Black Caucus and to move forward the structural alterations required for increased black visibility or participation within the power structure which gave the caucus its raison d'être. They called further for a movement away from the gradualist approach toward a recognition of the urgency of the situation. Clearly, the resolutions were assimilationist in substance. They were also attestations to the fact that the Caucus of Black Sociologists was being formed not by "bellicose radicals" given to meaningless rhetoric but by people who understood the nature of formal organizations, the conditions that engender subsystems, parallel structures, and processes which serve either to heighten or reduce alienation.

The statement made by the Caucus of Black Sociologists at the 1970 meeting of the ASA follows:

> The Caucus of Black Sociologists takes the position that traditional sociology as perpetrated by the establishment of the American Sociological Association does not address itself fully to the needs of the people

of the American Society; nor does it address itself to the crucial issues affecting the lives of people at home and abroad. The major focus of what we call empirical sociology is indeed extremely parsimonious and devoid of humanism.

Thus, Whereas we condemn the self-interested professionalism which is implicit in the conventions of the ASA and within present-day "mainstream sociology" and

Whereas, the Caucus is committed to re-directing the ASA and its sterile traditionalism on to a new path addressing itself to dynamic social change and the real needs of our society; and

Whereas the legitimacy of this view is derived from the often neglected sociological investigations of such scholars as Lester F. Ward, Albion W. Small, Charles S. Johnson, C. Wright Mills, and W. E. B. Du Bois;

It is therefore in this spirit and soul that we submit the following resolutions for acceptance and implementation by the 1970 Convention of the American Sociological Association.

Therefore, Be it resolved that the legitimacy of the Caucus of Black Sociologists be recognized as of 1 September 1970, as a functioning committee of the ASA.

I. 1. Be it further resolved that the ASA provide funds, office space, and other supportive services to facilitate the organization and maintenance of the Caucus of Black Sociologists, including a full-time executive secretary,

2. Be it further resolved that, effective immediately, appropriate steps be initiated to include a minimum of three (3) Black sociologists as members of the Council of the American Sociological Association, and that, from 1970 on, the ASA Council will include not less than three (3) Black sociologists.

3. Be it further resolved that every committee of the ASA shall include not less than one Black sociologist.

4. Be it further resolved that a committee appointed by the Caucus of Black Sociologists will serve as an advisory committee for the appointments of Blacks to the ASA committees.

5. Be it further resolved that the 1971 program chairman of the ASA reconstitute the allocation of sectional (session) chairman so as to have greater dispersion of Black sociologists so as not to restrict each and every one of them to a subsection implicitly or explicitly concerned with race and ethnic relations.

II. Be it further resolved that the ASA provide funds for the Caucus of Black Sociologists to undertake immediately a survey (with the Director appointed by the Caucus of Black Sociologists) to ascertain the status of Black faculty and Black graduate students and to determine what concrete efforts are being made to increase the number of such faculty and students in each department of Sociology in every American institution of higher learning containing same. It is expected that the first report will be made available and duly published in *The American Sociologist.*

III. Be it further resolved that research projects dealing specifically with Black people be directed by Black sociologists with professional competence in the research areas of concern.

Be it further resolved that the ASA urge both public and private funding agencies to direct all funds for sociological research on Black people to Black sociologists.

Be it further resolved that we demand research which validates social humanism, liberation, and the legitimacy of the struggle of oppressed people for self-determination.

IV. Be it further resolved that the ASA, in recognition of the long-standing significant contributions of W.E.B. Du Bois, Charles S. Johnson, and E. Franklin Frazier, initiate as of 1971, the *Du Bois-Johnson-Frazier Award* for distinguished contributions in the field of sociology by a sociologist, and that the criteria for the recipients of such an award will be established by the Caucus of Black Sociologists and duly publicized by the Caucus and by the ASA.

V. Be it further resolved that the ASA recognize the diverse expertise present among the constituency of Black sociologists by, inter alia, increasing Black representation in the ASA Visiting Scientists Program.

Be it further resolved that funds be provided immediately for teams of Black sociologists to conduct seminars for sociology faculties throughout the country, with such seminars focusing directly upon the integration of the Black perspective in sociology.[14]

Resolution I.2, the most controversial of all those presented by the caucus, narrowly received approval at the business meeting (a margin of five votes). What was not known by the nonblacks in attendance was that the defeat of resolution I would have been interpreted as hypocrisy and blacks would have bolted the organization. The arguments presented by adversaries to the motion centered almost exclusively upon the issues of "quotas" and constitutional constructionist sentiment. Both groups claimed support for the position that black sociologists should serve on the council but that their election should be based upon "universalistic criteria." The trouble with that argument is that the "universalistic criteria" have never been clearly defined. Furthermore, there is ample evidence that other factors tangential to or having absolutely nothing whatsoever to do with presumed scholarly reputation always operated in the national elections and are undoubtedly of greater importance in the final selection of leaders and other committee members. In the case of the final vote on this resolution, it was difficult if not impossible to separate those who understood the fundamental purpose of the resolution from those who would not have supported anything which originated with this caucus. The purpose of the resolution was to dramatize the need to have black representation on the council, especially since concrete steps had already been taken to assure the presence of women on the council. The women sociologists were a separate organizaiton, with no more than two black women affiliated.

The first two resolutions, dealing with black control of research and funds for research on black people, met a resounding defeat. This may be attributed to (1) the belief by many that such resolutions violated the rights and freedoms of all scholars, (2) the position that such policies would give undue weight to race as a qualification for scientific research or for the acquisition of funds, and (3) the unwillingness of many who controlled avenues of access to research funds to share them with others. The last rationalization of course has both a protective economic character as well as overtones of racism. Even in defeat, the essential point was made; black sociologists desired access to research funds and were simply tired of white sociologists making their reputations on black subjects through exclusive control over the funding mechanism.

As a result of council action, the Du Bois-Johnson-Frazier Award was established, effective 1971. It was agreed that the award would be given either to a sociologist or to an institution whose work in the development of black sociologists was in the tradition of these three scholars. A five-hundred-dollar prize would also be given the recipients (the first was Professor Oliver Cromwell Cox, in 1971). At its meeting on November 14, 1970, the council adopted the following motions:

1. That Council appoint a committee on the relationship of Black sociologists to the ASA, the purpose of the committee being to meet with representatives of the Black Caucus to work out mutually acceptable forms of cooperation, including affiliation, to seek means of support for the organization of Black Sociologists, and the Council further authorizes the expenditure of up to $3,000 for expenses;
2. That the ASA appropriates, against efforts to seek outside funds, $2,500 for costs other than travel to facilitate the proposed meetings of the ASA subcommittee and the leaders of the Black Caucus;
3. That Council expresses support for research which shows concern in design and goals for the values of social humanism, liberation, and the legitimacy of the struggle of oppressed people for self determination.
4. That Council instructs the Executive Office, administerators of the ASA Visiting Scientists Program to do everything possible to increase Black representation.[15]

Another resolution on the development of funds for fellowships and scholarships, offered jointly by the Opportunities Fellowship Group and the black sociologists, was referred to the subcommittee which subsequently met with caucus representatives. The members of the council subcommittee, Professors Morris Janowitz, Stanton Wheeler, Melvin Seeman, and Frank Myamoto, met with representatives of the Caucus of Black Sociologists on January 15, 1971. At the conclusion of these deliberations, the council subcommittee issued the following statement:

The members of the Council sub-committee met with representatives of the Caucus of Black Sociologists to implement the Council resolution of November 1970.

The sub-committee recommends that the Council accept and implement the principle that staff personnel be added to work on professional and academic problems related to the needs of the Blacks and other minority groups.

The focus of the duties of the position would be on assessing and developing the training, and professional status of sociologists. We recognize that the needs of the Black Caucus have a pressing priority, but the goal in the long run is the further advancement of the sociological profession.

As an interim step we recommend that the Council direct the

Executive Officer to explore the recruitment and financing of a part-time person from March until the Fall of 1971. The goal is to develop funding for a full-time person as long as this need is pressing in the sociological profession.

The Caucus of Black Sociologists has agreed to assist in seeking funds and nominating personnel to meet this staff requirement. The appointment will be made in the normal procedures and the person will be located in the national office of the ASA.

The sub-committee notes that the Executive Officer is collecting some descriptive data on the status of Blacks in the sociological profession and that such a report will be available by June, 1971.

The sub-committee also notes that the Executive Officer, in collaboration with representatives of the Black Caucus, is exploring the possibilities of the research design in depth to understand the assets and dilemmas of Black students and Black faculty members.[16]

The council accepted this statement at its meeting on April 29, 1971. Concrete steps for effective changes consistent with subcommittee recommendations were advanced. Thus, a search was begun for an executive specialist on minority affairs, the title suggesting the broadened scope of responsibilities. In December 1971, Professor Maurice Jackson agreed to accept the position and to assume duties in late January, 1972.

In the meantime, President Sewell had already appointed a Committee on the Status of Racial and Ethnic Minorities in the Profession whose charge was consistent with requests from the Caucus of Black Sociologists regarding the concerns of black professors and graduate students. Central concerns were issues of recruitment and training of black graduate students, the availability and awarding of stipends, progress through the Ph.D. program, the recruitment of black sociologists as well as matters pertaining to promotion, retention, and tenure. The first report of this committee was issued in the August 1972 issue of *TAS*.[17]

The responses made by President Sewell and council members were much more positive and effective than others at any previous times. Seventeen black sociologists were appointed to committees whose total membership in 1971 was 188; this was approximately 9 percent of the total. Three were elected to constitutional committees, for 11 percent of the total of 27 members. Two were appointed to membership on editorial boards (total 112). One was appointed to the council for the 1970-71 year.

Since 1970, one black sociologist was elected to the council and to the Committee on Committees. Two were elected to the Committee on Nominations and one each to membership on the 1971, 1972, and 1973 Program Committees. In addition, black sociologists serve on 75 percent of the combined total of constitutional, standing and ad hoc committees of the association. Three have served as chairmen of committees and one was elected to serve as a section chairman. Professor Jacquelyne J. Jackson was appointed in 1972 to the editorship of the *Journal of Health and Social Behavior*. Since 1970, the positive stance taken toward greater participation by black sociologists is noticeably reflected in their roles at the annual meetings.

The 1972 annual meetings in New Orleans illustrate the point. There, at least thirty-five black sociologists were active participants; that is, reading papers, serving as discussants or session organizers and as session chair-persons. They participated in sessions on the family; race and ethnic relations; historical sociology; the military; population policy; theory; sociology of education; social psychology; social class; women sociologists; and in the full range of sessions dealing with black community, separatism, black studies, and so on. The diversity of interests among black sociologists was never before more apparent.[18]

Since 1968, the ASA has continued to provide meeting space and other facilities at the annual meetings for activities of the Caucus of Black Sociologists. Special programs were sponsored by the caucus at both the 1971 and 1972 annual meetings. These were more or less traditional sessions but featured both white and black sociologists. The attendance at the sessions appeared to be much higher than the average for other sessions during the annual program.

Although black sociologists are included in the affairs of the ASA on a much broader basis than in the pre-1968 period, it is still somewhat difficult for them to be elected section chairmen or to be elected to high positions in the organization. Appointment to the various committees is a function of the attitudes of the people who serve as president and members of the council. It can be assumed that an overall increase in the number of black participants in programmatic and organizational activities of the ASA would have occurred without a black council member. However, it is highly doubtful that the proportion would have been as great without that presence or without interaction between the president of the association and the national chairman of the CBS. One strong explanation for this is the knowledge gap. Most white sociologists do not know black sociologists. Without someone to identify black sociologists who could be available for various roles, their observed greater participation would not, in all probability, have occurred.

As the essay by Epps and Conyers in this volume points out, a critical manpower shortage exists among black sociologists. It can only be alleviated by the implementation of bold policies designed to recruit, train, and sustain a much larger number of black graduate students in sociology. Perhaps by expanding the supply pool, the problem of visibility will be confronted in a realistic sense.

There is every reason to believe that the Caucus of Black Sociologists will not disband as goals of participation in the American Sociological Association are achieved. On the one hand, it is essentially a minority group bound together by an emotional quality, common interests, and sustained by patterned interactions. On the other hand, from a rational-system perspective of organizations, it is an instrument for the realization of well-defined goals. Thus, it is not likely to be a short-lived phenomenon since the issues that created its existence, though somewhat alleviated, are still present.

Notes

1   See Judith Kramer, *The American Minority Community* (New York: Thomas Y. Crowell and Co., 1970), chap. 1, for an explanation of this concept. The author is indebted to Professor Kramer's cogent analysis of the minority situation for the framework upon which this discussion is based.

2   Examples of these systems of classification of minority responses are found in James Vander Zanden, *American Minority Relations* (New York: The Ronald Press, 1971), part 5; and Peter Rose, *They and We* (New York: Random House, 1964).

3   Scanty evidence exists pertaining to the numerical strength of black sociologists in the American Sociological Association. The study by Conyers and

Epps, included in this volume, is a notable contribution toward providing much-needed data that illuminates our knowledge on this issue. It is estimated, however, that blacks make up approximately 2 to 3 percent of the total ASA membership. Given the long-established need for teacher-scholars of sociology in higher education, the ASA should have embarked thirty years ago upon a systematic program designed to increase the number of blacks in the profession. Several means could have been utilized to implement this plan: (1) encouraging alternative admission policies to graduate schools, (2) providing more financial aid to black students, (3) obtaining foundation support and governmental assistance for scholarship or assistantship purposes, (4) deliberate recruitment efforts at black undergraduate liberal arts colleges for potential graduate students, (5) arranging visiting professorships at predominantly black institutions to help train undergraduate sociology students (as in the arrangements at Fisk University with Robert E. Park and at Atlanta University with Wilson Record).

4   Despite the disjunctive character of this situation, it should be stressed that outstanding or widely known black sociologists, like widely known "leaders" in general, moved between two worlds—black and white—during the pre-World War II era. Often this duality was at great personal sacrifice, and the movement was constrained by the normative structure of the two different worlds. In a way, intellectuals, black and white, often share this same experience of duality and uncertainty.

5   Professor Jackson may be treading on soft ground in the absence of conclusive empirical evidence to support her claim. What is needed is comparative data of a substantive nature. Surely, it can be argued that her observation describes most sociologists, black or white, and that the tendency is to publish one or two articles and then to disappear from the world of publication. Of greater pertinence, perhaps, is the fact that, given the structure of limited and denied opportunity, many sociologists went into administration which, in many cases, did not allow sufficient time for empirical research. In that event and without stronger empirical evidence, her assertion may be unfair to authors who made a contribution, as measured by the publication of "refereed articles." Nevertheless, even with the acceptance of such disclaimers, the most salient point is the fact that black sociologists have not generally published in mainstream sociological journals.

6   Talcott Parsons, "The Editor's Column," *The American Sociologist* 1, no. 2 (February 1966): 68.

7   Minutes of the first business meeting of the 1968 American Sociological Association meetings, *The American Sociologist* 3, no. 4 (November 1968): 322.

8   Minutes of the first 1969 council meeting of the American Sociological Association, *The American Sociologist* 3, no. 4 (November 1968): 323.

9   Minutes of the second business meeting, 1969 meetings of the American Sociological Association, *The American Sociologist* 5, no. 1 (February 1970): 68.

10   Minutes of the 1970 council meeting, 1969 meetings of the American Sociological Association, *The American Sociologist* 5, no. 1 (February 1970): 62.

11   Ibid.

12   Letter from E. M. Volkart to Ernest Works, dated January 21, 1970.

13   Minutes, 1970 council meeting, p. 21.

14   Resolutions of the Caucus of Black Sociologists, presented at the 1970 Meetings of the American Sociological Association, Washington, D.C.

15   Minutes of the Council Meeting of the American Sociological Association, dated November 14, 1970.

16   Minutes of the Council Meeting of the American Sociological Association, dated April 29, 1971.

17   "Report of the Committee on the American Status of Racial and Ethnic Minorities In the Profession," *The American Sociologist* 7, no. 7 (August 1972): 30.

18   See the Program of the Sixty-seventh Annual Meeting of the American Sociological Association, New Orleans, Louisiana, August 28, 1972.

14

Wilson Record

RESPONSE OF SOCIOLOGISTS
TO BLACK STUDIES

During the late 1960s, the black power movement in the United States resulted in the introduction of black studies at a large number of colleges and universities.[1] By 1972, these programs had been in existence long enough to warrant some field research on their impact. These programs had a particular impact on sociologists, both black and white, who had specialized in teaching and research on race and ethnic relations. Of special relevance was the question of the personal and professional response of white sociologists, who in the main have been oriented toward an integrationist viewpoint in race relations.[2]

In 1972, with grants from the Metropolitan Applied Research Center and the American Philosophical Society, the author completed a series of interviews throughout the United States during a five-month period. The focus of the field study was upon colleges and universities which had had a wide range of experience with black studies; those selected for a site visit included public and private, large and small, religious and secular institutions, widely dispersed throughout the nation.

At each campus visited efforts were made to interview every sociologist, white or black, who at the time of the visit professed, or had professed in some previous period, competence in race and ethnic relations. The author also interviewed the black studies staff. Almost without exception interviewees were surprisingly receptive to questions about their experience, particularly as the interview proceeded. It was not uncommon for conversations to last several hours. The mood was reflective—sifting, sorting, at times almost purgative.[3]

Patterns of Response

Among persons interviewed on 70 campuses were 209 sociologists who at the time or in the previous few years considered race and ethnicity as a teaching or research field.[4] On the basis of the contents of these interviews, the sociologists could be sorted roughly into four categories with respect to response to black studies. The *embracers* are those who for various reasons regard black studies programs as essentially a plus for the campus. The *antagonists* opposed black studies from the outset and continue to combat the movement openly, while pursuing their own teaching and research in race realtions. They tend to think, or at least to hope, that the programs eventually will wither away. The *accommodators* may be no more enthusiastic about black studies than the antagonists, but they accept the programs as here to stay. They no longer oppose the movement, at least not openly, and they continue to practice their specialty, albeit often with more emphasis on research and less on teaching than before. The *dropouts* have left the field of race relations, withdrawing under the fire of black militants.

Table 2 shows the distribution of the 209 sociologists among the four categories of response. The sociologists are broken down by race, ethnicity (Jews and gentiles), sex, and age. The 209 are not, of course, a random sample of American sociologists who specialize in race and ethnic relations.[5] Instead, they are sociologists who happened to be located on the campuses which were selected to yield a varied group of colleges and universities, as described earlier.

Race, ethnic, sex, and age differences in response to black studies will be examined. But first the four basic patterns of response will be explored and the complexity of the sociologists' experience illustrated by quotations from the interviews.

The *embracers* are a mixed group and their reasons for embracement are sometimes poles apart. The 59 interviewees in that category include only a few black separatists, even among the 19 blacks. The category contains sociologists who would have preferred extending regular curricula to encompass black experience but eventually despaired of the establishment's ability to do so; radical sociologists who perceived black militance as a revolutionary tool which might be shaped to Marxist purposes; conservatives who welcomed black studies as a containment and decompression area;

traditional academicians for whom the black studies programs were a landing place for marginal or deficient black students combed out of sociology classes; and those who believed that only in a curriculum controlled by blacks could blacks achieve group identity and personal pride. These mixed purposes are illustrated in the quotations that follow.

Among those who welcomed black studies because of the "failure" of "conventional" race-relations sociologists to respond effectively to post-civil rights developments was a sociologist at a small, avant-garde school, who told me, "In 1956 I attempted to persuade the faculty of my department to offer more courses in the race and ethnic area, as well as to vigorously seek black faculty members. But I was voted down. Now the others wish they had listened to me. We might have forestalled the black studies movement, or at least slowed it down. We would have made sociology more relevant and maybe turned the black kids on. When black studies came along in 1969, I was already pretty disgusted with conventional race sociology and with this department. Not many of the black students sought me out, but when they did I told them to go ahead; that if *they* didn't do it, nobody else would. But I'm still a prophet without honor in my own department in spite of all that shot-calling seven years ago."

Somewhat similar views were voiced by a female white sociologist in a neighboring large state university. She pointed out that not all white sociologists had failed to anticipate the black power and the black studies movements; for example, a foresightful few associated in the 1940's with the Myrdal study, *An American Dilemma,* were skeptical about the depth and pace of the racial integration in which most of their colleagues had placed an optimistic faith. Black studies programs, she thought, might be able to fill an emotional as well as an intellectual gap for black and white students. Certainly it would not do any of them any harm. Nor would black studies necessarily be a disruptive force within the university. "What could be more conservative," she asked, "than to ask for a black studies department in the university or even a bachelor's degree? It really only says 'we blacks want to be like everybody else'."

A young white sociologist at a private university in the West also lamented the failures of his fellow race specialists, asking, "How could they be so blind to what was going on, these open-eyed experts?" If black students were "browned off" with sociology, they had every right to be. "We weren't doing very much to help them understand their condition or what they might do about it." While he had been consulted by the administration during the local black studies crisis, he did not feel that as a sociologist he had been of much help. "I had to admit that for all my training and research and experience I couldn't come up with very much. I think sociology can probably learn a lot more from black studies than black studies can learn from us." He concluded that "sociologists shouldn't be too critical of black studies, not until we have put our own house in order; not until we have done a lot more good work in both theory and research."

Other white sociologists were even more inclined to indulge in self-flagellation, concluding that in being either attacked or by-passed by the black studies movement "we got just about what we deserved." One sociologist at the urban branch of a major university in the Midwest lamented, "We really didn't know where it was at. We spent too much time in our offices and at the library. We weren't close to the black students, and maybe we didn't really want to be. Our understanding of the ghetto tended to be secondhand because we sent our graduate students to do the research we should have been doing, while we stayed in the study and pontificated on the nature of race."

One of his colleagues who was sitting in on the interview asked, "Why should we have been consulted by the administration? What could we have told them that would have been helpful in the circumstances?" He answered his own question: "Nothing! I don't think the black students regarded us either as a serious obstacle or as a useful resource. We were, rather, in their overused word, 'irrelevant'—probably the unkindest cut of all. They knew we could be ignored without penalty." As for the black militants, he concluded that they "certainly gauged the white sociologists accurately; too many of us were disarmed by a sense of intellectual failure and personal inadequacy; and we haven't recovered yet."

Radical sociologists were strongly disposed toward black studies from another perspective. Rejecting much of "conventional" sociological theory, particularly as it related to race relations, some radicals were eager to "restructure" the discipline to incorporate a strong Marxist emphasis on conflict, producing a "new" sociology. But that was only one task, for they aimed also to restructure the university and, ultimately, the society itself. Black studies might be fitted into each of those goals, however much it might for the time-being emphasize race to the exclusion of basic economic forces. One young radical told me that his major immediate objective was to take the treatment of race out of the hands of the "vulgar Marxists" and fit it into a truly sophisticated position that Marx and Engels at least implied if they did not in fact clearly specify.

Thus for the radicals black studies could be made to serve broad ideological and political purposes as well as more immediate black needs, in contrast to conventional sociological theory, which was conservative and consensus-oriented. As one young radical white sociologist stated, "You older sociologists simply don't realize yet how much you were, and still are, committed to the status quo in race relations. Your teaching and research haven't helped us to understand or to change race relations very much, despite your twenty years of opportunity. So what makes you think that you can do any better now or in the future? Black studies is a response to the bankruptcy of the 'American Dilemma' view of black-white relations." Concerning the influence of black studies in the university, what bothered him was "the possibility of too few, not too many, black studies programs. I am afraid that very quickly now these programs are going to be defanged, starved of funds, and absorbed into this academic bureaucracy without *anybody* crying out, least of all the white sociologists."

When supporting black studies movements on campus, the radical white sociologists often have followed informal and non-public routes. They contributed money, advised black students and black studies directors, defended black studies in departmental and regular committee meetings. They left the initiative to blacks, who tended to be highly sensitive to possible criticism of being dependent on whites and not sufficiently separatist or aggressive. In some instances even the radical whites appeared distressed by the blacks' rejection of them. They were quite impatient with suggestions that their behavior might be defined as patronizing by the black studies people. "We recognize the depths of prejudice in this society," said one of them, "and we realize that it resides in each of us, try as we might to evict it. But what we need to be concerned with is not personal emancipation but changing the whole damn social structure. And we ought to be able to work with black people and the black studies program."

Such a prospect was not embraced, however, by the black studies director at that same university, who noted that "the radical white boys over in sociology may mean well, but they really don't know where it's at with blacks. They can help us some, but not very much. Sure, I would like to change the system, but not in the way they seem to prefer. I want the system to work for the blacks. I am not sure just what white radicals want. A white capitalist and a white commissar are still, above all else, white. I am black twenty-four hours a day, year in and year out; that's the central fact of my existence. But you white sociologists, including the older conservatives, can flit from one interest or identity to another with the greatest of ease." To the author's suggestion that most white sociologists would have great difficulty, intellectually and emotionally, in adjusting to black separatism and black studies on campus, he responded, "Well, that's their problem. Blacks can't be expected to help them with their hang-ups. God! We have enough of our own."

The *embracers* also included some middle-aged sociologists teaching in second- and third-rank institutions who brought a certain religious dedication to their sociological work. Not only did they approve of black studies; they also in a number of instances pointed with pride to their having prodded reluctant black students to demand such programs. Such white sociologists have a strong "local," as opposed to a professional or cosmopolitan, orientation. They tend to inhabit schools with relatively small black enrollments, and to know the black students on an individual basis. A missionary spirit tends to pervade their relations to blacks; they seem to be little aware that their behavior, like that of the radicals, might be defined by blacks as patronizing. They complain not that blacks on campus are too militant but that they are too conservative.

"We have committed," remarked one of the religiously oriented white sociologists at a denominational school in the Southwest, "a lot of racial crimes against the blacks, and we ought to do several things: The first is to search our own experience and conscience and try to determine just who and what we are on race. The second is not merely to be available to blacks, but to seek them out. We ought to encourage them to challenge the system and help them in every way we can." Another observed, "If it weren't for me, I don't think we would have a black studies program on campus. I helped on my own while the faculty of the department did absolutely nothing. Even the other two men who did some teaching in the race area just ignored black studies as much as they could. I was up against the indifference of both my white colleagues and black students."

Other white sociologists favored black studies for quite different reasons. For some of them black studies was a program in which they could "cool out" critical and disruptive black students. "I don't bother with the militant black types much any more," said one. "I just tell them that if they don't like what we are doing, they can enroll in some of the black studies courses; and we have a lot of them. This takes the heat off." A colleague seconded the observation: "When Afro-American Studies was set up, I was strongly opposed to it, as were the other members of the department. However, I have changed my mind. It's a place you can send the black hotheads. If we couldn't do that, the regular race relations classes would become so chaotic I couldn't teach them."

Similar views were voiced by white sociologists who at one time in the black studies conflict had thought seriously of getting out of race relations altogether. "I had already notified the department chairman that I couldn't go on in Minority Groups," said one, "and I was retreading myself in criminology, which I used to teach. However, the chairman asked me to stick it out for another quarter, and I agreed to do so. The next time there was a black outburst in class I told the three black students involved that they ought to take courses in black studies and not bother with those I offered. The white students, by their silence and nods, seemed to back me. I guess the pressure got too much even for the most militant. I haven't been bothered much since."

Another white sociologist thought he might even come to some understanding with the black studies director. The two had met only once and, although the black studies program had been in operation for more than a year, had never really sat down and talked about black students and courses in the respective departments. Then the white sociologist approached the director, and they talked for a couple of hours in the inconspicuous and neutral territory of a faculty committee room. The black studies director was eager to increase enrollment in his department, and the white sociologist was eager to decrease the number of blacks in his classes. They made an arrangement which seemed to be working quite well at the time the two men were interviewed separately. "I 'dropped' the director's name when the black students acted up too much; they didn't quite know what to make of it. But after a while things seemed to go a lot better. Campus black militancy was peaking at about that time and maybe that explains the subsequent slacking off of disruption in my classes; but I don't think so, not all of it."

For some white sociologists black studies programs were acceptable from yet another perspective: as a kind of dumping ground for marginal students, black and white, whose grade point averages could be brought up to the required campus minimum in courses where the intellectual content was limited and the grading lenient. Not all black studies courses fall into that category, of course, but some of them do. Only rarely in the fieldwork of this study was a black studies department encountered whose GPA was as low as sociology's. In only one school was it lower. "It's very simple," a female white sociologist told me. "We get a lot of marginal students here and we are under all kinds of pressures to retain them and see that they get through. This campus is losing enrollment, and if it continues to drop, we will have a budget cut. There are all kinds of incentives for giving passing grades. However, the sociology faculty haven't departed very far from the standards of three or four years ago, with the exception of one man, since released, who gave automatic A's. We encourage the poor students to take black studies courses, even as a major; we know they can make it over there. No, I don't feel very comfortable with what we are doing."

Many of the black sociologists interviewed shared the same view. "Look," said one of them, a man in his early forties, "the GPA in sociology is one-and-a-half letter grades below that in black studies. Grading over there is loose, and I am embarrassed by it. The college has been getting very poor students under open admissions, and there's a lot of political pressure to keep them. We can take off some of the pressure and preserve our departmental standards by funneling the failing students into black studies. Now, if a good black student comes along, I try to get him into sociology; but the poor ones I encourage to go into black studies."

A department chairman on another campus indicated that whereas the sociologists had not taken an official position on the matter, there was an informal understanding that faculty advisors would facilitate such arrangements in their conferences with young blacks. "We will try to maintain standards until the pressures become overwhelming," he said. "So far, it seems to have worked very well. Since word has gotten around that sociology is tough, we don't have nearly as many black applicants as we did."

Even some of the sociologists who were convinced that black studies had only very limited intellectual content nevertheless believed that such programs might be highly beneficial for many of the new black students on campus. "Let's face it," said an older man at a public university in the Midwest, "many of the black kids coming here are lost, confused, angry—even numbed—by their experiences on this alien turf. They need a lot of support, a lot of help, and whites can't very well supply it, even if they are willing to try. Black studies can help these kids with some of their psychological and identity problems by providing a setting in which they can comfortably be black, sharing with other blacks some of their frustrations and misgivings. In learning a little about black history and culture, they can develop some pride—some self and group respect. That's what they need most." He continued, after a pause, "I am opposed to racial segregation, very emphatically; but I believe a case can be made for segregated black classes, to help these black youngsters 'get themselves together' as they put it. Yes, you can list me as being in favor of black studies."

At a large university in the border South, a white historian-sociologist stated that he had not been consulted at the time the black studies program was established. Nor had his offer to help in developing the program been accepted. A recognized authority on the history and sociology of American slavery, he was not involved while courses in his area of specialization were taught in the black studies curriculum by recently recruited black faculty whose major qualification, in his view, was the color of their skins. "But I still have to go along with the idea of a black studies program," he said, "even separate black classes taught only by blacks. We whites, regardless of how technically competent we are, are really handicapped when it comes to teaching blacks. And I'm not sure that we shouldn't have separate classes for whites in race and ethnic relations. Students in the two groups need to explore their feelings about each other. And contrary to what the sensitivity group-gropers say, that can probably be done better separately, at least at the beginning."

A different perspective came from a black sociologist at a predominantly black school who pointed out that, while he knew very little about what was going on locally in black studies, he would conjecture that its courses would have some psychological value for both blacks and whites. "The whites carry around a lot of guilt," he observed, "and need to be flagellated, while the blacks feel wronged and need to have revenge. Both groups can be satisfied by confrontation in black studies courses if you don't worry too much about course structure and academic content."

The same point was made by a female sociologist at a public university in New York City. "Maybe we should forget about black studies as an academic pursuit and simply look upon it as catharsis—as a means of helping both black and white students to cope with their racism. We could do a lot worse. If some of the race-centered emotional problems which students bring to class can be dealt with, then we can go on from there. The classes need not be taught by blacks; some whites might be able to do it, women probably better than men. For example, I haven't had any of the difficulties with black students which you report other white sociologists having. Perhaps the white male sociologist doesn't recognize how much he is threatened by blacks . . . and by women."

At a large midwestern university a black sociologist in his early forties, the author of a number of books on American blacks, took a different tack: "Black studies is the best thing that has happened for black students on this campus. At one time I thought sociology had a lot to offer, and many of the students thought so too. But sociology can't provide them an exciting way of studying their own past or of using that past to enhance identity. Sociology has too much of an on-the-one-hand-but-then-on-the-other-hand approach. Black studies are positive, upbeat; they go to the very core of the black student's ego needs. We should be expanding the program, not leveling off or retrenching. My patience with white colleagues who are unwilling to support black studies is wearing damned thin." Some black integrationists suggest that only after blacks are able to see themselves separately, as a distinctive cultural group, can there be any real integration.

The *antagonists*, like the *embracers*, are a variegated group, although they tend to have many common traits. Black studies programs were introduced on college and university campuses, literally hundreds of them, during the period from 1967 to 1972. While not all the programs were ushered in by oral confrontations and physical violence, such tactics were used at a wide range of institutions, from Cornell to San Francisco State, not only to initiate black studies programs but also to decide questions concerning development of curriculum, selection of faculty and staff, admission of students, and conduct of research. In many instances the more-or-less conventional methods for innovation in the university were either directly challenged or effectively circumvented by such militant action as occurred at Harvard, Duke, Ohio State, Berkeley, Washington, and Wisconsin, to name but a few examples.

"For fifteen years I have been on this campus," said one sociologist at an Ivy League school, "and I never saw anything like the black studies upheaval; it panicked the administration, muted most of the faculty, and enabled the militant blacks to get most of what they asked for. Nobody looked good in the end. None of the rules and procedures seemed to work anymore, and we didn't know what else to try when the old ways broke down."

For the integrationist white sociologist who had thought of himself as friend rather than foe, the separatist black movement's redefinition of the situation was a traumatic experience.[6] The result was serious and frequently unsharable problems of role, status, pedagogy, and profession within a rapidly changing and increasingly unpredictable academic setting. Over the years these white sociologists had been engaged in lecturing, researching and writing on racial issues, particularly those affecting blacks and whites in American society. Most of the sociologists believe that they had been sharply critical of established patterns of white superiority and black subordination. Moreover, in their citizen role and within the universities they thought of themselves as social activists who had tried to recast the racial balance.

They therefore could claim for themselves sensitivity to racial and ethnic developments as well as competence on the origins, character, and implications of those developments. Yet many of them who were in their forties and fifties and were well-placed in academic structures often found themselves directly in the line of black studies fire. Although white sociologists long had been inured to having their motives and competence called into question by conservative whites, they were stunned when militant blacks condemned them.

"I am anathema to the militant blacks on campus," declared one sociologist at a major university on the West Coast, "because I show something less than enthusiasm for the Afro-American studies program they are developing. While I have gotten threatening phone calls from white bigots over the years, I never thought I would get them from black bigots. It's getting pretty rough on me and my family, and I'm taking off for a year. Maybe things will be better when I return."

Even so, black studies evoked open opposition from only 45 (22 percent) of the 209 sociologists interviewed. One must take into account, however, among other things, the violence of the thrust, the demoralizaiton of some university members in the wake of a general upheaval, and the crisis of confidence that had begun to characterize social scientists during that period.

Who, then, are these 45 *antagonists?* A few are disillusioned radicals. "Like so much in the past couple of years," one well-known white sociologist wrote to me, "the idea [of black militance] has gone flat in the middle of what seems to me a total national paralysis of will and imagination. I think that I, like many other people of left-wing persuasion, people who could no longer buy the liberal image of America, have tended to side with the blacks because we were looking for a basic oppositional force, almost with desperation.... The end product of both student and black militance appears, to put it in extreme terms, to have been the elevation of a kind of lumpen mentality into the status of a radical life style." Several persons who were interviewed, having gone through a similar experience, had turned from early enthusiasm to open opposition.

Many *antagonists* have been in the race relations field for many years and have done research and writing; they are widely respected by colleagues in race relations and other sociologists and have turned out a number of graduate students, black and white who were professionally certified. They tend to believe that sociology has made contributions to both theoretical and empirical studies of race and expect it to continue to do so. The idea of black studies as distinctive, with its own concepts and methods accessible only to blacks, or of its being taught only by blacks, goes squarely against the universalistic criterion which they had sought to apply to their own work and by which they judge the efforts of others.

Said a white female, "Black studies as a college curriculum can't be justified. Now, black kids have all kinds of special needs, but black studies isn't one of them, or certainly not the most important. Most of all, young blacks on campus need to be able to read and write well, and many of them can't. This doesn't imply that I have no respect for their oral tradition, but what they need to concentrate on is basic tools. They already know what it means to be black, probably a lot better than many of their black teachers. We could help them more by placing less emphasis on black studies and more on providing black cultural centers, good counselors, and a lot of tutoring help for regular classes. Black studies is a diversion, a waste of time; the people who benefit from it most are those very marginal black faculty and administrators who use it as a springboard to the ranks of the middle-class. If the black kids want to dig into the black experience, let them do it later, from some disciplinary perspective."

That view was shared by a number of the white male *antagonists,* who pointed out that black students sometimes were all but forced by peer presssure to enroll in black studies courses, though their immediate needs were for "skills that will enable them to study well whatever subject they choose." In black studies courses white teachers were "frequently portrayed in an extremely unfavorable way," leading black students to lose confidence and respect for possible mentors.

"Part of it, of course, is political," said one sociologist at a public university in New York. "However, much of it is a result of marginal black faculty trying to look good, to reassure themselves and the black kids by condemning the whites. The sophisticated black kids see through this pretty well." Some *antagonists* reported that black students with whom they eventually managed to establish rapport confided that "you're not nearly as bad as I heard you were."

Other white *antagonists* referred to the materials used in the black studies courses as indicative of their poor quality and lack of balanced treatment. "They read Fanon but not Rustin," said one; "Malcolm X but not Kenneth Clark; Angela Davis and LeRoi Jones but not Roy Wilkins; the latter-day Du Bois but not Booker T. Washington; Marcus Garvey but not the mature Frederick Douglass. And a lot of the time they don't read anything." Some of the curriculum offerings "make no pretense at meeting university standards. They are out-and-out indoctrination exercises and there isn't much chance for student dissent. Nobody seems willing to do anything about these so-called courses, least of all the curriculum review committees. The only hope right now is that the brighter black students will drop out or demand that the courses be improved."

Many *antagonists* expressed disappointment at their university's approach in dealing with the black studies. Particularly distressing was their exclusion from decision-making about matters which seriously affected their work in the university. "The fact is," said one of them, "that we had to battle on two fronts, against the administrators and the blacks who got together at the expense of the historians and the sociologists, one of whom, by the way, was black in color if not in the current ideological persuasion."

He then described the subsequent fragmentation of the faculty group that had opposed the black studies measure. "The administration's capitulation really took the wind out of some of us. Others thought we were trying to buck an inevitable change and retreated. Some of our group, only a few, resigned and tried to locate at places they could respect, where they could work in a less frenetic setting. Some decided to stay on but to do no more work in the race field. As for me, as you know, I have stuck with it, and I don't intend to get out. This black studies fever is already cooling; things should be better next year."

Another *antagonist* on the same faculty told me much the same story, but added, "Smith is too modest to tell you how rough a time he really had or how he took the lead in trying to at least delay the black studies program, which was a real can of worms and quite smelly. He got a lot of abuse. When his opposition became public, the black militants and white radicals gave him plenty of trouble in his classes—picketing, cat-calls, walkouts, a lot of heckling, name it. Some of their organizations even passed resolutions demanding that he be fired, or at least censured. The administration was its usual tower of jelly. But old Smith is a really tough cookie; and now I think even some of the blacks grudgingly admire him—although you won't hear them saying anything like that publicly."

Other *antagonists* expressed concern about continuing to do sociological research in the race and ethnic field, noting that membership in the group to be studied was increasingly a prerequisite for obtaining funds and conducting research. They were distressed also by the possibility, some said the high probability, of black studies faculty receiving veto power over research proposals having to do with blacks and other minorities. "It's pretty clear now," said one of the *antagonists* at a college in the Boston area, "that whites are being discouraged from doing further research on blacks. If this continues and if fewer whites enter the field, as is now the case, within a couple of decades research about any minority group will become the monopoly of that group, and we will run the high risk of getting only insider, self-serving interpretations. We Wasps have to stick in there if a full range of sociological perspectives is to inform the race research of the future."

As could have been expected, the *antagonists* have encountered a great deal of hostility from the black studies movement. They seem to have defended their position (in contrast to the *accommodators* and *dropouts*), perhaps because of their lack of strong guilt feelings about the historical relationships of blacks and whites in this country, which seems to have disarmed a number of their colleagues. Another source of strength is their enthusiasm for sociology itself and the contributions which they believe it has made to the scholarly exploration of race. By and large the *antagonists* do not accept the idea that race and ethnic theory is only conservative white ideology. For them it has both autonomous and universal features, plus durability. Furthermore, their firmness, indeed their aggressiveness in some instances, does not hinge on strong colleague support. On the contrary, many of them were "loners" in their own departments, most of whose members seemed uneager to take on these ambiguous problems in which their own interests were not immediately involved. "Brown was basically right in opposing black studies," the chairman of a sociology department in an Ohio university reported, "but he was too righteous and wouldn't budge an inch. In the showdown, which he could have avoided, we couldn't do anything but support him; but I hope we won't have to go through *that* again."

Another trait of many *antagonists* is their respect for the work they themselves have done. In conversation they cite, defend, and sometimes criticize it, while complaining that their black critics are either unaware of or do not understand it. "I wrote [title of a book] in the mid-1960s," said a sociologist at a private college in the Midwest, "and it had some impact on professional sociology as well as public policy. If I were doing it today, I don't think I would change it very much. Right now race sociology is on a big pluralism kick, but that's a recurring theme and the emphasis can shift rather quickly. What we have to guard against is latching onto the latest fads in the field and forgetting the durable elements of our own tradition." Another *antagonist,* at a university in the Washington, D.C., area, expressed a similar view: "I haven't been seized by any urges to confess or apologize. I've done some good work in the social psychology of prejudice. So I didn't call all the shots in the civil rights or black power movement. Who did? Who could have?"

One of this man's associates was among those who saw some unintended positive values in the black studies challenge. "It forced us to reopen issues we thought were closed ... integration for example; and to look at a sentiment we thought had atrophied: black nationalism. It made us ask how applicable our general theories were to black-white relations since the breakup of the civil rights movement. Really, this is quite an exciting time to be working in race. But black studies has done a lot of harm, too. On balance, we may have been a lot better off without it. It's a gadfly, helpful in a way. But what a price we have paid!"

The tactics developed by the *antagonists* vary a great deal, depending on the person and the particular circumstances of his day-to-day interaction with blacks. They emphasized the importance of keeping control of the classroom or seminar or public lecture. A high value is placed on maintaining one's "cool," on displaying familiarity with even obscure persons or ideas which critical black students may inject into the dialogue. A serious acquaintance with the ideas of black scholars who have been critical of blac! eparatism and black studies—Kenneth Clark, Orlando Patterson, Martin Kilson, Arthur Lewis, Hylan Lewis, Andrew Birmmer, and so on—is important; familiarity with arguments for black studies is crucial.

These *antagonists* did not often accept the charge that they are "playing blacks against blacks, the white man's game." Instead, they believe they are committed to maintaining a classroom and campus atmosphere in which balanced explanation of all contemporary movements and ideas proceed without intimidation. Judged by his color and identified by black militant students as one of the oppressors, the white sociologist who is an *antagonist* believes that he is handicapped, sometimes to the point where he feels his ideas have no possibility whatever of receiving a thoughtful hearing.

Yet frequently *antagonists* seem able to overcome, to command a grudging respect, to be heard if not applauded. Concerning the issue of black studies, a sense of humor is a rare commodity in black-white encounters—"grim, grim, grim," as one of the *accommodators* put it. However, many of the *antagonists* seem to have retained some capacity for laughter—at the contradictions in racial ideals and realities, at the idiocy of many black-white situations, and above all at themselves. In the final analysis laughter, though sometimes emanating from gallows humor, may be the principal weapon helping to account for their persistence; a strong personal ego appeared important as well.

It is an interesting paradox that a commitment to academic standards has led some sociologists to embrace black studies and other sociologists to regard black studies with antagonism. The presence of a weak black studies curriculum is perceived by some of the *embracers* as an aid to preserving standards in the sociology department, as described earlier; on the other hand, it is seen by *antagonists* as a threat to standards in the university. The implication seems clear: it is by some of its "supporters" rather than by its open opponents that the black studies program has been read out of the university. That is to say, it is by *embracers* rather than by *antagonists* that the black studies program has been relegated to that peculiar group of campus activities, such as football and R.O.T.C., which the academic community can tolerate only because the activities have been institutionally defined as academically invisible. [7]

The third category of response was accommodation. There are 63 *accommodators,* who represent 30 percent of the interviewees. What shaped their response? A primary distinction between the *accommodators* and the *antagonists* is the former's acceptance of black studies as a fait accompli. They do not actively oppose the program. But neither have they dropped out of the race and ethnic field, even though most of them are white. Their lack of open hostility does not mean they are enthusiastic. Often they are quite critical in private conversation.

"Johnson, who teaches a course on black migration over in black studies, is a pompous black ass and ignorant to boot," said a white sociologist specializing in race and demography, "but I can't tell black students that, and certainly not the people who hired him. It would be dismissed as another instance of white racism or professional rancor. I asked him at a cocktail party once if he didn't feel squeamish about holding high rank and in effect being unqualified for his job. I smiled, of course. He said it didn't bother him one damn bit."

Said another *accommodator,* a social psychologist in a public university in Illinois, "In black studies the faculty members—as a group that is—are supposed to be very positive models for the black students—and for the whites. But that certainly isn't the case over there, with one partial exception. The teachers are poorly trained and are really quite ignorant of most things outside their limited backgrounds and immediate experiences. Once they have exhausted the rhetoric, all they can do is repeat themselves. What can they teach? Whom can they inspire? Maybe the street-wise kids who know a hustle, even on this university turf, when they see one. But who else?" He showed me a copy of a letter he had written to the dean cautioning against the appointment of marginal blacks to the black studies faculty two years before. His warning was not even acknowledged. "I decided right then to withdraw from the whole thing," he said, "and to let black studies run its course." At the end of the interview he added, in an afterthought, "These black kids may be bright after all . . . if they see through what the black studies program is doing to them.

One of the white female *accommodators* saw black studies as merely another of many marginal programs developed in the university over the years, about which the faculty was unable to do much. "Of course it isn't academically respectable," she shrugged, "but there are a lot of things around here that aren't—physical education, home economics, social work, business administration. We even offer a course in horseshoeing, called equestrian science, if you can believe it." Later in the interview she observed that she had found the pressure from blacks too much to handle in her minority groups class and had suspended the class "until such time as it can be conducted with some civility and the blacks can see me as something more than a mean white bitch. . . . The faculty of the department appreciated my dilemma, as did the chairman, and that made it easier for me. I'll keep my hand in by reading the literature and perhaps by some research, but I don't know when I'll get back into the classroom."

One interviewee was a white male *accommodator* at a public campus in northern California to whom a copy of the research prospectus was sent when an interview was requested. The interview got off on a startling note.

"Well, at last you're here. I am glad to meet you. You have played a pivotal role in my academic life lately, finally causing me to do something I had been wanting to do for a couple of years. I received your prospectus right at the end of the most difficult quarter I ever had in my course on the American Black—it used to be called the American Negro. The Black Student Union and the black studies kids had given me the roughest time ever. Immediately after reading the prospectus, I walked into the department chairman's office and threw the prospectus on his desk. I told him that it expressed my feelings exactly, and that I wasn't going to teach the damn course again."

The chairman apparently expressed no surprise, possibly because he, too, had found it a heavy burden to relate to blacks in the criminology and delinquency courses he occasionally offered. "He told me not to worry. The course will be deleted from the schedule but left on the books so I can pick it up again if I ever want to give it another try. I'll continue research in race, but now I want to go the comparative route and not focus so much on blacks. As for black studies, as long as you have as many blacks as we do there will be a demand for it; and the black studies office will continue as a center through which blacks attack the white faculty."

As a group the *accommodators* had not received extensive professional recognition. Those above age thirty are likely to have a fairly heavy investment in race relations. Though many of them intend to shift their research from blacks to other minority groups, they are by no means confident that the attacks from black studies people on campus will thereby cease.

"The militant nationalists who control black studies on this campus," said an *accommodator* at a university in New England, "use it as a base from which to attack white social scientists who dare to disagree with them. Black studies isn't an academic department; it's a guerrilla stronghold. Those of us who thought that when we abandoned the classroom we could pursue our professional interests without continued harassment may be in for some sad surprises."

Most of the *accommodators* manage to retain associations with a few black students on an individual basis—commonly seniors or graduate students whom the white professor got to know before black pressures against black student-white professor contacts mounted. "I have seen a great deal of Joe Wright lately," said one man who specialized in both race and education. "He's doing his M.A. over in education and thinks I can be of some help on his thesis, which is an evaluation of local Head Start programs. He doesn't come by during my regular office hours, of course. When he calls for an appointment he always suggests the late afternoon. The first time he came in, I asked if he was working or had a class conflict with my office schedule. After fumbling and hesitating a bit, he told me that it 'just wouldn't be a good idea if any of the brothers saw me spending time with white professors.' So he comes after everybody else has gone home. Even so, he makes sure the door is closed and he talks more quietly than usual. It's an odd arrangement, but I'm willing to go along. If our little conspiracy continues to work, I think I can help him to do a good job; he's a bright kid."

Black militants want to take over the teaching of black studies not only because they believe they know the realities of black culture in a way that only blacks can know them, but also because they believe the jobs rightfully belong to blacks. Some American blacks even question the propriety of appointing non-American blacks to those jobs. Here is an excerpt from the report of a recent conference of black studies directors:

One point of view was that whites should teach these [black studies] courses only to white students. . . . Also, despite white scholarly credentials in the subject area, politically-conscious Blacks should narrow the focus, due to the Black struggle, and protest the teaching of Black studies courses by whites. There was contention concerning the question of Africans who teach Black studies courses; this was viewed as limiting the number of jobs available to American Blacks. However, most participants disagreed with this viewpoint.

Black Africans and Jamaicans, being highly selected and British-trained, are often judged to be better qualified than most available black American scholars, and they are heavily represented in black studies faculties. Their ill-concealed conviction that American education, and black education in particular, is inferior does not greatly endear them to their students or faculty associates. One white *accommodator* reviewing black pressures for "black" jobs in colleges and universities noted ruefully, "It's a no-win game. Even if I supported every last demand of the black studies people except self-immolation, I would still be viewed as a white man filling a black man's job, not only telling lies but taking his bread."

What about the last group of sociologists, the *dropouts,* who constitute 20 percent of the 209 interviewees? They have tended to have traumatic experiences with black studies. Not so strong personally as the *antagonists* nor so resourceful as the *accommodators,* on the whole they have been inclined to withdraw when confronted by blacks who challenged their motives or competence. The initial hypothesis was that the *dropouts* would have only a limited personal and professional investment in the race relations field, which could therefore be abandoned without great sense of loss. However, that was the case for about a third of the group. The others had worked in the field five years or more and regarded race relations as their major area of competence. A few did indicate that their departure had not been prompted primarily by unfortunate experiences with black studies and black students, although they could recall a number of unpleasant encounters. They had changed their interests and found the field no longer "interesting," or were convinced that "class, not race, is really where the action is these days." One man stated that, in looking back on his decade in the field, he considered himself to have been presumptuous, even pompous, in studying blacks. "I am secretly embarrassed," he said, "I shouldn't have gotten into the field to begin with."

But what about those who had identified heavily and departed reluctantly? On some campuses where black militants were strong and violence-prone and where administrators were reluctant to take steps against them, the white *dropouts* were barred from their classrooms and could not continue. In other instances not only they but their families were threatened with physical assault. This was not reported as a widespread phenomenon. It occurred nevertheless, with enough frequency to lend credibility to the statement of a *dropout* sociologist at a major university in the East, which had experienced prolonged racial disturbances in 1968 and 1969: "I am out of the race relations field because I literally was driven out. Period."

An older sociologist at a small public campus wrote, "I am seriously considering giving up entirely the teaching of minority group relations after thirty years of it, and of related activities which caused me to be called a radical, a nigger-lover, and a communist. I feel almost entirely alienated now from anything black. It is too much of a hassle to try to be an impartial behavioral scientist when everything which is not praise is racist, and where the sole criterion for knowledge, understanding, or credibility is the color of your skin."

Another *dropout* at a private college in the West reported that while he had not been overtly threatened by blacks, he felt that the atmosphere created in the classroom caused him to lose face with students. "What happened was so unexpected, so far from my wildest imagination, that I really didn't know what to do. Within a short time I realized that if I continued, I would be involved in one unending confrontation with the blacks. Perhaps I am not a very strong person. Anyway, I just couldn't cope. When that term ended [in 1970], I vowed that I would never offer another course or do another piece of research or writing on blacks; and I haven't."

Probing in the interview revealed additional information. He said, "the leader of the disruptive black students in my class was also a member of the black studies committee and had been chairman of the BSU. After the second episode I went to the director of the black studies program and asked him if he couldn't persuade the black studies students to tone down their attacks. It was then that I learned that he was really *their* man, not his own, and certainly not the university's. Because black students had demanded of the university—and received—power over faculty appointments in black studies, he served at their pleasure. Of course, in this case he did nothing."

In most cases, disengagement came about slowly, in a series of steps taken almost imperceptibly by those who were reluctant to recognize that departure was for them ultimately the only feasible alternative. The process of disengagement—its psychological subtleties, its situational complexities, and its elements of tragedy for both blacks and whites could not be adequately documented in these interviews; however a few examples of the salient experiences can be presented.

One of the *dropouts* recalled that he began having difficulty with blacks and Puerto Ricans in his undergraduate classes in a New York City college as early as 1966. "I talked with my wife [also a sociologist] about it a lot," he recalled, "but always about how to *continue:* how to teach, how to relate, how to deal with conflict, what reading material to try, what term papers to suggest, what new research approaches to use. Over a period of two years I tried just about everything I could latch onto, with no improvement. I even went to some of the black studies faculty, but we didn't get anywhere. The substance of their message seemed to be that I was hopelessly disqualified because I wasn't black. I rather facetiously suggested that maybe I could get Nathan Hare to pronounce me an honorary black. They didn't laugh." He offered his last class in race in 1970 and is now studying "white ethnics."

At a branch of the University of Texas another *dropout* told me that the spring term, 1972, was the last in which he would offer a course in race and ethnic minorities. He had been under heavy pressure from both blacks and Chicanos. "Some of it is overt, but most of it is rather indirect—a certain ill-concealed contempt. Now, maybe that's their silent cry of distress, a call for help; but I don't see it that way. I have known for some time that the Chicanos prefer Chicano teachers, even poor ones, to me. Blacks prefer blacks. The image feedback to the Wasp sociologist is something less than ego-building." In trying to adapt to black student preferences, this man had eliminated term papers, essay examinations, and formal quizzes. "Eliminating myself was the only response acceptable to them. Far from opposing black studies," he concluded, "I'll be glad when the new program gets underway and they can all go over there."

One additional example of a white *dropout* is a young female sociologist at a public university in the Southwest. During the early and mid-1960s, while a graduate student at a West Coast university, she was very active in the free speech and civil rights movement. She had been jailed in Alabama, Oakland, California, and Mississippi, and she believed that her efforts would guarantee her acceptability to the black students. However, when the black power and black studies movement emerged on her campus, she was lumped with other white sociologists and strongly attacked as a white racist. Her participation in racial struggles was dismissed as a self-serving means of gathering materials for her dissertation, though she had written on a quite different topic. Some of the black women activists even charged that her principal motive had been to attract black men.

When her classes were disrupted, she became so distraught that she canceled the last four weeks of a minority groups course, basing final student grades on the mid-term and a take-home examination. As a Jew, she was particularly distressed by the black students' use of anti-Semitism as a weapon and by their inclusion of her in "the honkies who make a career of the black people's misery." The next year she offered only one course in the race and ethnic field, a comparative exploration of race, ethnicity, and poverty. While she was able to get through the term, she again found the experience so tension-ridden that she retired from the fray. As a result, she developed courses on the sociology of women—white women. "Although it is my first love, I won't go back to race. But maybe some day it will come back to me."

The four black *dropouts,* all male, abandoned the race and ethnic area for reasons that are disparate but in each case are related to experiences with black studies programs. A man who teaches at a Midwest university, located in a major industrial center with a large black population from which most of the black students were drawn, dropped out "because I was tired of constantly being called 'Oreo,' 'Tom,' and 'white man's nigger'." Black students, sometimes aided by radical whites, harassed him in his classes. He learned that they were encouraged by the black studies director, whose appointment he had opposed not only because of professional qualifications but also because the director had left his previous position under strong suspicion of a misuse of funds. "I am a rather conventional sociologist. And nobody can say I am anything but black, as that term has traditionally been understood. But 'black' as it is used in black studies is more of a political and ideological than a racial or even cultural designation."

When he complained of the harassment to the dean of arts and sciences, he was told to deal with the matter the best way he could. "The white administrators were afraid," he said. "It is that simple. I think they were relieved when I decided to drop the courses on race. Now I, too, am rather glad I did, because it has given me a chance to get into other areas which have interested me but which I never really had time to pursue. The department didn't seem to mind the loss of the courses. I don't think the faculty thought very highly of them anyway and they certainly didn't want any black-white, let alone black-black, conflict."

The second of the *dropout* blacks had been appointed to his position by a white department in a border state university during the early 1960s. "At that time, I was the house nigger, and I taught all the nigger courses. I never really wanted to do so, and I hoped I could move into sociological theory and medical sociology after I had done some time. But not much happened before the black studies movement came along several years later. When the BS curriculum was proposed, they asked me if I had any objections to their offering courses on urban black communities and the black family. Naturally I said no. The department was willing to go along, in part because I had several good offers from other schools, which gave me some leverage. So here I am teaching sociological theory and medical sociology. Now that's *real* freedom; that's *real* integration."

Another black *dropout* disengaged after having served as the first director of the local black studies program for almost a year. He accepted the position reluctantly and retained his regular appointment in the sociology department. Black students had been given a strong hand in the selection of faculty and curriculum; they later monitored the courses regularly and demanded that certain faculty members be censured or dropped from the program. "The usual charge was 'incompetence' or 'irrelevance,' but what they really objected to was any failure to spout the current black party line (Cleaver good, Karenga bad) or being too tough in assignments and grading. They were always complaining about the two Africans. To make a long story short, I bucked them for a time, and then I finally said to hell with it. I was so soured by the whole episode that when I came back to the sociology department I shucked off even the black sociology courses. I might become even less black than I am now if you damned whites would just stop trying all the time to stuff me in a black bag."

The 209 persons interviewed were classified as the basis of their reported behavior at the time of the interviews. Movement of white sociologists from one group to another has not been uncommon. For example, the ranks of the *accommodators* have increased at the expense of the *antagonists,* as black studies survived their early demise forecast by some bitter critics. Similarly some *accommodators* eventually gave up and entered the ranks of the *dropouts.* The *embracer* ranks have been reduced somewhat by the pressures of black militants. However, there has been little movement from these categories toward embracement.

Race, Ethnicity, Sex, and Age

It is important to emphasize again that the findings in this study are not based on a representative sample of sociologists. However, table 1 presents the social subgroups of the sample, distributed by their response patterns. Table 2 shows the four patterns of response broken down by social subgroup characteristics. On the whole, as would be expected, the tables show that blacks tend to be more receptive than whites to the black studies movement, younger sociologists more receptive than their older colleagues, and, in addition, gentiles more receptive than Jews, females more receptive than males.

Some demographic groups are clearly overrepresented. Blacks, for example, constitute 17 percent of the 209, a substantially higher proportion than for their membership in the ASA or their participation in sociology faculties. In the discussion that follows, the response of demographic subgroups is described internally, with respect to the 209 interviewees; that is, the distribution of the respective subgroups is compared to the distribution of the total group, among the four categories of response.

In table 2, the greater receptivity of blacks is revealed by the fact that although blacks are 17 percent of the total, they are 32 percent of the *embracers* and only 9 percent of the *antagonists*. Jews, on the other hand, though 25 percent of the total, are only 20 percent of the *embracers;* however they are 38 percent of the *antagonists* and 31 percent of the *dropouts*. Females are only 13 percent of the total but 27 percent of the *embracers*; they are 7 percent of the *antagonists* and 2 percent of the *dropouts*. Although age appears to have less force than race, ethnicity, and sex as a shaper of response, receptivity to black studies is tilted toward the lower age brackets. The two lowest age groups, which taken together contain 21 percent of the total, contain 29 percent of the *embracers,* only 13 percent of the *antagonists,* and only 17 percent of the *dropouts;* whereas the 50-59 bracket, with 23 percent of the total, contains only 15 percent of the *embracers* but 33 percent of the *antagonists*. It is worth noting, however, that both the 40-49 and the 60-and-over brackets contain more than their pro rata share of *embracers,* and the 40-49 bracket less than its share of *antagonists*.

The most accommodative sociologist appears to be the white gentile male. Apart from the age breakdowns, the only demographic subgroups for which the rate of accommodation is at least as great as their percentage of the total group are whites as a whole, non-Jewish whites (male and female), and males as a whole (table 2). With respect to the age subgroups, in table 2 the percentage of the total and percentage of *accommodators* are surprisingly well-matched. The composition of *dropouts* is also worth a separate examination. Here whites as a whole, male gentiles, and males are joined by Jews as subgroups for whom the rate of withdrawal is greater than their percentage representation in the total group of sociologists. Here again, for the age breakdowns the two columns are fairly well matched.

The same basic pattern found in table 2 can be seen from a different perspective in table 1, which shows the percentage rate of embracement, antagonism, accommodation, and withdrawal for each demographic subgroup. Whites break down into 23 percent *embracers,* 24 percent *antagonists,* 31 percent *accommodators,* and 22 percent *dropouts,* whereas the respective figures for blacks are 53 percent, 11 percent, 25 percent and 10 percent. With respect to sex differentials, only 24 percent of the males but 57 percent of the females are *embracers*; 23 percent of the males as against 10 percent of the females are *antagonists*; and the male *dropout* rate is more than five times that of females.

If race, ethnicity, sex, and age influence one's response to black studies, as seems at first to be the case for the 209 sociologists interviewed, can inferences be made as to what extent each demographic characteristic was an independent or distinctive force? The 36 blacks, for example, were more receptive to black studies than the 173 whites; but in what measure was the greater receptivity a function of race as distinguished from age or sex? The question is important because the age and sex distributions are different for blacks and whites.

Table 3 gives age breakdowns for the demographic subgroups. Although the average age of blacks (45.4) is virtually the same as it is for all sociologists (45.6), 30 percent of the blacks are under 35 and 44 percent under 40, as opposed to 21 percent and 32 percent, respectively, for the whole group. But the youth factor is not sufficient to explain a black embracement rate nearly twice as high (53 percent vs. 28 percent) or an antagonism rate only half as high (11 percent vs. 22 percent) as the larger group's, as shown in table 2. Females, whose receptivity tended to be higher than males', are a third of the blacks and only 13 percent of the whole. But again the differential between the embracement rates of black males and females does not seem large enough to account fully for the black-white differential, even when the age factor is observed. The black male embracement rate is higher than that of any age group and also higher than that of white females.

Similarly, females are relatively young. Their average age (41.7) is four years less than the total group's (45.6); furthermore, 32 percent—as opposed to 21 percent—are under 35, although 46 percent of the females are bunched in the 40-49 age bracket. Blacks are disproportionately represented in the female group—12 (43 percent) of the 28 women. The female and black embracement rates (57 percent and 53 percent) are very close, as are the female and black rates of antagonistic response (10 percent and 11 percent). Therefore if gender is an important determinant of response, as distinct from the age and race factors, that fact would be difficult to establish from these data, although the female's rate of embracement is twice as high as the male's for white gentiles, three times as high for Jews, and nearly half again as high for blacks.

A survey of sociologists that showed blacks, lower age-groups, and women to be more favorably disposed toward black studies would occasion little surprise. One might not have expected to find Jews among the least receptive subgroups. Can some variable other than ethnicity explain the small percentage of *embracers* and the large percentage of *antagonists*—to say nothing of the high *dropout* rate—among Jews?

Table 3 reveals that the 53 Jews in the group of 209 are older than the group as a whole. The average age for Jews is 48.5—3 years above the group average. There are no Jews below 30 and only 26 percent below 40, in contrast to 4 percent under 30 and 33 percent under 40 for the total group. Moveover, 44 percent of the Jews—as compared to only 35 percent of all sociologists—are 50 or older. The sex differential operates in the same direction insofar as receptivity is concerned. Whereas 13 percent of the total group are female, only 9 percent of the Jews are women. Still further, Jews are white. Thus, for the Jews, both their age and sex composition and their race constrain receptivity to black studies.

But even for this limited sample, ethnicity seems to be a relevant factor. As shown in table 1, Jewish males have the lowest embracement rate (19 percent) of any subgroup except the 50-59 age bracket (18 percent); Jewish males are 5 percentage points lower than all males. Jewish males and females taken together have a lower rate than any other subgroup except whites as a whole, white males, and age groups over 50. Moreover, the Jewish antagonism rate is impressively high. Both Jews as a whole and Jewish males have higher resistance rates than any other subgroup except the 60-and-over age bracket (although the 50-59 bracket is close). The Jewish rate, including female Jews, is 9 percentage points higher than the rate for all males, 10 points higher than for all sociologists, and 12 points higher than for all gentiles. The Jewish *dropout* rate (all Jews and male Jews) is also strikingly high. These figures suggest that ethnicity is indeed a distinctive force in shaping Jewish response to the black studies challenge.

Had the interviews taken place two years earlier, Jews almost certainly would have been distributed more toward embracement and less toward antagonism or withdrawal. That surmise is borne out by the interviews with Jews. Reasons for the shift are complex, and only some of the forces that seemed to be at work are indicated here.

The direct or indirect challenge to academic standards that black studies programs posed, as they developed on most campuses, was particularly abrasive to the scholarly tradition of Jews. Denigration of the cognitive skills and insistence that nonblackness is an insurmountable barrier to understanding black experience clashed head-on with the Jew's esteem for the traditional intellectual tools, in the use of which he had excelled, and with the classical academic perception of human experience as essentially universal. Black assault upon individual merit, traditionally defined, as the single criterion for entry and achievement rattled the age-old Jewish fear of quotas. Furthermore, the separatist thrust of the black studies movement offended a heavy Jewish commitment to integrationist ideology.

Perhaps more pointedly, the rhetoric of the black militants who typically promoted the black studies movement was often openly anti-Jew and anti-Israeli. The identification of some black militants with Africa bridged them emotionally to Muslims, to Arabs, and hence to oral attacks upon Israel. Moreover, the focus of many black studies programs upon the black ghetto as subject matter as well as action arena has brought the old tension between the Jewish shopkeeper/landlord and the black consumer/renter into the classroom and onto the campus podium for fresh examination. Attempts to apply colonial theories to black-white historical experience in the United States leave little doubt that the "colonizers" include Jews.

Over the preceding five or six years, as black militants had attacked educational, welfare, and other bureaucracies, they often found themselves confronting Jews as part of the establishment, as keepers of the status quo, and the universities in many cases now seemed no exception. Jews were being redefined in black minds not only as white but as "in." These are merely some of the developments which can be singled out either explicitly or implicitly from the interview materials as having driven a wedge between blacks and Jews.

In sum, this study has presented, on the basis of lengthy interviews with 209 sociologists from a representative group of 70 colleges and universities scattered over the United States, four basic patterns of response to the black studies movement: embracement, antagonism, accommodation, and withdrawal or dropout. The distribution of sociologists among the response categories by race, ethnicity, sex, and age indicate that age and, especially, race and ethnicity (Jewishness) appear to have been determinants of response. The force of gender is less certain. The finding that young sociologists, blacks, and perhaps women were more favorably disposed toward black studies might have been expected. The absence of Jews from the more receptive subgroups is surprising but reflects commitment to universalistic standards and sensitivity about the potentiality of quotas.

TABLE 1.
Distribution of Sociologists among Response Categories, by Subgroup, Social Characteristics

	No.	% of Total	Embracers (%)	Antagonists (%)	Accommodators (%)	Dropouts (%)	Total
All sociologists	209	100	28	22	30	20	100 %
Whites	173	83	23	24	31	22	100%
Non-Jews	120	58	24	20	36	21	101%
Male	108	52	21	20	36	22	99%
Female	12	6	42	17	33	8	100%
Jews	53	25	23	32	21	25	101%
Male	48	23	19	33	21	27	100%
Female	5	2	60	20	20	0	100%
Blacks	36	17	53	11	25	10	99%
Male	24	11	46	17	20	17	100%
Female	12	6	67	0	33	0	100%
Males	181	87	24	23	31	23	101%
Females	28	13	57	10	29	4	100%
Under 30	9	4	44	11	22	22	99%
30-34	36	17	36	14	36	14	100%
35-39	24	12	29	21	29	21	100%
40-49	67	32	31	16	31	21	99%
50-59	49	23	18	31	31	20	100%
60 and over	24	12	21	33	21	25	100%

TABLE 2.
Response Categories of Sociologists by Social Characteristics

	Total (%)	Embracers (%)	Antagonists (%)	Accommodators (%)	Dropouts (%)
All sociologists	100	100	100	100	100
Whites	83	68	91	86	90
Non-Jews	58	48	53	68	60
Male	52	39	49	62	57
Female	6	8	4	6	2
Jews	25	20	38	17	31
Male	23	15	36	16	31
Female	2	5	2	2	0
Blacks	17	32	9	14	10
Male	11	18	9	8	10
Female	6	14	0	6	0
Males	87	73	93	87	98
Females	13	27	7	13	2
Under 30	4	7	2	3	5
30-34	17	22	11	21	12
35-39	12	12	11	11	12
40-49	32	36	24	33	33
50-59	23	15	33	24	24
60 and over	12	8	18	8	14

TABLE 3.
Age Distribution of the 209 Sociologists, by Demographic Subgroup (percentages except for average-age figures)

	Total	Male	Female	Blacks	Jews	Gentiles
Under 30	4	4	7	8	0	5
30-34	17	16	25	22	13	18
35-39	12	12	4	14	13	10
40-49	32	30	46	31	30	33
50-59	23	26	11	14	29	24
60 and over	12	12	7	11	15	10
	100%	100%	100%	100%	100%	100%
Average age	45.6	46.2	41.7	45.4	48.5	44.3

Notes

1   As used here, "black studies" includes programs variously titled Black Studies, Afro-American Studies, African and Afro-American Studies, Black American Studies, Black American and African Studies, Black and Urban Studies, and so on.

2   In this study, "white sociologist," unless otherwise clearly indicated, refers to the white sociologist who specializes in race and ethnic relations.

3   It is perhaps significant that many interviewees have continued the dialogue through correspondence. Moreover, the author received thoughtful letters from forty-five or fifty sociologists whose campuses were not visited or who were away when visited.

4   Detailed notes were taken during the interviews and typed up immediately afterwards. All names of respondents are fictitious.

5   The 1970 Directory of the American Sociological Association lists 745 members with a race and ethnic relations specialty.

6   See Wilson Record, "Black Studies and White Sociologists," *The American Sociologist* 7 (May 1972): 10-11.

7   I am indebted to my wife, Jane Cassels Record, for this and many specific suggestions, plus invaluable assistance in organizing and interpreting the interview material.

Contributors

James E. Blackwell is professor and chairman of the Department of Sociology at the University of Massachusetts at Boston. His teaching career includes positions at Case-Western Reserve University, San Jose State College, and Washington State University. He is the author of *The Black Community: Diversity and Unity* (forthcoming, 1973); "Race and Crime in Tanzania," in *Phylon*; "Education and Development in Malawi," in *Perspectives on World Education*; and other articles. Professor Blackwell, who received his Ph.D. from Washington State University, was the first elected national chairman of the Caucus of Black Sociologists (1970-72),

Francis L. Broderick is Commonwealth Professor of History at the University of Massachusetts at Boston. Other administrative and academic positions include serving as chancellor of the University of Massachusetts at Boston (1968-72), Gordon R. Clapp Professor of American Studies at Lawrence University, and visiting professorships at Michigan State University and Catholic University of America. Professor Broderick is the author of *W. E. B. Du Bois: Negro Leader in Time of Crisis*; *Negro Protest Thought in the Twentieth Century* (with August Meier); *Black Protest Thought in the Twentieth Century* (with Elliott Rudwick); *Reconstruction and the American Negro*; and *Right Reverend New Dealer: John A. Ryan*. He recieved the A.B., M.A., and Ph.D. degrees from Princeton University.

James E. Conyers is professor of sociology at Indiana State University. He has also taught at LeMoyne College and Atlanta University. Professor Conyers is national chairman-elect of the Caucus of Black Sociologists, and past president of the Association of Social and Behavioral Sciences. He is the author of "Negro Doctorates in Sociology in America: A Social Portrait," in *Phylon* (Fall 1968); "Employers' Attitudes Toward Working Mothers," in *The Employed Mother in America*; "The Dependency Concept: Toward an Understanding of Its Causes and Reduction," in *The Journal of Social and Behavioral Sciences* (Spring 1970); and "Negro Leadership," in *Violence and Dissent in Urban America*.

Professor Conyers received his academic training at Morehouse College (A.B.), Atlanta University (M.A.), and Washington State University (Ph.D.).

G. Franklin Edwards is professor of sociology at Howard University. He received his A.B. from Fisk University in 1936, and his Ph.D. from the University of Chicago in 1954. He has served as visiting sociologist at Washington University and visiting professor of sociology at Harvard University. Among his publications are *The Negro Professional Class*; "Occupational Mobility of Negro Professional Workers," in *Contributions to Urban Sociology*; and "Marriage and Family Life Among Negroes," in *The Journal of Negro Education* (Fall 1963).

Edgar G. Epps is Marshall Field IV Professor of Urban Education at the University of Chicago. He formerly taught at Tuskegee Institute, Tennessee A & I State University, the University of Michigan, and Florida A & A University. He is editor of *Black Students in White Schools* (1972) and of *Race Relations: Current Perspectives* (forthcoming). Contributor of numerous articles to professional journals, Professor Epps was also the issue editor of *The Journal of Social Issues* 25, no. 3 (1969). Professor Epps received his Ph.D. from Washington State University.

Nathan Hare is the publisher of *The Black Scholar*. His teaching career includes positions at San Francisco State College and Howard University. He has published numerous articles on the black studies movement, and related subjects in the *Negro Digest, Black World*, and *The Black Scholar*. He is the author of *Black Anglo-Saxons* and *Black Consciousness* (forthcoming). Dr. Hare received his undergraduate training at Langston University and the M.A. and Ph.D. degrees from the University of Chicago.

Jacquelyne Johnson Jackson is currently associate professor of medical sociology at Duke University. She has taught at Southern University, Jackson State College, Howard University, and the University of Southern California. Her professional interests are primarily in gerontology and the sociology of black aging. Professor Jackson is the author of "*These Rights They Seek,* 'Social Gerontology and the Negro: A Review,' " in *The Gerontologist* 7 (1967), "Face to Face, Mind to Mind, It Sho Nuff Ain't No Zombie Jamboree," *Journal of the National Medical Association* 64 (1972), and numerous articles in major sociological journals. She is also the present editor of the *Journal of Health and Social Behavior*. She holds B.S. and M.S. degrees from the University of Wisconsin and the Ph.D. from Ohio State University.

Morris Janowitz is a member of the faculty of the University of Chicago. He received his A.B. from Washington Square College, New York University, 1941, and his Ph.D. from the University of Chicago, 1948. He has served as vice-president of the American Sociological Association and is a Fellow of the American Academy of Arts and Sciences. During the year 1972-73 he was Pitt Professor, University of Cambridge.

Butler A. Jones is professor and chairman of the Department of Sociology at Cleveland State University. He has taught at Talladega College, Ohio Wesleyan University, Oberlin College, and Hamline University. His publications include *Diplomatic Relations Between the United States and Chile, 1810-1822*; *The Introductory Social Science Course in the Negro College: An Analysis and Critical Commentary* (Bulletin no. 27. Stanford Social Education Investigation, 1943); "The Case Is Remanded," in "A Symposium on Law and Social Problems" *Social Problems* (Summer 1959). Professor Jones received his A.B. at Morehouse College, his M.A. at Atlanta University, and his Ph.D. at New York University.

Lewis M. Killian is a professor of sociology at the University of Massachusetts (Amherst). He has also taught at Florida State University, the University of Connecticut, the University of Oklahoma, and the University of Hawaii. His major publications include (with Ralph Turner) *Collective Behavior*; (with Charles M. Grigg) *Racial Crisis in America*; *The Impossible Revolution*; and *White Southerners*. Professor Killian received the A.B. and M.A. degrees from the University of Georgia and the Ph.D. from the University of Chicago.

Cy Wilson Record is professor of sociology at Portland State University. He has taught at Southern Illinois University, California State College (Sacramento), and served as visiting professor at the University of California (Berkeley) and Atlanta University. His publications include *The Negro and the Communist Party*; *Race and Radicalism*; *Minority Groups and Intergroup Relations in the San Francisco Bay Area*; *Little Rock, USA* (with Jane Cassels Record); and numerous articles on black-white relations in *British Journal of Sociology*, *Phylon*, *The American Sociologist*, and other journals. Professor Record holds the M.A. and Ph.D. degrees from the University of California (Berkeley) and the A.B. degree from Roosevelt University.

Richard Robbins is a professor of sociology at the University of Massachusetts at Boston. He has served as visiting professor at the University of Leicester, Hampton Institute, and Fulbright Professor at the University of Strasbourg. He is the author of *International Migrations* (with Donald Taft); *Desegregation and the Negro College in the South*; "Shadow of Macon County: Charles S. Johnson," in *Journal of the Social and Behavioral Sciences* (Spring 1972); and "Counter-Assertion in the New York Negro Press," *Phylon* (Fall 1949). Professor Robbins received the A.B. degree from Brooklyn College, the M.A. from Washington State University, and the Ph.D. from the University of Illinois.

Elliott Rudwick is professor of sociology and history and senior research fellow in the Center for Urban Regionalism at Kent State University. He has held other teaching positions at Bates College, Florida State University, and Southern Illinois University. He is the author of *W. E. B. Du Bois: A Study of Minority*

Group Leadership and *Race Riot at East St. Louis, July 2, 1917.* He collaborated with August Meier to write *From Plantation to Ghetto* and *CORE: A Study of the Civil Rights Movement.* He received M.S. and Ph.D. degrees from the University of Pennsylvania.

Charles U. Smith is professor and chairman of the Department of Sociology at Florida A & M University and holds an appointment as an adjunct professor at Florida State University. Professor Smith is the author of *The Tallahassee Bus Protest* and co-author of *Leadership in American Society: A Case Study of Negro Leadership.* He has also published a number of articles in *Social Forces* and the *Journal of Intergroup Relations.* He holds degrees from Washington State University (Ph.D.), Fisk University (M.A.), and Tuskegee Institute (B.A.).

Stanley H. Smith is dean of the University and director of graduate training in social gerontology at Fisk University. He has taught at Livingstone College (N.C.), Tuskegee Institute, and Meharry Medical College. He is the author of *Freedom to Work*; *Voting Rights and Economic Pressure* (with Lewis Jones); "Some Social and Economic Factors Relating to Periodontal Disease" (with Eugenia Mobley), in *Journal of the American Dental Association* (July 1967); and articles in other professional journals. He received his academic training at Fisk University (B.A. and M.A.) and Washington State University (Ph.D.).

Walter L. Wallace is professor of sociology at Princeton University and a consulting staff sociologist at the Russell Sage Foundation. He is the author of *Sociological Theory*; *Student Culture*; and *The Logic of Science in Sociology.* He is also a member of the council of the American Sociological Association. Professor Wallace received the Ph.D. from the University of Chicago, the M.A. from Atlanta University, and the B.A. from Columbia University.

William J. Wilson is associate professor of sociology at the University of Chicago. Previously, he taught at the University of Massachusetts, Amherst. He is author of *Power, Racism and Privilege: Race Relations in Theoretical and Sociological Perspectives,* and *America's Blacks* (forthcoming). He is also co-editor of *Through Different Eyes: Black and White Perspectives on Race Relations* and has contributed numerous articles to professional journals on race relations, sociological theory, and the philosophy of science. Professor Wilson received the A.B. from Wilberforce University, M.A. from Bowling Green State University, and the Ph.D. from Washington State University.

Index

407